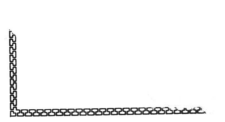

THE SETTLER ECONOMIES

AFRICAN STUDIES SERIES 35

The African Studies Series is a collection of monographs and general studies that reflect the interdisciplinary interests of the African Studies Centre at Cambridge. Volumes to date have combined historical, anthropological, economic, political and other perspectives. Each contribution has assumed that such broad approaches can contribute much to our understanding of Africa, and that this may in turn be of advantage to specific disciplines.

OTHER BOOKS IN THE SERIES

THE SETTLER ECONOMIES

Studies in the economic history of
Kenya and Southern Rhodesia 1900–1963

PAUL MOSLEY
Lecturer in Economics, University of Bath

CAMBRIDGE UNIVERSITY PRESS
CAMBRIDGE
LONDON   NEW YORK   NEW ROCHELLE
MELBOURNE   SYDNEY

Published by the Press Syndicate of the University of Cambridge
The Pitt Building, Trumpington Street, Cambridge CB2 1RP
32 East 57th Street, New York, NY 10022, USA
296 Beaconsfield Parade, Middle Park, Melbourne 3206, Australia

First published 1983

Printed in Great Britain at the University Press, Cambridge

Library of Congress catalogue card number: 82–12896

British Library cataloguing in publication data

Mosley, Paul
The settler economies. – (African studies series; 35)
1. Kenya – Economic policy – History
2. Zimbabwe – Economic policy – History
3. Kenya – Economic conditions – History
4. Zimbabwe – Economic conditions – History
I. Title   II. Series
338.9676'2   HC517.K4

ISBN 0 521 24339 4

TP

Contents

Contents

Maps

Tables

Tables

Tables

Figures

Preface

This book is a revised version of my PhD thesis, which was researched between 1976 and 1980 and finally submitted to Cambridge University in 1980. During those four years the focus of the research project broadened from the mere assembly of a data base for parts of the economic history of Kenya and Southern Rhodesia in the colonial period into a critique of certain versions of 'underdevelopment theory' which have now become a conventional wisdom for the interpretation of that history. The concepts and empirical validity of 'underdevelopment theory', of course, have recently been under scrutiny all over the underdeveloped world, not just in the countries examined here; I therefore hope that the book may have some interest for students of areas other than Eastern and Southern Africa.

Quite the pleasantest part of the job of writing the book is to thank those who helped me do so. I should have been lost without the patient and understanding help of Charles Feinstein in the painful early years of research. My present employer, the University of Bath, financed my visit to the National Archives of Rhodesia in 1978. John Lonsdale, Michael Redley and Carl Keyter helped enormously with encouragement, introductions to unfamiliar material and criticisms of half-baked ideas. The interviewees listed in Section E of the bibliography endured my questions with great courtesy, and filled some vital gaps in the documentary sources. Walter Elkan, the external examiner of the thesis, did his best to encourage me to get rid of some of the more tangled bits of exposition in the original version, and if the result does not have the Orwellian simplicity of his own prose, that is very much on my head. Lynette Latchem, as I have come to expect, did a lovely job of typing the final manuscript. Finally, Helen Weinreich-Haste lived with this piece of work from start to finish; she showed exemplary tolerance, in particular at those times when the raw materials for it spilled off my writing desk and threatened to invade the entire house, and I owe everything to her love and moral support.

May 1981   PAUL MOSLEY

A note on currency

The currency of both Kenya and Southern Rhodesia during the period of this study was the pound, which was kept at par with the pound sterling. The pound was divided into twenty shillings (except in Kenya between 1895 and 1921 when it was divided into fifteen rupees; but in this text all rupee values are converted into pounds and shillings). The shilling was divided, in Kenya, into one hundred cents, and in Southern Rhodesia into twelve pence. Money values in this book are thus given in one of three alternative forms:

£13
2 shillings} Kenya and Southern Rhodesia

Sh. 2.75 or 2.75 (Kenya)   two shillings and seventy-five cents

8s. 4d. or 8/4 (Southern Rhodesia) eight shillings and four pence

Abbreviations

For abbreviations used in references, see the bibliography. Briefly, the following system is used:
Archival sources and debates are referred to by means of the individual letters of the archive (or series) in question, as shown at the beginning of the bibliography. *Non-serial government publications and all secondary materials,* published and unpublished, are referred to by author's name, year and numbered section of the bibliography (e.g. B3, D1, as shown at beginning of the bibliography). *Serial reports* from statutory bodies are given the full reference in the notes.

The following abbreviations are used in the text:

BSAC   British South Africa Company
CNC   Chief Native Commissioner
DC   District Commissioner
KFA   Kenya Farmers' Association
MLA   Member of Legislative Assembly
NC   Native Commissioner
PC   Provincial Commissioner

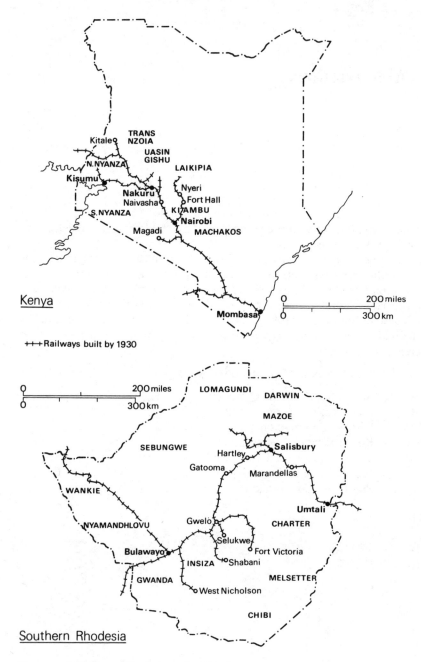

Kenya

+++Railways built by 1930

Southern Rhodesia

Kenya and Southern Rhodesia: principal place names.

xiv

1

Introduction

'Settler colonialism',[1] as practised in this century in countries such as Kenya, Southern Rhodesia, Algeria and South Africa, is a rather odd phenomenon: it throws out a challenge, by its very existence, to both the apologist for colonialism and to the 'underdevelopment theorist'. The former must come to terms with the restrictions placed on many parts of the indigenous economy in spite of the presence of a colonial administration nominally exercising 'trusteeship'; the latter must face the fact that settler economies quickly develop an economic nationalism of their own and to that extent fail to fit the classical-imperialist model of underdeveloped countries whose economic policy and development are dictated by the needs of the European metropolis.[2] In the last ten years, a large quantity of archive-based work has vastly increased our knowledge of such 'settler economies', in particular the two studied here.[3] But in fact most of this work consists of studies by historians of policy-making, since this is what the archives give most information about. By their very nature, such studies cannot shed any light on the development of the economy; this is often left to be inferred from a description of policy measures, rather than explicitly examined. Only the labour market has been at all intensively studied by economists on a time-series basis, and even there, the data base before 1945 is alarmingly weak.[4] As a result, our knowledge of the actual operation of the economy in settler states is at best based on questionable data and at worst on stereotypes, most of them falling within the general ambit of 'underdevelopment theory': the regression of the peasant economy, the stagnant real wage, the inefficient white farmer, the constraint imposed on industrial expansion by the peasant economy's decline. The research which produced these stereotypes has, at least, performed the service of driving out the more ancient colonial myth that underdevelopment in Africa was due to the absence of an economic spirit among Africans.[5] But it has not, as yet, provided a strong body of data concerning the operation of settler economies against which the stereotypes can be tested. The first

1

task of this study, therefore, is to build up the existing data base. We can then proceed to trace certain elements in the economic history of a couple of 'settler economies', Kenya and Southern Rhodesia. We do this over the entire colonial period from 1900 on, for reasons stated below: it follows that the number of elements we can choose is severely limited. We consider four here (African agriculture, European agriculture, the labour market, and secondary industry), but even within these headings specialisation has to be practised, so that the agricultural chapters are heavily biased towards cattle and maize. In addition, both the historical approach adopted and the character of the data available constrain the type of model that can be tested. For example, micro-economic models of motivation and factor allocation in African agriculture, such as those on which much of the litera-ture on agricultural underdevelopment has focused,[6] cannot be tested against the time-series data on which we rely here, and models of labour stabilisation cannot be tested without information on the breakdown of the labour force by earnings groups, which we lack. In both cases we have to fall back on cruder models and very limited methods of evaluating them, especially since the data are often so bad. However, even the limited evidence we are able to assemble is of such a type as to cast doubt on the four neo-orthodox stereo-types listed above. An important factor in the argument is that whereas the sources discussed above rely largely, in order to make such inferences as they do about the behaviour of the economy, on verbal evidence, e.g. the testimony of District or Native Commissioners, our own inferences are made largely from statistical evidence, much of it from archival material not previously explored for this purpose.

This study, therefore, is weighted towards the analysis of economic behaviour rather than policy-making, but the four chapters on economic behaviour are prefaced with a long chapter on the evolution of three facets of economic policy: land, railways and agricultural marketing. The purpose of this is to define the constraints within which economic behaviour operated. These constraints stemmed from past experience of policy and its influence on expectations as well as from present restrictions on economic activity. Much of this material must be explicitly developed within Chapter 2 from original sources since the existing literature (for example, that cited in note 3 above) frequently gives an inadequate picture. In particular, the element of conflict *within* the settler-producer group (Arrighi's 'white rural bourgeoisie')[7] and the influence which this conflict exercised over the eventual policy outcome have, with certain distinguished exceptions,[8] been glossed over, with the result that the making of economic policy is too often represented as a straightforward contest between European and African producer interests subject to intervention by the metropolitan power. This is to understate the influence of internal constraints on the policy-making process.

The historical development of the settler economies must, indeed, be seen as a process of mutual interaction between the economy and the political system, with the state of the economy (or its perceived state)[9] playing a part in determining policy and simultaneously being so much influenced by policy variables that a theoretical model which omits them often gives a picture which is the reverse of the truth.[10] For simplicity we may divide up this process of simultaneous causation into two 'legs':

$$\text{political system} \quad \underset{2}{\overset{1}{\longleftarrow\longrightarrow}} \quad \text{economy}$$

Relationships of type 1 – in which the state of the economy and other variables determine the evolution of policy variables – are dealt with mainly in Chapter 2 below, and relationships of type 2 – in which policy variables *inter alia* determine the evolution of the economy – are dealt with mainly in Chapters 3 to 6 below. The order of the chapters is designed, so far as is possible, to present a sequential argument: thus variables which are endogenous in Chapter 2 (land prices, railway rates, and marketing policies) are exogenous to Chapters 3 and 5, on African and European agriculture respectively; the productivity of African agriculture, which is endogenous to Chapter 3, is exogenous to Chapter 4 on the labour market; and the distribution of personal income, which is endogenous to Chapter 4, is exogenous to Chapter 6 on industrial development. A long period – practically the whole colonial period, in fact[11] – is examined, partly because the theories from the 'underdevelopment' stable which are reviewed – for instance, in the field of agricultural evolution and the development of the real wage level – are themselves long-period in character, and partly also in order to illustrate that matters which have been portrayed as static throughout the colonial period – for example, the response of economic policy to crisis in the economy and the inefficiency of European agriculture – in fact varied considerably through time. This implies, sadly, a large sacrifice of descriptive detail.

The function of this study is largely to analyse certain economic and political relationships for themselves rather than to serve as an essay in comparative economic systems. However, the analysis of Chapters 2 to 6 inevitably throws up the question of whether 'the settler economy' is sufficiently distinctive, either in terms of institutions or in terms of behaviour, to deserve classification as a species on its own. We consider this question in the concluding Chapter 7, largely on the basis of comparisons in the body of the text between the two 'settler economies' discussed here and other less developed economies of the kind most often presented as a contrasting ideal type, namely 'peasant export economies'.[12] Our conclusions are tentative; this study makes no pretence at a comprehensive coverage of the economy, and the data it uses are frequently not good enough for firm conclusions to be drawn from them. The validity of the data series presented is discussed in Appendices 2, 3 and 6, which consider the sources for the chapters which use archival material to supplement existing published series. On some occasions regression analysis is conducted between variables whose basis of measurement is far from ideal, on the grounds that the relationship in question is sufficiently interesting to warrant our saying whatever can validly be said on the strength of the available information. Where this is done, the fact is advertised and analysis is confined to an inspection of the size and significance of the regression coefficient, plus in some cases a search for factors systematically associated with the residuals from the regression. But it is possible that in some cases the errors in the data may be such as to invalidate the standard significance tests.

The orientation of the study is positivistic, in the sense that it searches for conclusions about the economies under discussion which hold good regardless of the investigator's value position, and also in the sense that it generally attempts to proceed by testing specified hypotheses. The conclusions it arrives at by this method frequently, as we have already indicated, challenge the conclusions reached on certain aspects of Kenyan and Southern Rhodesian economic history by members of the 'underdevelopment' school of historical and social science writing. It is therefore particularly important to acknowledge the influence of that school on the present work: most of the research reported on in this study owes its original stimulus to ideas formulated by its members, and in particular the practice of treating government policy as an endogenous variable, adopted in Chapter 2, owes much of its inspiration to the methodological introduction to Arrighi's *The political economy of Rhodesia* (1967 (D2)). More generally, in an essay originally published three years after *The political economy of Rhodesia*, Arrighi wrote the following words, in criticism of the earlier study of Barber (1961 (D2)) which had used a modified Lewis model to analyse the Central African labour market:

> Causal relations ... are not derived from historical analysis, but are imposed from within, that is, through *a priori* analysis; and a set of assumptions which yields the 'stylised facts' is held to have explanatory value, irrespective of its historical relevance. But since there will normally be many such sets, this methodology leaves room for considerable arbitrariness of choice and therefore for mystifications of all kinds. In view of this, the low scientific standards attained by modern 'development economics' and, for that matter, by economics in general should surprise nobody.[13]

It was a desire to respond to this challenge, more than anything, which prompted the present study.

1.2 BACKGROUND DATA

This section provides the bare minimum of background information as the main function of the study is analytical rather than descriptive and many good descriptive summaries of colonial Kenya and Southern Rhodesia

4

already exist. But it will be useful to provide some brief comparative material here under the three headings: distribution of land and people; agro-climatic; and constitutional. It will be useful to read the first two subsections in conjunction with Map 1.1.

Distribution of land and people

We have taken as our working definition of a settler society a country partly settled by European landowner-producers, who have a share in government, but who nonetheless remain a minority of the population and who in particular remain dependent, at least for labour, on the indigenous population (see note 1). This definition produces the following representative short-list of 'settler' societies in Africa and Asia. The current designation for the country, if different from its colonial name, follows in parentheses.

South Africa	Swaziland
Kenya	Bechuanaland (Botswana)
Southern Rhodesia (Zimbabwe)	Northern Rhodesia (Zambia)
Angola	Mozambique
Belgian Congo (Zaïre)	Algeria
Ceylon (Sri Lanka)	Malaya (Malaysia)[14]

This short-list forms the basis for Table 1.1, which compares these twelve countries by ethnic breakdown and share of whites in landownership and legislation. It is at once apparent that a feature of all settler societies was the ability of the immigrant group to obtain for themselves a disproportionate share in landownership. Kenya is near the bottom end of the list in terms of proportion of white population to the total; Southern Rhodesia is near the middle on this criterion, but exceeded only by South Africa in acreage of European-reserved land per head of white population.[15]

Agro-climatic data

As will be seen from Map 1.1, all the African 'settler economies' listed in the table satisfy the following conditions: a large part of the country is more than 3000 feet above sea level, and enjoys annual rainfall of more than twenty inches. These indices are highly correlated with one another and with a third precondition for large-scale European settlement, namely freedom from tsetse fly.[16] These were considered to be minimum conditions for successful agricultural settlement by white farmers. But at this point it is worth making a distinction between those colonies in Table 1.1 which enjoyed for the most part an average annual rainfall of more than forty inches, i.e. the Belgian Congo, Ceylon, and Malaya, and the others. For the first group was suitable essentially for plantation agriculture of crops such as tea, rubber and palm oil, and not for the pursuit of 'temperate farming' activities – cereal growing and cattle raising by Europeans. The second group, which

Map 1.1 Africa: 'settler economies', rain-sufficient regions, and land over 3000 feet above sea level. *Source*: Bennett 1962 (D3).

was not suitable for plantation agriculture, exhibits a distinctive pattern of economic policy; for whereas in plantation economies the production of food was an activity entrusted purely to indigenous producers,[17] in the others it was an activity in which competition between indigenous and white

Table 1.1. 'Settler economies' 1960: population, land and European representation on legislative body

Country	Population				Landownership			Representation on legislative body			
	Total (thousands)	Percentages of total			Total (thousands of square miles)	Percentages of total		Total member-ship	Percentages of total		
		European	Indigenous	Other		Alienated or reserved for Europeans	Other		European unofficials	European officials	Non-Europeans
Kenya	6 587	1.0	95.6	3.3	225	7	93	32	34	38	28
S. Rhodesia	3 070	7.1	92.2	0.5	150	49	51	30	100	0	0
Republic of South Africa	15 841	19.4	68.2	12.4	472	87	13	164	96	4[a]	0
Swaziland	252	2.8	96.4	0.8	7	51	49	no legislature	0	0	0
Bechuanaland	298	1.0	99.0	0	220	6	94	no legislature	0	0	0
N. Rhodesia	2 420	3.0	96.7	0.4	290	3	97	26	50	42[a]	8
Angola	4 550	3.5	96.5		481	3	–	26	69	31[a]	0
Mozambique	6 300	1.3	98.7		297	–	–	31	52	48	0
Algeria (excluding Saharan territories)	8 500	11.8	88.2		128	14	86	–	–	–	–
Belgian Congo (1958)	13 000	0.8	99.2		902	9	91	41	53	27	20
Ceylon	9 000	0.9	86.0	13.1	25	14[b]	86	95	3	0	97
Malaya	6 909	0.5	50.1	49.4	51	7[b]	93	52	0	0	100

– not available

Notes:

[a] In Northern Rhodesia and Angola two of the European officials in the legislature were nominated to represent African interests. In South Africa three European officials were nominated to represent African and four to represent Coloured interests.

[b] The entire area under plantation crops in Malaya and Ceylon, i.e. rubber, oil-palm, coconut, pineapple and tea, is taken to be under the ownership of European individuals or companies in 1960: this is a slight but not a gross over-estimate.

Sources: Population and landownership, African territories: Yudelman 1964 (D3). Tables 1 (p. 5) and 2 (p. 19); Gann and Duignan 1962 (D3). Appendix.

Representation on legislative body, African territories: Hailey 1957 (D3), Chapter 6.   Ceylon, all data: Oliver 1957 (D3); World Bank 1961 (D3).

Algeria, all data: Andrews, 1962 (D3); Saint-Germès 1950 (D3).   Malaya, all data: Silcock and Fisk 1963 (D3).

7

settler-producers was always present to some degree. Since indigenous producers could nearly always produce at lower cost, and immigrant producers were subject to diseases and climatic uncertainties not known in Europe, the immigrants' competitive position was weak; pressure for discriminatory action in restraint of such competition, at any rate in times of depression, was therefore also always present to some degree. To be sure, temperate farming activities never monopolised economic activity in the settler economies; parts of Kenya and Southern Rhodesia, to say nothing of the rest of the 'settler economy' group, were perfectly suitable for the growing of 'plantation crops' which were generally export-oriented and too capital-intensive for indigenous Africans to be able to get much of a competitive foothold.[18] Southern Rhodesia additionally supported mining activity which shared the same characteristics. But it is the existence of an economically insecure temperate foodstuff-growing white agricultural producer group, and of state action to protect it, rather than the much more frequently publicised intervention in the labour market[19] which marks off the true settler economy, as we shall henceforth call the first nine countries in Table 1.1, from the plantation economy.

Systems of government

All of the territories listed in Table 1.1 were, for the larger part of our period, parts of the empire of a European country. But this general statement masks enormous differences in the degree of self-determination which they possessed. The whole of South Africa from 1910 on, Ceylon from 1947 on, and Malaya from 1957 on enjoyed Dominion status within the British empire, i.e. effective internal self-government. At the opposite pole, the 'High Commission territories', Bechuanaland and Swaziland, had no internal legislative body at all for the whole country; rather, tax collection, public works and law and order were administered by a colonial bureaucracy under a Resident Commissioner subject to the direction of the High Commissioner for the United Kingdom in South Africa; this, incidentally, excludes them from that definition of 'settler societies' which is based on the representation of European producers in the legislative system.

   All the other territories occupy an intermediate position, i.e. throughout the period 1900–60 they were governed by a legislative council with some non-official representation on it, but its legislation was subject to some sort of metropolitan veto. The composition of these bodies changed frequently during the colonial period;[20] the position in 1960 is given in the right-hand column of Table 1.1. But within this intermediate group Southern Rhodesia stands on its own, since although nominally a colony it enjoyed after 1923, as Lord Hailey's survey puts it, 'so much the aspect of a Dominion that it is treated as lying within the sphere of interests dealt with by the Commonwealth Relations Office (the old Dominions Office) in the United Kingdom'.[21] Specifically, after that date it was governed by a thirty-member

Legislative Council elected by a franchise, the income and property quali-
fications for which excluded almost all Africans throughout our period.[22]
Any legislation passed by this Council which had the effect of discriminating
between the races was by an Order in Council of 1898, which remained in
force in the 1923 constitution, subject to the approval of the Secretary of
State for the Colonies. But this veto was never meaningfully invoked.

In all the other colonies in the 'intermediate' group, unlike Southern
Rhodesia, there was additional metropolitan restraint on the actions of the
legislature mediated through official representation on that body. But the
influence on economic policy, at any rate, of this restraint can be exaggerated.
The differences in policy, for example, between Southern Rhodesia with a
white unofficial monopoly on the legislature after 1923, and Kenya with no
white unofficial majority, were much watered down by white unofficial
majorities in Kenya on critical executive bodies such as the Board of Agriculture and Land Settlement Board, and white unofficial parity on the Inter-
Colonial Railway Advisory Committee.[23] In Chapter 2 these specific
differences in policy will be explored in detail, although the emphasis will
be on the policy out-turn rather than on the political and administrative
machinery by which it came into being. It will be noted from Table 1.1 that,
in general, the white unofficial element in the legislature was less in the
'plantation economies' than in the 'true settler economies'.[24]

To summarise, it is possible to whittle down our original short-list of
'settler economies', set up on the intuitive definition of territories where
European producers owned land and were dependent on the labour of
indigenous people, in either of two ways to make the definition of the species
more precise. The requirement that the white producers in question should
have representation on a legislative body excludes Bechuanaland and Swaziland. The more contentious, but more meaningful, requirement that they
should to some extent be in economic competition with indigenous food
producers excludes also Ceylon and Malaya, and arguably the Belgian
Congo. This second definition leaves Bechuanaland, Swaziland, South
Africa, Algeria, Angola, Mozambique, and Northern Rhodesia, in addition
to Southern Rhodesia and Kenya, as examples of 'settler economies'
proper. The expression 'settler economies' is intended, where used later
in this book, to refer to this group. The expression '*the* settler economies'
will in future be applied to statements intended to be true specifically for the
two countries, a case study of which takes up the whole of the rest of the
book: Kenya and Southern Rhodesia.

2

The political constraints on economic behaviour

2.1 INTRODUCTION: THE CONCEPT OF 'EXTRA-MARKET OPERATIONS'

In this chapter, by contrast with those that follow it, our focus is on the influence of economic factors on political variables. The dependent variables in question are three areas of economic policy – land policy, railway policy and marketing policy – which had important influences on the pattern of economic development, examined in Chapters 3 to 6 below. Each of these 'areas of policy' consisted essentially of intervention in the market for a critical factor of production. What kind of intervention materialises in any given historical case is, of course, a question of which groups have power to intervene in the market and what kind of intervention they perceive as being in their best economic interests. On these matters, however, as Rothschild has reminded us, conventional economic theory is silent:

> If we look at the main run of economic theory over the past hundred years we find that it is characterised by a strange lack of power considerations. More or less homogeneous units – firms and households – move in more or less given technological and market conditions and try to improve their economic lot within the constraints of these conditions. But that people will use power to alter the mechanism itself; that uneven power may greatly influence the outcome of market operations; that people may strive for economic power as much as for economic wealth: these facts have been largely neglected.[1]

This theoretical gap is particularly unfortunate in the context of societies in which, as Murray has noted in the Southern Rhodesian case, 'the administrative system favoured political agitation rather than more efficient production as the means for earning a bigger income'.[2] In what follows, no attempt is made to fill the hole in a formal sense. What is offered in this chapter, rather, is first, an elementary typology of 'extra-market operations', i.e. non-market means used to achieve economic ends;[3] secondly, three case studies in the use of such extra-market operations in the settler economies (section 2.2), and thirdly an attempt to search out 'reaction functions' or systematic response patterns of extra-market operations to economic

10

conditions (section 2.3). We hope that these exercises will supply, in addition to a narrative outline of economic policy-making, data which will enable the hole identified by Rothschild to be eventually plugged.

We begin the first exercise by asking who had an interest in manipulating which markets in the settler economies, and whence the power to do this was derived.

In every market we can identify at least three groups with potentially conflicting interests:

- the *producer*, wishing to maximise, or at any rate ensure a secure level of, profits;
- the *consumer*, wishing to keep down the unit cost of the things he buys. These things may or may not be inputs into a production process. If they are, he may well wish in addition to prevent other consumers (i.e. rival producers) from having them;
- the *trader*, wishing to maximise his own profits, and hence (at any rate until diseconomies of scale set in) to maximise the amount traded.

These diverse interests may then, as Table 2.1 shows, be pursued by means of a variety of different strategies; many, though not all, require support from government, the nature of which is spelled out in the second row of the table. Finally, the bottom row of Table 2.1 gives examples, for later reference, of the successful application of each strategy.

In the nature of the case, not all the strategies set out in Table 2.1 can be pursued at the same time: producers' desire for restriction of competition conflicts with traders' desire for an open market, producers' wish to keep the price of their output up conflicts with consumers' wish to keep the price of their inputs down, and finally, if producers are successful in setting up discriminatory arrangements for the marketing of their output of the supply of their inputs, there will be conflict *between* producers over rights of access to the dearest market or the cheapest source of supply. These are the three main foci of conflict over the nature and extent of extra-market operations.

Our principal argument in the sections which follow is: (1) Pressure on the state to implement extra-market operations was concentrated in periods when a loss was being made on agricultural exports, i.e. when the survival of the 'white agricultural bourgeoisie' was threatened. (2) However, the 'white agricultural bourgeoisie', in both settler economies, was inescapably characterised by both internal producer–consumer conflict and internal producer–producer conflict. This means that the sector of white agricultural capital must, contrary to the analysis of many scholars,[4] be seen not as one but as several sectors if the extra-market operations actually implemented are to be understood.

Table 2.1. *'Extra-market operations': objectives, strategies and resulting policies*

	Producer (acting on output side) Increase value of sales		Consumer		Trader
Agent and objective in market →	Increase selling price	Increase proportion of output sold on domestic market	Reduce buying price of input	Expand market (at constant price)	Maintain open market
Possible strategies ('extra-market operations') to achieve objective	Tariff protection	Exclude competition from domestic market	Confiscation (at zero or statutorily fixed price)	Withdrawal of allocation process from market by imposition of alternative (or 'developmental') criteria	Lobby against all measures threatening consumers' buying power (e.g. many, of the producers' measures)
Legislative backing required	Statutory monopoly	Segmentation of output into 'domestic' and 'export' pools	Government confiscation or statutory purchase order	Acts to 'apportion' input	
Historical case of successful application of strategy	Kenya: 1922 tariffs (p.208)	Rhodesia: Maize Control Acts of 1931 and 1934 (pp. 44–6); Kenya: Sale of Wheat Act 1930 (p.245)	Kenya: Confiscation: Crown land (p. 16); Compulsory purchase orders: Livestock control (p. 57)	Maize export rate on railways (pp.31–2); Rhodesia: Land Apportionment Act 1930 (p. 24); Kenya Highlands Order in Council 1939 (p. 25)	Chamber of Commerce pressure against maize control (p. 245)

2.2 THE EVOLUTION OF GOVERNMENT POLICY IN INPUT
MARKETS: THREE CASE STUDIES

Land

> Not long afterwards I read in an old explorer's book the phrase: 'Chief
> Mshlanga's country'. It went like this: 'Our destination was Chief Mshlanga's
> country, to the north of the river; it was our desire to ask his permission to pros-
> pect for gold in his territory.'
> The phrase 'ask his permission' was so extraordinary to a white child, brought
> up to consider all natives as things to use, that it revived those questions, which
> could not be suppressed: they fermented slowly in my mind.
> On another occasion one of those old prospectors who still move over Africa
> looking for neglected reefs, with their hammers and tents, and pans for sifting
> gold from crushed rock, came to the farm and, in talking of the old days, used
> that phrase again: 'This was the Old Chief's country', he said. 'It stretched
> from those mountains over there way back, to the river, hundreds of miles of
> country'. That was his name for our district: 'The Old Chief's country'; he did
> not use our name for it – a new phrase which held no implication of usurped
> ownership.
>
> Doris Lessing, *The Old Chief Mshlanga: Collected African Stories*
> (vol. I, London: Michael Joseph, 1973), p. 14.

'Imperium in imperio': concessionaire-dominated development to 1920

Almost the first act of European administrative penetration in the settler
economies was to restrict, indeed to outlaw, the market as the means by which
land should be transferred into the hands of the incoming European colonists. To understand how this came to be, it is necessary to examine the
contrast between intention and out-turn in the early years of colonisation.

In the original metropolitan intention, Rhodesia was to be a gold-mining
economy; Kenya a mere access route to Uganda and the headwaters of the
Nile, to be held in support of a larger imperial purpose, not developed.[5]
In both countries, however, the original intention had to be modified as
neither the costs nor the returns on the overhead capital invested to realise
these intentions matched the original projections. The Uganda railway was
expected in August 1895 to cost £1.75 million; these estimates subsequently
had to be revised upwards to £3 million in 1896, £4.93 million in 1900 and,
in the final reckoning, £5.53 million in 1902.[6] It was expected to carry about
the same value of imports as of exports, but by 1903 carried more than eight
times as much.[7] The gold deposits of Rhodesia, as is well known, failed to
yield the wealth which early publicists for the British South Africa Company
had led investors to believe was there for the taking. In each case military
expenditures in the first years of colonisation vastly exceeded original
estimates.[8] Such miscalculations required an emergency economic response
if the territories were to be prevented from becoming a long-term drain on
the colonial (and in Kenya's case also the Whitehall) government, and in

13

each case the one chosen as the 'least-cost' means of forcing development was the grant of large-scale monopoly concessions of land to white immigrants, very often to companies with a British or South African base. In Southern Rhodesia, 16 million acres – one-sixth of the whole country – was disposed of by this means in the years 1890 to 1896 alone, and this figure had risen to 21.5 million acres by 1913. In Kenya, following abortive schemes to settle Indian cultivators, Jews and Finns in the highland area,[9] the Governor, Sir Charles Eliot, decided to encourage British and South African white immigration in 1903 and as a result of the continuation of this policy by his successors some 5.03 million acres had been alienated by December 1914.[10]

These concessions were, by the standards of the time, both large and cheap. Something of their size can be inferred from the short, random list in Table 2.2.

These areas – the size of an average English county at the top end of the scale – represent *initial* allocations only, and many of the people in these lists were able to accumulate still more land by purchase from existing holders. In both countries strenuous attempts were made to prevent under-capitalised individuals from buying land, and openly in Southern Rhodesia,[11] covertly in Kenya, land acquisition by companies rather than individuals was encouraged. At the beginning of the First World War about half the alienated land of both settler economies was in the hands of concessionaire companies,[12] but as their governments depended on them not only for the bulk of primary production but also for much investment in infrastructure and agricultural processing,[13] they naturally came to assume a preponderant influence on the direction of economic policy. The BSAC's lament that the Liebig's Extract of Meat Company, to whom 1 200 000 acres of ranching land was sold in 1909, 'partakes somewhat of the nature of an imperium in imperio within Rhodesia, a highly undesirable state of things from our point of view',[14] applies *mutatis mutandis* to all the concessionaires listed in Table 2.2.

As for the price of these concessions, this was in all cases of government sales to 1912 nominal, and in many cases zero. The men of the 'pioneer column' who occupied Mashonaland in 1890 were given free land grants, under 'permit of occupation' from the British South Africa Company, of 1500 morgen (3150 acres). This system was later modified to give settlers the option of outright freehold purchase at a price of 1s. 6d. per morgen (8½d. per acre) in Mashonaland and 3s. per morgen (1s. 5d. per acre) in Matabeleland. Even in 1905 the ruling prices for land were 1s. 7d. per acre in Bulawayo, 11d. in Umtali and 7d. in Salisbury; this compared with 1904 average prices per acre of 16s. 3d. in the Orange Free State, 15s. 7d. in the Cape, and 11s. 10d. in Natal.[15] In Kenya the price was set at two rupees (Sh. 2.66) an acre in the prime highland areas of adequate rainfall, but Governor Eliot granted it free to 'pioneers' in areas where there was not yet any settlement. Pastoral land was in principle leased by the Crown at a

14

Table 2.2. *Kenya and Southern Rhodesia: some important land concessions before 1914 (acres)*

Southern Rhodesia		Kenya	
Liebig's Extract of		East African Estates	350 000
Meat Co.	1 200 000	East Africa Syndicate	320 000
Sir John Willoughby	600 000	E.S. Grogan and	
Mashonaland Agency	500 000	F.R. Lingham (forest	
Exploring Lands and		concession)	132 000
Mineral Co.	424 000	London and South Africa	
		Agency (sisal concession)	128 000
		Lord Delamere	109 562
		Scottish Mission	64 000
Average size of concession		*Average size of concession granted*	
granted (to 1921)	5 251	*(1903–5)*	5 488

Sources: Southern Rhodesia–answer in *SRLAD*, 10 May 1921, col. 530.
Kenya – PRO: CO 533/231, Memo by R.B. Wright, Lands Office, enclosed in Bowring (Acting Governor) to Colonial Secretary, 16 March 1920.

rental of one anna (1d.) per acre, but very often was sold outright to big concessionaires on leasehold terms which, in response to pressure from the purchasers, were made gradually easier as the years progressed.[16] The offer of such generous 'package deals' – cheap land on easy development conditions with secure tenure – was seen, rightly or wrongly, as the minimum supply price which the colonial administrations had to pay in order to attract well-capitalised settlers they wanted, who *ex hypothesi* were already enjoying a comfortable standard of living and who needed inducements greater than those offered in Canada and Australia to compensate them for the climatic and disease risks involved in agricultural pioneering.[17] But for the offer to be made it was necessary, in turn, to crush an incipient *free* market in land between coloniser and colonised, in which prices were far higher. This required a legal ban on that market, backed by physical force. This ban was chronologically the first, and one of the most significant, of the extra-market operations by which the settler economies were made viable.

Early settlers who came in advance of the main rush of concessionaires found that Africans were often willing to surrender land to them in return not only for trade goods, but also for cash. Thomas Watson of the Church of Scotland Mission, looking for a mission site in Kikuyu country, in 1897, noted of the Dagoretti region (ten miles west of modern Nairobi): 'All the land here is privately owned by some one or more of the natives and now they have learned to ask high prices for land compared with what they thought of two years ago.'[18] However, he pressed ahead with the purchase, completing it in May 1898 at a cost of 6.4 rupees (Sh. 8.50) per acre.[19] Similarly,

15

in the area which became Southern Rhodesia before 1890, some concessions were obtained by missionaries and prospectors, not of course from any central government but by 'asking the chief's permission' and paying a price negotiated with him.

As Doris Lessing's character, quoted above, noted, this model of transactions between occupant and purchaser of land did not long outlive the formal colonial occupation: concessions of the type described in the previous paragraph were incompatible with its persistence. A ban on all land dealings 'between Europeans of whatever nationality and natives' was imposed by the Kenya Crown Lands Ordinance of 1902, in the interests of 'preventing the exploitation' of the latter group. In Southern Rhodesia, as will be explained in more detail below, dealings between Africans and Europeans were technically legal until 1930 but socially almost proscribed. The supreme irony of the justification offered for the Kenyan ban appears most clearly when one compares the sums received by Africans on the open market in pre-colonial times with the sums they received when ordered to part with what had by the stroke of a pen been turned into 'Crown land'. Whereas direct dealings with missionaries had yielded them Sh. 8.50 per acre in Dagoretti, the Kenya government offered them at best Sh. 2.66 (2 rupees)[20] and at worst nothing; the BSAC, for its part, offered Southern Rhodesian Africans nothing in cash, and land in compensation only at its discretion.

Forced sales of this sort proceeded so fast as to threaten the subsistence of rural Africans. Given their inability to compete with incoming European colonists in the open market for land, the only sure way of protecting that subsistence seemed to be the creation of a sector of the land market into which Europeans could not enter. Such a sector, consisting of a number of patches of land confined to Africans (or 'native reserves'), was created as a temporary expedient, according to the patterns shown on Map 2.1. The task of delimiting the reserves was left in the first instance to local officials, who in both countries followed a wide variety of criteria. Palmer has described the Rhodesian case thus:

> The N/C Hartley, for example, made his reserves 'large enough for all purposes' on the grounds that it would be easier to reduce rather than increase them in the future; while the N/C Lower Gwelo decided, for reasons unstated, that his reserves should be 'as small as possible'. Some . . . paid careful attention to tribal boundaries and to the needs of extensive cultivators, while others failed or were unable to make such provision.[21]

In general, however, one cardinal principle was followed: land which was already occupied by Europeans, or which might in the future be required for European settlement, was not set aside as African reserve.

By the original imperatives of settlement, then, two separate markets, or rather non-market allocation processes, were set up in place of a free market in land between Africans and Europeans. But by the very act of settlement Europeans were turned from *consumers* of land (with a unanimous interest in acquiring it cheap) into *landowners*. This created two separate types of division within the European settler community.

In the first place, as Table 2.3 records, the beginnings of growth in white agricultural exports around 1910–12 caused land values within the European area to float upwards sharply. This caused two separate 'European land markets' to emerge: one in 'alienated land' in which private individuals sold each other land at prices well above those which had attracted the original

Table 2.3. *Kenya and Southern Rhodesia: prices of land in European areas, 1906–55 (shillings per acre)*

	Southern Rhodesia				Kenya	
	Price paid per acre of land in open-market private sales in alienated areas	Price paid per acre of Crown land sold by Estates Dept to incoming settlers			Price paid per acre of land in open-market private sales (a) on L.O. 487, Nakuru District	Price paid per acre of Crown land overall (Blue Book data)
	(a) Average auction realisation	Mazoe Dist.	Mashon- aland	Mata- beleland		
1906	–	–	1.62	3.33	–	2.83
1907	–	–	–	–	–	–
1908	–	–	1.75	1.44	–	2.81
1909	–	–	1.95	1.55	–	–
1910	–	–	1.95	1.15	–	3.10
1910–11	–	2.36	2.25	2.15	–	2.66
1911–12	–	3.67	2.90	2.25	–	4.12
1912–13	24.66	4.04	4.18		52.6	3.37
1914	–	–	6.50		–	3.08
1915	11.75	–	6.41		–	3.13
1916	–	2.19	–		30.1	–
1917	–	–	4.27		30.1	–
1918	–	2.35	–		46.0	–
1919	–	–	–		29.5	–
1920	–	7.00	–		67.5	–
1921	–	5.66	–		80.0	–
1922	–	9.43	14.2		67.5	–
1923	–	6.89	–		–	–
1924	–	–	–		–	–
1925	–	5.90	–		–	–
1926	–	4.01	–		–	–
1927	–	4.09	–		–	–
1928	–	7.07	–		–	–
1929	–	6.46	–		–	14.92
1930	–	8.36	–		–	9.64
1931	–	–				
					(b) Land Bank data Nakuru District	
1932	–	–	–		60.88	11.19
1933	–	–	–		65.57	10.11
1934	–	15.87	–		66.54	–
1935	–	19.98	–		63.06	7.98
1936	–	9.49	–		63.82	6.42

Table 2.3 (cont.)

	Southern Rhodesia				Kenya	
	Price paid per acre of land in open-market private sales in alienated areas	Price paid per acre of Crown land sold by Estates Dept. to incoming settlers			Price paid per acre of land in open-market private sales (b) Land Bank data Nakuru District	Price paid per acre of Crown land overall (Blue Book data)
	(b) Average realisation all districts	Mazoe Dist.	Mashon-aland	Mata-beleland		
1937	–	4.82	–		–	3.53
1938	–	–	–		–	4.33
1939	7.66	–	–		–	–
1940	6.80	5.19	–		–	–
1941	9.05	–	–		–	–
1942	9.75	3.54	–		–	–
1943	7.60	–	–		–	–
1944	11.75	–	–		–	–
1945	13.83	3.77	–		–	–
1946	14.92	3.77	–		–	–
1947	18.66	13.81	–		–	–
1948	30.92	–	–		–	–
1949	28.60	6.21	–		–	–
1950	36.00	5.80	–		–	–
1951	43.15	–	–		–	–
1952	43.25	18.42	–		–	–
1953	49.00	–	–		–	–
1954	54.66	–	–		–	–
1955	40.92	–	–		–	–

Note: Development conditions varied as follows:
Kenya: 1915 Crown Lands Ordinance: owner to spend Sh. 20 per acre on small allotments (1640 acres or less), Sh. 4 on large allotments, in each case within three years.
 1919 Soldier Settlement Scheme: owner to spend 10 rupees (Sh. 13.33) per acre on settlements less than 300 acres and 3000 rupees for the first 300 acres and thereafter 2 rupees for each additional acre on settlements more than 300 acres, in each case within three years. Minimum capital £5000.
 PRO: CO533/238, Pamphlet on information for intending settlers in Northey (Governor of Kenya) to Milne (Colonial Secretary), 13 December 1920.
Southern Rhodesia: 1912 – for every 1500 morgen (3175 acres), owner to spend £250, or place 10 head of cattle, or enclose 10 acres.
 1921 – for every 100 morgen, owner to cultivate 3 acres of land, or place 3 head of cattle.
 British South Africa Co., Annual Reports.
Sources: Southern Rhodesia, open market, to 1922 – British South Africa Co., Annual Reports; 1939–55 – Central African Statistical Office, Reports on the agricultural and pastoral production of Southern Rhodesia. Crown land – Mazoe, NAR: S 1089, Estates Dept (later Lands Dept) register of land sales; Mashonaland and Matabeleland, BSAC, Annual Reports.
Kenya, open market, 1913–25 – PRO: CO533/345, Grigg (Governor of Kenya) to Strachey (Assistant Under-Secretary, Colonial Office), 14 January 1926 (note that these data differ from those given for the same concession by Redley 1975 (D1), p. 10 who used Kenya Lands Office data); – 1932–6 – Kenya Land Bank, Annual Reports.
Crown land – Kenya, Blue Books, various.

settlers, and a second in 'Crown land' in which the government sold to newcomers. Until 1912 the price of 'Crown land' was kept cheap in the hope of attracting more highly capitalised companies to take up concessions,[22] but once prices began to rise sharply on the free market the BSAC and the Kenya government came to perceive the commercial foolishness of continuing to offer such a bargain, and the 'Crown land' price was allowed to float up towards the 'alienated land' price, in part through the medium of auctions. 'The British South Africa Company', warned the manager of its London Office, H. Wilson Fox, in 1913, 'finds that it has parted and is continuing to part with millions of acres of its land at what, judged by the standards of the very Colonies to which the Rhodesian people refer as models for imitation, are rubbish prices, and that the effect on population is comparatively inappreciable.'[23] Wilson Fox's hypothesis – that the low-price policy had encouraged land acquisition but, since this settlement was largely speculative, retarded development – found support in both colonial governments. In Southern Rhodesia auctions began in February 1913 'as an experiment'[24] and in Kenya in May of that year.[25] At the same time sale prices of non-auction Crown land rose, though not to anywhere near the commercial valuation. This policy inevitably set interests on opposite sides of the land market against each other. The small men, disappointed in their hopes of acquiring land at a nominal price, attacked the big landowners, and the big men, emphasising the productive side of their operations, attacked 'absentee speculators', sometimes going beyond this to a populist attack on the new government policies.[26]

The post-First World War settlement schemes barely moderated this conflict, and in Kenya definitely intensified it. The BSAC offered free land to ex-soldiers in Southern Rhodesia, but the other land companies who made land available to soldier-settlers could not be persuaded to emulate these concessions and sold to them, in most cases, at the full market price.[27] The responsible government of 1923 decided, after a couple of years when Crown land prices had been allowed to drift up sympathetically with the open market (Table 2.3), to reduce its average price of land from 7s. to about 5s. per acre, but prices remained higher and the government's stance less interventionist than, for example, in South Africa.[28]

In Kenya, where far more Crown land remained available for alienation to soldier-settlers, government intervention in the market was minimal. An original plan for the government to offer free grants to local soldiers on the Southern Rhodesian model was abandoned in favour of the recently established auction principle, only disabled ex-servicemen being offered land at concessional prices. New settlers were warned that 'from the outset, nothing was being given away'[29] and indeed, in areas of proven agricultural potential close to the railway, such as Nakuru, prices more than doubled (Table 2.3) before the collapse of crop prices in 1921–2 temporarily wrecked the settler's market in land. The soldier-settlers' protests were bitter, but for the moment impotent.

Superimposed on this conflict over land prices in the European area was a separate conflict over land use featuring much the same lines of cleavage. For, of course, very little of the land alienated in the years before the First World War was beneficially occupied, much less farmed.[30] It was common for a traveller passing through the European areas in the pre-war years to see 'hundreds of thousands of acres marked off in farms, with one white man as caretaker, and the natives there were paying rent to land companies'. The same observer proceeded to describe the economics of this system:

> In Matabeleland the average rent paid was £2 per head, so that £80 a year could be obtained from one farm, which amounted to 10% interest on £800. Very few of the settlers who came to this country could afford to pay more than £400 for a farm. Was it not a great temptation for a company, or an individual, who owned a lot of land, if he could draw £80 a year from each farm? Was he not likely to stick to the land rather than sell the farm for £400?[31]

Productive (and arable) farmers resented this practice of absentee landlords charging Africans rent for the right to occupy their land, or 'kaffir farming' as it was known, as it retarded settlement, created a risk of infection of their cattle from African squatter herds and appeared to diminish their labour supply. Absentee landowners (including a number of mining companies)[32] and the poorest white farmers such as those of Melsetter, Southern Rhodesia, who depended on African squatters as a source of ultra-cheap wage labour,[33] however, opposed any restriction of the practice. In Southern Rhodesia, a political victory went to them in the shape of the Private Locations Ordinance of 1908, which required that owners who occupied their land should take out a licence of 1s. per annum for each African adult male resident on their farm, whereas absentee landlords should pay 5s., and that there should be a maximum of forty adult males permitted on each farm of 3175 acres. In Kenya in 1919 a much weaker squatter ordinance – the Resident Native Labour Ordinance – was passed, which required all Africans resident on European farms to contribute three months' labour, but abstained from any attempt to curb the squatter population, on which indeed many white Kenyan farmers were critically dependent, in the interests of closer settlement and white livestock production.

The decision to settle a white agricultural population on the land in Kenya and Southern Rhodesia had thus set up three separate conflicts concerning how the land market should be managed: between European and African producer over the ultimate ownership of land, between government (or other European) seller and incoming buyer over the price of land, and between one type of European producer and another over the use of land. Of these, certainly the second and possibly the third had by 1920 been resolved in the interests of the small European producer very much more in Southern Rhodesia than in Kenya. They continued to simmer in the inter-war years, but attention was distracted from them by an intensification of, and pressures for a legal arbitration of, the first conflict.

20

Formal separation of markets, 1921–52

The hallmarks of land policy in the settler economies in the years before 1914 were its improvisatory quality and its domination by one interest within the European community. The grant of huge concessions was seen as necessary in order to attract a 'critical mass' of capital into the country, and so they were granted initially, as we have seen, more or less on whatever terms the applicant chose to ask for. But the concessions were granted *ad hoc*, as in due course were the reserves: the difference between 'African' and 'European' areas had a meaning in everyday parlance but not in law and indeed in Southern Rhodesia the African still possessed the famous right in law to 'acquire, hold, encumber and dispose of land on the same conditions as a person who is not a native'.[34] The barrier between the white and non-white land markets was kept in being only by administrative convention and by the inability of nearly all Africans and most Indians to afford the prices to which land in European areas had risen by the outbreak of the First World War. During the inter-war period, however, this barrier became and remained formal. In 1914 when the BSAC's twenty-five-year-old charter came up for renewal, the unofficial majority in the Southern Rhodesia Legislative Council was increased from two to six seats, substantially increasing the power of the new and aspiring settlers in relation to the BSAC itself and the old concessionaire group. In Kenya, the concessionaires actually tried to obstruct the formation of an elected Legislative Council,[35] and when this materialised in 1917 they were soon demoted to a position of some precariousness, winning only three of eleven elective seats in the 1919 election. The 'new men' seemed poised for the kind of successful assault on the privileges of the concessionaires, by means of taxation and development conditions, that would dislodge into the market some of the land currently locked up, and bring its price down. But their success was modest: an attempt to impose a tax on undeveloped land in Kenya was successfully beaten off in 1920 after a veto from the Colonial Secretary,[36] and a similar attempt in Southern Rhodesia only succeeded in 1928, after it had been watered down to virtual impotence by a reduction in the rate of tax to one per cent.[37] This failure of the 'new men' to turn their newly won political power into a greater degree of dominance over the European land market can be explained by the concessionaires' ability to convince them they would make smaller economic gains by attacking them than they would make by an assault on the land holdings of non-whites.

In Southern Rhodesia the 'threat from below' was posed as mainly an African one. One attempt to meet it had already been made by the Native Reserves Commission of 1913, which had achieved a reduction of the reserves by more than a million acres from those set out in Map 2.1, most of it largely in favour of the concessionaires.[38] Although the BSAC declined to sell to Africans, some private individuals were willing to do so, and by contrast with Kenyan experience, some Africans and Indians had grown rich

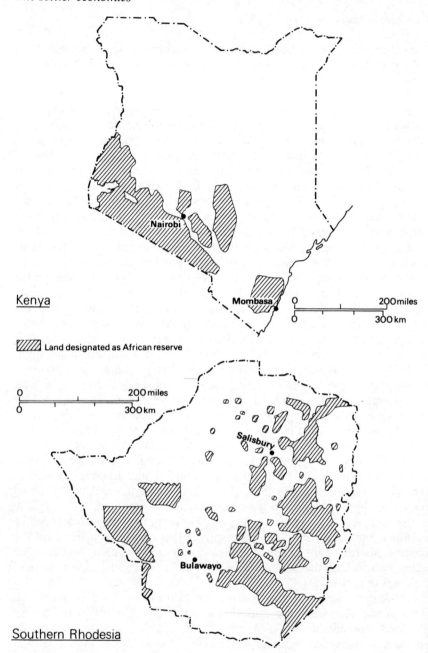

Kenya

Land designated as African reserve

Southern Rhodesia

Map 2.1 Kenya and Southern Rhodesia: disposition of African reserves, by Kenyan District Commissioners to 1915 and by Southern Rhodesian Native Commissioners to 1910. *Sources*: Sorrenson 1968 (D1), p. 161; Palmer 1977 (D2), p. 69.

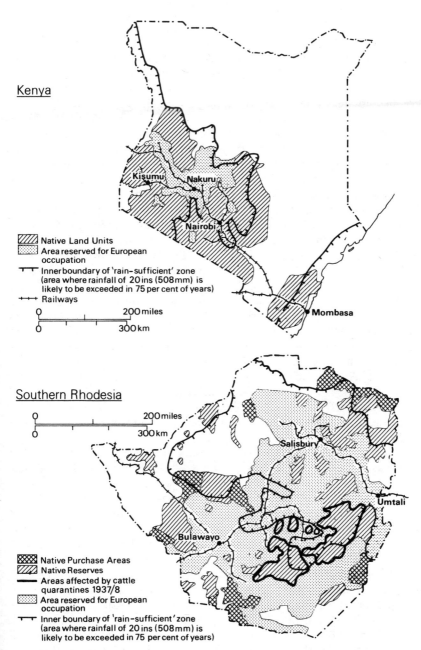

Kenya

Native Land Units
Area reserved for European
occupation
Inner boundary of 'rain-sufficient' zone
(area where rainfall of 20 ins (508mm) is
likely to be exceeded in 75 per cent of years)
Railways

0   200 miles
0   300 km

Kisumu   Nakuru
Nairobi
Mombasa

Southern Rhodesia

0   200 miles
0   300 km

Salisbury
Umtali
Bulawayo

Native Purchase Areas
Native Reserves
Areas affected by cattle
quarantines 1937/8
Area reserved for European
occupation
Inner boundary of 'rain-sufficient' zone
(area where rainfall of 20 ins (508mm) is
likely to be exceeded in 75 per cent of years)

Map 2.2 Kenya and Southern Rhodesia: boundaries of African and European area, as established by (Kenya) Highlands Order in Council 1939 and (Southern Rhodesia) Land Apportionment Act 1930. *Sources*: Great Britain 1955b (B1), map inside back cover, 'Population, tsetse fly and rainfall'; Southern Rhodesia 1939a (B2) for land distribution, Southern Rhodesia 1962 (B2) for 'rain-sufficient' areas.

enough during the period to 1914 to be able to buy farms, even sometimes when the seller had tried to put them off by quoting a higher price than he was asking of Europeans.[39] The settlers were thus glad to grab at the suggestion, long current in both Native Departments, that African purchases should be confined to areas where they would not damage European land values. For reasons which we have described this was a proposal which the old concessionaire group was also anxious to champion, and it frequently took the initiative in suggesting that certain areas of land might be reserved for African purchase.[40] But it also had the support of the missionaries, and of the Africans themselves, 1753 of whom were interviewed by the 1925 Land Commission and only eight of whom opposed the principle of segregation. It was the conviction of the Africans and their sponsors that they had more to lose than to gain from the continuance of an open land market which finally secured Whitehall approval for the Commission's recommendation to extinguish African purchase rights in the existing European areas. As compensation for this loss of rights the African community was allocated 7.4 million acres of 'Native Purchase Areas', adjacent in nearly all cases to the existing reserves, which were expected to suffice for the needs of the 'advanced' top decile of the African agricultural population.[41] This recommendation was the basis for the Land Apportionment Act of 1930, which for the first time created an exclusive European reserve of 49 million acres, whilst at the same time confirming the boundaries of Native Purchase Areas and existing reserves, which are set out on Map 2.2. An area of 17.7 million acres, most of it rocky, waterless and virtually unusable for agricultural purposes, was left unassigned in defiance of African and missionary demands that at least part of it be allocated to African communal use as an extension of the reserves.[42]

In Kenya, by contrast, the threat to the European land market was perceived as mainly Indian. Before the First World War many of the Indians originally recruited to build the Uganda railway had remained virtually to monopolise the business of trading with Africans which in Southern Rhodesia, by contrast, 'was at the time the most, if not the only, profitable activity carried out by the Europeans'.[43] They were thus in a position, unlike most Africans, to bid for a share in the land of the White Highlands. The anxiety which this provoked in the white community, never quite allayed by Lord Elgin's pledge of 1909 'that, as a matter of administrative convenience, grants in the upland areas should not be made to Indians',[44] was in 1921 whipped up into frenzy by, among others, the concessionaire group. Repulsed by the 'Devonshire declaration' of 1923, a White Paper which made it clear that the British government had no intention of granting responsible self-government to them in the forseeable future, the Kenya settlers were nevertheless successful, during the subsequent economic depression, in getting a Land Commission established to fix final boundaries of the African and European areas, on the model of the Rhodesian commission of 1925 and under the same chairman, Sir Morris Carter.

This gazetted 10.7 million acres as European reserve; made a net addition of 0.3 million acres to the African reserves, and created 0.6 million acres for African leasehold tenure; and recommended that in return for this 'all native rights outside the reserves should now be expunged'.[45] The most important difference between the Kenyan and the Southern Rhodesian position after the 1930s related to urban land. Whereas in Kenya since the Devonshire declaration the legal position had been that there could be no territorial segregation outside the White Highlands and the African reserves – allowing, in particular, an open market in urban land – all urban land in Southern Rhodesia under the 1930 Land Apportionment Act was European land, with the exception of those African locations which were owned by municipalities or private individuals: in urban areas these were kept extremely small, and security of tenure could seldom be achieved. Formally, therefore, the land market in both settler economies was by the mid 1930s segmented into a European area in which land was allocated by market forces and an African area in which it was communally allocated, with neither race having purchase rights in the preserve of the other. The reality, of course, was more complex, and in the rest of this section we consider what was actually happening to the land market in each area.

During the 1920s the number of African families occupying land designated as 'European', whether alienated or not, grew sharply (Table 2.4). We have seen that in the pre-1914 period the existence of these families had caused division between those white farmers who gained more from them in cheap labour and/or rent than they lost through stock disease (i.e. single-crop farmers and/or absentees) and those for whom the balance of advantage was the other way round (stock farmers and mixed farmers). But the legislation introduced to obviate this conflict – the Private Locations Ordinance and the Resident Native Labourers Ordinance – did not stabilise the position. During the inter-war period, white absentees became less numerous, white stock farmers became more numerous and the black squatter population more than doubled. Hence a steady pressure built up for stricter controls on squatter tenancy. These pressures were initially contained in two ways: in Kenya, settlers' associations were allowed to establish local squatter rules, and in Southern Rhodesia arrangements were made to phase out pure 'kaffir farming' agreements under the 1930 Land Apportionment Act.[46]

But in the post-Second World War period the squatter problem became more urgent. Very little attractive land within the European area remained unalienated,[47] so that space could only be made for new settlers by getting existing owners to sell. Additionally, such land could only be attractive to new settlers if available at a low enough price and with vacant possession. Hence post-war settlement policy, in both colonies, had two prongs: control of land prices, which in effect involved simply a continuation of wartime legislation, and the removal of those squatters from alienated land who were not part of a regular labour force. By now enough settlers had moved from

Table 2.4. *Kenya and Southern Rhodesia: distribution of African population by type of land tenure, 1922–51 (all figures in thousands)*

	Southern Rhodesia			On alienated land						Kenya		
	Total African population	In reserve	In Native Purchase Areas	In private location agreements (under 1908 Act)	On mission lands	Un-authorised	In labour agreements (under 1930 Act)	On un-alienated land	Permanent residence in mines and towns	Total African Population	In reserves and on un-assigned land	On alienated land (estimate)[a]
1922	788	503			103		–	161	21			
1926	848	553			113		–	159	23	2550	2435	115
1931	983	641			154		–	179	9	2970		
1936	1081	719	54		169			136	3			84
1941	1265	854	103		118		25	160	5	3410[b]	3309	81
1946	1533	1084	135	30	13	39	69	161	2	4060	3965	95
1951	1840	1258	237	10	19	58	93	159	5	5400	5305	95

Notes:

[a] All African population figures for the period before proper censuses were introduced are of doubtful reliability (for full details see Appendix 2 below), and should be used only for comparative purposes and not as an estimate of absolute magnitudes, which are almost certainly understated by the estimates in this table. The estimates of African resident labour in Kenya (final column of this table) are particularly shaky. In particular, they are incompatible with the suggestion that as many as 100 000 squatters were moved off European land between 1950 and 1955 (see p. 241 n. 50 below).

[b] Estimate for 1939.

Sources: Southern Rhodesia: *Annual Reports of the Chief Native Commissioner.*

Kenya: Total African population from non-native census estimates, as summarised in Great Britain 1955b (B1), Appendix VII. Estimate of population on alienated land is adult male resident labour as recorded in Kenya *Agricultural Censuses*, annual, grossed up by the conventional factor of $3\frac{1}{2}$ (on this, see Appendix 2 below). Estimate of reserve population is simply the difference between the first and third columns.

the position of prospective buyer to prospective seller of land to evince great alarm at the first proposal, so that whereas in 1918 proposals to restrain land prices had split the white agrarian bourgeoisie, being in general opposed by the concessionaire group and welcomed by small farmers, they now met almost universal rural opposition. 'Most country districts have told their elected members to wreck the [1948 Land Control] Bill', wrote one observer, 'unless the [Land Control] Board is to be controlled by the settler.'[48] This pressure was successful, in Kenya, in getting the compulsory purchase powers confined to undeveloped land; in Southern Rhodesia, as in 1919, the government made concessionary sales of Crown land but was unable to impose any restraint on the private market in agricultural land, whose average price doubled between 1945 and 1948.[49] Thus attention naturally switched to the second more vulnerable butt of settlement policy, the African squatter. Over 85 000 families of Southern Rhodesian Africans, who had not taken up labour contracts under the Land Apportionment Act, were shifted from European land during the years 1945–51, as were a large number, possibly 100 000 persons,[50] in Kenya. This process, comparable to the 'clearances' in the Scottish highlands in the second half of the eighteenth century, involved the movement of Africans to arid outlying districts, a reduction in their real incomes, and violent African resentment of Europeans, which in Kenya has been linked to the 'Mau Mau' uprising of 1952–4.

Within the African areas a market in land was growing *pari passu* with the destruction of the market in squatter tenures. The Rhodesian and Kenyan Morris Carter Commissions had both taken the view that reserve land should be allocated to African farm families not on the basis of their needs in a system of extensive cultivation (in which a large proportion, up to nine-tenths, of the land would be resting at any one time), but on the basis of their much smaller needs in a system of intensive cultivation in which little, if any, allowance for fallow land was made. The report of the Kenyan Commission had in fact openly stated:

> The greater the margin by which the population falls short of the optimum density requirement [sc. for intensive cultivation], the greater is the justification of Government for regarding unoccupied land as waste land of which it has the right and duty to make disposal in the way which it deemed best for the country at large.[51]

This policy decision naturally accelerated the speed with which reserve land became scarce. The tradition, prevailing within almost every African community, that no member of the community should be left without land to use meant that initially this scarcity reflected itself rather in subdivision of holdings than in the emergence of those holdings as commodities traded between Africans; imperceptibly, however, the latter tendency surfaced in the inter-war periods. In Southern Rhodesia this process of individualisation was channelled off into the Native Purchase Areas; in Kenya, where the trivial provision for African individual tenure in the Land Commission's

27

report has already been noted, it was perforce confined within reserves, particularly those which like Kiambu were themselves overspill regions for Africans who had migrated from other areas in response to population pressure. Already by 1933 the authorities looked on it with anxiety as a process which would make it harder for the squatters currently being expelled from the European settled areas to find lands, and hence were determined to put a lid on the market for reserve land if possible:

> Outright sale [of land] is a phenomenon which has appeared in the Kiambu District, and is probably a departure from original custom, which probably admitted of redemption as in the other districts. While it is not practicable to forbid it altogether, it must be regulated so as to prevent the land from getting into the hands of a few large landlords who might form latefundia [sic]. The sanction of the Provincial Commissioner should be required before an outright sale is recognised.[52]

The hope persisted throughout the period 1930–45, in both countries, that the 'restoration' of power to the chiefs, even if in some pre-colonial tribal societies individual heads of clans had not existed, would bring about agricultural improvement in the reserves on a basis of *communal* tenure: the emergence of a market in land was seen as an obstacle to the fulfilment of this objective, as it entirely removed the control of a critical factor of production from the hands of such authorities.[53] This hope was to prove futile. As will be related in more detail in Chapter 3, the condition of some reserves had deteriorated by 1939 to a point where they were in no sense self-sustaining: the colonial authorities were thus faced with the option, barring any extension of the reserves, of freeing the market in land within them or alternatively of accepting a serious decline in African rural income.

The first of these options was chosen. In Kenya the process of land registration, consolidation and enclosure was voluntary, undertaken only if all members of a village wanted it, and led to the registration of a number, indeed a majority, of sub-economic holdings[54] in order to keep the problem of landlessness as small as possible. But in Southern Rhodesia, under the Native Land Husbandry Act of 1951, the process was compulsory and the market was restricted to what agricultural officers defined as economic holdings. Farming and grazing rights, of a size which varied inversely with the fertility of the soil but were in no case inheritable, were granted to individuals. They might lapse at any time upon proof of inadequate husbandry, whereupon they would be auctioned off into the market. The effective demand for economic holdings of this sort greatly exceeded the supply; it was hoped that, by contrast with what was possible in the less industrialised economy of Kenya, the growth of off-farm employment could be sustained so as to take up the slack. In fact, it was precisely in the mid 1950s that off-farm employment began to cease to grow,[55] and the problem thus created was to lead to the suspension of land registration under the Native Land Husbandry Act in 1960. But by then the market as a means of land transfer had been irreversibly imported into the African reserves.

The parting of the ways, 1952–63

Throughout the period from the First World War to the mid-fifties, the land policies pursued in the two settler economies could be described, with differences of emphasis detailed in the previous sections, as identical; the achievement of possessory segregation between whites and other races, a progressive squeeze on African cultivators in white areas, and an attempt to canalise the pressure on scarce land resources in African areas by creating areas of individual African tenure. But, in two areas, sharp differences emerge in the 1950s. The first was the urban land market. In Kenya, Africans were in principle free to buy land anywhere, but the barrier of low incomes restricted their actual purchases to what became areas of slum landlord ownership in the areas of Pumwani and Kariakor in Nairobi, set apart for their occupation after a demand for zoning before the First World War. Those who could not be accommodated here or in municipal accommodation spilled out on to unoccupied Crown land beyond the city limits. In Southern Rhodesia under the Land Apportionment Act even the Pumwani option was not possible, and the policy adopted from 1946 on was to impose on municipalities the responsibility for building operations and on employers the responsibility for paying the rent on it; under such a system no urban African could have any security of tenure. In the 1950s the implications of this difference in the legal position became manifest.

In Kenya the fact that urban areas were non-racial made it possible for Africans to penetrate the European suburbs;[56] in Southern Rhodesia there was no such upward percolation in the housing market. The suggestion of the 1958 Urban African Affairs Commission that at least some non-racial areas should be created within the towns, and that Africans should be given more security of tenure there, was rebutted on the ground that this involved 'whittling away the Land Apportionment Act as quickly as possible', an act which had been seen by Europeans 'as a charter, almost a bill of rights in this country'.[57]

The second was the question of the rights of Africans to purchase land within the area reserved for Europeans, which was reopened by economic liberals in both countries in the 1950s. The repeal of the (Kenya) Highlands Order in Council was proposed by the East Africa Royal Commission in 1955, and although this proposal was resisted by much of the settler community, it gained substantial support, not least on the grounds that possessory segregation of land was actually keeping land values *down*.[58] It was eventually implemented in 1961. By contrast, the repeal of the Southern Rhodesia Land Apportionment Act, proposed by the Quinton Committee in 1960 and adopted by Sir Garfield Todd's United Federal Party as one of its main policies for the 1962 election, vanished from the realm of white Rhodesian politics when that party was defeated. From this contrast, more than any other, stem the subsequent differences in political evolution between the two countries.

29

Railways

> [The subject of railway rating] deals with the body politic, because by a system of
> railway rates you can make or mar a province, you can make or mar a race,
> really, because you can make your rates on a certain class of produce which is
> mainly grown by one race, more or less favourable, as the case may be.
>
> Sir Humphrey Leggett in Great Britain 1931 (B1), vol. II, p. 340

The concessionaire period: to 1920

The diverse origins of the settler economies were duly reflected in the two
countries' railway systems. Kenya's system was originally intended only
to provide quick access from the Indian Ocean to Lake Victoria and therefore consisted, until 1912, of one line between those points. By contrast,
Southern Rhodesia's was intended at first to exploit low-grade mineral
deposits, which generally could not bear the cost of carriage by non-rail
means for more than ten miles or so;[59] hence it spawned branch lines from
the start. In the period to 1914 the construction of railways was, where
possible, on a *laissez-faire* basis: the logic of the policy of concessionaire
development was, as we have seen (cf. note 13 above), that in return for the
grant of exceptionally cheap inputs – in particular land – the grantee would
itself undertake the burden of productive investment on its concessions.
This policy yielded quite a crop of additional branch lines in Southern
Rhodesia, but in Kenya, where hopes of profitable productive investment
were lower, resulted only in the ninety-one-mile line to the Magadi Soda
concession, completed in 1912. At this stage, the concessionaires, as in the
land market, met little opposition over the question of *where* railways should
be built. But the question of what should be paid for their services was a
live political issue from the start.

As a point of departure, it is possible to conceptualise the struggle over
railway rates in the settler economies in terms of a conflict between a monopoly supplier,[60] determined to raise price and restrict output to the profit-
maximising point, and a cluster of powerful settler-consumers (concessionaires and 'small men'), equally determined to use political pressure to force
this price down and if possible get output expanded as well by the provision
of more frequent services. This certainly was the way that the settlers themselves saw the matter.[61] But the available evidence, on a matter on which
the railway administrations were seldom forthcoming, is that they were in
fact output-maximisers,[62] subject to the constraint of avoiding a loss on
their overall operations. Persistently they expressed a wish to 'charge what the
traffic will bear', a nebulous phrase which, presumably, means that they
believed there was a 'critical railway rate' for all traffic, and that if rates
were pushed above this critical level the entire traffic would vanish. On the
opposite side of the market, the principal objective was of course simply
to push down railway rates as far as possible. Two rationalisations were
used in support of this argument: (1) in a situation where many trucks used

to bring imports up from the coast have to return empty for want of export traffic, the marginal cost of carrying exports down is small, and exports should only be charged this small marginal cost;[63] (2) the vague idea of 'the development of the colony'.

The conflict between these two pressure groups proceeded in the following fashion in the early years. As an initial step the railway authorities quoted rates for carriage which were approximately proportionate to value per ton (see left-hand column of Table 2.5); this was an attempt to charge in the absence of detailed data 'what the traffic would bear'. Since exports consisted of bulky raw materials and imports of manufactures, this policy immediately produced the structure of low export rates and high import rates which was always characteristic of the tariff books of the settler economies. At this stage, it was expected that, in terms of volume, 'down' freights to the coast would balance 'up' freights of imports. They did not,[64] and settlers were quick to suggest that this was due to crippling rail rates on exports. The railway companies, believing they had made an incorrect estimate of 'what the traffic would bear' and deferring to the settlers' superior political power,

Table 2.5a. *Rail rates for carriage of freight (shillings per ton-mile): Kenya and Uganda Railway, 1914–59*

Rate class	Description of goods carried	1914	1933	1943	1959	Thousands of tons carried in each rate class, 1959
1	Cotton cloth and piece goods, wines and spirits, cigarettes	0.59 (spirits) 0.39 (piece goods from Europe)	1.11			
				0.50	0.383	(103)
2	Cutlery, electric bulbs, glassware		0.87			
3	Blankets, bicycles	0.35	0.61			
4	Provisions, hardware	0.33	0.45	0.47	0.389	(45)
5	Petrol, paint	0.27	0.38	0.37	0.357	(252)
6	Bacon, ham, joinery, paper	0.28	0.28	0.29	0.313	(71)
7	Machinery and iron and steel in small quantities	0.14	0.20	0.20	0.29	(115)
8	Machinery and iron and steel in wagon loads		0.17	0.17	0.231	(428)
9	Raw materials (cement, diesel oil, timber etc.) in wagon	0.15 (cement) 0.20 (iron)	0.13	0.14	0.174	(288)
10	loads	0.18 (timber)	0.10	0.11	0.155	(843)
Exceptional			0.06	0.06	0.167	(934)
'Export':	Cotton (800 miles export rate)	0.04			0.12	
	Coffee (640 miles export rate)	0.075			0.24	(901)
	Maize (445 miles export rate)	0.019	0.024	0.023	0.082	

Note: 1914 data are given in per ton terms and are converted to per ton-mile terms using 1933 average length of haul.

Sources: Uganda Railway (1921–48, Kenya–Uganda Railway; 1948 and after, East Africa Railways and Harbours): *Administration Reports* 1914–15, 1933, 1943, 1959.

Table 2.5b. *Rail rates for carriage of freight (shillings per ton-mile):
Rhodesia Railways, 1905–58*

	Rate class	Description of goods carried	1905	1920	1925	1934	1958	Thousands of tons carried in each rate class, 1958
High value consumer goods	1	Cotton piece goods, manufactured tobacco	0.81	0.69		0.52	0.70	(11.2)
	2	Writing paper, cutlery and other household effects	0.62	0.69		0.43	0.58	(3.5)
	3	Hollow-ware, household utensils	–				0.49	(10.7)
	4	Paint, wire, dyes, petrol, most clothing		0.69		0.31	0.47	(8.1)
Lower value consumer goods	5	Cooking oil and other provisions	0.46	0.69		0.29	0.46	(5.5)
	6	Breakfast foods, wheat flour, rice	–	0.34		0.25	0.30	(13.0)
	7						0.28	(40.2)
	8	Iron and steel, machinery[a]	0.25	0.47		0.20	0.21	(20.8)
	9						0.18	(2.5)
Industrial inputs and high value exports	10	Hides and meat extract for export tractors, sugar, tobacco[a]	–	0.61		0.155	0.13	(42.3)
	11	Local timber and orange juice, ploughs, native hoes, cement[a]	0.16	0.25	0.24	0.075	0.11	(27.8)
	12	Cattle feeds, agricultural lime, salt, fertilisers (to 1945)		0.053	0.05	0.032	0.07	(50.7)
Low value exports and bulk inputs	13	Fencing wire, barbed wire, wheat, tobacco for export		0.14	0.10	0.032	0.06	(87.6)
	14	Fertilisers (after 1945)					0.055	(12.4)
		Special export rates						
		Maize to Beira (selling 32/6 or less)	0.034	0.038	0.027 ⎫	0.034	0.06	(641.3)
		(selling 37/6 or more)	0.034	0.038	0.038 ⎭			

– not available

Notes: [a] After 1945 the following changes in rates took place: machinery in full wagon loads was demoted to class 10; tobacco was carried at rate 10 plus 10 per cent; cement was demoted from class 11 to class 13; fertilisers were demoted from class 12 to a new class 14.   [b] Average length of hauls for different rate classes on Rhodesian Railways is unknown, but if as on East African Railways it was the higher-rated goods which travelled the longer distance (cf. Table 2.5a, last column) then the figures given here for the higher rate classes are over-estimates, and for the lower classes they are under-estimates.

Sources: 1905 – PRO: CO 417/407, High Commissioner Cape Town to Colonial Secretary, 9 January 1905. 1920, 1925 – Southern Rhodesia 1926 (B2), vol II, p. 103.
1934 – Railway Commission of Southern Rhodesia, Northern Rhodesia and Bechuanaland, *Annual Report*, Appendix 5.
1958 – Federation of Rhodesia and Nyasaland 1959b (B2), Appendix 4, p. 67 (rates are quoted for the average haul of 388 miles).

made repeated cuts, before the First World War, in their rates on the basic 'export staples': gold, coal and chrome in Rhodesia, beans and potatoes in Kenya, and maize in both countries. After increases in line with the cost of railway inputs during the First World War, further 'political' cuts in export rates were made to ease the plight of white farmers during the world depression in export prices in 1920–2.[65] These cuts required adjustment

Table 2.6. *Kenya, Southern Rhodesia and Nigeria: railway rates, 1920*

| | Carriage rates (pence per ton-mile; 330 miles) | | |
	Kenya	Southern Rhodesia	Nigeria
Consumer goods imports			
Cotton piece goods	7.00	4.12	2.90
Kerosene oil	2.15	2.42	1.18
Mainly European exports			
Maize	0.28	0.36	
Chrome		0.46	
Mainly African exports			
Groundnuts		1.00	1.55
Cotton, ginned	1.41	2.85	
Hides and skins	3.39	3.63	2.00

Sources: Great Britain 1921 (B1), pp. 117–20; Southern Rhodesia 1926 (B2) vol. II, pp. 103–4.

elsewhere in the system if the railway companies' cash flows were to be preserved: the freight rates on imports of consumer goods, for which demand was presumed to be inelastic, were pushed upward, as may be seen from Table 2.5. Even at this stage the trading lobby, particularly the Indians of Kenya, were up in arms at (though powerless to prevent) the consequent restriction on their sales to the (largely African) consuming public.[66]

A tendency to charge low freight rates for exports but high rates for imported consumer goods was apparent to some degree in all colonies.[67] But, as Table 2.6 shows, it went far further in Kenya and Southern Rhodesia than in Nigeria, an example of a 'peasant export economy' where the exporters were not as powerful a pressure group for influencing freight rates.

Intra-settler conflict 1920–45

As noted above, there was always some conflict, particularly in the 1921–2 depression, between concessionaires and small maize and tobacco producers[68] over rail rates. A quite separate focus of conflict between these two interests emerged in the 1920s: the routing of branch lines.

The most blatant example of this opposition of interests, and of the way in which it was usually resolved, was the Uasin Gishu line in Kenya. The Uasin Gishu is a plateau (see map, p. xiv) settled by many of the original South African immigrants who came to Kenya in 1903, and was over sixty miles from the nearest railway. It was therefore well outside the market zone, one of those areas where white settlers, as much the Africans around them, were living at subsistence level, 'on their dwindling capital, by taking in each other's washing, a hand-to-mouth existence'.[69] A line to connect this plateau up with the main line was surveyed in 1915; this was route 1 on Map 2.3b. This, as the map shows, did not join the main line by the quickest route, but cut the western wall of the Rift Valley, twenty miles north of the existing line, finally joining it at Nakuru. Furthermore, as McGregor Ross pointed out, it

> appeared to be traversing farms, for the most part unoccupied, which formed part of the allotment of 156 square miles [diagonally barred on Map 2.3b] which had been given to Lord Delamere in 1903. After crossing the Delamere concession it traversed two large blocks of forest comprised in a Concession granted to Mr Grogan. [Horizontally barred area on Map 2.3b.] It traversed them moreover in a manner almost ideal for the economic working of the forest areas. Transport of felled timber to the line would be, for the greatest part of the concessional area, down-hill. The line crossed enormous ravines low down in their course, entailing excessively heavy earth work and an inordinate amount of bridging.[70]

The First World War delayed the securing of loan finance for this project. By the time that it was revived in 1920 the representation of the 'small men' in discussions on economic policy had, as we have seen, greatly increased. Such men resented the determination of the concessionaires to route the arteries of communication in whatever way best served their estates, much as the landlords of eighteenth-century England had done in dictating the path taken by the turnpike roads. They used their majority on the Legislative Council to force through a resolution on 10 July 1920, recommending that the desired branch line should follow route 2 on Map 2.3b, joining the main line above the Rift Valley escarpment at a financial saving of some £600 000 and passing to the south of the estates of the 'landed barons'. However, a majority on the Legislative Council, in colonial Kenya, did not guarantee control over policy. In 1922, following a technical survey by a British engineer which was derived from sources with a direct interest in the early building of the railway along the original alignment,[71] construction was started on the compromise route depicted by the line marked 3 on Map 2.3b. The choice of this route is clearly the result of a deal having been struck between the big concessionaires and two groups of interests whom, given the altered balance of power after 1920, they needed at least to propitiate. One was the trustees of African interests in the Colonial Office, to whose attention it could be conveyed that the Nakuru route (3), when extended to Uganda, would cheapen the export of Ugandan cotton and coffee exports by reducing the incline up the Rift Valley escarpment; the other was the 'small men' themselves, who although publicly snubbed by the refusal of their persistent requests for an enquiry into the routing and cost of the Uasin Gishu line, could be privately conciliated by the promise of branch lines into their own regions, in particular the Kitale and Solai lines (4 and 5 on Map 2.3b). One Legislative Council member, J.E. Coney, who represented the area reached by line 4, was to allege in Council that the 'log-rolling' process had in fact been explicit.[72]

Much the same conflict of interest between 'old' and 'new' interests in relation to the construction of inter-war branch lines is apparent in Southern Rhodesia, although there the intensity of conflict was moderated by the fact that many of the branch lines, built before the war to serve mining

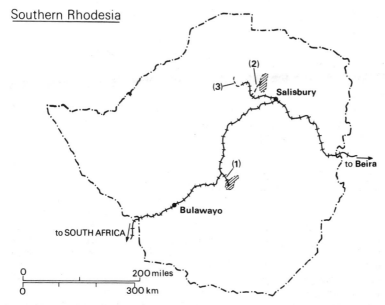

Map 2.3a. Conflict over branch railway lines, Southern Rhodesia, 1920s. (1) Selukwe chrome deposit (foreign-owned): (2) Umvukwes chrome deposit and proposed branch railway: (3) proposed Umboe branch railway.

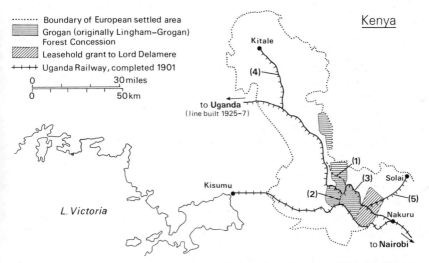

Map 2.3b. Alternative routes for Uasin Gishu Railway, Kenya, 1914–24. Uasin Gishu Railway: (1) alignment surveyed 1914/15; (2) 'Mau Summit route' surveyed 1918/19; (3) alignment eventually adopted. (4) Kitale line, built 1923–4. (5) Solai line, built 1924–5. *Source*: PRO: CO 533/206, enclosure in Bowring (Acting Governor of Kenya) to Milner (Colonial Secretary), 30 January 1919.

35

interests, survived to offer an 'external economy' to incoming agricultural settlers. The principal focus of conflict here was the suggested construction of a couple of branch lines to the north-west of Salisbury – one of them (3 on Map 2.3a) into the agricultural region of the Umboe Valley and the other (2 on Map 2.3a) into the Umvukwes chrome deposits. Captain Bertin, a Salisbury solicitor, argued that development of the Umvukwes deposits was being held up by the near monopoly of chrome mining held by Rhodesia Chrome Mines Ltd, under the control of the London-based businessman Edmund Davis, aided and abetted by the BSAC's control of the railways:

> We have this interlocking of directors and of people who control very large sums left for this and adjoining territories, which should be administered as a trust for the benefit of transport in this area of Africa. The people who are interested in the Selukwe chrome [1 on Map 2.3a; the only chrome deposit in Rhodesia being mined at that time; sc. Edmund Davis Associates] are the same individuals who are interested in the coal and the railways, and everything else. We shall have to alter that position in some way or another. It is suggested that the men in control of the Selukwe chrome do not want the Umvukwes chrome opened up. It will do them harm because it is chrome of a greater value [it was also a good deal closer to the nearest port at Beira].
>
> Which line should be built? Undoubtedly the Umvukwes. Yet this other one [sc. the Umboe] is forced upon us by the Railways and by the Beit Trustees.[73]

Bertin was casting the Umboe line in the same role which we have argued the Solai line filled in Kenya – i.e. as a sop to buy off the small farmer-settlers from opposition to the line of policy which the 'concessionaire oligopoly' really wanted to push through. However, in this particular case the Southern Rhodesia government was able to overcome the railways' restrictive bias by playing one foreign corporation off against another. Davis' principal rival, the Chrome Corporation of South Africa, had been buying claims off disappointed small-workers in the Umvukwes, and when that Corporation offered to pay the railways a rate of 2d. to 3d. per ton-mile on the branch line instead of 0.46d. ruling in the tariff book – and paid by the Selukwe producers – the railways' last objection to building the line was overcome.

Thus in both countries the competitive position of the 'small men' was bolstered by branch lines nearly all of which were to run at a loss – an inevitable consequence given that most of them carried mainly or exclusively maize, a traffic which in neither colony was carried at a rate which exceeded the estimated bare haulage cost. In 1930 in Kenya the sum of these losses ran to ten per cent of the country's public revenue.[74]

In the field of railway rates, the decisive influence on the rate structure during the inter-war period was the growth of motor road transport, which first became a significant enough factor to feature in public policy discussions in the middle 1920s. It took up two roles: the first, complementary to the railways as a supplement to the ox-cart and pack-donkey in bringing goods to market along those roads that were motorable; the second, competitive with them in bringing import traffics up from the coast. Since, in the 1920s, the top rail rate for consumer goods imports was something like three times the average ton-mile cost of road transport, such competition quickly made inroads on the railway's revenue. The railways devised three strategies in order to meet the threat. The first was to increase the volume of goods carried on the railways in order to lower unit costs of operation, particularly by exports to neighbouring countries. The second was a reduction of these top railway rates which were most vulnerable to road competition. The top railway rate, that charged for the import of high-value consumer goods such as cotton piece goods, was reduced between 1920 and 1940 from 1.03 to 0.40 shillings per ton-mile on the Kenya–Uganda railway and from 0.69 to 0.52 shillings per ton-mile on the Rhodesia Railways. The trading lobby, of course, had been pressing for cuts of this kind since the earliest days, and was by no means satisfied with those made in the inter-war period, as it could see perfectly well that by squeezing the rail rates concertina into a flat rate of, say, twenty cents per ton-mile in East Africa (or thirty cents on Rhodesia Railways, with its higher wages structure) all road competition on trunk routes could be eliminated.[75] But the balance of political power had by no means changed sufficiently against the primary exporters, who were of course still trying to stretch out the concertina from below, for such a drastic revision of rating policy to be contemplated. The concessional export rates remained at too low a level for rail rates on imports to be cut to a figure which would make them competitive with road transport. But those export rates were not reduced in response to pressure from exporters in the 1930s depression, as they had been in the depression of 1920–2.[76]

Such road competition as could not be abated by cutting import rates had to be combated by a third strategy, that of restricting road competition through licensing legislation which restricted the number of road transporters who could operate on a given route.

In Southern Rhodesia road operators were further constrained by being required, as a condition of the grant of a licence, to charge no less than the equivalent railway rate when operating parallel with the line of rail. The trading lobbies in both countries pressed persistently for the liberalisation of this system, but in this they were not successful until the end of the colonial period.

After the Second World War, shifts in the structure of the settler economies imposed further pressure on the pattern of railway freight rates. Industrialisation during the war caused many consumer goods which had once been imported to be produced at home. This reduced the proportion of the railways' total traffic that carried high freight rates: many trucks which went down to the coast with low-rated exports were now unable to recoup the deficit on the return trip since they came back with low-rated imports. This trend, occurring simultaneously with a continued erosion of the business of carrying the high-rated import traffics by licensed road transporters, left the railways with no option but to raise export rates – a step which was made politically easier for them by the increase of world prices during the Second World War to levels which made exporting a profitable proposition, temporarily, for all but the most inefficient producers. Subsequent increases in the general level of rates made necessary by the increase of the general price level in the 1950s were notable in that the lower rate classes were pushed up by more than the higher rate classes.[77] But against this trend, space was still found at the very end of our period for discretionary rail-rate reliefs to farmers.

To see the structure of rates which emerged, we may at this point refer back to Table 2.5. If we compare the figures for 1958/9 with the figures for 1914/15 and intervening years, we can see how far economic factors – i.e. the loss of the railways' monopoly position and the change in the composition of their traffic – managed to compress the original and largely politically determined rate structure of the railways. The compression is more dramatic on the East African Railways, where a differential of 30:1 in 1914 between the top and bottom rates per ton-mile had been squeezed to less than 3:1 by 1959, than on the Rhodesia Railways, where the difference between the top (cotton piece goods) and bottom (export maize) rail rates goes from 25:1 in 1920 to a still considerable 12:1 in 1958.

In concluding this case study it is worth briefly considering the welfare implications of the railway rating structure. E.A. Brett has argued that 'Public policy in Kenya was based upon the assumption that all communities should be made responsible for the well-being of the settler sector, and the railway was used as a primary means of operationalising this commitment.'[78] It will be apparent from our discussion so far that this judgment, which Brett is not alone in making,[79] oversimplifies the reality in both Kenya and Southern Rhodesia. In Table 2.7 we trace through time the rail rates charged for the carriage of a representative basket of goods produced and consumed by the European and African communities in both countries, using as weights the relative importance of the goods in question in consumers' budgets or in the productive structure, as the case may be. The relativities which emerge between the costs of rail freight for these 'representative baskets' are down in the table.

The data of Table 2.7 do not afford the basis for a scientific comparison of the welfare impact of rail rates. But they do suggest that if one compares consumer with consumer, or producer with producer, it was on balance the European who paid the higher rates until the 1950s.[80] African consumers certainly paid more than European producers at all times, but this reflects simply the practice of charging rail carriage according to the value of the article carried, and not, as Brett implies, discrimination intended to 'operationalise the commitment to the settler sector'. Both races paid high rates for consumer goods, both races enjoyed an exceptionally cheap export rate for their maize, and inasmuch as Europeans gained benefit from the system of rail rates, it was simply because they were responsible for most of the marketed production and only a small part of marketed consumption.

Table 2.7. *Kenya and Southern Rhodesia: ratios of average rail rates on 'representative baskets' of goods consumed by Africans and Europeans, 1914–59*

Kenya	1914	1933	1943	1959
European consumers/African consumers	1.15	1.37	1.01	0.96
European producers/African producers	1.33	2.03	1.95	1.29
European producers/African consumers	0.41	0.35	0.39	0.57
Southern Rhodesia	1920	1934	1958	
European consumers/African consumers	1.00	1.15	1.09	
European producers/African producers	1.86	2.11	0.82	
European producers/African consumers	0.72	0.30	0.33	

Sources: Rail rates, Table 2.5 above. Weights, from agricultural census, household budget survey or arbitrary assumption, as detailed below.
    The 'representative baskets' for each interest group are made up as follows:

Kenya
    African consumers: provisions, cotton piece goods, kerosene; weights from African price index (see Appendix 3 below).
    African producers: hides and skins, maize, wattle, cotton; 1951 weights from Agriculture Department *Annual Report* (B 3).
    European consumers: provisions, household requisites, petrol, wines and spirits, each with arbitrary weight of 25 per cent.
    European producers: coffee, sisal, wheat, tea, maize, beef, wholemilk butter; 1951 weights from Agriculture Department *Annual Report*.
Southern Rhodesia
    African consumers: basket as for Kenya. Weights from Southern Rhodesia 1959 (B 2).
    African producers: maize, millets, groundnuts, beef, hides; 1951 weights from *Annual Report of the Chief Native Commissioner*.
    European consumers: basket and weights as for Kenya.
    European producers: tobacco, maize, beef, gold, chrome, asbestos, coal; 1951 weights from *Annual Trade Report*.

The marketing system: maize and cattle

> *Chairman* Does the export price finally rule the internal price? [Is it not possible to] control the price by watching the demand and keeping back surplus? So as to keep the local market at a higher price, a reasonably high price? *Mr Dryden* There is a lot of this artificial manipulation in South Africa. As long as they have the Rand to call upon, they can do all sorts of weird things. I don't like this idea.
> NAR: ZBJ 1/1/2, Evidence to the Native Production and Trade Commission
> 1944, p. 826

Introduction

Whenever, in either of the settler economies before 1950, competition between black and white producers could be avoided, it was. If the pro-

39

duction of something required some indivisible input, the exclusion of African producers from the market was particularly simple, as poverty, exacerbated by lack of credit facilities, would prevent them from buying it, and market forces could then be left to work unhindered. But if this condition was not satisfied an 'indivisible input' could be *created* by requiring producers of a cash crop to buy an expensive licence, or by other administrative arrangements which introduced a handicap into the African cost structure without the appearance of overt discrimination of a kind which would attract Colonial Office intervention.

By a combination of these methods Africans were prevented, until the 1950s, from significant participation in the production of the settler economies' most important export crops: in Southern Rhodesia, tobacco (43 per cent of *total* exports in 1952) and in Kenya, coffee, tea, and pyrethrum (respectively 31, 6 and 3 per cent of total agricultural exports in 1952). In the case of tea and Virginia tobacco, 'natural' indivisibilities alone were almost sufficient on their own, as very few Africans could afford tea seeds or tobacco-curing barns[81] without Agricultural Department assistance which was not forthcoming; but in each of these cases, additionally, export was monopolised by a producers' cooperative which made it clear that it did not welcome African participation, and set its quality standards expressly so as to exclude it.[82] Pyrethrum production by Kenya Africans was discouraged by charging an annual licence fee which, in 1947, stood at 50s. or approximately half the average annual African disposable income from sale of crops and labour. African coffee growing was blocked first by fees and, when that proved insufficient, by administrative prohibition, until both were removed in 1949.[83] In Southern Rhodesia during the inter-war period, Native Department efforts to encourage African production of cotton and wheat, which had progressed fitfully during the early twenties, were sharply cut back on orders from above.[84] The official ideology in support of these restrictions on African cash crops – which occasionally had to be defended against a stray question in the Commons[85] – was that they helped to safeguard the African's food supplies, in face of his 'defective telescopic faculty'. It was stated in its plainest form by Kenya's Director of Agriculture in 1932:

> You might say that those areas in the Kikuyu Reserve which are suited to growing coffee had better grow coffee and nothing else to get the best return from each acre per annum, but then there is the question of the food requirements of the people. The native is not sufficiently advanced to grow coffee and sell it and with the proceeds buy food and other necessaries.[86]

Later this ideology acquired a couple of embellishments: cash-crop development led to land erosion[87] and exposed the African to price fluctuations with which he could not be expected to cope.[88] These views continued to be expounded despite the manifest success of African peasant production of coffee in Uganda and Tanganyika and tobacco in Nyasaland.

Not all African agricultural production for the market, however, could be restricted in this way. Some of it arose directly out of subsistence production activities, which could not be directly attacked without endangering the flow of hut-tax payments and of low-cost labour to the European areas[89] and were in addition hard to restrict, as they demanded no costly inputs. The most important activities in this category were maize growing and cattle raising. The very technical simplicity of these activities, however, made them also central to the European rural economy, and in particular to the business of encouraging new settlement, as they were among the few activities open to individuals of limited means and farming skills. Policy in such a context required the protection of the European producer against the competition of the African *without hitting the African too hard*, more particularly since there were influential economic sectors to whom maize and cattle were *inputs* and who welcomed the African's cheap supplies. It is the 'extra-market operations' involved in the reconciliation of these interests that we now examine.

The 'open economy': 1900–30

The most essential factor of production which the European economy required from the African, apart from labour, was food. In the pre-colonial economies, of course, the practice of exchanging food surpluses (for example, Kikuyu grain for Masai livestock) was of long standing;[90] the grafting of mines and plantations on to these economies thus involved in the first instance merely the addition of a cluster of 'food-deficit areas' to those already in existence. These foreign enterprises bought either direct from the African farmer or from a trader, in Kenya usually an Indian, who took the small loads (usually 35 to 60 lb) which the African producers brought in by donkey cart and head load, dried it in the sun, and sold it in 200 lb bags to miner, farmer or wholesaler. Their interest as consumers was to keep the price at which they bought as low as possible. Failing direct confiscation of standing crops, which seems not to have occurred after the early years of conquest, their best hope of doing this in the case of maize was to preserve a regime of free competition among traders, under which the price was free to float downwards towards the export parity; the rapid growth of African agricultural exports before 1914 is an index of the rate at which this trade expanded.

In the case of cattle the possibility of free competition of this sort in an open market was limited by disease. The four main diseases to which cattle were subject were rinderpest, contagious bovine pleuro-pneumonia (CBPP), African (or East) Coast fever and foot-and-mouth. Protection against rinderpest, in the state of knowledge of the early 1920s, was available through a vaccine; against East Coast fever, which was tick-borne, by regular dipping; against the other two only by slaughter of infected animals, fencing of non-infected areas, and quarantine of animals passing between clean and

41

infected areas.[91] However, the size of areas declared 'infected', the period of quarantine and, in the case of rinderpest and East Coast fever, the ratio of 'positive' treatment (vaccination and dipping) to 'negative' treatment (ordinary quarantine) were very much government policy variables. At one end of the veterinary policy spectrum lay Tanganyika, with a comprehensive intelligence service in the African areas, a policy of vaccinating against rinderpest (which had been banished from two-thirds of the country by 1934), government dip tanks and only local constraints on the stock trade.[92] At the other lay Kenya, with no Veterinary Department establishment in the purely pastoral reserves, no regular vaccination campaigns against rinderpest in African cattle, very few dip tanks on white farms[93] and, as a result of all this, a policy of quarantining entire reserves whenever disease broke out, with the result that the legal stock trade was confined to a trickle through the quarantine stations, a trickle which in normal years fell very far short of the natural increase in the African herd. The veterinary service was concentrated in European areas, with free rinderpest injections (Africans paid for theirs at quarantine stations) and quarantines confined to individual farms. This duality of standards was well exposed by a Colonial Office civil servant in 1934: 'It seems to me quite wrong that a huge area like the Masai reserve should be under quarantine. It is larger than the whole area occupied by Europeans, and no-one would contemplate placing the whole European area under quarantine because disease existed on some farms.'[94]

Southern Rhodesia was an intermediate case, with the same dual standards of veterinary service but far more localised quarantines and a policy of making grants to farmers to erect dip tanks on their farms and then allowing them to recover from Africans on their property the cost of dipping their cattle. In Southern Rhodesia 75 per cent of African cattle were dipped in this way by 1921. This contrast in dipping policy between the two countries owes something to the greater budget of the Southern Rhodesia Agricultural Department, but something also to land policy: it was possible to protect the White Highlands of Kenya, set in a compact block, by simply fencing them off from the pastoral reserves and providing manned 'drawbridges' in a way that simply was not possible in Southern Rhodesia where the main white belt was dotted with African reserves like currants in a cake (Map 2.2 above). Nonetheless, here too wholesale sellers of cattle could not find markets:[95] a summary picture of the situation in certain important pastoral reserves of the settler economies from 1913 to 1940 is given in Table 3.8 below.

As a result of these restrictions the marketing of beef cattle, though not controlled by any government authority before the 1930s, could in no sense be described as free, the supply of such cattle by Africans being as much determined by the government's quarantine policy as by what Africans wished to sell at the prevailing price. The consequences of this for cattle numbers and marketed offtake are explored in Chapter 3.4. For the moment it is necessary only to note that a growing surplus of live cattle in the African areas over what their owners wished to keep or were able to sell forced their prices down sharply in 1920 and kept them down throughout the boom of the 1920s. As a consumer of hardy breeding stock from the reserves, the European stockowner welcomed this development; as producer, however, it aroused his anxiety lest an opening of the 'drawbridges' by the Veterinary Department should bring down the price of slaughter stock in the settled areas.

Our discussion so far has in fact pictured European producers purely as consumers of African maize and breeding stock, with a consequent interest in a free market. Potentially, however, they were at the same time producing those commodities in competition with African producers, which gave them an opposite interest. But this conflict of roles was not immediately exposed: when the problem of white producers making losses on the home market first arose, in the decade 1910–20, it was met not by restricting African competition but by the formation of producers' organisations to seek export markets for any European production in excess of what would satisfy the home market at a remunerative price.[96] Except in 1921–2, these export markets were normally profitable ones, and there was thus no pressure to try and push Africans out of the rural (mine and plantation) markets, which they had always supplied at a fraction of the costs of European producers.[97]

Restriction of competition 1930–50

World prices began to drop at the end of the 1920s. By 1930 (see Table 3.6 below) most European farmers were therefore selling maize and beef in both local and export markets below their costs of production. This was widely perceived to be a situation critical for the survival of the entire European settler community, as maize growing and stock raising were seen to be among the few activities accessible to the small undercapitalised settler rather than the large international company. As such, they were perceived as both gateways to future settlement and keys to the land values on which the banks' ability to lend for further development depended.[98] Uniquely amongst settler economy outputs, they faced a substantial home market, and heavy African competition. The natural response was to raise prices in the former by restriction of the latter and also by a deliberate policy of encouraging export: the loss-making exports themselves could not be curtailed without flooding the relatively small home market. But this response met opposition, not only from Africans and their representatives in the church and the Colonial Office, but also from those producers who were major buyers of maize. Mere restriction of output by quotas on European producers was no solution, as a perplexed secretary of the Rhodesian Maize Association was to concede in 1933:

> I have been considering the suggested Quota Scheme, and I cannot for the life of me, see how you are going to evade, (1) the native question, (2) the large grower

with several farms. Whatever quota you may fix on it gives the natives the local markets. If you make regulations to exclude the natives, the Missionaries and the Home Government will kick. If you do not make the native carry his share of the disabilities of export the European growers will kick.[99]

Below we consider the various ways in which, from the 1930s on, this political dilemma of economic policy was confronted.

Maize

A policy of 'compulsory cooperation' had been advocated by the Rhodesian Agricultural Union since 1924: for whenever the export price which the Farmers' Cooperative was able to obtain fell below that obtainable on the home market farmers dodged the cooperative, sold directly on the local market what they could, and exported through the cooperative only what they could not otherwise dispose of. This policy was opposed not only by the consuming interests previously referred to, but also by farmers in Matabeleland and the Eastern Districts, who produced (or so they claimed) for their own consumption and little more, and saw little justice in being dragged in 'to share the burden of export'. Accordingly, when in 1931 a Maize Control Bill was finally put forward to establish a Maize Control Board as monopoly purchaser of maize, it covered Mashonaland and the Midlands only. It was nonetheless opposed by the Salisbury Chamber of Commerce, the Rhodesia Railways, and the Chamber of Mines,[100] which threatened to boycott maize offered to them by the compulsory pool. One rancher made it clear in the Legislative Assembly that he saw the solution of the problem as the elimination of the high-cost European producer, and the future prosperity of European agriculture as being based on maize grown at 4s. a bag – not by the European, but by the African producer.[101]

Included in the scheme for 'compulsory cooperation' were the African maize producers in controlled areas who, in principle, received the same price as Europeans, if they could deliver direct to the Board. Very few, however, were able to do so; thus instead of being able to sell to the highest bidder amongst local European farmers, miners and traders, African producers were now the unwilling clients of a monopsonist, the Maize Control Board, which appointed as their buying agents traders who had formerly had to compete for African maize. This not only reduced the price the African producers received but also increased their vulnerability to sharp commercial practices. The situation was thus described by a telegram from the Native Commissioner, Mazoe:

> Traders in reserve now in position of monopolists and dictate not only price, but medium with which to buy grain, which medium is trade goods only. stop. I anticipate difficulty in collecting native revenue this year. stop. In past years private consumers bought grain in reserve for cash, incidentally controlling to some extent the prices paid by traders.[102]

By this means the local selling price of maize in Southern Rhodesia was raised from 7s. 3d. to 8s. 7d. a bag between 1930 and 1932 (in Kenya, with no formal controls, it fell during the same period from Sh. 7.87 to Sh. 6.50 a bag). But the *payout* to producers in Mashonaland and the Midlands, when export sales had been taken into account, was a mere 5s. $3\frac{1}{4}$d. a bag. 'Prices obtained by growers in exempted districts', lamented the report of the Maize Control Board for 1932/3, 'must have been nearly double this figure.'

This was the Achilles heel of the 1931 control scheme. 'Maize poured in from the exempted areas'[103] where European farmers – and many Africans too – expanded their maize acreage, even at derisory yields of one or two bags to the acre, in order to avoid having to buy at the inflated Control Board price. Thus on 7 June 1933, when proposals for the continuance of control were put to the Legislative Assembly, the ending of exemptions was one of the amendments put forward. But this left the proponents of control with precisely the same opposition that they had faced in 1931. The key to its pre-emption lay in an apparently chance remark made by the (Liberal) MLA Max Danziger in that debate:

> In dealing with native maize, we must admit in the beginning that no differential legislation will be possible. Another fact which I think is axiomatic is that before control, the native always received a price for his maize which was less than the overseas parity. So if we continue to pay him the same amount that he has been receiving there will be no injustice to him and no hardship.[104]

Was it possible, he was speculating, to apply the principle of Pareto improvement and buy off the maize consumers' opposition to control by letting them buy maize at the prices they had paid before its inception, while at the same time letting Africans receive 'something almost equal to overseas parity?' This approach, in spite of its false premises,[105] was to prove the key to the policy eventually followed.

As it was desired to pay Africans just under export parity, the logical step might have seemed to be to export their maize, thus reserving the high-price local market to Europeans; this seems to have been the approach of the Rhodesian Agricultural Union. But this was overtly discriminatory, did nothing to square the opposition of maize consumers and would have involved a massive and costly reorientation of the distribution system, since Africans had by the 1920s been largely squeezed out of the urban, never mind the export, market. The only option that remained was to use African grain, paid for below export price,[106] to supply the consumers that had traditionally bought it: outlying miners, ranchers and tobacco farmers. How this was done is illustrated in diagram form in Table 2.8. The compulsory pool of traded maize was split, by the Maize Control Amendment Act of 1934, into an 'export pool' and a 'local pool'. Maize going into the export pool was paid for at export price net of operating expenses, and maize going into the local pool was paid for at the net local market price. Much of the local market was then supplied *out of the export pool*, through sales to ranchers and tobacco farmers at a price well below the Board's

45

standard local selling price. Direct dealing between African producers and white farmer-consumers continued to be allowed if the consumer paid to the Maize Control Board a tax known as a 'rake-off'. The size of this rake-off varied between 1s. 6d. and 5s. depending on the size of the competitive threat which African production posed to European production in the region in question. In areas where there were few European maize producers the rake-off would be small; in areas where there were many white maize farmers the rake-off would be large, particularly if they were frightened of African competition. The only direct consumers exempted from this tax were missions and 'certain struggling miners recommended by the Chief Mining Engineer'.[107]

The existing channels of African maize supply thus came in the 1930s to be used to sustain a kind of outdoor relief service for the European primary producing community in which every element of that community deemed to be 'in need' was supplied with cheap maize according to the Maize Control Board's estimate of its ability to pay; even the formal structure described above is only an approximation of the actual distribution pattern, as any consumer in special need could always petition the Control Board for regrading or for a reduction of the rake-off paid, and the minutes of the Control Board are replete with the details of such hearings.[108]

Consumer opposition to the extension of control having been bought off in this way, it remained to make sure that African participation in the local pool was restricted without any appearance of overt discrimination. This was done by giving the trader-producer who bought most of the African's output a 25 per cent stake in the local pool; the same fraction as that received by large European producers, delivering 6000 bags or more. Smaller European producers received a stake in the local pool of between 25 per cent and 75 per cent depending on the size of their production.[109] However, even in 1937 it was, in the words of the Maize Control Board, 'a common misapprehension' which has since been repeated by scholars[110] that the 25 per cent of African maize actually obtained the local price. In fact anything surrendered to trader-producers paid a 5s. 'rake-off',[111] which on top of transport, bagging costs and the trader's profits, brought the price actually received by Africans down to a below-export-parity price of (in 1935) 3s. or less. The only African maize which actually obtained the full local price was a proportion of that delivered by them (or by their Native Commissioners) *direct to the Board*; the size of the proportion was dictated by the African share of direct deliveries to the Board in the first two years of control (1931/2 and 1932/3). This was 20.44 per cent; hence in the 1934/5 pool year, for example, the African share of the local pool was calculated at 20.44 per cent of the 12 500 bags delivered by Africans direct to the Board in that year. This was a tiny proportion (0.44 per cent) of the 580 265 bags on which the local pool pay-out was made for that season.

These complex operations – which we attempt to summarise in Table 2.8, showing the Board's operations for a typical year – were to prevail until

1941/2. There was a threat that the screw would be further tightened in 1937/8, when the export price sagged again. The year 1938 was to produce a proposal to restrict the trader-producer's share of the local market from 25 per cent to 10 per cent[112] and two suggestions[113] that the right to market crops, like the right to own land, should be partitioned between the races, 'otherwise' (in the words of the second of these) 'the extinction of the European farmer through native competition must ... be merely a question of time'. But in 1939 this vision of the home market as the object of a zero-sum game, to be competed for between Africans and Europeans, receded as the export price picked up again (see Table 3.6); it continued to rise until it was well above that prevailing on the home market. As a consequence, the export and local pools were amalgamated, *de facto* as from the 1941/2 pool year and formally in 1944/5.

In Kenya, as in Southern Rhodesia, the fall in prices of the early 1930s was met by a plan for state control of maize marketing from the organisation which monopolised European exports; in this case, the Kenya Farmers' Association (KFA). This could broadly be described as the Rhodesian scheme of 1931 without exemptions: all maize, European and African, was to be compulsorily directed into a pool under the jurisdiction of the Board of Agriculture,[114] a part of which would be exported in order to sustain the internal price. In this way Africans who had, as in Southern Rhodesia, nearly been pushed out of the export market during the 1920s[115] could be 'forced to share the burden of export'. As in Southern Rhodesia the main consuming interest-groups – above all, in this case, coffee and sisal producers, but also urban consumers generally – protested,[116] and the scheme was not proceeded with. In 1935 a scheme for control was again put forward, this time without any central pool; every trader in maize was required to export a specified portion of it. This too was dropped, and so, finally, was a scheme to set up a fund which would guarantee the export price at Sh. 4.50 a bag, put forward in Legislative Council on 30 December 1935. Fundamentally, the reason remained the failure of the Coffee Board (and other consuming interests) 'to be convinced by the arguments which suggest that the native maize grower would be unable to satisfy the internal requirements of the Colony'.[117] A potent fear among the consuming and trading community at this time, which had previously been voiced on behalf of the Southern Rhodesia trading community by J.H. Smit, was that as the export surplus rose the local price would have to be pushed higher and higher to compensate for this, with a proportionate decline in local purchasing power.[118]

The only relief received by Kenyan European maize growers, therefore, was *ad hoc* cash hand-outs, plus the establishment of a Land Bank. Unlike their Rhodesian counterparts they did not obtain any increase in the internal price of maize until late on in the decade, because they were unable to control the internal market. The key to this failure was essentially their inability to disarm the opposition of major maize consumers to a higher supply

47

Table 2.8. *Southern Rhodesia: operation of maize market under Maize Control Amendment Act 1934 (figures are given for pool year 1935/6, crop year 1934/5)*

Origin	Quantity delivered (200 lb bags)	Pool destination	Pool price per 200 lb bag	Deductions from pool price	Price to producer per 200 lb bag	Ultimate destination	Price paid by purchaser	Proceeds to Maize Control Board (£)
African production								
Purchases by Board in reserves	3 535	Direct to Export Pool 3 535	5s. 10.25d	Variable 'rake-off'[b] transport charge, Trader's margin	2s. to 5s.6d[b]	*Exports* Sales to neighbouring countries	7s. 8.4d.	9 334
						Bechuanaland		1 454
						N. Rhodesia	7s. 7d.	
						Overseas	4s. 6.91d.	57 039
Sales to trader-producers	195 859	32 164 retained by traders for 'cross-entry sales', remainder allocated 75% to Export Pool. 25% to Local Pool				*Local 'production for export'* Chiller sales	6s. 4.78d.	13 992
						'Concession sales' to farmer-consumers[c]	9s. 4.41d.	33 556
Direct deliveries to the Board	4 902	49.8% to Export Pool 50.2% to Local Pool[a]				From traders direct to farmer-consumer on cross-entry terms	(Trader's price plus 1s. 4.79d. ('rake-off'))	2 250
Total African deliveries	204 296							

'Export Pool' 447 470 bags

Retained in store and unaccounted for: 22 640

Sales to trader-producers figures: 3 535, 32 164, 24 182, 3 809, 249 294, 277 285, 43 734, 71 647, 32 164, 147 545

98 341, 2441, 188 217, 2461, 40 923

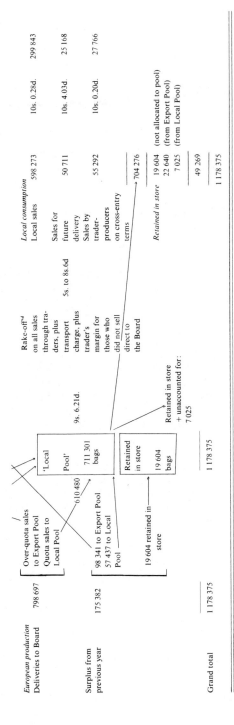

		Rake-off[d] on all sales through traders, plus transport charge, plus trader's margin for those who did not sell direct to the Board	*Local consumption*			

European production
Deliveries to Board 798 697

Over-quota sales to Export Pool
Quota sales to Local Pool 610 480

'Local Pool' 711 301 bags

Surplus from previous year 175 382
98 341 to Export Pool
57 437 to Local Pool
19 604 retained in store

Retained in store 19 604 bags

9s. 6.21d.

Retained in store + unaccounted for: 7 025

Grand total 1 178 375

1 178 375

Local consumption

Local sales 598 273   5s. to 8s.6d   10s. 0.28d.   299 843

Sales for future delivery 50 711   10s. 4.03d.   25 168

Sales by trader-producers on cross-entry terms 55 292   10s. 0.20d.   27 766

704 276

Retained in store 19 604 (not allocated to pool)
22 640 (from Export Pool)
7 025 (from Local Pool)

49 269

1 178 375

Notes:

[a] The preparation of African-grown maize *delivered direct to the Board* which participated in the local pool was set at 50.2 per cent, this being the proportion of European maize which participated in the local pool in the previous pool year.

[b] The average price received by African producers selling to the export pool varied with the deductions from the pool price ('rake-off', transport charges and traders' commission), none of which was in 1935 set at a standard figure. The range given is from NAR: S 1216/SC 1/100/242, Maize Control Board minutes, 21 May 1935.

[c] The range of concessionary rates to European producers broadened as the 1930s wore on, and by 1938 included special rates also for missions, 'struggling miners', and Melsetter District.

[d] The 'rake-off' was a variable charge on maize sold to farmer-consumers or traders. The baseline levels were 1s. 6d. (for export pool maize bought direct by farmer-consumers) and 5s. (for local pool maize bought from a trader) but these were frequently varied to assist a struggling white farmer or thwart a competitive African producer. See text, p. 46 and notes 108 and 111.

Source: Southern Rhodesia. Maize Control Board. *Annual Report* 1934/5 (but see note b)

49

price of maize by either of the successive methods employed in Southern Rhodesia, namely exemption of the major maize consuming districts from control and the bribing of major consumers with a concessionary price made possible through a two-pool system. The Coffee Board had made it clear in the debate previously referred to that its opposition to control was based on pragmatism rather than on the principle of *laissez-faire*, but its implicit request for a concessional price was not granted during the decade under discussion.

In 1937 and 1938, however, the same drop in world prices which had provoked blueprints for outright segregation of 'European' and 'native' crops in Southern Rhodesia caused a proposal very similar to the Rhodesian maize control scheme of 1934 to appear on the Director of Agriculture's desk.[119] This fell on more receptive ears than the KFA's schemes of the 1930s. Administrators were alarmed that the low prices of the depression, far from curbing African marketed production, had in fact been associated with a large increase therein, apparently producing a dangerous reduction in soil fertility. Plantation owners, seeing the import price rise sharply at the outbreak of war (it was in fact to quadruple between 1939 and 1944) were apparently more disposed to hedge their bet of 1935 that 'the native maize grower would be able to satisfy the internal requirements of the Colony'; both the likelihood (given erosion) and the cost of its being a losing wager had now increased. Quite apart from this, it seems clear that the coffee growers at any rate had been given informal undertakings that maize would be supplied to them below the KFA's official local selling price, after the model of the Rhodesian tobacco growers, and that this procedure would continue if the KFA were superseded by an official monopoly. The diary entry of a Trans Nzoia estate manager, later himself to become a member of the Maize Board, for 3 February 1940 reads:

> Called at the KFA. Mackintosh thinks he will be selling maize again within about a week as he does not think the downcountry people [sc. the estate consumers in Kikuyu Province] can have much left by now. He thinks Griffiths [General Manager of the KFA] offered the Thika people [coffee growers] maize at 9/- as a sop to get them to agree to maize control.[120]

It is not surprising, therefore, that by 1941 representatives of the main consumer groups (Stockowners' Associations and most importantly the Coffee Board) had joined the KFA, the chief Native Commissioner being the only dissenter, in resolving

> that [in order to guarantee that a certain minimum grain crop would come from European farms] there should be an annual Government guarantee of a suitable economic flat rate per bag f.o.r. based on [agreed] costs of production for a specific quantity of European-grown maize. Native-grown maize should be left to find its own level on a free market.[121]

The main stumbling-block to formal control had now been overcome:

this resolution, more overtly discriminatory than the '1934 Southern Rhodesian model' originally proposed, was duly implemented when in December of the same year the Chief Secretary persuaded the Legislative Council 'to vote as a subsidy from the public funds such amount as may be necessary to provide a guaranteed minimum return of Shs. 8/50 per bag' (sc. for European producers).[122]

The offering of an official government guarantee required the setting up of an official Maize Control organisation to purchase the maize; the head of this organisation was granted a monopoly of such purchases by the Defence (Control of Maize) Regulations of 1942, taking the European crop through the KFA and the African crop through the licensed buyers set up by the Ordinance of 1935. Maize sales from African squatters to European farmers continued to be permitted as the sole exception to this monopoly, on payment of a rake-off to the Board of Sh. 2.10.[123] All the essential features of the Southern Rhodesia system as it stood in 1942, with export and local pools effectively amalgamated, were therefore replicated, with the exception that the variations in trader mark-ups and transport costs to which Rhodesian African producers were at this time subject were ironed out by the offer of a fixed buying price to the African producer. The system of fixed prices, in short, was pushed two stages back down the chain by which maize reached the Board from the producer, and the upshot was the price-structure shown in Table 2.9.

This scheme looked non-discriminatory to the foreign (e.g. Colonial Office) eye, but contained a number of potentially discriminatory elements: the standardised 'quality difference' between European and African pro-

Table 2.9. *Kenya 1942: price structure for maize*

	Shillings per 200 lb bag
Basic price to African producer	4.90
Quality difference	0.50
Trader's commission, to cover buying and bagging expenses	0.50
Cost of bag	1.20
Storage	0.50
Transport to railway	0.60
To Native Development Fund	0.75
Maize Control's buying price at railhead, i.e. price to European producer	8.95
Maize Control's mark up	2.55
Maize Control's selling price	11.50

Source: C.J. Wilson (Chief Native Commissioner), *KLC Debs.*, 21 August 1942, col. 312.

duction often did not correspond to any actual difference; the African producer was always charged for a new bag when he could in practice get a second-hand one for just over half the price;[124] and the land conservation services supplied in return for the 'Native Development Fund deduction' seldom corresponded to what small African farmers would otherwise have spent their marginal seventy-five cents on.

The effects of maize control on both Southern Rhodesia and Kenya are described in a little more detail in Chapter 3. It is sufficient here to note that what it essentially involved was, in both countries, (1) *a taxing away of the increment above export parity which some Africans enjoyed by virtue of their access to local markets,*[125] which taxation made possible (2) *a high local selling price,* often a large multiple of the producer price. The Kenya Chief Native Commissioner (CNC) put this in a nutshell:

> Now Sir, the problem facing thousands of natives at the moment is that yesterday they were being paid Sh. 6 or more [other versions suggest Sh. 7] for a bag of maize and today they are being told that Government will not let them be paid more than 4/90; yet when they have to buy maize meal they have to pay 80 per cent or more above the price which they used to pay.[126]

This operation of taxing the local sales which yielded such increment was to require some spectacular distortions of resource allocation. As the CNC noted,

> There should be nothing to prevent the Sotik area from supplying the thousands of bags of maize required by the Kericho tea companies. The ludicrous position has been reached that because that area could not guarantee to supply the quantity required under the contract with the tea companies, maize was imported by rail from Nakuru to Lumbwa [about 60 miles] and brought 22 miles to Kericho by road. In 1941, 5500 tons of maize and maize meal was exported from that very area [i.e. Sotik] 52 miles by road through Kericho to Lumbwa station, then railed to other points of distribution, probably Nakuru.[127]

But efficiency of territorial resource allocation, a basic criterion for many economic enquiries into the settler economies of the 1950s,[128] was never a matter of importance for the settler minority groups within the territories.

Beef: cowboys, Africans and the Liebig Company
Although similar to the maize industry in that European and African marketed output were almost level pegging in both countries throughout the period under consideration, the beef industry differed from it in three respects: the importance of disease considerations on the supply side, the heterogeneity of the product (a 100 lb ox was a remote substitute for a 700 lb animal), and finally the fact that the product could be stored for years without deterioration. The first of these factors, during the period up to 1930, had been used to prevent Africans from competing in the (urban or overseas) market for heavy animals; but the third, particularly after 1925, was to preclude this being any sort of final solution to the economic predicament of white ranchers. For, from this date onwards, cattle numbers were

to build up much faster in African areas than in European,[129] precisely as the result of the application of a differential quarantine policy. The 'overhang' of African cattle was seen as a threat by white ranchers because of illicit breaches of quarantine and the fact that some European producers were too undercapitalised to fatten their cattle up into the higher grades where they were safe from African competition, and to the administration because it jeopardised the African's rural subsistence.

A means of disposing of this overhang elsewhere than on the local market was therefore urgently needed. Some fanatical stockowners were to suggest destruction of African cattle.[130] But the consensus of more moderate opinion was in favour of a two-pronged attack: the development of an export trade in chilled meat outside Africa to enliven the domestic market for the higher grades of cattle, after the precedent of maize; and the construction of an extract and canned beef factory to take off the African cattle surplus.

The first prong of this attack appeared in Kenya as a practical possibility only briefly, between 1917 and 1924, never thereafter to enter the realm of practical politics during the colonial period. In Southern Rhodesia, however, where there was more land, at lower prices, within the 'ranching belt', an export footing had already been created by the Imperial Cold Storage Company. But in 1928 that footing was being held at a loss, and the ICSCo 'asked the Government for an export bounty as the only way it could successfully tender' for a contract to supply 8000 tons of beef to Italy during 1929. This bounty, of a value averaging 15s. a head (effectively 2s. to 2s. 6d. per 100 lb liveweight)[131] was payable to any exporter, not just the ICSCo, and a number of ranchers tried their hand, more or less unsuccessfully, at using it to place beef on the British market. It was financed firstly by a 2s. 6d. slaughter levy, then by a combination of this and a 3d. stock tax, finally in 1935 by a 10s. levy on all cattle slaughtered within the colony.[132]

As with maize, the principle was invoked of taxing local transactions – many of which were of course in African hands – in order to finance exports essential only to the European minority. Moreover, like all specific taxes, the levy was regressive in effect, hitting the vendors with thin, poor quality cattle to sell (most of whom were African) harder than vendors with fat cattle to sell (most of whom were European).

As such the levy did nothing to resolve the problem of the 'African overhang'. This required the provision of a meat factory, and this in turn required that the Liebig's Extract of Meat Company or one of its competitors be persuaded to extend its already profitable ranching operations (see p. 14 above) forward into manufacturing within Africa.

The first attempt to persuade them to do so, in Kenya in 1922, ended in failure, the sticking point being the government's unwillingness to engage in potentially costly extra-market operations in order to guarantee African supplies:

> Dr Gunther and Mr Holt came out to Kenya to investigate the possibility of establishing a meat industry in this country on behalf of Liebig's ... I am given to

understand that they came out here and had a look, and found in those days that the natives would not sell their cattle under some perfectly exorbitant price; £5 or £10 had been mentioned to me, so they found they could not possibly buy stuff at reasonable prices unless Government exercised compulsion. This Government would not, certainly not with the Masai. In those days compulsion might have involved all sorts of things, like patrols of the K[ing's] A[frican] R[ifles] *which would be far too expensive.* Anyhow, Government was not prepared to exercise compulsion on the natives to sell stock, and so Liebig's went home.[133]

What the Kenya Government of 1922 had refused, the Southern Rhodesia Government of 1933, faced with a new far worse overstocking position, was quite willing to countenance.[134] In return for Liebig's undertaking to erect a factory capable of treating 25 000 head of cattle a year, the company received not only 'full remission of customs duties, a 10 000 acre "Depasturing" farm for the factory at a rental of £1 per annum, free veterinary services from the Government, and a subsidy [of 1s. $1\frac{1}{2}$d. per 100 lb liveweight] for as long as chilled and frozen meats received bounties',[135] but the critical assurance of an adequate supply of cattle at a price satisfactory to it.[136] This in 1933 was around 6s. per 100 lb liveweight, at a time when the ICSCo was offering 10s. and some farmers were realising 21s. on the open market.[137] The fundamental problem for the authorities, therefore, if they wished to keep Liebig's in operation, was how to funnel African cattle from good markets into one very comfortably the poorest of all.

Gradually they developed four weapons in their arsenal of extra-market operations. The first was the ancient expedient of quarantine: from early in 1936 onwards, a large area (see Map 2.2), encompassing most of the native reserves within fifty miles of the Liebig factory at West Nicholson, was put in quarantine for foot-and-mouth,[138] a state in which it was to remain for two and a half years, giving the Liebig factory a monopoly[139] on African sales from this area. The second was the slaughter levy, previously described, which taxed at the rate of 10s. per animal – i.e. a higher percentage the poorer the animal – all animals outside the quarantine area *not* going to Liebig's. The third, most ingenious of all, was Liebig's practice of sending agents into quarantined reserves under the guise of independent bidders, who would stage a mock auction against one another (Liebig's buyer the while remaining silent) while at the same time taking care not to go above a price – on the balance of evidence, somewhere between 4s. 6d. and 5s. per 100 lb in 1938 – which was pitched some way below Liebig's advertised buying price. In this way Africans could be persuaded that they could get no better price than the one which Liebig's had decided to offer,[140] and Liebig's could give the impression of paying a price higher than one they were in fact paying.[141] The last resort was physical force, or the threat of it: the evidence, not surprisingly, differs wildly, but it seems clear that Africans were frequently forced to stand aside while their cattle were taken and a nominal payment for them was thrown on the ground, or persuaded that it was against the law for them to refuse to sell their cattle at whatever price the Liebig's buyer offered.[142] By this miscellany of methods – of which the quarantine was the vital one, as it segregated the stock market in the main Liebig's catchment from the stock market elsewhere in the country – Liebig's were able to obtain African cattle, though not in the numbers they had desired,[143] at about half the free market price, that is, at about half the f.o.r. export parity (Table 2.10a). Nor were they the only commercial enterprise to benefit from such operations. The Cold Storage Commission – the parastatal organisation which had taken over the ICSCo's assets in 1938 – had a gentleman's agreement with Liebig's to take over any cattle surplus to their requirements, which Liebig's could of course afford to provide at a price well below the Cold Storage Commission's advertised buying price.[144] When, therefore, in 1937 the Kenya government – faced in a sense with the same dilemma in a still more acute form, as no chiller trade had been developed – decided to resolve it in the same way by turning to Liebig's, Liebig's were well prepared. They had an even stronger hand to play than they had had in 1933 *vis-à-vis* the Southern Rhodesia government, since by 1937 the market had grown to the point where Liebig's could consider opening a second factory in Southern Rhodesia. This second

Table 2.10a. *Prices paid for African cattle, per 100 lb liveweight, Southern Rhodesia 1938 (shillings)*

	By Cold Storage		
By Liebig's buyers to Africans in quarantine area*	From Liebig's	From Europeans in prohibited area	On open market from Africans immediately outside quarantine area
5/6 to 7/-[a]			
4/- to 6/-[b]	7/6 max[f]	8/4[c]	9/4[c]
4/7[c]			
5/-[d]			
3/10[e]			

Note: *This column should be read in conjunction with note 141.
Sources:
[a] NAR: ZAX 1/1/1, Evidence of J.C.R. Gurnall (Managing Director, Liebig's Rhodesia Ltd) to Commission on Sales of Native Cattle, pp. 28 and 41.
[b] NAR: ZAX 1/1/2, Evidence of J.M. Nash (cattle buyer from Liebig's) to Commission on Sales of Native Cattle, 14 November 1928, p. 164.
[c] NAR: ZAX 1/1/1, Evidence of R.D. Gilchrist MLA to Commission on Sales of Native Cattle, 1 November 1938, p. 64.
[d] NAR: ZAX 1/1/1, Evidence of A.S. Cripps to Commission on Sales of Native Cattle, 7 November 1938, p. 92
[e] NAR:ZAX 1/1/1, Evidence of A. Gelman, General Manager of the Cold Storage Commission, to Commission on Sales of Native Cattle, 8 November 1938, p. 69.
[f] NAR: ZAX 1/1/1, Evidence of A.R. Jackson, trader, to Commission on Sales of Native Cattle, 7 November 1938, p. 106.

Table 2.10b. *Prices paid for African cattle, per animal, Kenya 1938 (shillings)*

By Liebig's buyers in Machakos District	Average all buyers destocking sales in Machakos District	Free market price in Machakos District
12.0[a]	16.83[c]	35.0 to 60.0[c]
10.0[c]		55.0 to 60.0[b]
		50.0 to 100.0[a]
		(in Masai Province)

Sources:
[a] Isher Dass, *KLC Debs.*, 17 August 1938, col. 231.
[b] KNA: PC/SP 1/2/2, Annual Report, Masai Province, 1938.
[c] KNA: DC/MKS 1/1/27, Annual Report, Machakos District, 1938, p. 31. The quoted Liebig's price is that for animals bought by Liebig's at Sultan Hamud (the railhead for Machakos District).

factory constituted an additional bargaining card in Liebig's hand as it now faced the Kenya government, and enabled it to exert still more stringent conditions. In the first place, they only offered a buying price of 4/- per 100 lb – i.e. a range whose uppermost point was at the bottom of the range of buying prices quoted by witnesses to the Southern Rhodesian Commission on Sales of Native Cattle. In the second place, Mr Brinton (the general manager of Liebig Rhodesia Ltd) emphasised

> that it would greatly assist his directors in reaching a decision as to the relative merits of building a second factory in Kenya or building a second factory in Southern Rhodesia were they to receive an assurance that the Kenya Government would do all in its power to ensure that the cattle were forthcoming. He had been informed that there were in existence rules for the culling of cattle, which might be applied in certain areas were a suitable market available, and that the Veterinary Department, in collaboration with the Administration, were engaged in laying down stock quotas for particular native grazing areas.[145]

The Kenya government took the hint, gave Liebig's the 'assurance' requested,[146] and concessions similar to the Southern Rhodesia government's to boot.[147] The most promising area for applying the 'rules'[148] mentioned by Mr Brinton was Machakos, where the level of over-stocking in relation to the available acreage was particularly severe, and where (unlike other areas such as Masailand) there had been no attempts to increase offtake by opening new quarantine stations and stock routes in the middle 1930s.

The government was at this point faced with the classic dilemma of economic policy in settler states: 'If we destroyed [cattle] without paying compensation to the owners, that would have been an intolerable injustice, and if we had destroyed them and paid anything like the market value it would have been an intolerable burden on our finances.'[149] In Machakos, the dilemma was resolved by compulsory sales of African cattle at a price

56

which, as Table 2.10b illustrates, bore no relation to the free-market price. This led to a protest march of 2000 Wakamba into Nairobi, which has been frequently described (van Zwanenberg and King 1975 (D1); Forbes Munro 1975 (D1); Wrigley 1965 (D1)). The crucial point for the purposes of our present argument is that the Kenya arm of Liebig's, lacking one of the four 'inducements' which had driven the cattle of Southern Rhodesian Africans through their portals at the desired price (i.e. exemption from a slaughter levy), and finding a second (its quarantine monopoly) very much diluted by the existence of a thriving local market within the reserve, was forced to lean on the government there to deploy a much more liberal dose of the fourth, namely force. The costs of this kind of 'extra-market operation' were far greater than they had been in the era of conquest: not only was the resistance more concerted, but it was also widely publicised in the English newspapers,[150] and questions were asked in the House of Commons. The outcome was a denial of the original assurance of adequate supplies to Liebig's by the Kenya government,[151] and abandonment – for the moment – of the policy of compulsory destocking. Not for the last time, a settler-producer group had found that the costs of attempting to subvert the market to their own advantage actually exceeded the costs of accepting the market on its own terms. The price of cattle to Liebig's, after this defeat, rose dramatically, and caused Liebig's Kenya operations to become, for a time, so unprofitable that their factory had to close from March 1939 to February 1940.

The dual price structure for beef, which had, in the first instance, been set up to try and guarantee the economic viability of the Liebig Company's operations in each country (see Table 2.10), was to persist during the war years in both countries. During this period each African reserve was compulsorily required to deliver a quota of stock to a government statutory body (in Southern Rhodesia the Cold Storage Commission, in Kenya the newly established Livestock Control) at a price very close to the Liebig's price, which in turn continued to bear much the same relativity to the free-market price as it had done in pre-war years. Additionally, during the war years, there began the payment of different prices for different 'grades' of animal. But since the grades were themselves correlated with weight, what this implied was a doubling – or more, depending on the arbitrary differential adopted between the price per pound offered for the top and the bottom grades – of the premium received by producers of heavy animals. And since there were in 1939 endless empty acres in the European area of both countries, whereas many of the African reserves were becoming heavily over-stocked,[152] the racial distribution of gains from the institution of this policy is not hard to anticipate. The buying price structure of the two statutory bodies in 1948 is set out in Table 2.11.

The steep taper of the Southern Rhodesian price structure, as described above, offered an ideal opportunity for inserting an invisible input, namely extensive ranching land, which most Africans had no hope of obtaining,

57

Table 2.11. *Southern Rhodesia and Kenya:*
guaranteed prices for cattle per 100 lb liveweight, 1948

Grade	Southern Rhodesia	Kenya
GAQ	23/1	}25.0
FAQ	17/9	
Compound	11/-	}18.50
Inferior	8/5	

Sources: Southern Rhodesia – *Annual Report of the Chief Native Commissioner* 1948: 'Report of the Native Production and Marketing Branch'.
Kenya – 'The beef cattle of Kenya' by C.A. Long, in Matheson and Bovill 1950 (D1), p. 131.

into the cost structure of the upper part of the livestock market, and thereby segmenting it, much as quarantine policy had done before, and precisely in the same way that the indivisible input of transport costs (plus rake-off if required) had segmented the maize market. The only problem, from the point of view of European producers in the 1940s, was that few of them could afford this input and at the same time the cattle required to realise its value. Accordingly the Cold Storage Commission decided to give them a helping hand, which at the same time protected the urban market from a glut of destocked cattle:

> To slaughter [the destocked cattle] as bought would have meant the loss of many tons of beef, and would have dislocated the market for European stock. It was, therefore, decided to place these cattle with farmers for grazing. In very few cases could the farmers pay for them ... A Grazier Agreement was, therefore, introduced under which cattle were delivered to [farmers] who undertook to maintain and care for them and return them for slaughter at a date to be stipulated by it.[153]

This extension of the activities of the Land Banks was no more than a boost to what had always been happening informally, but particularly since the destocking sales began. Together with the tobacco boom it was the major means by which European agriculture in Southern Rhodesia was made secure in the post-war years.[154]

Guaranteed prices, and the export loss problem once again: 1947–63

Maize
It is easiest to see the elements of continuity and change in maize marketing after the Second World War by looking at Table 2.12, which shows the price structures for maize prevailing in 1942 – where our previous section ended – and, for convenience, 1957.

The basic variable which changed during the Second World War was domestic demand, which expanded so much that it became possible for the first time to unload the year's crop onto the local market without pushing the local price below the level considered economic by European producers.

This state of affairs, which had come about as the result of an extraneous boost to the economy, was one which the European farmers' organisations – the RNFU and KNFU – wished at all costs to preserve. Accordingly, they entered into negotiations with their respective governments at the end of the war with a view to securing a guaranteed price for maize which would secure an acceptable margin above 'costs of production'. This they succeeded in doing, in agreements negotiated in Southern Rhodesia in 1945, and in Kenya in 1951.[155] These agreements, designed to ensure a comfortable living for the European producer, dominated the entire price structure. Policy goals which were incompatible with them – such as, in Kenya, the prevention of exports as recommended by the Food Shortage Commission of 1943[156] – were over-ridden. The European price thus negotiated, with appropriate deductions, determined the African price, as shown in Table 2.12, and in Southern Rhodesia the prices of other crops which could be planted as substitutes for maize by Africans were set in relation to the maize price so as to ensure an appropriate balance between African plantings of maize and other crops. The system represented a consolidation of the *ad hoc* measures first adopted in Southern Rhodesia in the 1930s, except that there was now no rationale for a system of separate export and local pools. By 1950, also, two elements of cost intervening between African and European producers – the transport charge and the trader's commission – had been standardised for all producers as fixed deductions, thus cancelling out the advantage hitherto enjoyed by producers near the railway line and by those facing less avaricious traders. The 'rake-off' on maize delivered to Southern Rhodesia farmer-consumers or to the Maize Control Board's local pool was commuted to a 'Native Development Fund levy', the proceeds of which were to be used on land conservation, water development, and other services in the reserves; a similar levy had, of course, already been instituted in Kenya. The wide spread between producer and consumer prices remained, and with it the temptation to sell on the black market. So did the concessionary prices to meat exporters using maize as an input.[157]

This structure remained unaltered until the middle 1950s, at which point the export realisation once again fell below the statutory 'guaranteed' price (Table 3.6 below). Once again the problem arose of who should pay the loss on export. In Uganda and Tanganyika, at the same time, the problem was met by dissolving monopoly control boards. In the settler economies nothing so drastic happened, but it is testimony to the increased strength of the maize consumers' lobby in the economy that the producers were this time unable to unload export losses onto them through an increased local producer price. In Kenya in 1955, and in Southern Rhodesia in 1959, after an interim during which the export loss was shared between government

Table 2.12. *Kenya and Southern Rhodesia: price structures for maize, evolution early 1940s to late 1950s*

Kenya (shillings and cents per 200 lb bag)	1942	Institutional changes in intervening years	1951[a]	Institutional changes in intervening years	1957/8[a]
Basic price to African producer	4.90		22.85		22.43
Quality difference	0.50		0.60	Consolidated with traders' margin in 1952	
Export loss cess	—		—	Instituted 1955/6	5.–
District Council cess	—		—	Instituted 1952	2.–
Trader's commission, to cover buying, bagging and storage expenses	1.–	⎫ Made variable 1947. Equated railage system adopted within Nyanza Province only	2.–		3.10
Cost of bag	1.20	⎬	2.50		2.70
Transport to railway	0.60	⎭	1.40	1958: equated railage system replaced by graduated transport charge	1.30
To Native Development Fund	0.75		3.45	To African Betterment Fund	3.45
Maize Control's buying price at railhead, i.e. price to European producer	8.95		32.80		39.98

Southern Rhodesia (shillings/pence per 200 lb bag)	1940	1948		1957
Basic price to African producer	variable (probable range 5/- to 6/-)	19/3		23/9½
Trader's handling margin	variable	Standardised 1946	Made flexible in 1955	3/11 (maximum)
Cost of bag	1/6 (average)	Standardised 1948		3/2½
Transport to railway	variable	Standardised 1948		5/2
'Rake-off'	variable (min. 1/6, max. 5/-)	Abolished 1948		—
To Native Development Fund	—	Instituted 1948		3/11
Maize Control Board's buying price at railhead (i.e. effective price to European producer)	10/6¾ (local pool) — 6/10 (export pool)	30/-		40/-

Note: ^a After 1947 maize prices to African producers varied between regions on account of variations in transport charges, and, subsequently, variations in district council cesses. For 1951 and 1957/8, Kenya data refer to North Nyanza District, the main region of African surplus production, only.

Sources: Johnson 1968 (C), Table 13, p. 199; Southern Rhodesia, Maize Control Board, *Annual Report* 1940/1; C.J. Wilson, *KLC Debs.*, 21 August 1942, col. 312; Kenya 1952 (B3), p. 38; Kenya 1958 (B3), pp. 21–6.

and producer subject to a floor price, the maize producers accepted responsibility for part of the losses on export. These were henceforth paid by them through a special cess on each bag delivered; the rest of the export loss was met by subsidies and by an increase in the domestic *consumer* price. The predictable result of the latter development was a sharp increase in direct sales from Africans to farmer-consumers, many of them illegal,[158] and a queue of influential consumers for concessionary prices from the statutory boards. It came to be recognised as a test of one's political clout whether or not such prices could be secured.[159]

The partial elimination of the export subsidy was the limit of the concession the maize producers were forced to make to market forces. The system of pre-planting prices well above export parity to producers remained, in spite of recommendations by independent commissions that these prices be slid down to the export parity level, if not left to the free play of market forces;[160] so also did the subsidy on the consumer price. These features of the maize marketing system in Kenya and Zimbabwe remained in 1981.

Beef

Just as the 1935–45 period had provided European maize farmers with a windfall which they wished at all costs to retain – the institution of guaranteed prices – so also it had offered their rancher counterparts the windfall of an embryo dual price system, with Liebig's (later government statutory bodies also) taking much of the offtake from the African herd at a depressed price from which European ranchers were protected by the grading system, and, in Southern Rhodesia, by export subsidies also. In Southern Rhodesia this situation was preserved by maintaining the Cold Storage Commission monopoly on purchases from Africans: the buying price at the weight and grade sales could be set at an arbitrarily low figure,[161] in return for which the Commission committed itself to accept all cattle offered to it. In Kenya neither the Livestock Control set up in the war to ensure supplies of meat for the forces, nor its successors, the Meat Marketing Board (1946–51) and the Kenya Meat Commission (1951–) which took over the Liebig Company's assets, were capitalised on a scale which would enable it to make a similar commitment.[162] As a result these institutions throughout the post-war period found themselves competing with perfectly legal markets in the African reserves, offering up to double the 'government price' for a given animal.[163] Consequently, once the wartime power of requisition lapsed, rather crude methods had at first to be employed to secure adequate supplies from the African areas. The buyer who had bought at compulsory sales in Masailand continued to tour the district after the war with 'Livestock Control' still written on his lorry, and a Masailand DC was murdered in late 1946 by an African whom he had tried to persuade to sell a bull.[164] In Masailand these methods were soon abandoned; in other pastoral areas, however,[165] the para-statal organisation which took over the Livestock Control's stock routes (African Livestock Marketing Organ-

Table 2.13. *Hypothetical profits on local sales of beef by Southern Rhodesia Cold Storage Commission, 1961/2 buying season*

Grade	Average producer price (offered by Cold Storage Commission)	Average local selling price (at auctions)	Gross profit /loss	Plus 'fifth quarter realisation'[a]	Less average operating costs	Net profit or loss	
						per 100 lb	as a %
	per 100 lb cold dressed weight						
Rhodesia's Best	175/5	135/2	−40/3	27/1	17/10	−32/-	−18%
Imperial	157/5	132/7	−24/10	27/1	17/10	−15/7	−10%
Standard A	139/5	129/7	−9/10	27/1	17/10	−0/7	−0.4%
GAQ	120/3	118/-	−2/3	27/1	17/10	+7/-	−6%
FAQ	106/5	109/3	+2/10	27/1	17/10	+12/1	+11%
Compound	89/10	102/1	+12/3	27/1	17/10	+21/6	+24%
Inferior	64/-	96/7	+32/7	27/1	17/10	+41/10	+65%

Note: [a] Realisation on offal, hides and by-products; average across all grades.
Source: Federation of Rhodesia and Nyasaland 1963b (B2), p. 35.

isation – ALMO) was granted a monopoly of legal purchases from Africans. This was a formalisation of precisely the arrangement which had funnelled a 'satisfactory' portion of the African herd at 'satisfactory' prices into Liebig Rhodesia's works in 1936–8; and it is significant that 'only in Samburu where a [destocking] quota system is in force [was ALMO] able to purchase adequate numbers'.[166]

In 1956 a marked freeing of the market is apparent in both countries. The Kenya government greatly expanded its practice of holding auction sales in reserves, and the Cold Storage Commission grudgingly succumbed to political pressure – among Africans, the lack of an open market for cattle was a grievance second only to land shortage – and initiated auctions of its own. The data on prices paid at these auctions give us, for the first time, an indication of how much the lower grades were subsidising the higher (Table 2.13).

The institution of these auctions pushed up prices in the lower grades so far as substantially to curtail the Commission's beloved grazier scheme; as its annual report for 1956 relates, it

> endeavoured persistently but unsuccessfully to enter into fresh agreements with the Native Department [to purchase African cattle]. It was clear that the Department, having witnessed the success of auction sales, was reluctant to accept all alternative methods of disposal in which competition was not the price-determining factor.[167]

63

However, it did not cause the Commission substantially to modify its weight and grade buying price structure. As a result it continued to be able to isolate European producers at the 'top end' of the market from the influence of market forces, with the familiar consequence of bringing forward 'a superfluity of the top grades which the local market is unable or unwilling to absorb (even at the subsidised selling price) and to throw a rapidly increasing percentage of these grades on to the export market. This can presently only be sold at a loss.'[168]

As in maize, so in beef, a familiar constraint to the settlers' economic ambitions reappeared in the middle fifties: the scope for market manipulation in time of depressed export prices was limited by the extent of the (domestic) market. This limitation, well perceived by the witness to the Native Production and Trade Commission quoted above, is an important theme in our concluding section.

2.3 CONCLUSION: SCOPE AND DETERMINANTS OF EXTRA-MARKET OPERATIONS

Two main themes have lurked beneath the surface of the preceding narrative. The first is quantitative: changes in the character and intensity of extra-market operations tended to cluster at periods of crisis in the European agricultural economy. The second is qualitative: the nature of these policy changes, so far from representing an ever-increasing pressure by a unified white agrarian capitalism on the African peasant economy, was constrained and conditioned by internal conflicts within the white agrarian capitalist group, which sprang from the fact that such capitalists frequently found themselves on opposite sides of the same market (land, maize, beef to some degree) or alternatively on the same side as competitors (branch railways). This final section attempts to formalise and refine these hypotheses.

The settler agricultural economy encountered, during its colonial history, crises of two types. First, there was a crisis of *existence* during the early years of the twentieth century. The response to this was to try and attract a white agricultural population onto the land, which in turn required a number of extra-market operations if that population was to have a hope of viability. Secondly, there were three crises of *export loss*, during the years 1920–2, 1929–34 and 1955–8 approximately, during which period many agricultural exports, in particular maize and beef on which our discussion centres here, were unprofitable; these too brought forth extra-market operations from the government. The policy response to those crises, as discussed in this chapter, can be schematised as Table 2.14.

A first possible explanation of government behaviour in those crises might be that government responded automatically to the stimulus of export loss in the same instinctive way as Pavlov's dogs responded to the sound of their bell.[169] But a closer scrutiny of Table 2.14 and Appendix 1 suggests that actually the government's use of extra-market operations was not in fact a constant response to a given stimulus, but rather that each of

Table 2.14. *Kenya and Southern Rhodesia: economic stimuli and political responses, 1903–60*

		Nature of 'response'							
		Land policy		Export rail rates on maize		Marketing policy			
						Maize		Cattle	
Years	Nature of 'stimulus'	Kenya	S. Rhodesia	Kenya	S. Rhodesia	Kenya	S. Rhodesia	Kenya	S. Rhodesia
1903–9	Need to establish white agricultural economy	Price of Crown land held at Sh. 2.66 per acre (p. 14)	Price of Crown land cut, 1908 (p. 14)	Reduced in 1904 and again in 1909 (p. 32)	Cut by 40% in 1910 (p. 32)	–	–	–	–
1920–2	Export loss	– (Also moves towards formal possessory segregation)	Cut in price of Crown land, 1923 (p. 19)	Cut by 25%, 1922 (Table 2.5)	Cut by 21%, 1922 (Table 2.5)	–	–	Abortive approach to Liebig Co., 1922 (p. 53)	Imperial Cold Storage Co. sets up in business, 1924 (p. 53)
1929–34	Export loss	Land Bank established 1930 (p. 47)	–	No change (though some subsidies were mediated through refunds of rail rates) (Table 2.5)	No change (Table 2.5)	Subsidies (Maize Control eventually implemented 1942) (pp. 47–52)	Maize Control Act 1931; Amendment Act 1934 (pp. 43–9)	Liebig's set up in business, 1938 (p. 56)	Liebig's set up in business, 1933. Export Levy & Beef Bounty Acts, 1931, 1935 (p.54)
1955–60	Export loss	–	–	*Increase in average export rate of 25%, 1953–9* (p. 243)	*Increase in average export rate of 35%, 1954–60* (p. 243)	*Reduction in subsidy to maize farmers* (pp. 59–62)	*Reduction in subsidy to maize farmers* (pp. 59–62)		Freeing of market; auctions instigated in African areas (p. 63)

– no significant change

Sources: Chapter 2 (figures in brackets after each entry are references to the page where the policy measure in question is discussed).

them was used with progressively declining strength over the colonial period. Thus, restraint in the government land price to attract settlement was a critical instrument of economic policy in 1903–10 in both settler economies, but an unimportant instrument in 1920–2 and thereafter. Cuts in rail rates were important in 1903–10 and 1920–2 (indeed in Southern Rhodesia between 1919 and 1925 the export rail rate was made *contingent* on the export price of maize), but insignificant in the latter two periods. State control of the marketing of maize was critical in the 1930s – the first time it was seriously tried – but was in fact loosened in the next period of export loss crisis after 1955.

These gradually increasing predictive failures reflect two things. In the first place, of course, they reflect factors which are not present in the crude Pavlovian model; thus, for example Crown land pricing policy became an instrument of gradually decreasing effectiveness as more and more of it was sold, and cuts in export rail rates became an instrument of gradually decreasing practicability as road competition made it less and less possible to compensate these cuts with increases in import rates. But the failures also reflect the presence of internal political constraints, which grew in number as the economy became more complex. Thus a policy of restraint on the price of land was easy to implement in 1903–9 as it involved crushing no opposition save that of powerless Africans, but much harder to implement thereafter as once most of the fertile Crown land was sold a policy of restraining its price involved downward pressure on the profits of far from powerless white concessionaires, as was discovered in the post-war settlement periods of 1918–20 and 1945–7. A policy of responding to crisis by cuts in the export rail rate on maize was relatively easy to implement in 1920–2 when maize dominated European agricultural exports, but much harder in the 1930s, by which time the opposition of the coffee and tobacco farmers had grown, and downright impossible in the 1950s, which duly saw a squeezing of the railway rate structure. The policy of protecting European maize farmers by shoring up the price on the home market met immediate opposition from maize consumers, and could only be implemented in a modified form in which those consumers were bought off with cheap maize; even this modified form of market manipulation was not contemplated in the final 'export loss crisis' of the 1950s.

To be sure, governments in the settler economies frequently tried to carry through their desired extra-market operations by buying off the opposition. For example: (1) a potential conflict between concessionaires and small men over land prices in 1919–20 was defused by the concessionaire group taking the lead in pushing for formal possessory segregation of land; (2) a potential conflict between maize farmers and other producers over rail rates in 1920–2 was defused by pushing up the rail rates on imported consumer goods to pay for subsidised export rates; (3) a potential conflict between maize growers and consumers over maize control was defused, in Southern Rhodesia in 1934 and in Kenya in 1942, by in effect bribing those consumers who had power with cheap maize; (4) a potential conflict between the Southern Rhodesia Cold Storage and the white ranchers was defused by using the Liebig market as a low-cost source of supply for itself which could subsidise the higher grades.

But the scope which governments had for squaring the opposition to a planned extra-market operation in this way was itself limited. There were two kinds of constraints. The *economic* limit was the size of the market in which extra-market operations were being used to influence the distribution of the gains from trade. Thus, to take the simplest case, the size of the market for railway services was limited by road competition which could be controlled but not eliminated, and this in turn limited the extent to which cuts in export rail rates, financed by increases in import rates, could be used to respond to export-loss crises. The size of the domestic market for maize was limited by domestic demand, and this in turn limited the extent to which it could be used as a buttress against export losses. The scope for extra-market operations, as was perceived by the witness to the Commission quoted above,[170] is limited by the extent of the market.

In addition to this there was a *political* limit on the extent to which extra-market operations could be deployed, which was simply the extent to which the ultimate losers from them, usually but not always the Africans, were content to acquiesce in that role. As Africans became more politically conscious over time this limit moved inwards so as to reduce the colonial state's room for manoeuvre. Kenya Africans who had allowed their cattle to be conscripted below the market price in 1914–18 protested so violently against the imposition of a similar measure in 1938 that all compulsion was dropped. Southern Rhodesia Africans were in 1956 able to squash the reintroduction of 'weight and grade' sales in a similar way. In the middle 1950s, finally, white coffee and tobacco farmers who had subsidised white maize production in earlier years now refused to do so, with the result that the maize industry was forced to pay for its own export losses.

Our conclusion then is that the simple Pavlovian model of policy will only do as a first approximation to the modelling of colonial economic policy in settler economies. Its applicability is constrained at a first level by internal political opposition to the 'obvious' methods of preserving the core of the settler economy; even if this opposition can be squared, it is then limited by the extent of the market and by the acquiescence of the losers in the extra-market operations ultimately adopted. The difference of this general mode of approach from that used by Marxist writers such as Arrighi and Good will perhaps be clear. Whereas they see the main, indeed the only, division within the white community as being 'that between international capital [sometimes portrayed as "speculative"[171]] and local capital,' we see, initially, a split between concessionaire companies and individual enter-prises, but increasingly the development of political fault-lines between economic *sectors*, both of which imply that the category of white capital must be seen not as one sector but as several if policy is to be properly under-

67

stood. Secondly, they neglect the *economic* (though not the political) constraints on extra-market operations. Less obvious will be our difference with a writer such as Murray who analyses Southern Rhodesian politics along sectoral lines but who sees, rather on the analogy of Peacock and Wiseman in developed countries, a gradually increasing role for the state in the economy.[172] In fact this role reached an apogee in the Second World War, and thereafter diminished.[173] Historians of both the political left and the political right have, unusually, been united behind the contention that the role of the state in nurturing the white agricultural economy gradually expanded;[174] our contention is that both schools are wrong. After the Second World War, in fact, the state's increased willingness to raise its stake in agriculture was counter-balanced by its reduced power to do so without coercion of a type whose likely costs cancelled out the advantages.

APPENDIX 1: A 'STIMULUS-RESPONSE' MODEL OF GOVERNMENT ECONOMIC POLICY RESPONSE IN SETTLER ECONOMIES

In a paper concerned with macro-economic policy in a developed economy (Mosley 1976 (D3)) we have put forward the following naive model in which government policy interventions are seen as being 'triggered' by crisis in the shape of an unsatisfactory state of the economy. If x_i is any instrument of economic policy, y_j is any target, and y_j^* is its desired value,

$$\Delta x_i = f(y_j - y_j^*) \text{ when } y_j < y_j^* \text{ (i.e. } y_j \text{ has not reached its satisfactory value)}$$

$$\Delta x_i = 0 \text{ at other times} \quad (\text{i.e. } y_j > y_j^*)$$

i.e. the policy authorities respond, to a degree proportionate to the size of the perceived 'crisis', during crisis periods only; at other times they are inert.

The purpose of this appendix is to see whether the model can be applied also to the very different circumstances of less developed economies where policy-making is dominated by a white minority group. We may use the 'extra-market operations' discussed in this chapter – government intervention in the land market, railway rate policy and maize and cattle marketing – as examples of x_i; y_i is some indicator of the health of the European agricultural economy. Our approach here to the definition of a 'crisis period' is to choose periods when maize cultivation – the activity of which was believed to supply the centre of gravity of the white agricultural community[175] – was unprofitable, i.e. in the present case,

y_j = average level of maize profitability on export market

$y_j^* = 0$

Regression analysis applied to the variables described above yielded the following result. (Land policy is not incorporated in the analysis, as it was not used as an instrument of short-term policy intervention, certainly after 1919.)

Dependent variable: changes in export rail rate on maize

Kenya: $\left\{\begin{array}{l}\text{change in export}\\ \text{rail rate on maize}\\ \text{per ton-mile}\end{array}\right\} = 0.15 - 0.069^{**} \left\{\begin{array}{l}\text{change in export}\\ \text{loss per bag of maize;}\\ \text{in shillings}\end{array}\right\}$

$$r^2 = 0.3613$$
(crisis periods)

$= 0.10 + 0.025 \left\{\begin{array}{l}\text{change in export}\\ \text{loss per bag;}\\ \text{in shillings}\end{array}\right\}$

$$r^2 = 0.0478$$
(non-crisis periods)

Dependent variable: level of subsidy to maize farmers

Kenya: $\left\{\begin{array}{l}\text{level of subsidy}\\ \text{on maize (£000)}\end{array}\right\} = 145.7 + 28.7^{**} \left\{\begin{array}{l}\text{export loss per bag}\\ \text{of maize, in shillings}\end{array}\right\}$

$$r^2 = 0.497$$
(crisis periods)
no relationship (non-crisis periods)

Southern Rhodesia: $\left\{\begin{array}{l}\text{level of subsidy}\\ \text{on maize (£000)}\end{array}\right\} = 134.7 + 219^{**} \left\{\begin{array}{l}\text{export loss per bag}\\ \text{of maize, in shillings}\end{array}\right\}$

$$r^2 = 0.345$$
(crisis periods)
no relationship (non-crisis periods)

Definitions

Crisis periods are periods of export loss on maize, i.e. 1920–2, 1929–35, 1955–9.

Non-crisis periods are all other years between 1914 and 1960.

Export loss on maize is estimated average cost of maize production (as estimated under 'sources' below), less estimated f.o.r. export price, times − 1 (i.e. it is positive when a loss is made on export, and negative when a profit is made on export).

** denotes that the regression coefficient is significant at the 1 per cent level.

Number of observations

fifteen (crisis periods)
thirty-two (non-crisis periods)

Sources of data

Export price of maize: Table 3.6

Average cost of maize production: linear trend drawn through the data in the following table.

Year	Kenya (shillings/cents)	S. Rhodesia (shillings/pence)	Source
1907		3/6	British South Africa Co.
1913	6.30		PRO: CO 533/210, evidence of F.W. Baillie to Economic Development Commission 1917.
1917	10.60		PRO: CO 533/210, evidence of A.C. MacDonald to Economic Development Commission 1917.
1918		10/6	PRO: CO 417/602, report of RAU Congress, 17 March.
1921		9/-	PRO: CO 417/619, report in *Rhodesia Herald*, 8 March 1921.
1930		8/-	Southern Rhodesia 1931 (B2)
1934	6.05		Huxley 1957 (D1), Chapter 9; Pandya, *KLC debs.*, 28 November 1934.
1950	20.0		Matheson and Bovill 1950 (D1), p. 68.
1955		$28/10\frac{1}{2}$	Federation of Rhodesia and Nyasaland, *Maize production costs on some European farms: interim report on the results for 1955/6.*
1959	30.53		Based on average costs per acre given by Farm Economic Survey Unit 1961b (B3) and average yields per acre there quoted.

Export rail rates on maize: Kenya–Uganda Railway, *Administration reports*, various; Railway Commission of Southern Rhodesia, Bechuanaland and Southern Rhodesia, *Annual reports*; PRO: CO 417/659, evidence of R.S. Newett contained in Connaught to Churchill, 8 April 1921.

Subsidy on maize exports. Southern Rhodesia (after 1950): Federation of Rhodesia and Nyasaland 1963a (B2), p. 3; (1930s) Maize Control Board, *Annual reports*. (Subsidy is taken as (50 per cent of pool price less export price) times number of bags marketed by Europeans, 50 per cent being the average European stake in the local pool.)

Kenya: Kenya 1966 (B3). For the guaranteed price period after 1942 subsidy is taken as guaranteed price less export price, times number of bags exported; for the period of the 1930s the subsidies were given *ad hoc*, and information is obtained from *KLC Debs*.

The hypothesis set out at the beginning of this Appendix, i.e. that the 'stimulus' of export losses elicits a 'response' in the shape of cuts in the export maize rail rate and in the pumping in of subsidies on maize cultivation, gets some support. In the case of subsidies on maize cultivation, the hypothesis holds true almost by definition: there were subsidies, significantly related with the size of the export loss, in years of export loss, and no recorded subsidies in other years. In the case of rail rates, a long enough run of data to test the hypothesis exists for Kenya only, and this gives a significant relationship of the expected sign between change in export rail rates and charge in export loss in crisis periods, and an insignificant relationship, of perverse sign, in non-crisis periods. However, the explanatory strength of the hypothesis grows weaker all the time; an attempt to explain why this happens is made in the text, pp. 66–7.

3

African agricultural development

Chairman What resources have the Natives today from which you could find funds to promote their interests?
Chief Native Commissioner The biggest source today, I think, is cattle. And the price of maize today is higher than it has been for some considerable time. They are fortunate in having surplus crops for sale.
Chairman What other sources of wealth have the natives?
Chief Native Commissioner Labour.

NAR: ZBJ 1/1/1, Evidence to the Native Production and Trade Commission,
1944, p. 7.

3.1 INTRODUCTION: A THEORETICAL PERSPECTIVE

Background

The purpose of this chapter is to examine the extent and causes of development in African agriculture in the settler economies, in the light of the policy-induced constraints discussed in the last chapter.

We begin by setting out, in Table 3.1, some aggregative data on developments in the African agricultural economy. These cover the only variables of which we have estimates running right through the colonial period: namely in Southern Rhodesia, total production of grains (maize, millets, wheat, groundnuts, rice), in Kenya, agricultural exports of African origin, and in both countries, the African cattle herd. They are not of a reliability which enables firm inferences to be made from them. However, it can be said that they offer no support to the more extravagant allegations of continuous agricultural decline made by commentators of the 'underdevelopment' school: for example, Arrighi's reference to a 'progressive decline' in the overall productivity of the African peasantry,[1] Good's suggestion that 'a disintegration of the peasantries ... occurred in all the [settler] states of Africa with varying time-span and intensity';[2] and, most forthright of all, Palmer's statement that by the end of the 1930s 'the agricultural economy of the Shona and the Ndebele, like that of the Kikuyu and most South African peoples, had been *destroyed*'.[3] On the indices portrayed in

71

Table 3.1. *Kenya and Southern Rhodesia: African agricultural development, a general overview*

Southern Rhodesia

	(1)	(2)	(3)	(4) – (3)/(1)	(5) = (2)/(1)	(6)
Years	Total African population (000s)	Grain production (000 bags; five year average centred on year stated)	Cattle population (000 head)	Cattle per head of African population	Estimated grain production per head of African popula- tion (200 lb bags)	Estimated grain production per head of African population (index: 1914 = 100)
1902	514	1676	55	0.11	3.26	112
1911	705	2190	330	0.46	3.11	107
1914	716	2070	406	0.56	2.89	100
1916	745	2248	491	0.65	3.01	104
1921	778	2799	854	1.09	3.59	124
1926	834	2770	1197	1.43	3.32	114
1931	986	2832	1623	1.64	2.87	99
1936	1088	2917	1547	1.42	2.68	93
1940	1224	2997	1718	1.40	2.44	84
1945	1473	3967	1911	1.29	2.69	93
1950	1755	3830	1832	1.04	2.18	75
1955	2145	6350	1900	0.88	2.96	102
1960	2475	5854	1953	0.79	2.38	82

Note: ^{a}interpolated figure
Sources: (NB complete data arrays for cols. 1, 2, 7 and 8 are displayed in Table 4.3 below.) Cols. 1–6: Southern Rhodesia, *Annual Reports of the Chief Native Commissioner*, various (note: in col. 1 the CNC's estimate is used throughout, even though better census estimates exist for 1960, in order to have an internally consistent series). Col. 7a: before 1948: estimate published in non-native census; after 1948: estimate based on census data (n.b. data for 1921–40 are almost certainly biased downwards; for

columns 6 and 12 of Table 3.1, the African agricultural economy of Southern Rhodesia appears about as prosperous in 1955 as it was in 1914, and that of Kenya twice as prosperous.[4] But between these years there is no smooth trend to be seen in either direction: there are periods of decline, indeed, in the late 1920s, 1930s and late 1940s in Southern Rhodesia and in the late 1920s and 1940s in Kenya, but there are also periods of growth, concentrated in Southern Rhodesia in the early 1920s and early 1950s and in Kenya in the early 1920s and 1930s. This contrasts with the African reserves of South Africa, where agricultural output per head of African population certainly fell between 1918 and 1970 (Knight and Lenta 1980 (D3), Table 1) although it has been recently suggested (Simkins 1981 (D3)) that most of this fall was concentrated in the years after 1955.

During the 1950s an important qualitative change occurred. African peasant production had been 'pinned in' by deliberate policy to the pro- duction of low-value cash crops, until that time, to a far greater degree in

Kenya

Years	(7) Total African population (000s) (a) Con- temporary estimates	(b) Back pro- jection from 1948 census	(8) Value of exports of African origin (£ 000; five-year average centred on year stated)	(9) Cattle population (000 head)	(10) = (9)/(7) Cattle per head of African population	(11) = (8)/(7) Exports of African origin per head of African population (£)	(12) Estimate of exports of African origin per head at constant prices, i.e. previous columes deflated by price of export maize (index: 1914 = 100)
1902							
1911	3000		173	1005	0.34	0.072	
1914	2650		189			0.071	100
1916							
1921	2480	3671	218	2372	0.95	0.087	92
1926	2550	4119	472	3200	1.25	0.185	182
1931	2970		358	4742	1.59	0.120	157
1936	3210[a]		468			0.145	268
1940	3410	4790	904	4500	1.31	0.26	295
1945	4060		1205			0.29	192
1950	5400		2695	5500	1.01	0.49	89
1955	6883		4745	6300	0.91	0.68	221
1960	8366		8265			0.99	340

discussion see Appendix 2). Cols. 8 & 9: Kenya Agriculture Department, *Annual Reports*, various. Col. 12: Table 4.3 below. (NB for years before 1922 African and European agricultural exports are given in the same table, and the exports treated as African here are beeswax, coconuts, copra, millets, peas and beans, sesame, groundnuts, hides and oilseeds, and a notional 50% per cent of maize exports.) Before 1920 rupee values are converted to sterling at the rate of £1 = 15 rupees. Price index of export maize for col. 12: Kenya 1966 (B3)

the settler economies than in African colonies with a negligible settler presence.[5] But in Kenya, under the Swynnerton plan of assistance to inten-sive agricultural development in African areas, this restriction was now removed, and high-value export crops such as coffee, pyrethrum and tea came to occupy a large proportion of the cultivated acreage. Such encourage-ment of high-value African cash crops did not occur in Southern Rhodesia, which experienced a brief cotton boom in the early 1950s but where by 1960 the African economy had virtually reverted to the production of low-value food-grains only (Table 3.2). As a consequence there was a sharp bifurcation in the fortunes of African agriculture in the two colonies at the end of our period.

Theoretical perspectives

The debate concerning the causes of agricultural underdevelopment in sub-Saharan Africa and elsewhere has in recent years shifted from socio-

Table 3.2. *Kenya and Southern Rhodesia: African marketed crop production, shares of grain and 'pure cash-crops'*

	Southern Rhodesia					Kenya							
	Value of African marketed crop production (£000)	Percentage share of				Value of agricultural exports of African origin (£000)	Percentage share of						
		Grain crops	'Pure cash-crops'				Grain crops		'Pure cash-crops'				
			Total	Cotton	Turkish tobacco			Total	Cotton	Coffee	Pyre-thrum	Wattle	Other
	(1)	(2)	(3)	(4)	(5)	(6)	(7)	(8)	(9)	(10)	(11)	(12)	(13)
1912/13	–	–	–	–	–	199	65.2	34.8	18.5	0	0	0	16.3
1930	–	–	–	–	–	208	59.1	40.9	10.6	0	0	20.1	10.2
1951	510	87.2	12.8	12.8	0	2328	52.7	47.3	16.5	2.3	0.4	16.3	11.8
1961	2168	97.8	2.2	1.8	0.4	7740	25.7	74.3	6.5	36.3	7.9	1.9	21.7

– no data

Notes: 'Grain crops' are defined as: maize, millets, sorghum, groundnuts, wheat, rice. 'Pure cash-crops' are defined as: cotton, tobacco, wattle, coffee, coconuts and derivatives, pyrethrum, vegetables.
Southern Rhodesia data cover only those African crops marketed through a statutory board and exclude sales of, for example, vegetables. To this extent the contrast between columns (2) and (7) is overstated.

Sources: Kenya Agricultural Department, *Annual Reports* 1913, 1930, 1951 and 1961; Southern Rhodesia, *Annual Report of the Chief Native Commissioner* 1961: 'Report of the Under-Secretary, Native Production and Markets Branch'.

logical barriers to efficient resource allocation,[6] through an emphasis on risk aversion and the persistence of 'survival algorithms',[7] to the political and economic burdens laid on peasant agriculture by competition from capitalist farmers.[8] We shall come back to the second and third of these hypotheses later; but for the moment, we adopt a different approach. This is to see whether the experience of African agricultural change in the settler economies corresponds at all with the idea put forward by William Allan and, in its most complete form, by Ester Boserup: namely that population pressure is a critical independent variable in agricultural change.

Boserup's approach may be briefly summarised as follows. As population pressure builds up in a particular community it will force that community progressively to shorten its fallow period and thus make more intensive use of existing land. By this means the community is projected through a series of discrete technological steps, from forest-fallow systems in which the soil rests for twenty to twenty-five years between plantings and the characteristic tool is the axe, through bush-fallow, hoe-cultivation systems with a six to ten year rest period, to short-fallow systems involving plough cultivation, a resting period of a year or less, and in many cases the use of a planted fallow or manure to make the soil revive more quickly. (These technical regimes may each be represented as 'survival algorithms', in Lipton's approach.) Since, in Boserup's view, the sedentarisation of agriculture (implicit in the switch to a short-fallow system) is a precondition for the specialisation of labour, and sedentarisation is most likely to take place under the stimulus of increasing population pressure, she is easily able to reach the conclusion that 'primitive communities with sustained population growth have a better chance to get into a process of genuine economic development than primitive communities with static or declining population, provided of course that the necessary agricultural investments are undertaken'.[9] Population pressure on the African agricultural economy, as was related in Chapter 2, built up rather rapidly in the colonial period, both by natural increase and by land policy.[10] We therefore have in Kenya and Southern Rhodesia a potentially good testing ground for this theory, although the fragility of the data throughout the colonial period will mean that any conclusions must be tentative.

Boserup's analysis is limited by the fact that it considers only one form of adaptation to a population density above the critical level, namely

(1) altering the input mix required to produce a given output.

Other possible forms of adaptation, however, include

(2) increasing the output of existing production activities by increasing the area planted and/or pastured, and marketing a greater output above subsistence;

(3) altering the output mix, by increasing the proportion of cash crops to subsistence crops;

75

or if agriculture is no longer considered as a closed system,

(4) migrating into employment outside African agriculture, in order to secure a subsistence by non-agricultural means.

In this chapter, long-period technical adjustments of type 1 above, in relation to agricultural production, are considered in section 3.2. Short-period adjustments of output, step 2, are discussed in section 3.3 in the case of maize, and section 3.4 in the case of beef cattle. Adjustments of type 3 were in large measure, as we have seen, precluded by official policy until the 1950s. Adjustments of type 4, migration into the labour market, were of course, critical, but involve our going outside the territory of agricultural production as such; they figure as independent variables in the supply functions of sections 3.3 and 3.4, and are discussed in more detail in our next chapter.

3.2 LONG-PERIOD CHANGE AMONG CROP PRODUCERS

The consequences of land scarcity, 1900–45

The state of African agriculture in 1900 is characterised by multiplicity of cropping,[11] the use of the short-handled hoe and the axe as tools of cultivation, and some system of fallowing without deliberate application of manure. In Southern Rhodesia it was common for Africans to practise the form of shifting cultivation known as *citemene*, in which new lands for cultivation were created by burning the small branches of trees around the stem and planting seed in the ash, with a fallow period of about fifteen years.[12] In Kenya, by contrast, some African areas had population densities higher than any known in Southern Rhodesia.[13] Here, shifting cultivation proper, of the kind in which the dwelling house moves with the cultivated plot, had already been replaced by bush-fallow, with a two to three year resting period in which the bush was cropped by animals. The early explorer, Joseph Thomson, passing through Northern Nyanza in 1887, noted that there 'almost every foot of ground was under cultivation. Yet the people seem to have some idea of the rotation of crops, for they allow land to lie fallow occasionally, such parts being used as pasture ground for cattle and sheep.'[14] These patterns of land use, later to be commended as an efficient adaptation to the prevailing factor endowments of abundant, mostly poor, land and scarce labour,[15] were deplored by the agricultural-science establishment of the time, and much of the sparse advice which African agriculturalists did receive from the colonial governments before the First World War adjured them to abandon them.[16] Masefield notes that:

> Dr Willis, a distinguished Director of the Ceylon Botanic Gardens, in a textbook of tropical agriculture written in 1908, did no more than express the orthodox scientific attitude of the time when he described shifting cultivation as 'utterly

76

destructive of the natural capital of the country' and extolled the merits of continuous cultivation (referring of course to the perennial crops of the European planters).[17]

The Africans' practice of shallow planting, which was to be encouraged in the same way as long-fallowing after the menace of soil erosion had become evident, likewise attracted official disapproval, as the following passage from a Kenya Provincial Commissioner's report makes evident: 'All these tribes in their methods of cultivation have the same fault, and that is none of them turn the soil over to a sufficient depth. The surface of the land is, what one might term, "scratched" and the seed is dibbed in.'[18]

This pattern of agriculture was confronted, from the moment of colonial conquest, with a drastic reduction in the area of land available for the exclusive use of Africans. Meanwhile, as a glance back at Table 3.1 will verify, African population grew steadily after 1920. The implication of this, of course, was a sharp increase in population densities, which migration into employment on European farms and mines could not do much to mitigate. The overall development in population in the settler economies, with some indication of the regional variations around the national mean, is given in Table 3.3. These increases in population required an increase in food output and the instrument generally used to secure this was the plough. The areas where the plough first became widespread were, in both countries, those where population pressure was most intense: in Southern Rhodesia, Victoria district and the highland areas of Matabeleland and, in Kenya, Nyanza Province followed by Kikuyu land.[19] This is entirely in accordance with the basic Boserup model. But Boserup herself makes the caveat that the probability of an agriculturalist actually acquiring a plough – or any indivisible input – depends not only on his need for it (which is determined, on her argument, by population pressure) but also on his ability to pay for it,[20] since, unlike the hand-hoe and hand-axe characteristic to the bush-fallow system, it had to be bought with cash income from outside the village economy, and was in most districts, until after the Second World War, only available to the more prosperous farmers.[21]

Let us, therefore, consider the statistical relationship between plough ownership, population density and per capita cash income. The results of a regression for 1913 and 1938 – the first and last years for which we have appropriate Southern Rhodesian data – are:

$$\text{for 1913: } Z = 61.99 + 5.17\,(P/L) + 6.00\,Y_g + 32.08^{**}\,Y_c \qquad (3.1a)$$
$$\qquad\qquad (0.62) \quad (1.68) \qquad (1.01) \qquad (2.97)$$
$$r^2 = 0.4445, D.W. = 0.8508$$
$$\text{for 1938: } Z = 2534.7^* + 4.83\,(P/L) + 66.2^*\,Y_g - 73.2\,Y_c \qquad (3.1b)$$
$$\qquad\qquad (2.55) \qquad (0.32) \qquad (2.09) \qquad (1.21)$$
$$r^2 = 0.1356, D.W. = 1.6902$$

where Z = number of ploughs owned by Africans in each district;

(P/L) = population per acre of arable reserve land in each district;

Table 3.3. *Kenya and Southern Rhodesia: African population densities*

	Estimate of African population	Estimate of land available for Africans to cultivate (square miles)	African population per square mile of available land	Population densities in specific reserves			
				Marandellas	Mrewa	Victoria	Mazoe
Southern Rhodesia							
1890	400 000	(150 000)	(2.7)				
(1900–8: *ad hoc* delimitation of reserves by Native Commissioners)							
1911	700 000	33 420	20.9	11	2	13	8
(1915: Native Reserves Commission)							
1921	778 000	33 740	23.1	14	7	23	13
(1925: Morris Carter Commission)							
(1930: Land Apportionment Act)							
1931	986 000	45 414	21.7	21	9	22	17
(1941: Land Apportionment Amendment Act)							
1941	1 390 000	47 892	29.0				
1951	1 970 000	47 892	41.1				
Kenya				Kiambu	N. Nyanza	Machakos	
1897	2 500 000						
1911	2 650 000						
1921	2 480 000	47 995 (Reserves as gazetted by Crown Lands Ordinance 1915)	51.6	52	81	25	
						33	
1931	2 970 000	47 995	61.9	69	93	42	
(1934: Morris Carter Commission)							
1941	3 410 000	48 149	70.8				
1951	5 400 000	48 149	112.1	215	236	64	

Note: Figures for Kenya exclude all unassigned land, such as Northern Frontier District.

Sources: Total population data – Table 3.1. Estimates of land available for Africans to cultivate – Southern Rhodesia 1962(B2), Johnson 1968 (C), Table 2, p. 40; Kenya – Great Britain 1934a (B1) Chapter 3. Population densities in specific reserves – Southern Rhodesia, *Annual Reports of the Chief Native Commissioner*, various (NB a blow-up factor of 3½ is used to go from reported figures of taxpayers to total population, see Appendix 2). Kenya – KNA:DC/KBU series, DC/MKS series and DC/NN.1 series, District Annual **Reports** for Kiambu, Machakos and North Kavirondo (subsequently N. Nyanza), various.

78

Y_g = total production of grain per head in each district, in 200 lb bags;

Y_c = cattle holdings per head of population in each district.[22]

The effect of the population density variable on plough ownership is in each year of the expected sign, though this effect is not statistically significant. Also, the only significant 'income' proxy variable in each case – cattle holdings in 1913 and crop-yield in 1933 – has the expected positive sign, although the results are marred in each case by the fact that the other 'income' variable exhibits a negative sign. Additionally, the population and crop-yield data are poor, so that these results should not be regarded as a rigorous test of the hypothesis.

It is an interesting extension of this approach that a number of observers considered the process of acquisition of ploughs to be subject to a 'band-wagon effect': the implement conferred such prestige on its owner that once a significant cluster of people in a district owned one others would rush to emulate them independently of their absolute income level, on the analogy of the Duesenberry model of consumer behaviour.[23]

> There is no question that the younger generation of native is being pushed by his womenfolk into the use of the plough and this slovenly method of agriculture. The man with a plough and oxen has a better chance of a 'pick' in the marriage market than the one without ...[24]

> The young Native ... instead of growing perhaps ten bags of grain on one acre of land, prefers to follow the example of his elders and scratches up four or five acres of land to produce the same crop. He ... knows, no doubt, that by adopting better methods he could grow more grain on less land, but he does not wish to be different from his fellows or to offend against public opinion ...[25]

These passages point not only to a sociological element in the process of agricultural change, but also to Native Commissioners' awareness of a far more serious dent inflicted by the data on the Boserup model, namely the fact that in many cases the advent of the plough was not an agent of 'Agricultural Growth' – in the sense of raising the productivity of a given acre of land – but rather a means of reducing the labour input involved in producing a given output,[26] which often involved an extension of the acreage.[27] This was commented on cynically by a number of observers in terms of the usual settler ideology of 'the lazy African', but understandingly by a few. These few saw that shallow ploughing, which gave low yields *per acre*, might yet be a more effective element in a survival algorithm than the deep ploughing favoured by the agricultural officers, as the retention of the tree-stumps gave protection against soil erosion.[28]

Although, therefore, the first response to population pressure was land-extensive rather than land-intensive, it was inescapable that when the limit of available cultivated lands was reached, and yet population densities continued to grow – a situation reached in many African reserves by the early 1930s – an intensive response was the only one left if food supplies were to be safeguarded, in spite of its associated increase in labour cost.[29]

This intensive response was overwhelmingly of a capital-saving kind: earlier planting, and weeding (both of which involved a higher labour input), rotation of crops, use of farmyard manure. In the Nyanza Province, Kenya it was reported in 1938 that

> there is a good deal of progress to report in the gradual development of the crofting system. The use of manure and compost is spreading; the acreage under planted trees continues to increase; and the drive relating to soil control measures is making people more conscious of their duty towards the land they work themselves.
> *Most attention in these aspects has been devoted to the highly populated areas of the Province.*[30]

In the Marandellas District, Southern Rhodesia, 'Methods employed are showing definite signs of improvement. More and more natives are realising the value of manuring their lands, and kraal manure instead of being allowed to go to waste is becoming a much sought after commodity.'[31]

Quite separately from this, there is clear evidence that until the 1940s all but the very richest African agriculturalists were prevented by sheer poverty from acquiring industrial input such as manufactured fertilisers or farm carts;[32] for most, the plough was the only purchased input, in distinct contrast to the experience of African peasantries which gained access to lucrative cash-crops at this time, such as Uganda and the Gold Coast.

The Kenyan Provincial Commissioner's evidence quoted above is consistent with the basic Boserup hypothesis that population pressure was the principal factor causing these capital-saving innovations to be adopted. We wish to test this hypothesis more formally, but we have no district-by-district data on input of this kind, which was home-produced and not bought in like the plough. Hence we must as dependent variable use some measure of productivity. Output of grain in bags per acre is the one most consistent with the spirit of Boserup's analysis, but output per man is in a sense the best indicator of agricultural prosperity, and the one used in Table 3.1 above. We consider both.

On Figure 3.1 we plot, once again for 1913 and 1938 (the beginning and end years of the period for which we have data on all African districts of Rhodesia) a scattergram relating grain yield per acre to persons per arable acre of land (as an indicator of population pressure),[33] omitting districts whose boundaries changed during the period. The data confirm, in broad terms, the basic hypothesis of positive and increasing correlation between population pressure and agricultural productivity, the regression equation relating the two variables being of the expected sign, but insignificant, in 1913:

$$Y = 1.98** + 0.047\,X; \; r^2 = 0.0868, \; D.W. = 2.09 \qquad (3.2a)$$
$$(3.57) \quad (0.92)$$

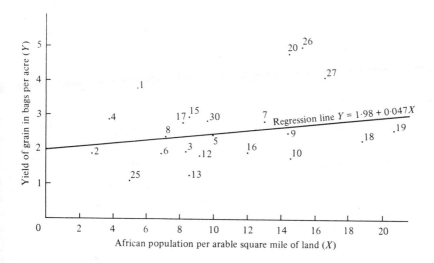

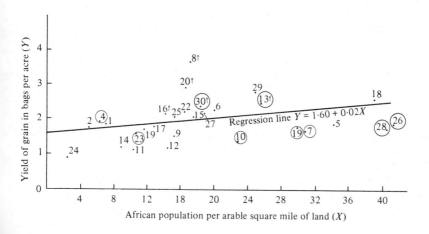

Fig. 3.1 Southern Rhodesia, African reserve areas: arable acreage per capita and grain productivity. (a) 1913; (b) 1938. Circled numbers show districts in which 66% or more of the land was allocated to Europeans under the 1930 Land Apportionment Act; arrows show districts in which the grain yield rose between 1913 and 1938. *Districts*: 1 Charter, 2 Darwin, 4 Hartley, 5 Lomagundi, 6 Marandellas, 7 Mazoe, 8 Mrewa, 9 Mtoko, 10 Victoria, 11 Chibi, 12 Chilimanzi, 13 Gutu, 14 Ndanga, 15 Umtali, 16 Inyanga, 17 Makoni, 18 Melsetter, 19 Bulawayo, 20 Bubi, 21 Bulalima-Mangwe, 22 Gwanda, 23 Matobo, 24 Nyamandhlovu, 25 Wankie, 26 Gwelo, 27 Belingwe, 28 Insiza, 29 Sebungwe, 30 Selukwe. *Sources: Annual Reports of the Chief Native Commissioner* 1913 and 1938; Southern Rhodesia 1930a (B2).

but positive *and* significant in 1938:

$$Y = 1.60** + 0.020* \ X; \ r^2 = 0.3387, \ D.W. = 2.30 \qquad (3.2b)$$

where Y = yield of grain in bags per cultivated acre of reserve land in a given district;
X = African population per arable square mile of reserve land in that district.[34]

If, in order to get rid of the tautology inherent in the fact that an increase in population density means an increase in families per acre, and hence an increase in yield per acre even at constant technology, we re-run (3.2) with grain yield per head as the dependent variable, we get a similar pattern:

For 1913: Yield per head = 16.17** + 0.207 (population per arable
    (4.18)   (0.64)   square mile)
$r^2 = 0.0146$ (3.2c)

For 1938: Yield per head = 3.04 + 0.834** (population per arable
    (1.55) (9.32)   square mile)
$r^2 = 0.7563$ (3.2d)

These are encouraging results for the Boserup hypothesis; but the fact that they are based on data which are far from ideal means that they should be regarded as providing modest support for the hypothesis, and by no means finally confirm it. Moreover, high population density, as the six districts in the bottom right-hand quadrant of Figure 3.1b bear witness, was far from being a necessary condition of high productivity: we return to this phenomenon later.

In Kenya there is no equivalent to the regular statistical return of African districts collated by the Southern Rhodesia Chief Native Commissioner. But the data we do have, for the period up to 1950 approximately, tell much the same story. In the first place the one empirical survey to consider the variables appearing in Figures 3.1a and 3.1b – arable acreage in relation to food production – in the inter-war period, which looked at the three districts of the Kikuyu country, gave the findings shown in the first table. Secondly, the data on population density and marketed output per head

District	Usable acreage per capita	Output of food crops for own consumption, per capita (value in shillings)
Kiambu–Nairobi	2.45	121
Fort Hall	2.17	139
Nyeri	1.60	160

Source: S.H. Fazan, 'An economic survey of Kikuyu proper', in Great Britain 1934b (B1), vol. I, p. 974.

(there are no data on total output) for the major regions of African production in 1948 are associated in the positive, but not very tight manner
shown in the second table. However, the looseness of fit is not surprising
since a lot of the variation in the right-hand column reflects inter-district
differences in output prices, which are not relevant to the Boserup model.

	African population density per square mile, 1948	Sales of African agricultural produce outside the district per head of African population, 1948 (£)
Fort Hall	411	2.60
Kiambu–Nairobi	351	5.35
Nyeri	272	1.40
N. Kavirondo	236	5.13
C. Kavirondo	185	5.65
Kericho	99	0.16
Teita	10	0.03

Source: Population density data – Great Britain 1955b (B1), Appendix VIII.
Sales outside the district – KNA: District Annual Reports 1948, for the
seven districts listed.

Having looked at the underlying pattern, let us now consider the deviations
from it; the regions in which the 'stimulus' of high population pressure
failed to elicit the expected 'response' of high grain yields. These can be
arbitrarily represented, in the Southern Rhodesian case, by the six points
in the south-eastern quadrant of Figure 3.1b. What was the cause of this
failure?

Clearly the 'rogue variable' causing deviations from the Boserup regression
line is not income this time, if we are right in supposing that variations
in output are caused by inter-district variations in the use of 'home-produced
inputs' rather than variations in purchased input. Nor, to judge from the
statistical analysis, does it seem to be the proportion of land in Native
Purchase Areas or male absenteeism: factors which were indeed to become
important after the Second World War.[35] But it may well have something
to do with cultivators' relationship to agricultural demonstrators, since
from the 1920s on they were the main source of recommendations to insert
these inputs into the production pattern. These demonstrators, mostly
African to reduce suspicion,[36] had been percolating into the African
reserves since the 1920s,[37] distributing seeds, proposing farm layouts which
reduced fragmentation, and employing advertising methods heavy with
the symbolism of modernisation and 'adoption'[38] to persuade farmers to
use the 'new' (i.e. the more intensive) methods. Differences in the welcome
they received are well documented, the demonstrators being listened to in

some reserves 'with indifference and in some cases hostility'[39] and in others with great enthusiasm.

A plausible hypothesis is that these differences in response (and hence in yields) *within* the category of high-density districts in settler economies is connected with a feature of these economies densely documented in contemporary reports on them, namely the effect of past experience of land policy in the different districts. For example, the report of the Southern Rhodesian Native Production and Trade Commission of 1944 maintained that the main obstacle to Africans' adoption of the new output-raising techniques of production recommended to them was their fear

> that any success will be a reason for depriving them of a portion of the Reserves set aside for them or a ground for refusing their demands, which are insistent, for an extension of the Reserves. One Native, a member of an authorised Native Council and therefore a man of some standing, said ... 'My fear is that if I were to go to a demonstrator and be taught, my land would be cut and I would be given a very small area to plough ... We feel that if we follow these people there is a danger that some of our land will be taken away from us.'[40]

Likewise, an Agricultural Officer in evidence to the Kenya Land Commission of 1933 reported that

> Five years ago the Kikuyu looked on the agricultural officers with the greatest suspicion and would have nothing to do with them. The issues of good seed were refused and there were absolutely no chances of doing any work on their shambas [holdings] to show them improved cultural methods because they thought the land would be taken from them.[41]

One would expect this fear of land confiscation to be greatest in those districts where a large part of the land had been made over to Europeans, more particularly since much of this land had not been occupied by them even in 1945. This hypothesis finds striking support in the Rhodesian case from Figure 3.1b, from which it appears that of those six districts which depart from the basic Boserup pattern by having *high* population density (more than sixteen persons per square mile) but also *low* grain yields (less than two bags per acre), five (Victoria, Bulawayo, Mazoe, Gwelo, Insiza) are amongst those where more than two-thirds of the land was alienated to Europeans. In these districts, it seems, fear of inability to reap the rewards from more intensive production intervened between the cultivator and a rational (in the colonial authorities' eyes) response to the teachings of demonstrators. By contrast, only one of the five districts where maize yields improved between 1913 and 1938 was among those where more than two-thirds of the land had been alienated to Europeans.[42] In Kenya it may also be that this 'policy anticipation effect' contributes to the explanation of the large inter-war difference in crop sales per head between Kikuyu districts (where land alienation to Europeans was substantial, though nowhere on a Rhodesian scale) and Nyanza Province (where it was insignificant).[43] The evidence of the Agricultural Officer quoted above suggests that this is likely. This fear of counter-moves by the government seems to have inhibited a number of cultivators from ever setting foot on the ladder which leads to higher risks and higher yields, on to which they would otherwise have been forced by increasing population pressure.

All this implies a picture of 'rational producer response' more complex than that commonly presented, for example in Lipton's approach (1968 (D3)), of a 'game against nature', in which the producer does the best that he can given the worst that the elements can possibly inflict on him. For although the idea of the African agriculturalist as participant in a game is a highly fruitful insight for whoever would wish to understand his behaviour – an insight missed, of course, by the colonial authorities – what all previous formulations of this idea seem to have overlooked is that in settler economies, at any rate, he was involved in a game not only against nature, but against the government. A straight extrapolation not only of the land policies adopted in parts of Kenya and Southern Rhodesia in the first thirty-five years of this century, but also of the Rhodesian policies on maize and cattle market-ing[44] could on its own have rationalised the expectation that any move by him towards greater commercialisation of his farm operations would be met by a counter-move on the part of the policy authorities, designed to restrict his land holdings, or his market outlets, or both.[45] Any rational strategy by an African agriculturalist to protect his economic position, or Liptonian 'survival algorithm', would in such a context obviously embrace measures to shield himself against the effect of such counter-moves (such as passive resistance to agricultural demonstrators). The same of course applies, theoretically speaking, to any economic actor on whose behaviour government policy is believed to be contingent.[46]

Epilogue 1945–63

During the period up to the Second World War African peasant producers in both settler economies were fairly firmly pinned into the production of grain crops (cotton in Western Kenya and wattle in Central Kenya provide limited exceptions to this rule). It is therefore a reasonable assumption that the relative prosperity of particular districts was largely determined by productivity in grain crops, and the argument so far suggests, with the important exception noted in the previous paragraphs, that in this period productivity was determined at least in part by population density. By the end of the colonial period this was no longer so: for example, in 1961, Nyanza Province, overwhelmingly the most densely populated of the African regions of Kenya, exported less than half as much agricultural produce, in per capita terms, as the far less populous Central Province (Table 3.4).

To be sure, this reflects in part a change in our measuring-rod for peasant prosperity, which is now value of sales rather than physical productivity. But even in physical terms the population density model had lost much of its predictive power by 1960.

85

Table 3.4. *Kenya, principal African districts:*
sales of agricultural produce outside the
district, per head of African population
(value in shillings)

	1929	1945	1961
Central Province			
Kiambu–Nairobi	5.35	19.04	
Fort Hall	2.60	22.72	41.80
Nyeri	1.40	14.20	
Nyanza Province			
Kericho	0.16	3.10	
N. Kavirondo	5.13	5.80	
(subsequently			
N. Nyanza)			17.30
C. Kavirondo	5.65	7.04	
Coast Province			
Teita	0.03	2.60	30.6
Index of agricultural			
export prices, 1929 = 100	100	111	254

Sources: 1929, 1945 – KNA: DC/KBU, DC/FH,
DC/NYI, PC/NZA series, Annual Reports for districts
listed. 1961, sales data – Agricultural Department,
Annual Report 1961; population data – 1962 census
estimates as recorded in Kenya, *Statistical Abstract* 1962.
Index of agricultural export prices – Table 4.3 below.

Two reasons for this have been suggested. The first runs in terms of
absenteeism. It is certain that participation rates of Africans in modern-
sector employment rose substantially in the war and post-war periods,
particularly as a result of a boom in secondary industry.[47] This both took
more adult males away from the reserves, and took them away for longer
periods, as secondary industry, much more than mines and plantations,
demanded 'stabilised' labour. The verbal evidence is eloquent that this
had damaging effects on the regions which sent the greatest proportion of
migrant labour. An agricultural officer in Maragoli, one of the most densely
populated (and once prosperous) of all African farming areas in Kënya,
described the position thus in 1955:

> The general picture can only be described as Malthusian – a teeming population
> with a very high birth-rate, trying to live on small holdings whose size and fertility
> is fast dwindling through continual subdivision and over-cropping. The present
> pattern can best be described as a 'Dependents' Dormitory', i.e. the majority
> of families in the division have a breadwinner outside. The present estimated
> average holding is between three and four acres ... This is already below the

86

critical figure of four acres reckoned by the Agricultural Department as a necessary minimum to support a family and provide a small cash surplus . . . [More-
over] land is being subdivided amongst sons not merely as shambaland but as
'Residential Plots', on which they will settle their families, and on which they will
build the best house they can afford. The present pattern, in fact, is one of 'sub-
urbanisation of the reserve'; not villagisation, as there is no planning involved,
but merely an increasing density of housing . . . One of the most distressing
aspects of the Division is the fact that the people as a whole have lost faith in
agriculture as a means of subsistence. This is a social and economic tragedy in a
country whose fertility was once a legend . . . It is no exaggeration to say that only
the old, the women and the stupid are actively engaged in farming in the
Division . . .[48]

Barber, also, is emphatic about the damaging effects of absenteeism
after 1945, although without direct evidence, and he argues that it is directly
correlated with population pressure.[49]

The second explanation runs in terms of a differential rate of uptake of
those high-value cash crops – i.e. essentially non-grain crops – which at
last came to be grown in substantial quantities after the Second World
War. These are coffee, pyrethrum, tea, sisal, cotton and sugar cane in
Kenya; cotton, tobacco, rice and groundnuts in Southern Rhodesia.

Table 3.5 is a first attempt to test for the relative importance of these
two factors in Kenyan African agriculture. It ranks seven major African
agricultural districts at three different periods according to the indicators,
population density, absenteeism from the district and proportion of 'pure
cash crops' to total sales outside the district.

Reliable inference from Table 3.5 is difficult for several separate reasons:
the population density data for 1929 and 1945 are not good; there is a
likelihood, as noted above, of intercorrelation between population density
and absenteeism; finally the absenteeism variable itself may well mean a
different thing in the Kiambu–Nairobi region (where employment in Nairobi
on a nearby coffee estate need not necessarily have meant absence from
the family farm for long periods) and in Nyanza Province (where it almost
certainly would have done). In the light of these caveats the only two observations that can safely be made from the combination of the value of sales
data in Table 3.4 and the criteria by which the same districts are ranked in
table 3.5 are as follows.

First, in 1929 population density and the cash-crop ratio are so tightly
intercorrelated that it is impossible to disentangle their influence on sales
of agricultural produce per head with the data available. By 1961 however,
they have become separated, and of the two the cash-crop ratio is clearly
the dominant influence on the value of sales. Secondly, it is impossible
from the available data to ascertain any statistical effect, one way or the
other, of absenteeism on sales of agricultural produce per head.

In Southern Rhodesia the available data for 1951 – the only year in which
we have district-level information on all four of the variables in Tables 3.4

Table 3.5. *Kenya, principal African districts: population density, absenteeism and cash-crop sales, 1929, 1945 and 1961*

	1929 Ranking on criterion of			1945 Ranking on criterion of			1961 Ranking on criterion of		
	Population density	Absenteeism	Ratio of 'pure cash-crops' to total sales	Population density	Absenteeism	Ratio of 'pure cash-crops' to total sales	Population density	Absenteeism	Ratio of 'pure cash-crops' to total sales
Central Province									
Kiambu–Nairobi	4	1	1	4	1	2	2	–	1
Fort Hall	3	3	4	3	3	1			
Nyeri	5	5	5	5	5	3			
Nyanza Province									
Kericho	6	2	no cash-crop sales	6	2	6			
N. Kavirondo (subsequently N. Nyanza)	2	4	3	2	4	5	1	–	3
C. Kavirondo (subsequently C. Nyanza)	1	6 =	2	1	6	4			
Coast Province									
Teita	7	6 =	no cash-crop sales	7	7	7	3	–	2
Other Coast Province districts									

– no data

Note: 'Pure cash-crops' are defined as: coffee, tea, wattle, cotton, pyrethrum, sisal.

Sources: Population density and sales outside the district – KNA: DC/KBU, DC/KBU, DC/NYI, DC/FH, DC/KER, DC/NN. 1 series, Annual Reports for districts listed for 1929 and 1945; Agricultural Department, *Annual Report* 1961. Absenteeism (i.e. males aged 15–40 in employment), 1929 – PRO:

and 3.5 – tell a very similar story. The data is sufficiently disaggregated – covering all thirty districts considered in Figure 3.1 – for us to be able to run a regression of agricultural sales per head on population density, absenteeism and the 'cash-crop ratio'. This gave the result:

$$Y = 0.29 - 0.00014\ D + 0.0069\ A + 0.013^{**}\ C; \quad r^2 = 0.5369$$
$$(0.82)\quad (1.68)\qquad (1.02)\qquad (5.37)$$

where Y = sales of agricultural produce outside the district per head of African population;

D = African population density per cultivated square mile;

A = male absenteeism ratio for the district, calculated as:

population recorded on – population recorded as being
tax registers   present on the day of the survey
_____
population recorded on tax registers
for the adult male population

C = proportion of 'cash-crop' sales to total sales outside the district, where 'cash-crops' are defined as: cotton, rice, tobacco and groundnuts.[50]

These data, again, suggest that the cash-crop percentage was an important determinant of rural prosperity after 1945, and that absenteeism had no significant effect one way or the other. One suspects, however, the presence of multi-collinearity between all three independent variables, hence it would be dangerous to draw excessively firm conclusions from the analysis.

It can certainly be said that within the rural African economy at this time a double pattern of differentiation was emerging. Firstly, between individuals: those Africans who had managed to acquire land holdings by the 1930s (either formally in the Rhodesian Native Purchase Areas, or informally in the Kenya reserves by occupation and enclosure)[51] often developed into full-time farmers, with substantial capital assets and a year-round pattern of labour input. Others were caught in a vicious circle of low income, need to migrate to urban employment, low farm productivity and low income which became more intense as subdivision proceeded. (The Rhodesia Native Land Husbandry Act of 1951, formally, and District Commissioners in Kenya, informally, imposed floors on family land holdings, but these merely accentuated the emerging problem of landlessness.)[52] The study by Massell and Johnson graphically tabulates in the Rhodesian case the dichotomy in patterns of farm operation which had developed between the (relatively) prosperous Native Purchase Area farmer and the (usually migrant) reserve cultivator by this time.[53]

Secondly, however, differences were emerging between regions. This was no longer simply, as in the inter-war period, the difference between heavily and lightly populated regions. In Kenya, the leadership among African agricultural regions passed from Nyanza to Central Province, largely as a result of the latter Province's quicker uptake of the cash-crops that Africans became able to grow at the start of the 1950s. This 'quicker uptake' was partly a political matter, and partly a matter of relative suitability of different regions for pyrethrum, coffee and (at the very end of the decade) tea.[54] It had the effect of raising some outlying districts such as Embu and Meru, which by reason of distance from rail had been reduced to complete pauperism during the depression of the 1930s, but which were very suitable for coffee, to very high places in the league table of rural prosperity by the end of the 1950s. In Southern Rhodesia, Hartley District, by no means one of the most prosperous African farming districts in the inter-war period (cf. Figure 3.1), was emphatically the most prosperous in the early 1950s, having by far the greatest African cotton acreage.

To sum up this section, the basic hypothesis propounded by Boserup, that population pressure could be a stimulus, indeed a necessary (though not sufficient) condition for agricultural development, seems to fit the facts of the settler economies up to the Second World War approximately, in contrast to the perspective of underdevelopment theory which sees that pressure, imposed by the land policies of the colonial governments, as squeezing the African agricultural sector almost out of existence. But a closer survey of the facts requires us to modify the basic hypothesis in five ways: (1) the plough was an instrument, often, of extending the cultivated area and not of intensification; (2) capital shortage barriers often intervened between Africans and their desired response to land shortage; (3) also intervening, in areas thickly settled by Europeans, was a fear of land confiscation by them which made them, in particular, unreceptive to the advice of agricultural demonstrators; (4) partly because of this African farm families were often forced into an alternative response, migration into off-farm employment, which contemporary observers allege had come to damage the agricultural economy (the statistical results are inconclusive) by the 1950s; (5) the relative intensity of African cash-cropping by region, which was partly a political and partly a climatic variable, had come to exert a dominant influence on the inter-regional pattern of agricultural prosperity by 1961.

3.3 SHORT-PERIOD RESPONSE 1: THE SUPPLY RESPONSES OF MAIZE PRODUCERS

Supply response among crop producers

Technical adaptation of the type described in the previous section involved costs: new tools, and generally an increased labour input as well. *A priori*, therefore, the theory sketched out on p. 75 above would assume that it was a last resort, adopted if and only if other expedients failed to secure the basic objective of ensuring survival. As noted above, the most obvious expedient in the event of changes in the farm family's income target, or falling productivity of the soil, was a change in the amount marketed. In this section we examine such changes in the case of maize, which by the 1920s had become rural Africans' main subsistence crop (replacing millets in this role) in addition to being a source of cash income. We wish to see if the supply responses of African producers corresponded to any principle of rational behaviour, and whether they differed between periods or regions.

So far this task has not been attempted, to my knowledge, for maize in the economies under consideration, in spite of what is now a vast literature on the supply responses of peasant producers. This is, in a way, not surprising. For once there is no great problem with the data, as, after the establishment of statutory marketing boards, these are quite reliable.[55] But there are serious problems of interpretation. First, what independent variables apart from the price of maize do we consider as determinants of supply response;[56] and secondly, how do we interpret the marketed supply of a product such as maize which is both a subsistence crop and a cash-crop, so that the income/leisure choice *and* the choice of how much of the output to consume intervene between the producer and his decision on how much to sell?[57]

Our approach is, for the first problem, to use the price of major cash-crops in maize producing areas – cotton in Kenya, and groundnuts in Southern Rhodesia – and an index of the modern sector wage rate as indicators of alternative income opportunities to extending surplus maize production; and for the second problem to examine the relative response of African and European producers to price. One would expect large producers to have a lower income elasticity of demand for own-consumption maize than small producers, and hence to deliver more to market out of a given output. In passing it will be possible to examine the hypothesis, which not only governed colonial policy towards maize marketing but also some academic writing, that African marketed surplus was determined purely by weather conditions and hence was far more unstable than European production, which was price responsive.[58]

The two parts of Table 3.6 set out the basic data underlying the growth of the maize industry in Kenya and Rhodesia, and the two parts of Table 3.7 set out the results of regression analysis designed specifically to test the hypothesis stated above. (In Kenya, this is done for the area now known as 'Western Province' only, because of the inadequacy of data for the whole country before 1942.) The correlation coefficients obtained are generally low on account of our deliberate omission of non-economic variables which have an obvious effect on maize production (notably rainfall) and those significant results which we do obtain present an often confused picture. Nonetheless, the following two points can be made.

First, that taking the period as a whole, there is a consistently positive response of African recorded maize deliveries to price (Table 3.7a, equations 2 and 3; Table 3.7b, equations 7 and 8), but this is significant only in equations 3 and 8, and then only at the 90 per cent level. These findings are, however, inconsistent with the conventional wisdom of the colonial authorities, that maize was simply dumped on the market by African producers as an

Table 3.6a. *Southern Rhodesia: maize exports, sales and prices, 1930–61*

| Crop year | Prices paid (shillings/pence per 200 lb bag) on local market | | | Quantities delivered to marketing board (thousands of 200 lb bags) | | Exports (thousands of 200 lb bags) | Imports (thousands of 200 lb bags) | Import cost (shillings/pence per 200 lb bag) |
	(1) To European producer[a]	(2) To Africans at store	(3) On export market	(4) European	(5) African	(6)	(7)	(8)
1930/1	6/6	–	5/2	1183	317	701	0	0
1931/2	5/3¼	–	5/1	831	107	1302	0	0
1932/3	8/5	–	6/10	1150	222	255	0	0
1933/4	7/7¾	–	6/4	805	204	609	0	0
1934/5	8/6½	–	5/11	1409	442	396	0	0
1935/6	8/3¾	–	7/8	1491	591	1065	0	0
1936/7	7/11¼	–	7/-	952	309	1303	0	0
1937/8	9/3¼	5/- to 7/-	7/8	740	325	275	0	0
1938/9	9/7½	5/- to 9/4	7/9	1059	389	48	–	–
1939/40	8/11½		6/11	682	136	552	50	9/10
1940/1	11/3¾		–	686	208	0	0	0
1941/2	12/3		–	906	320	0	495	12/6
1942/3	13/6		14/-	960	448	104	374	19/8
1943/4	15/6		16/-	866	469	267	0	0
1944/5	16/6		–	795	302	0	0	0
1945/6	18/6		–	394	203	0	24	20/6
1946/7	25/-		–	1970	655	0	20	22/-
1947/8	30/-	19/3	–	705	370	0	1766	42/11
1948/9	30/-[b]	18/5–23/9	–	988	855	0	117	42/11
1949/50	35/-	23/9	–	465	200	0	434	40/1
1950/1	37/6	24/3	–	1402	662	0	81	40/-
1951/2	45/-	28/-	–				1577	70/6

Year							
1952/3	41/6	27/-	—	1364	909	0	91	74/1
1953/4	40/6	25/6	—	1735	890	0	167	49/1
1954/5	40/6	25/-	—	1780	706	0	13	49/4
1955/6	41/6	25/7	26/4	2419	1395	940	0	0
1956/7	40/-	23/9½	34/3	2708	831	2396	0	0
1957/8	41/6	22/10	34/3	2432	536	2313	0	0
1958/9	36/3½	22/2	34/3	2653	728	2360	0	0
1959/60	24/8	24/8	34/10	1866	513	2624	0	0
1960/1	31/6	20/-	33/2	4169	1186	1765	0	0

– data not available

Notes:

a Payout figures for European producers are averages, and do not indicate what individual producers received because of varying quotas of different classes of producers in the local pool. These producer prices include government subsidies and good farming bonuses.

b The government producer price was guaranteed from the 1948/9 crop year onwards. The level of guaranteed prices was announced in May of each year.

Sources:

Cols. (1) and (3) to (8) – Federation of Rhodesia and Nyasaland 1963a (B2).

Col. (2), 1937/8 and 1938/9 – NAR: S 1215/1090/172, Maize Control Board minutes 1938.

1947/8 to 1960/1 – Guaranteed minimum price; from *Annual Report of the Chief Native Commissioner 1961*: 'Report of the Under-Secretary, Native Economics and Markets Division'.

Table 3.6b. *Kenya: maize exports, sales and prices, 1929–63*

Crop year	Guaranteed bulk price[a]	Subsidy or cess	Price to European farmer	KFA pool payout	Price to Africans at Bungoma[c]	On export market[d]	European	Total	Sales from Western Province[e]	Calendar year	Exports (thousands of 200 lb bags)	Imports (thousands of 200 lb bags)	Import cost (shillings per 200 lb bag)
	Prices paid (shillings per 200 lb bag)						Quantities delivered (thousands of 200 lb bags) — African						
1929/30				12.40		13.78	1859			1929	428	11	16.58
1930/1				7.87		9.14	1650			1930	1244	–	14.86
1931/2				6.19		8.06	763			1931	1041	23	7.75
1932/3				6.50		8.16	1140			1932	288	23	8.25
1933/4				3.50		6.71	747			1933	633	4	4.84
1934/5				6.90		8.50	–		14	1934	246	25	6.15
1935/6				5.68	3.00	5.51	1012		35	1935	671	11	3.94
1936/7				4.32		5.74	–		88	1936	813	8	3.50
1937/8				7.20	7.50	9.75	968		113	1937	407	12	8.15
1938/9				6.33	5.25	7.86	–		132	1938	658	1	6.00
1939/40				6.33	5.30	7.87	618		42	1939	563	16	6.72
1940/1				7.32	5.02	no export	–		131	1940	0	23	6.91
1941/2				8.50	4.75	9.38	311	716	295	1941	283	2	9.61
1942/3				8.96	3.39	8.96	361	338	309	1942	155	1	7.38
1943/4	10.80	–	10.80	7.52		12.22	600	641	182	1943	46	–	15.96
1944/5	11.40	(+2.85)[b]	(14.25)	8.63		12.59	528	983	333	1944	24	11	29.27
1945/6	11.40	(+2.85)[b]	(14.25)	8.40		15.19	552	655	316	1945	603	–	20.29
1946/7				9.45		15.98	508	1002	610	1946	195	0	0
											…5	10	18.51

94

Season									Year			
1949/50	21.00	+2.40	23.40	12.25	26.28	737	1690	1218	1949	35	–	0
1950/1	21.00	+7.80	28.80	13.65	41.68	736	982	850	1950	345	0	0
1951/2	30.30	+4.70	35.00	22.82	58.59	755	1092	668	1951	227	0	0
1952/3	38.25	0	38.25	29.75	62.40	638	738	416	1952	764	0	0
1953/4	38.72	0	38.72	30.17	50.82	784	1483	1111	1953	120	336	55.15
1954/5	38.15	−3.00	35.15	27.70	39.40	1202	1221	810	1954	514	0	55.63
1955/6	38.15	−3.00	35.15	26.85	38.55	887	691	425	1955	864	0	0
1956/7	39.98	−2.00	37.98	30.33	37.70	867	721	247	1956	47	0	106.67
1957/8	39.98	−5.00	34.98	27.33	36.81	1015	835	287	1957	253	606	36.96
1958/9	37.00	−10.00	27.00	22.00	34.08	893	938	266	1958	1095	1	119.98
1959/60	35.60	−3.60	32.00	23.10	35.91	779	880	437	1959	608	0	111.34
1960/1	35.50	0	35.50	24.30	34.62	880	706	351	1960	103	0	92.56
1961/2	35.50	0	35.50	31.40	35.20	869	774	263	1961	2	1125	40.92
1962/3	35.50	−11.50	24.00	28.60	30.56	1150	1083	316	1962	963	282	37.41

– data not available

Notes:

a Guaranteed price was announced in February each year to apply to deliveries after the harvest from the main large farm planting in March.

b In the 1944/5 and 1945/6 seasons European growers were paid a maize subsidy of Shs. 7.50 per acre, plus an extra Shs. 7.0 for every bag delivered over and above 400 000 bags; the subsidy recorded is calculated from this information.

c Bungoma, in the northern part of Western Province, is the centre of the most commercialised region of African smallholder maize production. The local market price at Bungoma is, after the institution of Maize Control in 1942, the guaranteed bulk price (i.e. the European bulk price recorded in col. 1). plus/minus any subsidy or cess, less the trader's commission; a charge for a portion of the agent's expenses; and the Agricultural Betterment Fund cess. For details of the price structure, see Table 2.12.

d Export values are given f.o.b. Mombasa and as such are not strictly comparable to the f.o.r. values given in the third part of col. 1.

e Note that the administrative boundaries changed during this period contemporaneously with modifications in marketing arrangements. Thus the figures for *before 1946* are for North Nyanza District (which corresponds to the present Kakamega and Bungoma Districts put together); *1946/7 to 1954/5* are for Kakamega District (the old North Nyanza District, renamed); *1955/6 to 1958/9* are for Elgon Nyanza (corresponding to the present Bungoma District) and North Nyanza (corresponding to the present Kakamega District); *1959/60 to 1962/3* are for Western Province, minus an estimate for Busia District (supplied by the DAO Busia) giving us, once again, Kakamega and Bungoma Districts put together.

Sources: Export price, exports, import prices, imports – Kenya 1966 (B3). Deliveries to Maize Marketing Board (African and European totals) – Kenya Government Sessional Paper no. 6 of 1957/8, 'The maize industry', supplemented by Maize Marketing Board, *Annual Reports.* Bungoma prices, Western Province deliveries, before 1946 – KNA: DC.NN.1 series, Annual Reports, North Nyanza District. 1946/7–1954/5 – personal communication from Mr G. Stern, Crop Production Division, Ministry of Agriculture, Nairobi (from 1946–54, District Agricultural Officer, Kakamega). 1955/6–1958/9 – Nyanza Province Marketing Board Annual Reports. 1959/60–1962/3 – Maize and Produce Board Annual Reports. Prices to European farmers, KFA pool payout prior to 1942 – Kenya 1943(B3). 1943–1963 – from Munro 1973(C) Table A-11.

impulse reaction to crops in excess of their subsistence needs (cf. note 58 above). In both cases the predictive power of the relationship is increased by adding the modern sector wage rate as an explanatory variable (equations 3, 4 and 8), though in Southern Rhodesia the effect of this on maize production is, unexpectedly, positive. In Southern Rhodesia the fit is further improved by taking the price-ratio of maize to groundnuts, rather than the raw maize price, as the basic independent variable; a similar exercise in Western Kenya using the price of cotton as an additional independent variable yielded insignificant results.

Secondly, that the *stability* of European deliveries was not, contrary to the belief of contemporary policy-makers, significantly, if at all, greater than the stability of African deliveries. Coefficients of variation, as derived from the series presented in Table 3.6, were as shown here. Actual policy

Kenya		Southern Rhodesia	
Guaranteed price period 1941/2–1962/3		1929/30–1960/1	Guaranteed price period 1948/9–1960/1
European deliveries	31.9%	59.0%	50.1%
African deliveries	33.1%	60.8%	40.8%

was based – or at any rate justified to sceptical enquirers – on the opposite assumption (cf. note 58 above).

The effects of 'maize control'

In the final section of Chapter 2.2 above we argued that the major immediate effect of the introduction of monopoly maize marketing in Southern Rhodesia (1931) and Kenya (1942) was to eliminate those pockets of well-above-export parity maize prices which had survived the coming of the railway and the competitive European producer, to the benefit of African producers in up-country regions. The general depressive effects of this policy on maize output by Africans can now be inferred from the quantitative estimates of their response to price made in Table 3.7. For example, if Southern Rhodesian Africans had been paid in the crop year 1938/9 the average price paid to Europeans (9s. 4d. per bag rather than 5s. 3d.),[59] then one would expect, using equation 2 in that table, that their output would have been 189 000 bags more,[60] worth, at that price, £85 050. It is of course possible that the increase might not have been as great: the regression equation is subject to disturbance, and the hypothetical policy of 'no maize control' would have led to a different price for Europeans as well as Africans. But it is quite clear that at the higher price more would have been produced.

Apart from this general effect on African maize production, two distributive effects are worth mentioning. In the first place, the offer of a flat buying price which as such could take no account of local surpluses and deficits accentuated the African producer's strong desire to recapture the local market, which maize control had largely removed from his legal grasp, by illegal 'direct-to-consumer' sales on the black market. Often these sales crossed regional boundaries, and tales of petrol tankers, on their way from the maize-surplus areas of Nyanza and Western Provinces to the maize-deficit areas of Central Province, splitting open after a crash to reveal a cargo of maize are part of the folklore of recent Kenyan economic history. For obvious reasons it is not possible to ascertain the magnitude of black market sales, but we can gain some idea of their significance by considering data on one important element of the black market price available to African producers in Kenya – namely the price available across the border in Uganda. As Figure 3.2 shows, the price in Buganda (the main maize consuming region in Uganda) is significantly associated with the residual from the insignificant regression equation (7) in Table 3.7b relating deliveries from Kenya's Western Province to the Maize Control or equivalent, to the Maize Control's buying price at Bungoma, the centre of the Western Province producing area. The regression equation in the absence of the Uganda price is, we recall,

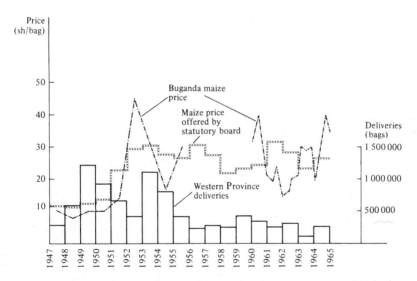

Fig. 3.2 Western Province of Kenya: deliveries of maize to West Kenya Marketing Board, Marketing Board buying price, and price across the border in Uganda, 1947–65. *Sources*: as for Western Province data in Table 3.6b. Uganda, Ministry of Agriculture and Cooperatives, *Monthly Price Bulletin*, and Miracle 1965 (D3), p. 135. The inspiration of a graph in Yoshida (1966 (D1)), who however used 1960–5 prices in Eastern Uganda only, is acknowledged.

Table 3.7a. *Southern Rhodesia: results of regression analysis relating maize deliveries to price offered and other variables*

Equation no.	Period covered by analysis	Dependent variable	Regression coefficients on independent variables					r^2	D.W.
			Constant	Price offered to European producers (shillings per 200 lb bag)	Price offered to African producers (shillings per 200 lb bag)	Price offered to African producers as a proportion of groundnut price	Index of money wages in agriculture and mining combined (1914 = 100)		
1	1930/1–1961/2 (32 observations)	European deliveries to Maize Control Board	655.8** (2.69)	29.06** (3.20)				0.2549	0.73
2	1948/9–1961/2 (14 observations)	African deliveries to Grain Marketing Board	−338 (−0.44)		46.1 (1.44)			0.1477	2.25
3	1948/9–1961/2 (14 observations)	African deliveries to Grain Marketing Board	−899 (−1.14)		52.9 (1.75)		8.05 (1.66)	0.3191	2.68
4	1948/9–1961/2 (14 observations)	African deliveries to Grain Marketing Board	−718 (−1.59)			2051.4** (2.86)	13.4** (2.85)	0.4997	2.81

Note: Figures in parenthesis below coefficients are Student's *t*-statistics; **denotes significance at 1% level, *at 5% level.

Source: Table 3.6a above, except for groundnut price which is from Southern Rhodesia, *Annual Report of the Chief Native Commissioner* 1961: Report of the Secretary Table 105.

98

Regression coefficients on independent variables

Equation no.	Period covered by analysis	Dependent variable	Constant	Price offered to European producers (shillings per 200 lb bag)	Price offered to African producers at Bungoma	Export price of cotton (shillings per 100 lb)	Wage rate in modern sector (shillings per month)	r^2	D.W.
5	1929/30–1962/3 (34 observations)	European deliveries	814.9** (6.50)	0.61 (0.11)				0.0247	0.91
6	1942/3–1962/3 (22 observations)	European deliveries	452.2** (5.52)	10.6** (3.74)				0.4124	1.59
7	1938/9–1962/3 (25 observations)	African recorded maize marketings, Western Province	320.2** (2.72)		0.77 (1.27)			0.0687	0.98
8	1942/3–1962/3 (22 observations)	African recorded maize marketings, Western Province	494.6** (3.47)		0.18 (1.67)	2.37 (0.10)	− 0.85* (2.11)	0.1904	1.36

Note: Figures in parentheses below coefficients are Student's *t*-statistics: **denotes significance at 1 per cent level, *at 5 per cent level.
Sources: Table 3.6b above, except for wage rates in modern sector which is an arithmetic average of the money wage rates in public services and agriculture presented in Table 4.9c.

$$Q = 320.2 + 0.77P_k\,; \quad r^2 = 0.0687 \text{ (equation 7, Table 3.7b)}$$
where Q = maize deliveries from Western Province,
P_k = price offered by statutory Board's agent in Western Province.

With the Buganda price inserted as an additional independent variable it becomes

$$Q = 792^{**} + 1.45\,P_k - 11.72^*\,P_u\,; \quad r^2 = 0.19$$
$$\quad\;\,(2.78)\quad(0.91)\quad\;\;(2.03)$$
where P_k = official Maize Board buying price in Kenya,
P_u = price in Buganda.
*denotes significance at 5 per cent level.
**denotes significance at 1 per cent level.
Numbers in parentheses below coefficients are Student's t-statistics.

Black market sales were not only a response on the seller's side to a flat and (in his perception) low price offered by the marketing board; they were also a response to a third factor influencing the regional allocation of maize production, namely the statutory Board's selling price. This invariably contained an element of monopoly profit.[61]

The wide gap between buying and selling price was a feature of the system throughout the period of formal maize control in both countries. Once described by a Kenya Chief Native Commissioner as 'the most barefaced and thorough-going attempt at exploitation the people of Africa have ever known since Joseph cornered all the corn in Egypt',[62] it had the natural effect of inducing consumers of maize to grow large quantities of it, even in areas not well suited for growing it (e.g. Machakos district in Kenya and the Matabeleland districts of Rhodesia), in order to protect themselves from being thus exploited if forced into buying maize on the open market. In general this hindered any tendency for maize production to be concentrated in the hands of the most efficient growers, and in particular it upset the balance between arable and animal farming. In 1949 in the highly populated rural districts of Kenya:

> The necessity for extensive crop production has reduced the role of farm animals from a dominant to a secondary one. The Kikuyu, Nandi, Kavirondo, Lumbwa, Meru, Embu and Machakos reserves are no longer areas producing surpluses of animal products, but are consuming areas of animal products imported from other parts of the country.[63]

Secondly, it must be said that the effects of maize control were not confined to the producer price or the relationship between this and the consumer price, but ramified, like land policy, into all those areas of agricultural behaviour which involved a response to government initiative. We have already noted that when maize control was introduced in Southern Rhodesia, it aroused such resentment among African cultivators that many of them would no longer listen to the teachings of extension workers.[64] But even when this obviously discriminatory system was replaced by a one-pool system in Southern Rhodesia (later to be copied in Kenya), cultivators continued to voice violent opposition to statutory deductions from their payout. This suspicion of the marketing system may well have had an adverse effect on their productivity.

3.4 SHORT-PERIOD RESPONSE 2: THE CASE OF AFRICAN BEEF CATTLE

Whereas the official conventional wisdom tended to treat the African's supply response as maize grower as unresponsive, one way or the other, to price stimuli (note 58 above), it insisted that, as cattle owner, his supply response was perverse. The annual report of the Rhodesian Cold Storage Commission for 1941, for example, maintains that: 'In the reserves the native still regards his cattle as an indication of his wealth, and numbers mean more to him than quality. He only sells to cover his immediate needs, and consequently, the tendency is for increased prices to reduce the number of cattle offered.'[65] And in 1933 the District Commissioner, Machakos asserted that

> Stock prices remained very low. This should be taken as a blessing in disguise in a District such as this, because it tends to dispel the illusion often cherished by natives as to the high value of their stock; and also because it necessitates a greater number of animals being sold to obtain a given sum of money, thus helping to reduce numbers.[66]

At first sight this conventional belief appears to be borne out – in some but not all cases – by the data of recorded cattle sales and prices. The estimated regression equations connecting the two variables are:

For Kenya, Masai districts 1924–52 (selected years):
Cattle sales = 14 149 − 18.4 (price offered per animal in shillings)
$$r^2 = 0.0050$$

For Southern Rhodesia, deliveries to Cold Storage Commission 1948–61:
Cattle sales = 22621−185.13 (price offered, shillings per 100 lb cold dressed weight)
(African third grade only) $r^2 = 0.2557$

Source: Table 3.8 and 3.9 below, which see for details of original data.

However, it is perhaps even more dangerous in the case of cattle than in the case of maize to analyse supply response by means of a simple inspection of current price and current marketed supply. As with maize, slippage between increases in real income and increases in supply is caused by demand

101

Table 3.8a. *Kenya, Masai districts (Narok and Kajiado): sales of cattle and certain explanatory variables, 1924–52*

| | | | | Possible explanatory variables: | |
| | No. of head of cattle sold to | Price paid for bullocks at Narok | Cattle | District clear (O) or subject (X) to quarantine | Year of compulsory |
Year	traders	(sh./head)	population	regulations	sales (C)
1924	10 000	30.0	618 000	X	
1925	2 793			X	
1926	–			X	
1927[a]	11 100	50.0		X	
1928	7 683	40.0		X	
1929	–	50.0		X	
1930	6 856	38.0		X	
1931	10 732	30.0	790 000	X	
1932	11 884	23.0		X	
1933	14 567	–	b	X	
1934	11 117	15.0	b	X	
1935	15 006	40.0	440 000	O[c]	
1936	–				
1937		35.0 to 70.0			
1938	19 127	55.0 to 60.0		O[f]	
1939	–	–		O	
1940	–	–		O	
1941	17 760	31.90 to 56.0		O	C
1942	20 178	28.79 to 37.90		O	C
1943	25 653	–		O	C
1944	25 785	–		O	C
1945	–	48.75	650 000		C
1946					C
1947	–	–			d
1948	12 000	86.0			
1949	10 974	85.70		X (rinderpest)[e]	
1950	5 681	–		X (pleuro-pneumonia)	
1951	5 341	130.0		X	
1952	4 961	170.0		X	

– no data

Notes:

[a] In this year auction sales were begun in the Masai reserve as an experiment, but abandoned the same year following a boycott by Nairobi butchers.

[b] 1933 and 1934 were years of catastrophic drought: the Annual Report for the latter year states that 'by the end of the year the countryside was littered with the carcasses of dead cattle in such numbers that scavenging birds and animals were unable to deal with them and they dried in the sun to parchment-covered skeletons'.

[c] In this year, for the first time, the quarantine restriction on export to Kikuyu and South Kavirondo districts was lifted, and these became the largest legal markets for Masai cattle.

[d] Compulsion may have been perceived, even though not legally experienced, in this year

102

for own-consumption; as with maize, difficulty in identifying the supply curve arises from the fact that it is apt to shift at the same time as the demand curve. As with maize, advertised official prices paid for African cattle were highly unreliable indicators of the selling opportunities open to African herdsmen, on account of the continual influence of local markets set up in evasion first of the quarantine rules and later of the low prices paid by the statutory boards, offering very different income opportunities from those boards.[67]

But in addition, the identification problem is exacerbated by repeated government intervention to ban, restrict or increase cattle sales, which had the effect of bodily shifting the supply curve, as documented in Chapter 2 pp. 54–8, 62–4. The African supplier of maize never found himself deprived of a market for his maize[68] or forced to sell a fixed quota of it at a statutory price; the African supplier of cattle did. It is thus certain that what the series of cattle prices and cattle deliveries in both countries traces out before 1946, when compulsory destocking ended, is not a supply curve, but the intersection of a demand curve and a supply curve that was subject to frequent policy-induced jumps.

Also cattle, unlike maize, served the function of productive asset in addition to being a source of cash. The implications of this for supply have been stated in two alternative forms. The strong form, having been asserted at least as early as 1904, must rank as one of the earliest hypotheses of development economics; this contends that the cattle owner will seek to maximise cattle holdings,[69] and will therefore sell cattle to traders only if forced to do so by destitution or government command. The weaker form merely asserts that since cattle were a durable asset and, moreover, one which frequently yielded a higher return than readily available financial assets,[70] they were often held back from the market in periods even of rising prices in the hope that prices might rise further.[71] Given their role as reserve asset, this would be particularly likely to happen if the cattle herd had been depleted by drought or disease below its normal size.

How far do these considerations explain the observable pattern of African cattle sales? Table 3.8 sets out the available data for the inter-war period, and the Kenyan figures, for which we have the longer series, are graphed in Figure 3.3. The principal impression which emerges from Figure 3.3 is that policy variables on the *demand* side of the market, rather than forces

owing to the practice of the Meat Marketing Board buyer of driving around the reserve in a Livestock Control lorry (see p. 62).
[e] February – June and October – December only.
[f] In this year Liebig's Extract of Meat Co. opened their meat processing plant which relied exclusively on African cattle deliveries.
Sources: KNA: PC/SP 1/2/2 and 3 and ARC (MAA) 2/3/41 II, Annual Reports, Masai Province (subsequently Narok and Kajiado Districts) for the year 1924–52; some supplementary information from Great Britain 1934b (B1), vol. III, pp. 3105–79.

Table 3.8b. *Southern Rhodesia: sales of cattle and certain explanatory variables, 1918–40*

Year	No. of cattle sold to Europeans			Price at		Possible explanatory variables	Government policy variables	
	National total	Selected districts		Ndanga	Bulalima-Mangwe	African livestock numbers (national total)	Numbers of cattle under quarantine[d]	Other measures
		Chibi	Ndanga					
1918	—	2 600	5 000		120/- to 240			
1919	—	1 500	3 500		180/- (oxen)			
1920	—	1 600*	1 600	80/- to 100/-				
1921	—	1 400	200	50/-	60/- (oxen)			
1922	—	—	200		35/- (all cattle)	845 498		
1923	—	—	100		20/- (all cattle)	927 343	—	
1924	—	—	50			1 005 277	—	
1925	—	1 123			60/-	1 095 841	—	
1926	27 144	2 355	—			1 192 466	—	
1927	22 860		630			1 370 567	—	
1928	32 000	3 000	—			1 420 913	—	
1929	59 214	5 000	—	100/- (all cattle)		1 495 803	—	
1930	79 248	—	—			1 558 075	—	
1931	41 156	—	—			1 628 299	—	
1932	31 642	None[a]	3 900	15/- to 25/- (all cattle)		1 755 610	156 300	
1933	81 081		3 512	20/- (all cattle)	1 748 621	1 748 621	251 701	
1934	71 985	10 074	2 926	40/- to 55/- (large oxen)		1 708 461	487 493	b
1935	62 601		1 226[a]	15/- to 30/- (cows)		1 708 465	411 321	
1936	94 580	10 953	2 815	15/- to 30/- (cows)		1 653 462	329 851	
1937	105 357	7 988	2 464	45/- } (600 lb cows)	57/- } (600 lb oxen)	1 547 623	341 777	
1938	156 851	12 077	4 302	45/- }	57/- }	1 582 062	421 251	
1939	87 518	7 997	2 997			1 555 806	184 055	c
1940	93 893	8 135	3 043			1 570 310	146 953	

– no data

Notes:

[a] Sales affected by foot-and-mouth disease in this year.

[b] In this year Liebig's Extract of Meat Co. opened their meat processing plant at West Nicholson, which relied largely on deliveries of African cattle.

[c] This was the year in which forced culling of cattle began in some districts; see p. 54 above.

[d] Districts under quarantine were:

1931	Chilimanzi
1932	Bulalima-Mangwe
1933	Bulalima-Mangwe; Msiza
1934	Ndanga; Chibi; Gwanda; Nyamandhlovu; Belingwe
1935	Ndanga; Chibi; Bulalima-Mangwe; Gutu; Bikita
1936	Ndanga; Chibi; Matobo; Melsetter; Gutu; Bikita
1937	Ndanga; Chibi; Matobo; Melsetter; Victoria; Bikita
1938	Ndanga; Chibi; Matobo; Melsetter; Victoria; Bikita; Charter
1939	Charter; Insiza
1940	Charter; Hartley

Sources: Prices – NAR: N 9/1/25 and S 235/501 – 17, Native Commissioners' Reports, supplemented for 1937/8 by evidence of A. Levy to Commission on Sales of Native Cattle, ZAX 1/1/1, p. 108; also file S 138/38 for data marked*. Cattle numbers – NAR: ZBJ 1/2/2, memorandum by C.A. Murray to Native Production and Trade Commission 1944. State of quarantine – Southern Rhodesia, Veterinary Department, *Annual Report*

105

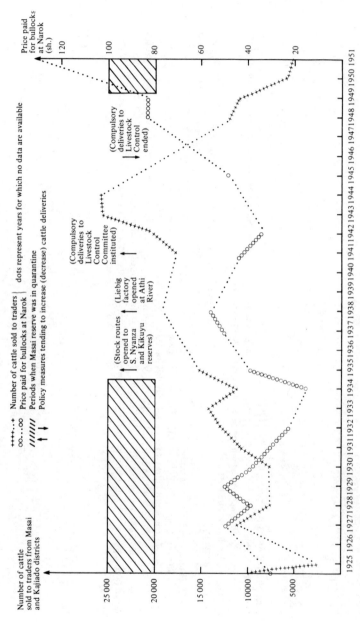

Fig. 3.3 Masai districts of Kenya: sales of cattle, government policy measures and price of bullocks at Narok, 1924–51.
Source: Table 3.8a.

106

on the supply side, exert a major influence on cattle sales. Thus cattle sales fluctuate wildly about a static trend from 1924 to 1934, during which the pastoral districts were under perpetual veterinary quarantine; increase in 1935 when the stock routes through Kijabe and into South Kavirondo were opened; increase again in 1938 when the Liebig factory opened; reach peak levels during the period of compulsory deliveries in war time;[72] and drop back dramatically when the compulsory Livestock Control was dissolved, and still further when quarantine was once again imposed in 1949. Price appears to play little part; but then it seldom had much scope within which to operate, as the Masai's attempts to respond to temporary periods of high prices by sending more cattle out of the reserve quickly hit a policy-imposed barrier. The following tale is representative:

> Auctions were organised at Kajiado in June 1928 ... The average price realised was Sh. 74/- a head, mainly owing to competition from Tanganyika buyers. The Nairobi buyers considered the price too high and thereafter boycotted the sale ... The auction therefore had to be discontinued ... It is clear that if full advantage is to be taken of the surplus stock in the Masai Province the quarantine regulations which have bolted and barred all outlets except Ngong must be released ...[73]

It is possible that the 'previous peak price' hypothesis explains the low deliveries in the latter part of 1928 and 1930. In Southern Rhodesia the available time-series of data in the pre-statutory board period is much shorter, but it is notable that the sharpest increases in numbers of cattle marketed, in 1933 and 1938, coincided with government policy actions: the opening of the Liebig factory and the beginning of officially sponsored pressure to destock, respectively. Quarantine regulations, although used as a tool of policy for the first time in the 1930s, have less effect on the total of cattle marketed than in Kenya, since, as is apparent from Table 3.8b, they covered at most only over a quarter of the colony's total African cattle herd.

We may now turn to the post-Second World War period, during which in both countries quarantine regulations exerted an insignificant effect on marketed supply and marketing was in the hands of a statutory board. These are set out in Table 3.9.

The influence of government compulsion is once again apparent in the drastic fall-off of deliveries after the removal of compulsory destocking regulations in 1946/7; indeed, it took until 1960 in Southern Rhodesia to build up to the level of cattle deliveries achieved in wartime, and in Kenya the wartime level of deliveries to the statutory authority was nowhere near being achieved even by 1963. More puzzling is the fact that when, in 1951–3 in Kenya and in 1956 in Southern Rhodesia, the marketing board's statutory buying price was sharply raised, marketed supplies did not respond. This may be because prices in local African markets retained a sufficient premium above statutory board buying prices to remain a more desirable outlet to

Table 3.9. *Kenya and Southern Rhodesia: deliveries of African-owned cattle to statutory board, 1941–63*

Sales to Kenya Meat Commission				Sales to Southern Rhodesia Cold Storage Commission				
	Price per head (3rd grade) (shillings/cents)				Price per 100 lb liveweight, net of levy and marketing charges (compound grade; (shillings/pence)			
No. of head sold	Buying price	Buying price relative to buying price of maize (index 1957 = 100)	Policy measures	No. of head sold	Absolute buying price	Buying price relative to buying price of maize (index 1957 = 100)	Policy measures
1941	78 600	(32.0 to 56.0)						
1942	97 000	(28.0 to 32.0)		Compulsory destocking sales (1941–6)				Compulsory destocking sales (1943–7)
1943	101 014							
1944	133 553							
1945					141 445			
1946					161 671			
1947					202 815			
1948					85 365			
1949					103 981	14/8		
1950					75 901	19/0		
1951	13 118	140.0			112 253	19/0		
1952	14 707	183.0	102		110 063	21/11	48	
1953	12 606	218.0	94		95 800	24/6	56	
1954	15 103	211.0	89		120 455	24/6	60	
1955	18 279	215.0	99		106 640	24/6	59	
1956	17 211	226.0	107		109 670	24/6 to 34/9	72	Auctions instituted
1957	17 250	237.0	100		116 186	36/1 to 42/8	100	
1958	16 880	248.0	116		139 551	27/0 to 39/8	91	
1959	25 531	225.0	130		139 644	34/1 to 47/4	99	
1960	36 903	220.0	121		213 469	29/3 to 39/8	108	
1961	42 457	213.20	112					
1962	48 676	238.0	96					
1963	53 628	238.85	106					

Sources: Deliveries of cattle – Cold Storage Commission of Southern Rhodesia and Kenya Meat Commission, *Annual Reports*.
Cattle prices. Southern Rhodesia – *Annual Reports of the Chief Native Commissioner*; Kenya – Kenya Meat Commission *Annual Reports*.
Maize prices – Tables 3.6a and b above.

sellers; documentary evidence from Machakos District, Kenya,[74] suggests that in that district this was certainly so.

Contrariwise, in the years after 1957 deliveries increased very sharply in both countries, in spite of the absence of any obvious price stimulus. One possible explanation of this runs in terms of the role that cattle play as a buttress to crops; in the years 1956/7 to 1959/60, African maize deliveries (Table 3.6) were relatively low and maize prices *as a proportion of cattle prices* (Table 3.9 above) were also depressed. It may have been this fact which convinced Africans who owned both arable land and cattle that this was an opportune time to sell more cattle to the statutory boards even though *absolute* cattle prices were not rising. But in the absence of documentary information or other crucial explanatory variables, and in particular the price of cattle in local reserve markets, this must remain mere conjecture.

On the evidence of Sections 3.3 and 3.4, therefore, it appears that African food producers' supply responses can be interpreted by means of a rational model of economic behaviour if and only if policy-induced phenomena such as the black market and (in the case of cattle) statutory compulsions and restrictions, are taken into account. The Boserup model, in the earlier part of the chapter, only gave a satisfactory picture of African farmers' *technical* adaptations if constraints imposed by policy were added into the model; the same, here, seems to be true of their supply response. Colonial officials, as we have seen, were frequently able to paint a mystifying picture of Africans' economic behaviour as being 'irrational' or 'lazy' and to explain the underdevelopment of African agriculture in these terms.[75] The fault in their reasoning lies, as we can now see, not so much in the data which they used as in the model which they projected onto those data. Many of the data which we have on African cattle sales and cattle prices, for example, do indeed trace out a negative pattern; but to go from this pattern to the inference that Africans sold few cattle because prices were high is to make the mistake of picturing the African agriculturist as a free agent in the market.

In fact the behaviour of the African agriculturist in settler states was, as we have seen, constrained by the policy authorities' intervention at every step. 'Rationality' for him therefore involved, not the free choices of producers in textbooks, but the question of how he might do best for himself in a policy environment that could not be taken as given, but might well hit back at him if he appeared to do too well. If 'rational economic man' is defined not as a trader in an impersonal market but as a player in a game with a hostile colonial government, he can readily be seen, on the evidence so far presented, to have been alive and well in colonial Kenya and Southern Rhodesia. Nor, contrary to the contention of many 'under-development' writers, was the game one which he always lost.

APPENDIX 2: A NOTE ON THE DATA FOR CHAPTER 3

The data used to compile the tables of Chapter 3 are of variable reliability; variable also, there-fore, is the strength of the inferences that can be made from the figures set out there to hard con-clusions about trends in the African agricultural economy. In this appendix we offer more

The settler economies

information about the methods by which the sources cited in the tables obtained their figures, so that the reader can judge as accurately as possible how much confidence is to be put in a particular row or column of data.

Output and sales figures

In general it is possible to divide the data in Chapter 3 into three categories of reliability.

Category 1
Data collected by a marketing board or customs authority. In this case we can be fairly certain that the figures are reliable, as the body supplying them kept properly audited books of all transactions passing through its hands. Into this category fit the statistics in Table 3.1, columns 3, 8 and 11; also Tables 3.2, 3.6, 3.7 and 3.9.

Category 2
Data collected by administrative officers from traders. These are less reliable than Category 1 data to the extent that many traders in remote districts did not keep properly audited accounts.[76] As with the data of Category 1, it is important to be aware that they cover only sales through registered trading stores, and exclude both black market sales (after 1931 in Southern Rhodesia, and 1942 in Kenya, when statutory boards for the handling of maize and other grains were set up) and legal person-to-person transactions. But in principle there are no errors arising from guesswork or sampling. In this category fall the 'sales outside the district' recorded by Kenya District Commissioners, which are used in Tables 3.4, part of 3.5 and 3.8.

Category 3
Data collected by an administrative officer from traders, and then 'grossed up' on the basis of field surveys to give an estimate of total output, as in Table 3.1, columns 2 and 5. This type of data is the least reliable of the three categories, as it contains an element of sampling error; the most assiduous Native Commissioners would cover about 10 per cent of the plots, the laziest perhaps 4 or 5 per cent. Wide though the margin of error may therefore be on either side of the point estimate of absolute output supplied by the investigator, our contention is that these data nonetheless give a useful picture of the inter-district difference and even more of the change over time in yields, as in Southern Rhodesia the method of investigation was standardised across all Native Commissioners. This is the purpose for which they are used in Table 3.1 and equations 3.1 and 3.2.

Acreage figures

These are supplied for Southern Rhodesia only; there are no Kenyan estimates except those made for the Kenya Land Commission in 1934. The tendency was, as with crop estimates, for the Native Commissioner to estimate the acreage/population ratio for a sample of villages in his reserve and then to apply this ratio to the estimated population figures (q.v. below). Thus in the Victoria area in 1921 'the usual figure taken [was] that every adult is cultivating three acres',[77] whereas other estimates varied from 2.5 to 6 acres.

Cattle numbers (Table 3.1, columns 3 and 10)

In Southern Rhodesia these data are of quite high reliability, as each beast had to be compulsorily dipped, and the fees which African cattle owners paid for this service (as the administration saw it) were an important auxiliary source of public finance in addition to hut tax. The figures for column 3 of Table 3.1 are thus in every case based on a full count of all legally owned African cattle in Southern Rhodesia.

110

The same claims, alas, cannot be made for the figures in Kenya where dipping was not compulsory. Periodic statements of cattle numbers were made by the Kenya Veterinary Department, which are recorded in Table 3.1, but these appear to have been based purely on informed guesses by District Officers and are therefore of doubtful value for purposes of analysis. Until the beginning of aerial surveys in the post-colonial period there are no reliable statistics of Kenyan livestock numbers.

Population data (Table 3.1, columns 1 and 7; Table 3.3; part of Table 3.5)

In both Southern Rhodesia and Kenya current estimates of the total African population were built up by multiplying the number of adult male African taxpayers by a blow-up factor which represented the estimated average ratio of total population to adult males. The level of this blow-up factor was in Kenya always, and in Southern Rhodesia during the period up to 1913, left to the discretion of the individual District (or Native) Commissioner to estimate on the basis of a sample of total population/adult males ratios in such villages as his staff could find time to visit. In 1913 the Chief Native Commissioner of Southern Rhodesia issued an instruction to the effect that 'in the absence of a census, the indigenous population should be calculated on a basis of three and a half times the total number of indigenous taxpayers',[78] but many Native Commissioners continued to use their own judgment, which pointed to a general upward revision of the blow-up factor between the early years of this century and the 1930s. The same occurred in Kenya, where central coordination of estimation procedures had never been attempted, but the assumption used by the 1934 Land Commission was that male polltax payers were 49 per cent of the total adults, females representing the other 51 per cent, and that 37 per cent of the population were children. This gives a blow-up factor of 3.24 approximately.[79] For Southern Rhodesia the frequency distribution of blow-up factors is set out in Table 3.10.

Table 3.10. *Southern Rhodesia: frequency distribution of population/taxpayer ratios, 1921, 1926, 1931*

Ratio	1921	1926	1931
3.1	1		
3.2	2		
3.3	2		
3.4	2	2	
3.5	8	12	4
3.6	2	1	6
3.7	3	2	4
3.8	3	4	2
3.9	2	1	1
4.0	1	2	3
4.1	2	3	2
4.2	1	2	1
4.3	1		3
4.4			1
4.5		1	
4.6 or more	1	1	1

Source: Johnson 1969 (D2), Table IV, p. 10.

Table 3.11. *Kenya and Southern Rhodesia: estimates of population by various methods*

Southern Rhodesia Total indigenous population			Kenya Total African population		
	Chief Native Commissioner's estimate (thousands)	Census estimate (thousands)		Estimates published in non-native census[a] (thousands)	Census estimates (thousands)
1901	489.6		4000	(1902)	
1911	692.9		3000		
			2650	(Blue Book)	
1921	778.0		2480		
			2330		
1926	850.1		2550	(1925)	
1931	986.8		2970		
1936	1088.7				
1939			3410		(4790)[b]
1941	1257.8				
1946	1546.8		4060		
1948					5251
1951	1838.3				
1956	2219.9				
1961	2557.3				
1962		3090			8366

Notes:
[a] Estimate for 1926 was made by the Chief Native Commissioner.
[b] Back projection from 1948 census result by census team, using UN Model Life Tables.

It should be noted that although sampling errors in relation to the blow-up factors are the principal source of error in the estimates the base itself is not exempt from suspicion. Many Native and District Commissioners claimed 100 per cent accuracy, or close to this, for their hut counts which formed the basis of tax registers,[80] but for several districts the tax registers sometimes show spurts which cannot easily be accounted for by migration or natural increase.[81]

In Kenya in 1948 and 1962, and in Southern Rhodesia in the later year, a full census of the African population was held for the first time. All these censuses reported a figure for total African population substantially in excess of that put forward by Native and District Commissioners. This carried the additional implication that Native and District Commissioners' estimates of African population in earlier years were also under-estimated – i.e. that the blow-up factors had been set too low. Table 3.11 demonstrates the point.

These figures suggest that in the year of the first African census (1962 and 1948 respectively) the established methods had been understating the African population by about 25 per cent.

One possible approach, therefore, to building a consistent series is simply to up the official pre-census figures of the African population by 25 per cent in each year: this is the approach adopted by Johnson (1969 (D2)) for Southern Rhodesia. Unfortunately, however, as Goldthorpe notes, it cannot be taken as certain that the same, or roughly the same, proportional error prevailed throughout. It would be rash to assume, for instance, that the same proportion of able-bodied men have avoided paying hut or polltax throughout British rule in Kenya, and this factor would clearly affect the completeness of the register and hence the estimates of population.[82] This being so it is probably preferable to project directly back from the reliable population estimates we do have and whatever assumptions may be sensible regarding birth and death rates, then to tack an arbitrary 'blow-up factor' of our own onto the official estimates.

This has in fact been attempted by Lury (1965 (D1)) for Kenya. Looking first at the death rate Lury adopts a United Nations suggestion 'that population projections could be made using a reduction in mortality equivalent to an annual gain of 0.5 years in the expectation of life at birth'.[83] He also suggests that birth rates fell by 4 per cent between 1921–31 and by 5 per cent between 1931–9. On these assumptions his back projection of the population of Kenya to 1921 (before this date, in view of uncertainties about the effects of the 1914–18 war and the succeeding influenza epidemic, he is understandably unwilling to go) is:[84]

1921   3 671 000 (official figure 2 483 000)
1931   4 119 000 (official figure 2 967 000)

If we apply these same assumptions to the African indigenous population of Southern Rhodesia we reach the following population estimates (Johnson's estimates, based on a 25 per cent blow-up of the CNC's estimates, are next to them for comparison):

	Our estimate	Johnson 1969
1921	1 277 000	972 500
1926	1 353 000	1 110 000
1931	1 434 000	1 275 000
1936	1 575 000	1 465 000
1941	1 731 000	1 685 000
1948	2 109 000	2 109 000
1954	2 427 000	2 427 000
1962	3 090 000	3 090 000

These estimates are very much in excess of the ones set out in cols. 1 and 7b of Table 3.1 above, but the original Native/District Commissioners' estimates are used there in order to have a consistent series for the entire colonial period. To the extent that the figures in Table 3.1 do overstate the true growth in population between 1900 and the Second World War, one of the main judgments drawn from the table, i.e. that there was no long-term decline in the prosperity of the African rural population over that period, is reinforced.

113

4

The labour market

Objectives

In Chapter 2 we examined the nature of the 'extra-market operations' by which settler-producers attempted to secure inputs into their production process and markets for their produce at prices favourable to them. But perhaps the most important 'extra-market operations' of all were those carried out in the market for an input so far not discussed, namely African labour. These gained much prominence in the literature following Arrighi's insistence (1973 (D2)) that in Southern Rhodesia 'unlimited supplies of labour',[1] so far from existing as a state of nature in the pre-colonial economy, were in fact created by such operations. Subsequent work on the colonial labour market (Clarke 1975 (C)), van Zwanenberg 1971 (C), Phimister 1974 (D2), van Onselen 1976 (D2)) has intensified the focus on these operations, using in the third of these cases a regional and in the fourth an industrial emphasis. However, these studies are deficient in at least two respects. Firstly, they offer very little statistical evidence for the period before 1945: only Arrighi, for example, puts forward any time series for wages during this period.[2] Secondly, none of them works with a formal economic model. The purpose of this chapter is to try and make good some of these deficiencies of fact and theory. In this section, we offer summary data on African money and real wages, using in part the information given by Native and District Commissioners, a source not used for this purpose by the writers cited.[3] In section 2, a very simple model of labour-market adjustments in primary economic activities – mining and agriculture – is built up in which the 'extra-market operations' considered by these writers are interpreted, by analogy with those considered in Chapter 2, as an impulse reaction to a crisis situation, namely labour shortage.

African wages and employment: data

Summary estimates of African employment and wages by sectors are set out in Table 4.1 and 4.2 respectively. In reading Table 4.2, which gives estimates of wage levels, it is particularly important to note the following points.

114

Table 4.1. *Kenya and Southern Rhodesia: sectoral distribution of African employment, summary (all data in thousands)*

	Southern Rhodesia		Other			Kenya			Other		
Year	Mining	European agriculture	Manufacturing and construction	Services (includes public sector)	Total	Mining	European agriculture	Services	Manufacturing and construction	Public sector	Total
1911	38.6	13.5	{23.7	}	75.8						
1921	37.6	62.5[a]	{14.0	}	114.1						
1923							70.9[b]	{	67.4	}	138.3
1931	35.2	72.1	{56.9	}	164.2		79.6[c]	{	61.8	}	141.4
1941	84.0	101.6	99.9		285.5	20.3	100.6	{	87.1	}	208.0
1951	63.7	212.4	104.4	149.7	530.2	5.5	203.1	58.0	52.0	89.3	407.9
1961	48.5	234.2	126.1	215.2	624.0	3.5	252.0	79.7	60.5	167.0	562.7

Notes:

[a] Almost certainly an over-estimate.
[b] Agricultural census estimate; includes resident labour.
[c] Blue Book estimate.

Source: Tables 4.8a and b.

115

Table 4.2. *Kenya and Southern Rhodesia: indices of African wage levels, summary*

Southern Rhodesia

	Indices of money wages (1914 = 100)			Indices of real wages (1914 = 100)		
	(1)	(2)	(3)	(4)	(5)	(6)
	European agriculture	Mining	European agriculture and mining: composite index	European agriculture	Mining	European agriculture and mining: composite index
1899	105	89	94	b	b	b
1903	100	–	127	b	b	b
1906	114	128	120	b	b	b
1911	–	–	–	80	–	–
1916	101	–	101	74	–	74
1921	116	96	106	45	37	41
1926	140	–	111	74	–	59
1930	125	–	100	92	–	82
1935	85	71	78	78	65	72
1939	105	84	94	99	77	95
1946	144	120	138	72	60	70
1951	282	210	264	98	73	91
1956	481	415	464	126	109	122
1961	500	523	505	140	125	121

Kenya

	Indices of money wages (1914 = 100)			Indices of real wages (1914 = 100)		
	(7)	(8)	(9)	(10)	(11)	(12)
	European agriculture	Public sector employment[a]	European agriculture and public sector; composite index	European agriculture	Public sector employment	European agriculture and public sector: composite index
1906	71	–	77	b	b	b
1911	80	–	86	b	b	b
1916	85	–	85	62	–	62
1921	91	–	91	35	–	35
1926	122	200	141	65	104	75
1930	112	135	118	76	91	80
1935	75	150	93	69	137	85
1939	86[a]	–	108[a]	78[a]	–	103[a]
1946	149	220	172	77	117	91
1951	176	520	290	61	179	100
1956	294	820	469	77	216	123
1964	454	1820	909	104	417	208

– not available

Notes:
[a] 1938 data.
[b] No estimate of real wages before 1914 is attempted on account of the absence of suitable price data.
Source: Tables 4.9a – c.

First, that food and housing, of a kind which varied very widely according to time and place,[4] were generally supplied free to African labourers on farms and mines, but not in urban employments until legislation was introduced to require some urban employers, who did not provide free housing, to pay their employees a housing allowance.[5]

Second, that the data provided for the years before the Second World War are based not on a complete enumeration of employees, but on an estimate of the modal level of wages by informed observers. These were made either centrally (by the Native Affairs Department in both countries, and in Southern Rhodesia by the Chamber of Mines) or locally by Native and District Commissioners. The latter estimates are particularly important, indeed almost our only source, for ascertaining the course of rural wages, on which very little has so far been written.[6] Full details of methods of computation are given in Table 4.9a below.

Third, that the estimate of 'real wages' provided is based up to 1939 not on a price index of all commodities consumed by Africans, but rather on a composite index of the *import prices* of certain goods which we know to have made up an important part of the cash expenditure of Africans (namely cotton piece goods,[7] cotton blankets, cigarettes and manufactured tobacco, soap, sugar, salt, matches, boots and shoes) and the *consumer price* of maize, their main food.

Fourth, that the type of average estimated by the figures of Table 4.2 changes between the pre-1945 and post-1945 period. The pre-1945 figures are estimates of *modal* African wages, that is, of the wages received by the largest group of African labour; the unskilled and untrained labourers. Conceptually these estimates are very close to the 'wage on entry into the labour force' which is the crucial variable in, for example, the Lewis model of economic development with unlimited supplies of labour,[8] although the basis on which they were computed by Native Commissioners, etc., is far from systematic. By contrast, the post-war figures, although better computed, are estimates of *mean* African wages (total wage bill divided by number of workers), which incorporate, of course, semi-skilled and skilled African workers. It follows, therefore that these figures are biased upwards from the true unskilled worker's wage, to a degree which is not systematically known, but which appears, from the accompanying figures, to be fairly small.

	Money wage index, Kenya agriculture and public services (1914 = 100)	Minimum wages of unskilled workers at Magadi Soda Company (shillings)	
1926	141	13.0	1924
1946	172	20.0	1946
1956	469	39.0	1957

Sources: Money wage index from Table 4.2, column 9; wages of unskilled workers at Magadi, from Hill (1961) (D1), pp. 98 and 165.

On the assumption that mean and modal wages of Africans did not differ significantly, we have proceeded, in Table 4.2, to chain the post- and pre-Second World War series together, but this source of weakness in the data must be borne in mind throughout.

For these reasons the real wage data in columns 4–6 and 10–12 of the table must be seen as imperfect series, imperfectly deflated.

Given these reservations and the gaps in the data of Table 4.2, the following seem to be the only conclusions that can safely be drawn about the trend of African real wages in the settler economies.

1. Before the First World War in Southern Rhodesia there is a surge in money and, probably, real wages in the mining industry, peaking in 1902. Arrighi has noted this,[9] but he fails to note that the boom in wages in the mining industry did *not* spill over into agriculture, in which wages remained almost static between 1900 and 1914.[10]

2. Real wages fell sharply in both world wars. The period 1914–21, in which in both countries real wages fell to less than half of their pre-war levels, is quite the most dramatic period of falling real wages in the colonial history of either territory;[11] it was to take black agricultural workers, at any rate, until 1939 to recover the ground lost at this time.

3. Real wages *rose* during the decade of the 1930s, in apparent contradiction of Arrighi's contention that this was the period when, for the first time, conditions of 'unlimited labour supplies' prevailed in the Southern Rhodesian economy.[12]

4. Real wages of African unskilled workers in primary industries were, at the end of the 1950s, barely above their 1914 levels. The real wage index for Southern Rhodesia miners and agricultural workers stood at 120 in 1959 (1914 = 100) and for Kenyan agricultural workers and public sector employees it stood at 136, but it seems likely that some of the increment was due to an increased penetration of African workers into the ranks of the skilled and semi-skilled after 1945.

This is about as far as we can go on the basis of the raw data themselves. To proceed further we need to set them against some sort of theoretical picture of how the labour market worked. In the most famous model (Lewis 1954 (D3)), the modern sector wage rate is determined by average product in subsistence agriculture, and the modern sector's demand for labour by the rate of expansion of the capitalist sector and by the wage rate; but in the simplest version of the model 'unlimited supplies of labour' ensure that this demand is always met without increases in the real wage rate of unskilled labour. Formally,

$$w_u = \alpha w_r \qquad (4.1)$$

conventional restriction

$$1 < \alpha < 1.5$$

$$l_d(u) = f(Y_u, w_u) \qquad (4.2)$$

conventional restriction

$$f'(Y_u) > 0, f'(w_u) < 0$$

$$l_s(u) = l_d(u) \tag{4.3}$$

where:

w_u = modern sector wage rate,
w_r = average product in agriculture, } defined in real terms
Y_u = value of product in modern sector,
$l_d(u)$ = modern sector demand for labour,
$l_s(u)$ = supply of labour in modern sector.

In the simplest version of the model, w_r and Y_u are autonomous, and w_r is a constant, giving three equations in three unknowns.

We consider these three components of the market for unskilled labour – wage determination, the demand for labour and market adjustment – *seriatim* in the three parts of the next section.

4.2 THE MARKET FOR UNSKILLED LABOUR IN MINES AND PLANTATIONS

Wage determination and the existence of a 'supply function'

The dependent variable of the first equation of the above model (4.1), average product in agriculture, is composed partly of sales of agricultural produce and partly of subsistence income. Such data as we have on this variable are set out in Table 4.3; in Kenya, these consist only of exports of African origin (i.e. a part of the marketed surplus) which must then be deflated by the price of a bag of maize to give an estimate of real agricultural product.

In Figure 4.1 this variable is graphed against the real wage series summarised in Table 4.2. From 1930 in Southern Rhodesia, and throughout the period in Kenya for years where data exists, the expected positive correlation between movements in the modern sector wage index and the estimated level of average real agricultural product does exist. To this extent it is possible to give some credence to the Lewis-type equation (4.1) in which supply-side factors above determine the level of modern sector wages,[13] though not of course to his assumption that the real wage remains constant. To this extent also it is possible to make a connection between the evidence of Table 4.2 and that of Table 3.1. Taken together, these suggest, first, that there was no secular decline in either African agricultural production or real wages over the colonial period taken as a whole, contrary to Arrighi's hypothesis that the flow of Southern Rhodesian African labour into the market was based on a 'progressive reduction in the productivity'[14] of the peasantry. Secondly, both series fluctuate about a static trend with peaks

119

Table 4.3. *Kenya and Southern Rhodesia: rural population and agricultural production, 1914–60*

	Southern Rhodesia				Kenya					
	(1)	(2)		(3)	(4)	(5)		(6)	(7)	(8)
	Estimated total African production of grain (thousands of 200 lb bags)	Estimated African population (thousands)		= (1)/(2ii) Grain production per head of African population (200 lb bags)	Estimate of exports of agricultural produce of African origin (£000)	Total African population (thousands)		= (4)/(5ii) Sales of African agricultural exports per head of African population (£)	Deflator for (6): export price of one 200 lb bag of maize (shillings)	African agricultural exports per head deflated by export price of bag of maize (index, 1925 = 100)
Year		(i) rural^a	(ii) total			(i) Contemporary estimate	(ii) Back projection from 1948 census			
1914	2132	716	718	2.97	189	2650	—	0.071^b	7.53	—
1915	2751	—	725	3.79	—	—	—	—	—	—
1916	1598	—	733	2.18	—	—	—	—	—	—
1917	2480	—	741	3.34	—	—	—	—	—	—
1918	2278	—	745	3.05	—	—	—	—	—	—
1919	2724	—	762	3.57	258	—	—	—	13.73	—
1920	3311	—	770	4.30	309	—	—	—	12.14	—
1921	3289	—	778	4.22	84	—	—	—	10.07	48
1922	1188	767	792	1.50	182	2330	3716	0.048	13.46	56
1923	3483	776	806	4.32	261	—	3761	0.069	10.23	111
1924	2740	786	820	3.34	430	—	3806	0.112	12.37	120
1925	2892	805	834	3.46	546	—	3851	0.141	12.37	100
1926	2707	825	850	3.18	476	2550	3896	0.122	10.78	109
1927	2836	863	877	3.23	460	—	3941	0.116	10.11	119
1928	2675	895	904	2.95	477	—	3986	0.119	12.26	111
1929	3050	913	931	3.27	543	—	4031	0.134	13.78	72
1930	3034	952	958	3.16	403	—	4076	0.098	9.14	59
1931	2659	974	986	2.69	222	—	4119	0.053	8.06	81
1932	3298	999	1016	3.24	273	2970	4202	0.064	8.16	102
1933	2123	1040	1026	2.06	355	—	4285	0.082	6.71	104
1934	2781	1073	1046	2.65	301	—	4368	0.069	8.50	95
1935	2610	1099	1066	2.44	357	—	4451	0.080	5.51	189
1936	2991	1078	1088	2.74	472	—	4534	0.103	5.74	182
1937	3270	1134	1148	2.92	652	—	4617	0.141	9.75	124

Year										
1938	2935	1172	1188	2.50	561	–	4700	0.119	7.86	138
1939	3160	1198	1218	2.68	513	3410	4790	0.107	7.87	138
1940	–	1185	1238	–	–	–	4840	–	–	–
1941	2798	1178	1257	2.22	1031	–	4890	0.210	9.38	226
1942	3098	1198	1317	2.35	999	–	4940	0.202	8.96	228
1943	3688	1242	1377	2.67	881	–	4990	0.176	12.22	146
1944	3878	1391	1437	2.69	1007	–	5040	0.199	12.59	160
1945	4171	1419	1487	2.80	1119	–	5090	0.219	15.19	146
1946	4133	1531	1546	2.67	1296	–	5140	0.252	15.98	159
1947	–	1524	1600	–	1725	–	5190	0.332	18.01	186
1948	4620	1645	1660	2.78	1720	–	5251	0.327	23.20	173
1949	3645	1653	1710	2.13	2113	*Agreed estimate*		0.397	26.28	153
1950	3772	1743	1768	2.13	2991	5000		0.553	41.68	134
1951	2719	1823	1838	1.48	3289	5700		0.576	58.59	100
1952	4394	1886	1910	2.30	3367	6000		0.561	62.40	91
1953	5732	2000	1982	2.89	3534	6300		0.560	50.82	162
1954	5938	–	2062	2.87	5381	6600		0.815	39.40	186
1955	5505	–	2142	2.57	4986	6883		0.724	38.55	190
1956	7640	–	2219	3.44	4613	7200		0.642	37.70	172
1957	6938	–	2289	3.03	5216	7500		0.697	36.81	204
1958	6050	–	2359	2.56	5781	7800		0.743	34.08	221
1959	6303	–	2409	2.60	7531	8100		0.932	35.91	263
1960	4651	–	2475	1.87	8265	8366		0.987	34.62	289

– not available

Notes:

[a] In 1933–6 estimated rural population actually exceeds estimated total population. The most likely reason is that some foreign African immigrant workers got themselves included in the count of rural population. In col. 3 we use the total population series, although it is conceptually less desirable for the purpose, in order to have a longer run of data.

[b] Note that this estimate is made from the contemporary estimate, not from a back projection; controversy about population trends before 1921 makes such a back projection meaningless.

Sources:

Cols. 1 and 2 from Southern Rhodesia, *Annual Reports of the Chief Native Commissioner.* (NB col. 2a is sum of Africans in reserves on alienated land and on unalienated land.

Col. 4 from Kenya Agriculture Department. Annual Reports with interpolations from Trade Reports (for a fuller note on this series see notes on col. 8 of Table 3.1 above).

Col. 5: contemporary estimates from Great Britain 1955b (B1), Appendix VII, p. 464; back projections to 1921 from Appendix 2 above. (The latter series is used for cols. 6 and 8 in order to have an internally consistent series.)

Col. 7: Kenya 1966 (B3).

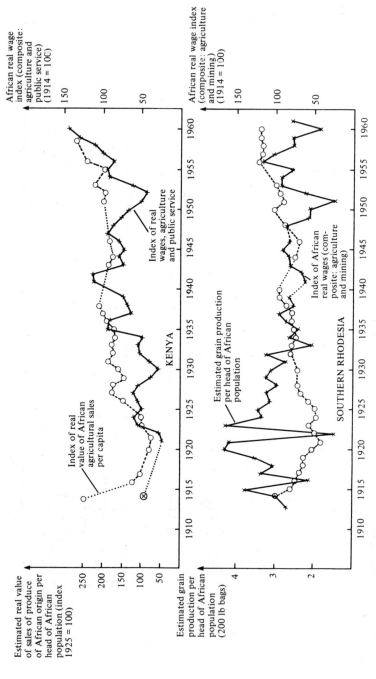

Fig. 4.1 Kenya and Southern Rhodesia 1914–60: estimate of African per capita income from wage employment and peasant agriculture. *Source*: Table 4.3, cols. 3 and 8; Table 4.9b, col. 4; Table 4.9c, col. 4.

122

in the years before 1914, in the late 1930s and in the middle 1950s. This final peak turned, in Kenya, into sustained growth. At the same time, conditions in the rural economy are far from providing a complete explanation of changes in the modern sector wage level, as Figure 4.1 also bears witness. The most glaring anomaly is the case of Southern Rhodesia between 1914 and 1930, in which there is initially no observable relationship between grain yields and real wages. To be sure, the data, in particular on grain yields, are far from reliable; but it is perhaps worth investigating whether any systematic factor can be brought forward to account for these periods when urban and rural real incomes were apparently forced apart. An obvious candidate is demand-side pressures, in particular the gap between the supply and demand for labour. That is, we now wish to consider the following modified version of hypothesis (4.1):

$$w_u = \alpha w_r + \beta(l_s(u) - l_d(u))$$ (4.1')

This requires us to modify assumption (4.3) of the Lewis model, that the market for unskilled labour always closes automatically. But this should not worry us too much, since as has been extensively recorded 'labour shortage', as perceived by employers, was a persistent feature of the market for unskilled labour. Hence we suspend (4.3) and consider in its place the supply function:

$$l_s(u) = \gamma\left(\frac{w_u}{w_r}\right)$$ (4.3')

We now test the model consisting of (4.1'), (4.2) and (4.3'), taking these relationships in reverse order.

If the participation rate (labour supply as a proportion of the labour force) is taken as the appropriate measure of $l_s(u)$, then the least-squares estimates of (4.3') are as follows:

Southern Rhodesia: $\frac{L_i}{N_i} = 41.4^{**} + 0.0018\left(\frac{w_u}{w_r}\right)$; $r^2 = 0.0003$ (4.3a)
(10.46) (0.037)

(twenty-one observations, i.e. 1921–38 and 1944–7)

Kenya: $\frac{L}{N_i} = 30.1 + 0.007\left(\frac{w_u}{w_r}\right)$; $r^2 = 0.0249$ (4.3b)
(13.96)(0.57)

(eighteen observations, i.e. 1922–39)

where: L_i = African male workers of indigenous origin[15] (Southern Rhodesia); *source*: Table 4.8a, column 1a.
L = African male workers (Kenya); *source*: Table 4.8b, column 1a.
N_i = Estimate of number of males between fifteen and forty on tax register (both countries); *source*: Table 4.8a and b, column 1b.

w_u = Real wage index (1914 = 100); *source*: Tables 4.9b and c, col. 4.

w_r = (Southern Rhodesia) estimate of total grain production per head of African rural population; *source*: Table 4.3, col. 3.

(Kenya) estimates of *exports* of African origin deflated by the export price of maize, per head of total African population; *source*: Table 4.3, col. 8.

** denotes significance at 1 per cent level. Numbers in parenthesis below coefficients are Student's *t*-statistics.

The link between participation rates and the rural–urban differential as revealed by these figures can only be described as tenuous. There is no support for the 'backward bending supply curve of labour' hypothesis so much beloved of colonial officials mean employers[16] and indeed one or two recent academic contributions.[17] The correlation between participation rates and the rural–urban differential is, indeed, positive, but it is weak and insignificant – especially during the years 1927–30 in Kenya and the 1930s in Southern Rhodesia – and, in particular, there is no support at all for Arrighi's contention (in the context of Southern Rhodesia) that 'the conditions affecting the supply of African labour altered *continuously* and in the direction of greater responsiveness to wage employment opportunities'.[18]

In the case of Southern Rhodesia there exists a possible *ad hoc* explanation of the discrepancy between the actual movement of the participation rate in the 1930s and its expected movement, as forecast by hypothesis (4.3′). This lies in the extraordinary growth during that period of what would now be called the African informal sector: self-employment, mostly within the reserves, in petty trade and manufacturing. In this sector, which is discussed in more detail in Appendix 5 below, self-employment is recorded as growing as follows during the early 1930s:

Year	Number of Africans engaged in self-employment in reserves	Year	Number of Africans engaged in self-employment in reserves
1930	864	1934	2081
1931	1586	1935	2991
1932	1884	1936	3649
1933	1992	1937	3709

flattening out thereafter.[19] It is possible that this rapid growth could have been partly responsible for the fact that after 1931, unlike previously, the participation rate ceases to move sympathetically with the real rural–urban income differential; but in the absence of more and better data, this conclusion must remain speculative.

124

The demand for labour

Turning, therefore, to equation (4.2), the principal feature to emerge from a casual look at the data on African employment and output is that there was a very tight link between these two variables during the period up to approximately 1955, but that this relationship collapsed in the middle 1950s, after which period large increases in output took place with scarcely any increase in employment, particularly in the non-agricultural sectors. Let us first consider the relationship between employment and output before 1955. There are two reasons in particular for the 'tightness of fit'. One was the undercapitalisation of many employers, which in turn was partly the result of the progressive relaxation of the colonial governments' settlement policies to admit 'small men'. This meant that all variations in the cost structure which were implemented in response to changes in output had to be mediated through changes in the workforce rather than through changes in capitalisation or technology.[20] The other was the high proportion of African workers who could be hired or fired without notice. This applied, obviously, to casual and to immigrant contract labour; less obviously it applied also to resident labour on farms, for under the terms of the (Kenya) Resident Native Labourers Ordinance of 1919 and the Rhodesian Private Locations Ordinance of 1908[21] it was possible for the farmer or, if he owned a private location, the industrialist or miner also to keep his resident labour idle for weeks and months at a time on his land, using them only on the days he needed them and paying them only when they had completed a thirty day ticket. (This led to frequent, and justified, complaints[22] that an artificial shortage of labour was being created by legislation originally intended to relieve it and that employers were keeping in addition to the labour force they really required what Tow has aptly called 'an inventory of spares'.)[23]

To make progress in estimating (4.2), we now wish to establish to what extent the employment figures recorded in Table 4.1 actually correspond to the demand for African labour, that is, to the amount of labour which employers *desired* to hire. The assumption we shall make is that the demand for labour was equal to actual employment in those years for which the Southern Rhodesian Chief Native Commissioner (or in Kenya, the Labour Section of the Department of Native Affairs) did not report a shortage, that is, in all years for which data are graphed on Figure 4.2 *except*:

Kenya	*Southern Rhodesia*
1925	1914–20
1926	1925–9
1935–9	1938–9
1946–54	1946–55

Deleting data for these years from the data graphed in Figure 4.2 we derive the following estimate of a 'demand for labour' function for European agriculture in Kenya and mining in Southern Rhodesia respectively:

(4.2a) *Kenya: European agriculture*

$$l_D = 76.4^{**} + 0.24^{**}\,Q; \quad r^2 = 0.8068, \quad D.W. = 1.7250$$
$$(11.33)\quad(7.64)$$

Number of observations = 16
(i.e. 1923–4, 1927–34, 1954–7, 1959–60)

where l_D = employment of African males in European agriculture in years of 'adequate labour supply' as defined above (thousands).

Q = estimate of real value of exports of non-African origin, i.e. value of non-African exports in £000 deflated by the export value of a bag of maize (1925 = 100).

(4.2b) *Southern Rhodesia: mining industry*

$$l_D = -1.64 + 0.82^{**}\,Q; \quad r^2 = 0.9118, \quad D.W. = 0.4559$$
$$(-0.61)\quad(15.41)$$

Number of observations = 23
(i.e. 1909–13, 1921–4, 1930–7, 1940–5)

where l_D = employment of African males in European agriculture in years of 'adequate labour supply', as above defined.

Q = index of mineral production (1938 = 100).[24]

The estimated relationships (4.2a) and (4.2b) provide a sufficiently close fit to the data to warrant our trying to derive estimates of the demand for

Table 4.4. *Kenya and Southern Rhodesia: supply and 'demand' for African labour, 1909–60*

	Kenya: European agriculture				Southern Rhodesian mines			
	(1)	(2)	(3) Excess demand			(4)	(5)	(6) Excess demand	
Year	Supply of African adult male labour (actual employment; thousands)	'Demand for labour' (estimated from equation 4.2)	Arithmetic sign of difference between cols. 2 and 1	CNC's (or Labour Dept's) estimate	Supply of labour (actual employment; thousands)	'Demand for labour' (estimated from equation 4.2)	Arithmetic sign of difference between cols. 5 and 4	CNC's estimate
1909			*		32	29	−	
1910			*		37	30	−	
1911			*		38	32	−	
1912			*		34	33	−	
1913					33	36	+	*
1914					36	45	+	*
1915					37	50	+	*
1916					40	55	+	*
1917					38	53	+	*
1918					32	42	+	*
1919					30	43	+	*

Table 4.4. (cont.)

	Kenya: European agriculture				Southern Rhodesian mines			
	(1)	(2)	(3) Excess demand		(4)	(5)	(6) Excess demand	
Year	Supply of African adult male labour (actual employment; thousands)	'Demand for labour' (estimated from equation 4.2)	Arithmetic sign of difference between cols. 2 and 1	CNC's (or Labour Dept's) estimate	Supply of labour (actual employment; thousands)	'Demand for labour' (estimated from equation 4.2)	Arithmetic sign of difference between cols. 5 and 4	CNC's estimate
1920					36	43	+	*
1921					37	44	+	
1922					35	50	+	
1923	70	93	+	*	36	53	+	
1924	87	85	−	*	41	54	+	
1925	78	100	+		39	54	+	*
1926	84	101	+		40	64	+	*
1927	102	111	+	*	40	67	+	*
1928	114	107	−		43	73	+	*
1929	110	98	−		46	74	+	*
1930	125	121	−		45	68	+	
1931	120	111	−		35	46	+	
1932	104	109	+		36	39	+	
1933	105	114	+		48	44	−	
1934	106	101	−		62	54	−	
1935	no data				76	59	−	
1936	100	156	+	*	84	65	−	
1937	no data				90	83	−	
1938	111	139	+	*	87	88	+	*
1939	no data				83	84	+	*
1940	no data				85	82	−	
1941	100	112	+		84	79	−	
1942	122	117	+		81	80	−	
1943	120	102	−		78	73	−	
1944	118	107	−		75	69	−	
1945	118	108	−		71	64	−	
1946	108	113	+	*	70	61	−	
1947	122	124	+	*	69	59	−	*
1948	no data		no data	*	58	64	+	*
1949	139	115	−	*	56	71	+	*
1950	159	114	−	*	59	72	+	*
1951	154	116	−	*	63	73	+	*
1952	141	118	−	*	61	73	+	*
1953	141	111	−		59	80	+	*
1954	141	119	−		62	80	+	*
1955	157	138	−		59	91	+	*
1956	134	151	+		60			
1957	148	143	−		60			
1958	no data							
1959	157	156						
1960	171	165						

Sources:
Cols. 1 and 4 – Table 4.8.
Cols. 2 and 5 – Estimated from equations 4.2a and b by substitution of appropriate value of mining production index (in the case of col. 5) and European agricultural production index (col. 2).
Cols. 3 and 6 – Arithmetic difference between previous two columns. Years marked* are years of excess demand for African labour according to the Chief Native Commissioner (or, in Kenya after 1945, Labour Department).

labour in the industries under consideration by simple substitution. These are set out in Table 4.4, side by side with the figures for actual employment, so that by simple subtraction an estimate of 'shortage' can be derived.

These estimates of labour shortage do not tally exactly with the estimates of Native Commissioners, as reported on Table 4.4: thus in Kenya, 1924 was a 'labour shortage' year according to the Chief Native Commissioner but not according to the analysis of Table 4.4. The same is true of 1947 in Southern Rhodesia. Given the clumsiness of the methods employed in both cases, this is not surprising. But if the years which both sources agree were periods of labour shortage are graphed back onto Figure 4.2, certain slippages in the employment/output relationship become understandable: for example, 1935–7 in Kenya, and 1925–9 in Southern Rhodesia, when output for the sectors under examination rose sharply without any significant increase in employment. These estimates of labour shortage are now used to consider the response of the economy (and political system) to labour shortage, in relation to the simple hypothesis set out in equation (4.1).

The market for unskilled African labour: adjustment processes

Adjustments of the wage level

Can the wage equation (4.1′), which allows the unskilled African wage to respond to demand conditions in the modern sector, explain the movement of real wages any better than the simple Lewis-type equation (4.1) under which it is determined purely by the level of agricultural productivity? To answer this question, we look at the deviations of the actual level of real wages from the level predicted by equation 4.1, to see if in any way they were correlated with excess demand.

This is done in Table 4.5. As the data on which it is based are broken series and in any case deficient in quality, any conclusions derived from them can only be regarded as tentative. But for what they are worth their implication is that increases in real wages played a considerable role in resolving situations of excess demand for labour in the primary industries of the settler economies throughout the colonial period.[25] The data are given here.[26]

Kenya		Southern Rhodesia	
Number of years of excess demand for labour in European agriculture	Number of years in which real wage rate in African agriculture rose	Number of years of excess demand for labour in mining	Number of years in which real wage rate in mining rose
5	4	5	3
(1923, 1927, 1936, 1938, 1946)	(all except 1936)	(1927, 1938–9, 1951–2)	(1927, 1938, 1952)

Table 4.5. *Kenya and Southern Rhodesia: real wages in relation to the state of the labour market, 1909–58*

	Kenya		Southern Rhodesia	
	(1)	(2) Estimated level of African real wages in European agriculture (index: 1914 = 100)	(3)	(4) Estimated level of African real wages in mining (index: 1914 = 100)
Year	Excess demand for labour in agriculture		Excess demand for labour in mining	
1909				
1910				
1911			−	
1912			−	
1913			+	
1914		100	+	100
1915			+	
1916		62	+	
1917		51	+	
1918			+	
1919			+	
1920		40	+	
1921		35	?	41
1922			?	37
1923	+	50	?	43
1924	?	50	?	
1925	?		?	
1926	?	65	+	44
1927	+	75	+	52
1928	−	74	+	
1929	−	68	+	
1930	−	76	?	
1931	−	81	?	
1932	?	68	?	72
1933	?	76	−	68
1934	−	81	−	64
1935	no data	68	−	65
1936	+	66	−	69
1937	no data	64	−	69
1938	+	69	+	77
1939	no data	77	+	77
1940	no data	80	−	77
1941	?	78	−	
1942	?		−	
1943	−		−	
1944	−		−	
1945	−		?	
1946	+	67	?	60
1947	+	77	?	72

Table 4.5. (*cont.*)

	Kenya		Southern Rhodesia	
	(1)	(2) Estimated level of African real wages in European agriculture (index: 1914 = 100)	(3)	(4) Estimated level of African real wages in mining (index: 1914 = 100)
Year	Excess demand for labour in agriculture		Excess demand for labour in mining	
1948	no data		+	
1949	?		+	
1950	?		+	79
1951	?	61	+	73
1952	?	59	+	80
1953	?	66	+	83
1954	—		+	
1955	—	70	+	
1956	?	77	no data	109
1957	—			116
1958	—			

+ Year of excess demand for African labour on both indicators considered in Table 4.4
− Year no excess demand for African labour on both indicators considered in Table 4.4
? Labour supply position ambiguous. i.e. indicators in Table 4.4 give contradictory indications
Sources :
Cols. 1 and 3 – Table 4.4 above.
Cols. 2 and 4 – Table 4.9 below.

Clearly the labour markets of the settler economies did not approximate to the South African model in which the supply of labour was augmented, in times of labour shortage, not by raising wages but purely by enlarging the recruiting area,[27] contrary to the contention of Arrighi and others.[28] This is not, however, to suggest that wage increases were the only or even the principal means of adjustment in the settler economies. Political mechanisms of course had their place also, as was inevitable in an environment where small-scale farmers not only could not afford to increase wages in time of labour shortage but risked social ostracism within the local Farmers' Association if they did so, or even the threat of legal action for enticement.[29] What were these political mechanisms, and how well can they be correlated with the measures of excess supply and demand developed in Table 4.4? We proceed to discuss them *seriatim*; a summary picture is offered in Table 4.7.

Non-wage adjustments

We may begin by examining the political response to the first labour shortage crisis in European agriculture in both settler economies, that of 1908–11.

130

This does not figure in Table 4.5, as statistics of agricultural labour did not then exist, but all verbal sources testify to the fact that it was seen as threatening the viability of the infant settler agricultural economy in both territories.[30] The response in both Kenya and Southern Rhodesia was to set up a commission of enquiry – the Southern Rhodesian Native Affairs Commission of 1910 and the Kenya Native Labour Commission of 1912. Employer witnesses, in their evidence to these commissions, were almost as unanimous in their recommendations for government action to augment the labour supply as they had been divided on issues of land policy. As may be inferred from the stylised summary of the attitudes of different interest groups presented in Table 4.6, all European producer groups favoured an increase in tax rates and limitation of the size of the African reserves, with the organisations of small miners and farmers being marginally more hawkish than the others.

Of these measures, land policy has been fully discussed in Chapter 2 above, and we return briefly to it in the next sub-section. Variations in tax rates were, as Table 4.7 shows, not being used as instruments for the control of the labour supply in Southern Rhodesia after 1903, or in Kenya after 1920 when a tax increase was rescinded following the first organised riot of urban Africans that the colony had experienced. However, there is fairly firm evidence that increases in the *intensity* of tax collection by Native (District) Commissioners and their African staffs often followed from instructions to make a special effort to maximise the tax take in years of labour shortage.[31] Also, even though there was no increase in *personal* tax rates on Africans after the 1920s, the introduction of state-buttressed monopoly marketing, as discussed in Chapter 2 above, had the effect of introducing a tax on African marketed agricultural output at a time (late 1930s and early 1940s) when labour shortage was beginning to emerge again after the inter-war depression. Sometimes, as with the Rhodesian cattle levy, this tax was overt, sometimes, as with maize control, concealed in the differential between the African's farm-gate price and the price paid to European producers (and all consumers). But in either case taxes of this sort, which fell on agricultural but not on labour income, were of course a more effective instrument for channelling rural Africans into the labour market than the poll tax, which did not discriminate between sources of income.

Legislation

There are three types of legislation that are relevant to the quantity and price of labour supplied to the modern sector: compulsory labour legislation, resident labour (or 'squatter') legislation and registration certificate (or 'pass law') legislation.

So much is made of forced labour as a coercive measure distinctive to settler economies[32] that it is important to point out here that its use on the one hand in Kenya and Rhodesia, and on the other in the 'indirect rule'

Table 4.6. *Southern Rhodesia, Native Affairs Commission 1910 and Kenya, Native Labour Commission 1912: summary of opinions expressed by witnesses on labour supply*

	Kenya			Southern Rhodesia		
	Reserves	Tax	Other policy recommendations	Reserves	Tax	Other policy recommendations
General Manager, Uganda Railway	No comment	Increase	No comment			
Commissioner of Public Works	No comment	No comment	Planters' and Farmers' Associations should form a recruiting society and fix wages collectively			
Agricultural interests *Large concessionaires* Lord Delamere	Curtail	Do not increase, except perhaps as a once-for-all basis	'Do not continue policy that every native should be a landholder' Introduce identification law Provide locations on outskirts of towns			
Mining interests Salisbury Chamber of Mines (mostly large mines)				Quite adequate in size	Increase	No comment
Smallworkers' and Tributors' Association				Limit in number	Increase or decrease poll-tax according to labour situation	Severe penalties for leaving reserves without permission
Agricultural interests Landowners' and Farmers' Association (mostly concessionaires)				Need immediate definition, with provision for those at present on farms	Increase but reduce for employees	No comment
Mashonaland Farmers' Association (mostly small farmers)				Confine Africans to reserves	Double	Government to require all able-bodied men to work 3 months per

132

Small farmers			Salisbury Chamber of Commerce	
Mr Fletcher (coffee planter, Kiambu)	Too large	Increase, but remit for employees	Introduce identification law	Increase	Minimum 3 months notice before leaving
Mr Hewitt (coffee planter)		Increase, but remit for employees	Control by pass laws Do not encourage African agriculture		

Sources: Kenya 1913 (B3), Minutes of oral evidence, witnesses 3, 16, 18, 36, 91. Southern Rhodesia – Lee 1974 (C), p. 116; also NAR: SA 5/1/4. Minutes of Salisbury Chamber of Commerce meeting, 2 July 1910.

133

peasant export economies of Uganda and British West Africa, were remark-
ably similar,[33] being largely confined to government public works employment during the first forty years of this century, plus conscription for
essential services during wartime. In Southern Rhodesia there was in fact less
legally compulsory labour than the colonial norm between 1900 and 1940,
the practice being formally abandoned in 1900 following Colonial Office
pressure.[34] Commonly, however, Administrators (and subsequently Prime
Ministers) made *ad hoc* requests to Chief Native Commissioners to secure
workers for mines and farms which badly needed help; and the state-backed
recruitment organisations took a great deal of the task of securing labour
for less popular employers off the shoulders of the government. In Kenya,
by contrast, there was no such organisation, and in consequence the government needed to rely on large amounts of compulsory labour during the
expansion of infrastructure of the 1920s. This need was greatest during
1921–3, in which period one-eighth of the entire labour force was compulsorily recruited,[35] but dwindled to nothing by 1938 (column 11 of Table
4.7) although conscription was reintroduced during the Second World
War.

Resident labour legislation, on the other hand, was distinctive of the
settler economies. It followed from the fact that in these colonies the government early on alienated for the sole use of Europeans more land than
Europeans could beneficially occupy. For this policy left many Africans
short of land – at any rate in the areas which they had ancestrally occupied –
and since many European employers experienced chronic labour shortage
at a subsistence wage, the logical next step was to make these two factors
of production the subject of a statutory exchange, requiring the African
to render a quota of labour if he wished to continue to occupy alienated
land. The instrument by which this exchange was mediated was, in Rhodesia,
the Private Locations Ordinance of 1908, restricting the number of Africans
who could reside on European land.[36] In the same year a rental of £1 per acre
of Crown (unalienated) land was imposed, the net effect of the two measures
being to drive many Africans living outside the reserves either back into the
reserve or alternatively into employment on European farms. A dramatic
improvement in the labour supply situation was reported: 'the majority
of farmers now have their full complement', reported the NC Chilimanzi
in 1913, 'thanks mainly to the Private Locations Ordinance'.[37] But the
African squatter on European land was not, at first, *required* to work for
any period. This contrasted with the practice in Kenya, where by the Resident
Natives Ordinance of 1919, imposed at a time of acute labour shortage
after the First World War, *all* Africans resident on European land were
required to render three months' labour-service to their employer. Under
the Land Apportionment Act of 1930 Southern Rhodesia moved over to
the Kenyan model of making labour agreements compulsory for African
squatters; rental agreements under the Private Locations Ordinance were
gradually phased out as the number of labour agreements grew,[38] the

process not being finally completed until the mid 1950s. But the squatter system was a long-term measure, not an impulse response to labour shortage. The data of Table 2.4 suggest that, if the figures can be believed, there is no significant relationship between the degree of labour shortage as measured by Table 4.7 and the number of Africans squatting on European land.

Finally, in Kenya from 1916 until 1946, and in Southern Rhodesia from 1902 to 1958, Africans who ventured outside the reserves were required to bear a registration certificate or 'pass'. The principal function of the pass was to keep down the wages of Africans at times of labour shortage when they might otherwise have been pushed upward. Employers were required to enter on the certificate the period of employment an employee had spent with them and the wage he had been paid; this made it unnecessary for an employer ever to pay a worker more than his 'supply price' and often prevented employees from receiving the wage increases they might otherwise have received on changing employers. But no more than the other measures we have described was the registration certificate a means of short-period adjustment of labour deficits. To find these we have to move on to the other two measures on our list.

Recruited labour

Undoubtedly the most important means of closing the gap between labour supply and demand at subsistence wages was the practice of recruiting labour, usually from outside the country in the Rhodesian case, on fixed-period contracts. In both cases the recruiting organisation was private,[39] but whereas in Kenya the business was atomistic, carried on as van Zwanenberg puts it by 'a mixture of adventurers and alcoholics, often living dangerously on the fringes of their profession',[40] in Southern Rhodesia it began as a mining employers' monopsony in 1903, and continued as such until 1933 with the BSAC acquiring a controlling interest. Even after the rebirth of the recruiting business in 1946 there were only two companies in the field, one dealing exclusively with the needs of agriculture. Altogether the Rhodesian organisation was a high-priced, highly capitalised affair compared with its Kenyan counterpart.[41] But both organisations performed essentially the same function, namely that of tapping rural areas of potential labour supply (most of them outside the country in the case of Southern Rhodesia) which had a lower supply price than the national average;[42] and then distributing the labour, which once having enlisted was no longer free to choose its place of employment, amongst those employers who lacked it, which would of course include the unpopular employers whom 'free flow' labour had scorned. The operations of recruiters in the settler economies have been so well covered by van Zwanenberg (1971 (C), Chapter 9) for Kenya and van Onselen (1976 (D2)) and Clarke (1975 (C)) in Rhodesia that in what follows we confine ourselves to the relationship between numbers of Africans recruited and the state of the labour market as measured by Table 4.5.

Table 4.7. *Kenya and Southern Rhodesia: labour surplus and shortage in primary industries in relation to various non-wage methods of market adjustment, 1900–63*

	Southern Rhodesia						Kenya				
	Measures of non-wage adjustment						Measures of non-wage adjustment				
	(1)	(2)	(3)	(4)	(5)	(6)	(7)	(8)	(9)	(10)	(11)
	Excess demand for mine labour	Legislation[g]	Tax level[a]	Female labour[b]	Recruited labour[c]	Compulsory labour[d]	Excess demand for agricultural labour	Legislation[g]	Tax level[e]	Child and female labour in agriculture	Compulsory labour
1900		Registration of African workers began 1902	10/- per head				no data				
1901			10/- plus 10/- per wife								
1902											
1903			20/- per adult male						variable		
1904											
1905											
1906					4.9				4/- per head		
1907		Private Locations Ordinance 1908			14.1						
1908					15.8						
1909					16.8						
1910					20.4			Masters and Servants Ordinance 1910			
1911	–				9.3				4/- per head		
1912	–				14.6						
1913	+				13.4						
1914	+				9.5						
1915	+				11.1			Registration of Natives			
1916	+				6.5				8/-		

136

Year		Legislation					Legislation		
1919	+			10.1		⟶	Resident	8.7	10.5
1920	+			16.8			Native	11.4	25.5
1921	?		0.6	9.8			Labour	10.1	19.3
1922	?			4.4		+	Ordinance	16.5	15.2
1923	?			6.0		?	1918 16/-	20.1	13.3
1924	?			8.6		?		19.7	12.8
1925	?		1.6	9.0		?	12/-	19.7	12.9
1926	+		1.6	7.4		+			9.7
1927	+			8.3		−			9.1
1928	+			7.5		−		22.0	5.7
1929	+					−		22.5	7.4
1930	?	Land Apportionment Act 1930	1.0	5.8		−		22.0	4.5
1931	?			1.2		−		18.2	3.5
1932	?			0		?		18.2	3.8
1933	−					?			2.8
1934	−	Industrial Conciliation Act 1934	1.8			no data		19.7	1.2
1935	−					+			1.3
1936	−					no data			
1937	−					+	1937 Trade Union Ordinance — Variable^e		
1938	+					no data			
1939	+					no data			
1940	−					?			
1941	−		3.7		10	?			
1942	−				10	−			
1943	−				11.4	−			
1944	−		13.5		11.4	−		90.9 (entire economy)	18.8
1945	?					+		84.2	
1946	?					no data	1946: end of statutory requirement for Africans	90.6	
1947	?					+	to carry	87.9	
1948	+					no data	passes	76.5	
1949	+			0.3		?		71.0	
1950	+	Land Apportionment Amendment Act 1950^f	41.7	4.0		?		59.9	

137

Table 4.7. (*cont.*)

	Southern Rhodesia						Kenya				
	Measures of non-wage adjustment						Measures of non-wage adjustment				
	(1)	(2)	(3)	(4)	(5)	(6)	(7)	(8)	(9)	(10)	(11)
	Excess demand for mine labour	Legislation[g]	Tax level[a]	Female labour[b]	Recruited labour[c]	Compulsory labour[d]	Excess demand for agricultural labour	Legislation[g]	Tax level[e]	Child and female labour in agriculture	Compulsory labour
1951	+				10.3		?			78.0	
1952	+				13.6		?			82.5	
1953	+				14.5		?			93.4	
1954	+				19.8		—			101.5	
1955	+				24.1		?			109.1	
1956		no data	40/- per adult male		20.4		—			123.1	
1957					25.8		—			123.7	
1958		1958: end of			28.7						
1959		statutory			26.0						
1960		obligation			21.7						
1961		for Africans			14.4						
1962		to carry passes.			11.2						
1963		Industrial Conciliation Amendment Act: Africans allowed collective bargaining rights			7.9 8.6						

138

+ , − , ? See Table 4.5

Notes:

a Note that the tax rates quoted here are simply those which *all* adult Africans had to pay; grazing and dipping fees were in addition levied on those who used European land, and tax was payable on dogs after 1923. The 20/- increase per head levied in 1956 was specifically set aside for African education.

b There are no reliable statistics on child labour in Rhodesia; an attempt was made to register juvenile employees in 1926 by means of the Native Juvenile Employment Act, but this was described as 'more or less moribund' by the NC Mazoe in 1931 (NAR: S 235/509, District Annual Report for 1931) and in the *Annual Report of the Chief Native Commissioner* for 1933 as 'practically a dead letter, because of the neglect of employers to comply voluntarily with its provisions, and the practical difficulties of forcing them to do so'.

c These figures cover only Africans recruited on contract by the statutory bodies, the Rhodesian Native Labour Bureau and its post-Second World War successor, the Rhodesian Native Labour Supply Commission.

d This was exclusively used for food production. The Agricultural Department *Annual Report* mentions only its use in 1944 and 1945; the 1942 and 1943 figures are from Clarke 1975 (C), p. 155.

e Collection at the rate of 1 rupee per hut [Sh. 1.33] began at the Coast very late in 1901; the rate was raised to 2 rupees the next year. The rate was raised to 3 rupees in the Kisumu and Naivasha provinces in 1903; as fresh districts were brought under administration the district commissioner introduced taxation, usually only at the 1 rupee rate at first, increased to 2 rupees in the second year.' Clayton and Savage 1974 (D1), p. 28. The 3 rupee rate became general in 1906. The Sh. 4.0 poll tax introduced in 1910 was payable by those not liable to hut tax. In 1936 following the report of the Pim Commission the African hut and poll tax was graduated in what was intended to be a progressive fashion, with the Sh. 12.0 maximum rate payable only by what were seen as the most prosperous tribes, and less by others: e.g. the Masai paid Sh. 10.0, the Meru and Elgeyo Sh. 8.0, and the Turkana Sh. 3.0.

f The Land Apportionment Amendment Act of 1950 provided for the removal within five years of all Africans resident on European land but not working for Europeans.

g The list of legislative measures in this column is necessarily arbitrary as there is no firm criterion for what measures were relevant to the labour market. Note however that all legislation touching urban labour, e.g. minimum wage legislation, is excluded from the scope of this table.

Sources:

Cols. 1 and 7 – Table 4.5

Cols. 3 and 9 – Southern Rhodesia, *Annual Reports of the Chief Native Commissioner* and Kenya, Native Affairs Department, Labour Section (subsequently Labour Department), *Annual Reports*.

Cols. 4–6 and 10–11 – Table 4.8.

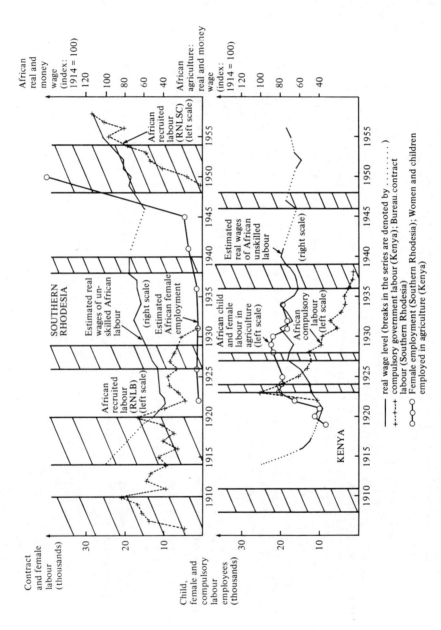

Fig. 4.2 Kenya and Southern Rhodesia 1905–60: periods of excess demand for African unskilled labour, with wage and non-wage responses. *Sources*: Table 4.7 (1905–11 in Kenya is added to these on the strength of contemporary ... ... which the regression method described above can be used): Table 4.9

African real and money wage (index: 1914 = 100)

120
100
80
60
40

African agriculture: real and money wage (index: 1914 = 100)

120
100
80
60
40

SOUTHERN RHODESIA

Estimated real wages of unskilled African labour

(right scale)

Estimated African female employment

African recruited labour (RNLB) (left scale)

African recruited labour (RNLSC) (left scale)

Estimated real wages of African unskilled labour

(right scale)

African child and female labour in agriculture (left scale)

African compulsory labour (left scale)

KENYA

Contract and female labour (thousands)

30
20
10

Child, female and compulsory labour employees (thousands)

30
20
10

1910 1915 1920 1925 1930 1935 1940 1945 1950 1955

1910 1915 1920 1925 1930 1935 1940 1945 1950 1955

——— real wage level (breaks in the series are denoted by ....)
+++++ compulsory government labour (Kenya); Bureau contract labour (Southern Rhodesia)
○—○—○ Female employment (Southern Rhodesia); Women and children employed in agriculture (Kenya)

140

The top part of Figure 4.2 is a graph of numbers of Africans recruited by the Rhodesian Native Labour Bureau and its post-war reincarnation, the Rhodesian Native Labour Supply Commission. The correspondence between the troughs in the recruited labour series and the periods of adequate demand (1910–14, 1920–5 and 1929–38) is good, with the recruited labour series dipping sharply in each of those periods and dropping to zero in the third; clearly, recruited labour was laid off whenever there was no shortage. This may seem strange, given the lower wage it was paid, but the capitation fee and the lower productivity of labour which tended to stay for shorter periods in the workplace[43] clearly offset the advantages of this cost-differential from the employers' point of view. Likewise, there are peaks in the recruited labour series towards the end of the periods of labour shortage: 1905–10, 1914–20 (not 1925–9) and 1945–55. During the first four years of the last three labour shortage periods there is, in fact, no movement in the trend number of recruited labourers, confirming the impression that for most employers the taking on of contract labour was an expedient only contemplated if other means of closing the gap between supply and demand proved unsatisfactory.

In Kenya we have no time series on recruited labour, which given the penumbral nature of the recruiting profession in that colony, described above, is not surprising. But we do know that the period of maximum activity of the labour recruiting profession in Kenya was in the middle twenties, that it then dwindled almost to nothing in the depression and revived again during the middle to the late thirties.[44] These data square with the pattern of labour surplus and shortage presented in Table 4.7 and Figure 4.2.

Female and juvenile employment

A form of cheap labour somewhat neglected by historical writings on the colonial economy is the labour provided by women and children, which could be obtained principally for certain tasks in agriculture, but was also employed in manufacturing and even mining[45] for a good deal less than the going rate even for an adult male obtained by a recruiter.[46] The Kenyan data record a rapid increase in female and child labour in agriculture during 1921–2 (which are 'shortage' years on the Chief Native Commissioner's definition but not on the definition of Table 4.4), no real trend thereafter until 1945, but during the labour shortage period which followed a rapid and continuous increase in both African female and juvenile employment. The Rhodesian data, which one suspects very much understate the case, tell a similar story in respect of female employment (data on child employment are not given), i.e. employment more or less static until the late thirties, then rising dramatically during the war and the post-war period. Some of this sudden upsurge in female and juvenile employment may simply reflect improved reporting; but it reflects also the discovery at a time of labour shortage that a large part of the potential labour force had in fact been underused as a means of responding to increased demand

141

without raising the overall cost structure, and indeed the newspapers and legislative council debates of the period 1940–55 in both countries are full of moral and practical justifications of its increased use.[47]

Conclusions

We are now in a position where, with the aid of Table 4.7 and Figure 4.2, we can pull the threads of the argument in this section together. For, whereas in Arrighi's view 'political mechanisms were of crucial importance in closing gaps between (labour) supply and demand',[48] what we can now see is that genuine political mechanisms requiring the intervention of Government (legislation, tax increases and in Kenya forced labour) were only of importance in this role up to the mid-twenties. After that the role was filled by the induction of categories of labour a little more expensive than free flow labour, but not as expensive (on a short-term calculation) as the alternative expedient of a wage increase; i.e. recruited labour in the inter-war period, and female and juvenile labour in particular in the post-Second World War period. But secondly, whereas Arrighi suggests that from the inter-war period onwards economic mechanisms were redundant as a means of adjusting to an excess demand for unskilled labour,[49] the real wage series portrayed on Figure 4.2 suggest in fact a continuous increase in the willingness of employers to raise real wages in situations of excess demand for labour, *but often only as a last resort should the previously mentioned expedients have failed.* Thus in Kenya, a situation of labour shortage began to emerge in 1909 but money wages of African farm workers only began to increase in 1911 (we have no data on real wages); in the second labour shortage period beginning in 1923 real wages rose after a lag of only one year accompanied by big increases in both compulsory and female/juvenile labour;[50] a third labour shortage emerged in 1936, and real wages did not rise until 1938, after big increases in privately recruited labour; a fourth shortage developed in 1946, and the real wage rate increased at once, together with imports of contracted labour from as far afield as Ruanda-Urundi.[51] The Southern Rhodesia story is similar: real wages of black miners were almost certainly substantially *cut* during the first two periods of labour shortage (1905–9 and 1914–20);[52] rose gently in the third period of shortage, 1926–9, but not in the fourth, 1938–9. In the fifth period, 1948–54, real wages rose more or less continuously. But they then continued to rise in the late 1950s, a period of excess supply of labour, suggesting that even in the extractive industries the practice of 'labour stabilisation', in fact current in large foreign-owned enterprises since almost the beginning of the colonial period, was starting to percolate into substantial areas of the economy.

In Chapter 2.3 above, we argued that the level of subsidy on the maize price, and to some extent the structure of export rail rates, could be seen as a conditioned governmental response to situations of 'crisis' on the output side of the settler economy. Similarly we would argue that the 'package' of responses discussed in this section – first non-wage responses as a rule, then real wage increases if this failed – could be seen as a conditioned employer response to labour shortages, which were a situation of crisis on the input side for those who had not the capital to adjust factor proportions – or even raise money wages – at all easily. However, the nature of the responses to crisis, as in the case of the responses to export loss discussed in Chapter 2, changed over time. Whereas before the First World War (Table 4.6 above) labour shortages led to proposals from employers for reductions in the reserves and tax changes, the shortages immediately before and after the Second World War provoked proposals, from the more conservative employers, for urban influx control and government recruiting, and from the more liberal employers, for improvement of housing and minimum wage policies.[53] Nobody suggested squeezing the reserves or raising African tax rates. The reason for this change in response was simply that the *cost* of this kind of crude extra-market operation had risen: Africans were now more politically organised, and had shown this in demonstrations such as the Mombasa dock strike of 1947 and the Bulawayo general strike of 1948. As in the market for cattle, discussed earlier, so in the market for labour the system of procurement by compulsory purchase order from the African reserves had to be definitively abandoned after the Second World War. The reason was that once the political costs of such procurement were added to the financial costs, a crude over-riding of market forces was no longer the least-cost method of obtaining labour.

APPENDIX 3 A NOTE ON THE DATA FOR CHAPTER 4

This appendix presents information, by analogy with Appendix 2, on the principal sources used to compile the statistical material in Chapter 4. We discuss here all the *new* series presented in Chapter 4; but the argument also makes use of some data on agricultural sales and productivity, for a discussion of whose reliability the reader is referred to Appendix 2.

Employment data (Tables 4.8a and b and summary Table 4.1)

Kenya

Between 1922 and 1935 the Native Affairs Department estimate of African employment was calculated from Monthly Labour Returns. These returns were requested from all employers, but the response rate was low, and they were received only from 50 to 65 per cent of all known employers, and the number of known employers was rather less than the number of actual employers. Although coverage increased over time, official records show that the response rate diminished, so that the increases in employment shown are probably not due to increases in coverage. For 1922–5 there was some confusion as to whether resident labourers were to be included. From 1927 on, resident labourers and daily-paid casual labourers were definitely excluded.

The Agricultural Census estimates of total, female and child labour employed in European agriculture (Table 4.8b, columns 2a, 3a, 3b) are probably the best we have for the pre-Second World War period: the number of establishments which they had to cover was higher than for the Monthly Labour Returns, and the response rate was somewhat higher, probably of the order of 95 per cent on average (interview V. Liversage, 24 November 1979 (E)). These estimates *included* an estimate for resident labour.

I have not been able to ascertain how the Blue Book estimates of agricultural public service and domestic labour (Table 4.8b, cols. 2b, c and d) were compiled. The logical assumption would be that they came from Special Labour Returns, which excluded resident labour, but this makes the Blue Book estimate of agricultural labour for 1937 hard to understand, as it is more or less the same as the 1936–8 average estimate of agricultural labour (*inclusive* of squatters) provided by the Agricultural Census. In the absence of information about the source of the Blue Book estimates, I have not included them in the analysis of Chapter 4.

From 1936–47 estimates of total employment came from a Special Labour Census, which excluded male juveniles, female employees, resident labourers, daily-paid casual labourers, and those in the armed services; from 1948 on, enumeration of employees was taken over by the Kenya unit of the East African Statistical Department, which now included in its estimated total the figures for female, juvenile and resident labour. The overall non-response rate had, by 1960, been brought down to about 10 per cent (East Africa Statistical Department 1961a (B3), p. 12).

Southern Rhodesia

As in Kenya, the position until 1937 is that information on African employment comes from two sources: (a) what was intended to be a comprehensive enumeration of all employees, which fell foul of rather low response rates (conducted by the Native Department), and (b) a rather more reliable enumeration of employment in one sector; in this case mining. From 1903 on the Government Chief Mining Engineer provides excellent data on total employment, division by racial categories and by origin (contract or 'free flow'); the data in column 2a are from this source. Until 1937 there was no regular enumeration of African farm-workers in European agriculture; the figures given in column 2c for 1911, 1921 and 1931 are taken from the decennial census of the non-African population.

After 1937, regular monthly enumeration of African employees in all sectors begins. After 1951 the published figures, contrary to previous practice, include female and registered juvenile labour. Information on employment in European agriculture becomes much more reliable due to an increase in the scope and staffing of the European agricultural census in 1951; non-response rates fell dramatically after this date, and overall were down to less than 3 per cent in 1960.

Data on money wages (Tables 4.9a–c and summary Table 4.2)

The estimates of wages before 1945 presented in Table 4.9 cannot be considered even as reliable as the estimates of employment in Table 4.8. There are two reasons for this. First, the estimates of agricultural wages set out in Table 4.9 are based not on a complete enumeration of employees but on an estimate of the *modal* wage of unskilled labour in given farming districts reported by the local Native (District) Commissioner. In defence of this crude method we can, however, say (a) that the market for unskilled African labour within particular European farming districts was fairly free, with very good knowledge among both employers and employees of what wages were being offered on neighbouring farms, and strong social pressures being exerted by employers upon one another in clubs and local Farmers' Associations to prevent the payment of wages above the current norm (see note 29), and (b) that it is the best available; even in the United States at this time enumerators seeking information on the level of farm wages in particular states had to proceed by making annual enquiries on the 'general level' of farm wages rather than by a complete enumeration of wage bills.[54] Secondly, it is to be noted that the data in Table 4.9 capture only the value of cash wages plus a maize ration of 2 lb per diem. They exclude, therefore, trends in the level of non-wage benefits going beyond this, in particular meat supplies and housing (also, on some large farms, primitive educational and medical facilities); they also exclude trends in hours worked. The evidence on these matters is so sparse as to preclude our trying to use it to adjust the existing money wage series, but suggests in each case a modest once-for-all improvement in the late 1920s and 1930s.[55] On working hours, frequent reports suggest that the inter-war norm was an excessively long day, slightly shortened before the Second World War. Thus when in 1938 the Cold Storage Commission in Southern Rhodesia took over the assets of the old Imperial Cold Storage Company, 'the old compound, which all who saw it agree was disgusting, [was] replaced by neat rows of clean iron huts, with special quarters for the married natives, adequate rations extending to the wives and families of workers, and hours decreased from 4 a.m. to 7 p.m. to a new schedule of 7 a.m. to 5 p.m.' (*Rhodesia Mines and Industries*, February 1941, p. 17).

To the extent that this intuition is correct, however, one of the general arguments of Chapter 4, namely that there is no evidence of a secular decline in real African labour incomes after 1914, is strengthened.

After 1946 in Southern Rhodesia, and 1951 in Kenya, the monthly enumeration of employees undertaken by the Central Statistical Office included a question about the total wage bill: this gives us an 'average African earnings' figure which is more soundly enumerated than the pre-1939 data, but less conceptually desirable as an indication of the earnings of African unskilled labour (see p. 117 above) because it is an average which incorporates the earnings of the skilled and semi-skilled. Non-response rates for these data are of the same order of magnitude as those for employment, i.e. about 5 per cent by 1960.

Prices of goods consumed by Africans (basis of real wage estimated in Tables 4.9b and c)

No estimate of the household budgets of rural Africans was made before 1939. Hence any attempt to estimate movements in prices of goods consumed by Africans must rely on import prices. In deciding what items to include in an index of the price of 'goods consumed by Africans' we are driven back to the accounts of traders themselves (e.g. in evidence to the Southern Rhodesian *Native Production and Trade Commission*, 1944) and those observers who kept an interested eye on their operations, i.e. the Southern Rhodesian Native Commissioners, the Kenya District Commissioner and the British Board of Trade (in publications such as the *Report on the trade and commerce of East Africa*, annually from 1922). From these accounts we have selected the following short list of items as being particularly important in their consumption:

cotton piece goods	sugar
cotton blankets	salt
cigarettes and manufactured tobacco	matches
soap	boots and shoes

An index of the import parity prices of these goods, c.i.f. Mombasa (the price level and relative salience of the goods cited in the Southern Rhodesian import statistics differs scarcely at all from this series) from 1914 to 1939 (1914 = 100), is as follows. The weights used in the calculation of the index are based on the value of *total* imports, not the expenditure on these items by Africans, which is not recorded. These weights are updated in 1921 and 1931. Note finally that with an index running over a period as long as this there are problems of quality change, e.g. during the 1920s the expensive leather footwear imported principally from Britain was largely replaced in the African market by rubber and canvas footwear imported principally from Japan.

	Index of import prices of goods consumed by Kenyan Africans, c.i.f. Mombasa	For comparison: index of retail prices of foodstuffs consumed by Southern Rhodesian Europeans[a]
1914	100	100
1915	148	
1916	117	
1917	145	
1918	195	
1919	254	
1920	226	160.9
1921	306	
1922	226	
1923	211	
1924	233	
1925	224	
1926	202	108.8
1927	173	108.5
1928	166	111.3
1929	158	110.7
1930	158	103.4
1931	122	97.5
1932	120	93.9
1933	111	92.3
1934	121	91.2
1935	108	90.6
1936	105	89.5
1937	104	94.7
1938	108	
1939	101	

[a] *Source*: Southern Rhodesia, *Annual Yearbook* 1938

In 1939 an index of the prices of goods 'mainly consumed by Africans' becomes available in Kenya. It is based on the Mombasa prices of the following commodities (the weights attached to each commodity follow, in parentheses):

Maize flour (*posho*)	(14)	Fuel	(15)
Beef	(14)	Soap	(3)
Vegetables	(14)	Clothing	(10)
Sugar	(4)	Household utensils	(1)
Tea	(6)		
Other foods	(16)		

The value of this index from 1939 to 1953 (1939 = 100) can then be calculated.

146

	Index of import prices of goods consumed by Kenyan Africans, c.i.f. Mombasa	For comparison: linked index of retail prices of goods consumed by Southern Rhodesia Europeans.[a,b]
1939	100	100
1947	198	198
1948	207	213
1949	215	224
1951	289	261
1952	325	272
1953	324	285

Note: [a] This only goes back to 1947. 1939–47 change is assumed to be the same as for Kenya Africans.
Source:
[b] Clarke 1975 (C), vol. II, pp. 173 and 188.

After 1953 the index peters out. However, it is possible to continue it using the weights noted above and the prices recorded in quarterly issues of the *East Africa Economic and Statistical Bulletin* and this procedure gives values for 1955–8

	Linked index 1939 = 100	For comparison: Southern Rhodesia European linked price index, 1939 = 100
1955	390	296
1956	379	310
1957	380	320
1958	400	331

Finally, in 1958 a new index of prices of goods consumed by Africans – based this time on Nairobi – was started.

	New index	Linked index 1939 = 100	For comparison: Southern Rhodesia European linked price index, 1939 = 100
1958	100		
1959	100	(400)	340
1960	101	(404)	348
1961	104	(416)	357
1962	106	(424)	365
1963	109	(436)	369

The immediately apparent difference between our own index and those previously published is in their volatility: thus, whereas it seems to be true for both Europeans and Africans that prices were about the same in 1939 as they were in 1914, and that they were about four times this level in 1963, the price increases during and after the First and Second World War seem to have hit the African consumer much harder than the European. It is tempting to assume that since the African index before 1939 is based on a deliberately restricted list of imported items (excluding, for example, locally produced maize, whose price barely doubled between 1914 and 1919,

147

whereas import prices rose by 250 per cent) it must exaggerate the price changes to which Africans were subject. But there is contemporary evidence to suggest that this is, in fact, untrue (see note 11) and it is also possible to exaggerate the salience of locally produced food in the budget (by contrast with the consumption) of the African farm-worker or miner before 1939, as his rations – mainly maize – were nearly always provided by the employer. Our procedure here for 1914–39 is to compile a composite index from the import price index set out above (with an arbitrary weight of 75 per cent) and the f.o.b. export price of maize (with an arbitrary weight of 25 per cent). The sources for maize export prices are as for Table 3.6, plus, in the case of Southern Rhodesia data before 1930–1. Southern Rhodesia 1931 (B2). Appendix D. This composite index is set out here; it is used as the deflator to compile the real wage tables set out in full in Appendix 4, and in summary form in Table 4.2 above.

Year	Kenya	Southern Rhodesia	Year	Kenya	Southern Rhodesia
1914	100	100	1927	163	172
1915	150	150	1928	165	167
1916	137	137	1929	164	146
1917	158	158	1930	148	137
1918	197	197	1931	118	109
1919	236	261	1932	117	115
1920	199	209	1933	106	108
1921	262	219	1934	–	–
1922	214	268	1935	118	112
1923	192	197	1936	98	104
1924	214	214	1937	110	106
1925	209	208	1938	102	109
1926	187	190	1939	101	101

After 1939, in the absence of a price index for Southern European Africans, we use the composite index of prices of goods consumed by Kenyan Africans, set out above, as a deflator in both countries.

APPENDIX 4 DETAILED TIME SERIES ON WAGES AND EMPLOYMENT: KENYA AND SOUTHERN RHODESIA 1905–63

This appendix gives a full statement of the data used to put together Tables 4.1 and 4.2. Sources are given in summary form only; a discussion of their reliability is at Appendix 3 above.

148

Table 4.8a. *Southern Rhodesia: recorded African employment and industrial distribution, 1906–63 (figures in thousands)*

Year	(1) Total African employment					(2) Distribution of African employment by sector			(3) Distribution of African employment by type of labour			
	(a) African adult males in employment		(b) As % of males on tax register		(c) Non-indigenous males as % of total adult male workforce	(a) Mining	Non-mining		Contract labour (RNLB)			Female labour
	Total	Indigenous	Total^a	Indigenous			(b) Total	(c) European agriculture	(a) Total	(b) mines and other	(c) % farms	
1906						19.8			4.9	100	0	
1907						27.7			14.1	100	0	
1908						30.8			15.8	96	4	
1909	58.6					32.7	25.9		16.8	75	25	
1910	66.0					37.8	28.8		20.4	75	25	
1911	75.8					38.6	37.2	13.5	9.3	82	18	
1912	72.8					34.6	38.2		14.6	56	44	
1913	73.1		35.8			33.4	39.7		13.4	49	51	
1914	81.0		39.3			36.3	45.0		9.5	48	52	
1915	81.6		38.7			37.9	43.2		11.1	60	40	
1916	80.1		37.1			40.2	39.6		6.5	46	54	
1917	83.3		41.9			38.6	44.9		10.0	47	53	
1918	79.3		40.6			32.1	46.4		7.3	56	44	
1919	79.9		38.8			30.6	50.1		10.1	55	45	
1920	95.1		45.5			36.8	52.2		16.8	41	59	
1921	114.1		54.1			37.6	76.5	62.5	9.8	37	63	0.6
1922	131.6	41	60.6	31.2	68.7	35.6	96.0		4.4	34	66	
1923	137.6	47	63.7	34.3	64.9	36.6	101.0		6.0	50	50	
1924	142.1	50	65.3	35.2	64.7	41.3	100.8		8.6	35	65	
1925	147.1	55	66.7	37.4	62.5	40.8	107.5		9.0	35	65	1.6
1926	171.9	77	45.0	45.0	54.6	40.8	133.1		7.4	40	60	
1927	179.9	82	77.1	45.5	56.7	40.6	137.8		8.3	24	76	
1928	177.8	83	73.5	46.8	53.1	43.7	134.1		7.5	33	67	

Table 4.8a. (cont.)

	(1) Total African employment					(2) Distribution of African employment by sector			(3) Distribution of African employment by type of labour			
	(a) African adult males in employment		(b) As % of males on tax register		(c) Non-indigenous males as % of total adult male workforce	(a) Mining	Non-mining		Contract labour (RNLB)			Female labour
Year	Total	Indigenous	Total[a]	Indigenous			(b) Total	(c) European agriculture	(a) Total	(b) mines and other	(c) % farms	
1929	161.6	71	66.1	44.0	55.9	46.8	116.1		–	35	65	
1930	156.7	68	63.2	43.5	56.4	45.3	111.4		5.8	47	53	
1931	164.2	69	65.0	42.0	57.9	35.2	129.0	72.1	1.2	12	88	1.0
1932	157.2	73	61.2	46.4	53.5	36.0	121.3					
1933	176.5	75	68.4	44.9	57.7	48.2	123.0					
1934	184.0	80	65.0	43.4	57.0	62.3	121.9					
1935	204.6	684	70.4	41.1	58.8	76.2	127.2					
1936	221.4	98	76.4	39.8	60.1	84.0	137.3	83.2				
1937	243.6	94	89.6	38.6	61.3	90.6	153.1	87.8				
1938	255.7	96	92.7	37.6	62.3	87.7	167.9	92.0				
1939	242.1	96	85.8	39.6	60.3	83.5		93.6				
1940	249.5	101	87.6	40.5	59.4	85.8	163.7	96.1				
1941	285.5	119	96.6	41.7	58.2	84.0		101.6				3.7
1942	295.3	134	91.3	45.4	54.5	81.8		110.4				
1943	310.7	138	100.5	44.5	45.2	78.4		114.3				
						Mining	Services (all)	Manufacturing and construction	European agriculture			
1944	293.7	138	100.2	47.0	52.9	75.1	86.7		123.6			
1945	298.4	142	111.4	47.5	52.4	71.6	77.1		130.6	Contract labour (RNLSC)	13.5	
1946						70.6	74.9		135.8			
1947	387.0	183	111.8	47.5	58.4	69.8	71.6		147.4			
1948	373.1	177	104.7	44.8	57.8	58.9	66.4	72.3	147.3		0.3	
1949	391.8	166	106.2	42.4	60.0	56.9	58.9		165.7		2.3	
											4.0	41.7[b]

150

Year		Mining	Services		Manufacturing and construction	European agriculture	
			Domestic	Other			
1951	530.2	63.7	70.2		104.4	212.4	13.6
1952							14.5
1953							19.8
1954	559.0	62.4	76.1	85.0	119.7	220.1	24.5
1955	579.0	59.6	79.2	91.2	121.4	227.4	24.1
1956	611.0	60.9	99.3	85.4	135.6	230.0	25.1
1957	628.0	60.7	107.0	88.0	144.8	227.7	28.7
1958	635.0	57.1	113.5	90.9	143.0	231.5	26.0
1959	635.0	52.5	119.3	92.7	139.3	233.5	21.7
1960	647.0	52.3	119.3	94.1	138.6	242.3	
1961	624.0	48.5	120.7	94.8	126.1	234.2	11.2
1962	613.0	44.1	118.2	95.2	115.2	240.8	7.9
1963	610.0	40.9	115.0	94.9	106.6	257.3	8.6

– no data

Notes:

[a] Figures may exceed 100% as some labour came from other countries.

[b] This figure almost certainly over-estimates the growth in female employment between 1945 and 1949, although it was certainly rapid. The figures before 1945 probably under-record female employment, particularly in agriculture.

[c] From 1950 on, employment figures are given for 'total persons in employment', not for adult males only

[d] 'Other services' includes transport, electricity and water, commerce.

Sources:

1905–12 – Annual Reports of the Chief Native Commissioner, Mashonaland and Matabeleland.

1913–47 – Annual Reports of the Chief Native Commissioner, supplemented by Annual Yearboks of the Colony of Southern Rhodesia, 1924, 1930, 1932, 1938, 1947.

1947–53 – Barber 1961 (D2), p. 222.

1954–63 – Southern Rhodesia, Monthly Digest of Statistics, Sept. 1963 and Sept. 1964.

Contract labour – before 1931, Rhodesia Native Labour Bureau. Annual Reports; after 1947, Clarke 1974a (D2), table 6, p. 119.

Table 4.8b. *Kenya: recorded African employment and industrial distribution, 1919–63 (figures in thousands)*

	(1) Total African employment			(2) Distribution of African by sector employment					(3) Distribution of African employment by type of labour			
	(a) African adult males in employment[b]		(b) African adult males in employment (NAD estimate) as a percentage of adult male tax-payers	(a) Mining	(b) European agriculture		(c) Domestic service	(d) Public sector	(a) Female (agriculture only)	(b) Child	(c) Compulsory (i.e. ordered Native Authority Amendment Ordinance 1922)	(d) Squatters (adult males only)
Year	Native Affairs Dept.	Blue Book estimate		Native Affairs Dept estimate	Agricultural Census estimate	Blue Book estimate	Blue Book estimate	Blue Book estimate	Agricultural Census estimate	Agricultural Census estimate		
1919	95.0								3.9	4.8		
1920	90.0								4.9	6.5		
1921									4.2	5.9		
1922	119.1		28.6						6.6	9.9	10.5	
1923	138.3		31.7		70.9				8.3	11.8	25.5	
1924	133.9		29.3		87.0				8.4	11.3	19.3	
1925	152.4		30.4		78.5				6.0	13.7	15.2	
1926	169.0	164.3	33.6		84.6	64.8	18.9	34.3			13.3	
1927	147.9	160.4	28.0		102.0	76.8	22.4	32.5			12.8	32.9
1928	152.2	177.0	29.0		114.3	92.3	20.0	24.3			12.9	
1929	160.1		30.3		110.6	91.1		19.9			9.7	
1930	157.4	128.3	29.7		125.8	90.6	18.0	20.0	3.9	18.1	9.1	
1931	141.4	157.0	26.6		120.2	79.6	16.7	30.7	3.3	19.3	5.7	
1932	132.1	150.5	24.4		104.1	77.6	16.7	27.1			7.4	
1933	141.0	146.0	26.0	8.0	105.0	79.7	15.0	26.5	3.5	14.6	4.5	
1934	145.0		26.9	10.9	106.8	89.0	15.0	23.2	3.5	14.7	3.5	28.9
1935	150.0	155.2	26.3	13.6	no census	90.0	17.0	23.9	no census		3.8	
1936	173.0	165.0	30.1	11.0	100.9	106.3	18.0	28.1	10.9	8.7	2.8	24.1
1937	183.0		31.2	7.5	no census	111.5	17.3	32.7	no census		1.7	28.0

East Africa Statistical Department estimate[c]

Year		East Africa Statistical Department estimate								
1941	208.0	257.3		20.3	100.6		44.7	14.6	51.2	23.3
1942	247.4	261.5		17.0	122.5		63.0	27.4	64.2	23.7
1943	248.4	264.7					63.5	28.1	62.8	26.7
1944	249.7		18.8		118.0		57.9	28.1	62.8	34.6
1945	259.2	294.9			118.3	30.0	64.8	28.3	55.9	31.9
1946	252.2	287.1			108.1		66.1	34.7	55.8	27.3
1947	265.5	300.8			122.1	28.8	81.2	33.8	54.1	26.6

Private sector employment

Year		Mining and quarrying	European agriculture	Manufacturing and construction	Services[d]	Public sector employment			
1948[e]	385.5	8.5	189.1	43.8	60.7	88.6	30.5	44.9	27.9
1949	394.9	8.3	201.9	52.3	62.9	92.1	32.7	38.3	27.6
1950	420.7	5.5	203.1	52.0	58.0	89.2	24.2	35.7	25.5
1951	412.4	5.8	202.6	58.7	65.4	97.0	34.4	43.6	27.4
1952	434.5	4.7	211.2	52.2	66.6	113.7	40.3	42.2	27.6
1953	453.0	5.5	218.8	62.1	74.0	130.5	49.5	43.9	25.5
1954	491.0	7.5	245.6	67.6	82.3	147.5	57.2	44.3	27.4
1955	558.0	8.7	233.0	71.2	79.2	148.7	64.7	44.4	23.6
1956	540.1	7.5	251.0	66.9	82.1	146.8	79.5	43.6	23.4
1957	554.7	6.1	249.5	63.6	79.6	137.8	83.0	40.7	
1958	534.7	5.1	251.7	60.2	82.4	134.8			
1959	537.0	4.8	271.8	60.8	85.3	135.7	74.7		
1960	560.0	3.5	252.0	60.5	79.7	167.0	81.8		
1961	589.8	3.5	245.5	57.9	105.9	168.5			
1962	581.3	3.1	219.7	51.1	113.9	157.3			
1963	536.1								

153

Table 4.8b. (cont.)

Notes:

[a] 1939 and 1940 figures are interpolated to fill a break in the series, from the graph (page unnumbered) 'Registered natives in employment, Kenya Colony', in Kenya, *Report of the Native Labour Census 1946* (Nairobi, 1946).

[b] Agricultural Census estimate of agricultural employment *includes* daily paid and squatter (resident) labour. Native Affairs Department: estimate of total African employment (col. 1a) *excludes* such labour, hence the row totals within col. 2 for a given year frequently add up to more than the figures for total employment in that year given in col. 1a. Blue Book estimates of African agricultural employment probably (it is not stated) exclude such labour, which would provide an explanation of the difference between this and the Agricultural Census estimate in the 1920s; but in the 1930s the Blue Book figures converge on the Agricultural Census estimates, making this explanation no longer plausible. For more discussion of this discrepancy see Appendix 3 above.

[c] 1941–7: East Africa Statistical Department, estimates of total employment: these are Special Labour Census estimates *including* military employment.

[d] The figure given in this column covers *all* services. i.e. commerce, electricity, water and transport in addition to domestic service.

[e] From 1948 on, employment figures relate to total employment, not to adult males only.

Sources: For 1920–40 – Kenya, Native Affairs Dept, Labour Section, *Annual Reports*; Kenya. *Blue Books*, various; Kenya, *Agriculture Censuses*, various.

For 1941–63 – East Africa Statistical Dept (Kenya Unit) 1961a (B3); East African High Commission, *Economic and Statistical Bulletin*, various issues, Tables E3 and E4; child, female and squatter employment from Kenya Labour Dept, *Annual Reports*.

Table 4.9a. *Kenya and Southern Rhodesia: African agricultural wages, 1898–1946*[a]

	Southern Rhodesia						Kenya					
					Unweighted average, all districts					Unweighted average all districts		
							Kiambu District (mainly coffee farms)	Trans Nzoia District (mainly maize farms)	Machakos District (fruit farms, sisal plantations)	Excluding allowance for value of food		Including allowance for value of food[cd]
Year	Marandellas District	Mazoe District	Mrewa District	Victoria District	Excluding allowance for value of food[b]	Including allowance for value of food[c]				Series 1	Series 2	
1898	11/-											
1899		10/-		15/-	15/-(1)	19/-						
1900					12/3(9)	16/3						
1901					14/2(3)	18/2						
1902												
1903	12/6				10/-(1)	18/-				4.0		8.0
1904												
1905												
1906	10/-				12/6(2)	20/6					5.40	13.4
1907					13/-(2)	21/-					5.40	13.40
1908									5.30		5.40	13.40
1909									5.30		6.0	13.0
1910		10/-			10/-(1)	18/-				4.0	7.0	15.60
1911					14/-(2)	22/-					7.0	15.0
1912									8.00	7.0	10.80	18.80
1913											10.50	18.80

155

Table 4.9a. (cont.)

156

	Southern Rhodesia						Kenya					
					Unweighted average, all districts					Unweighted average all districts		
										Excluding allowance for value of food		Including allowance for value of food[cd]
Year	Marandellas District	Mazoe District	Mrewa District	Victoria District	Excluding allowance for value of food[b]	Including allowance for value of food[c]	Kiambu District (mainly coffee farms)	Trans Nzoia District (mainly maize farms)	Machakos District (fruit farms, sisal plantations)	Series 1	Series 2	
1914					10/-(1)	18/-					10.80	18.80
1915					13/9(1)	21/9			6.70			18.80
1916					10/3(3)	18/3	6.10				8.0	16.0
1917					10/-(1)	20/-	7.15				7.0	15.0
1918					10/-	20/-						
1919					12/6(1)	22/6						
1920			20/-		16/9(8)	22/9						
1921			15/-		15/-(2)	21/-				10.0*e	8.0††	15.0
1922					17/-(5)	22/-	10.0				10.0*	17.0
1923	12/6				18/3(7)	23/3	8.0					
1924	12/6		13/9		16/3(2)	21/3	10.0					
1925	17/6	12/-			14/3(3)	19/3	12.0					
1926					20/2(5)	25/2					18.0	23.0
1927	20/-		22/6		21/3(2)	26/3	13.0	12.0	16.0	12.0	18.0	23.0
1928							13.0	12.0		12.0	18.0	23.0
1929					20/-(1)	25/-					18.0	23.0
1930					17/6(3)	22/6			17.0			21.0
1931	9/-			10/-	13/-(4)					16.0	16.0	21.0
1932	11/-		15/-	10/6	12/3(3)	17/3				16.0	16.0	21.0

cuts

8.0

Year					9.0	11.0			11.50	16.50
1938									11.50	16.25
1939	12/6									
1940										
1941						11.0				
1942							10.0**	20.0		
1943						10.0	10.0**	20.0		
1944										
1945	12/-(2)	17/-				12.0	12.0**	24.0		
	14/-(5)	19/-								
1946	19/9					16.0	16.0**	28.0		

Notes:

ᵃ All data given are *cash* wages per month (or thirty-day ticket) in shillings paid by employers who also provided food and, nominally, housing (though African employees were often expected to build their own shelter). If a range is quoted by the informant, the mid-point of this range is taken.

ᵇ The 'unweighted average, all districts' is an average of African agricultural workers' wages across all districts that reported a figure. The number in brackets following all entries in this column is the number of districts reporting a figure for agricultural wages in the year in question. Where a range for wages is given, the mid-point is taken.

ᶜ The following arbitrary additions to cash wages are made to arrive at an estimate of the total monthly value of African agricultural workers' earnings:

4/- for 1895–1903   (Source: Clayton and Savage 1974 (D1), p. 49)

8/- for 1904–14

5/- for 1925–33

12/- for 1945–6   (Source: Kenya *Blue Books*)

For intermediate years the gaps are filled by allowing the notional 'ration allowance' to vary in proportion to the price of maize. this being over-whelmingly the most important element in farm workers' rations.

ᵈ The cash element of the Kenya rations – included series is an unweighted average of series 1 and 2, if both series report a value for the year in question.

ᵉ In 1921, the level of agricultural wages was cut, by agreement between European farmers, from Sh. 12.0 to Sh. 8.0 cash element (for an account of this episode, see Huxley 1935 (D1), vol. II, p. 81); the figure given is an average of these two values.

Sources: Southern Rhodesia districts – NAR: N 9/1/4–23 and S 235/501–18, Native Commissioner's Annual Reports, 1898–1946. Kenya districts, district level data – (Kiambu and Machakos) KNA/DC/MKS/1/1–30 and DC/KBU/9–37 respectively. (Trans Nzoia) Native Affairs Dept, Annual Report. with interpolations from the diaries of S.H. Powles, a Trans Nzoia maize farmer (RH: Mss. Afr.s. 1121). Kenya National level data – Series 2 is from Kenya, *Blue Books*, various. Series 1 is a Native Affairs Department series, compiled from (before 1914) Kenya 1913 (B3) and (after 1914) Kenya, Native Affairs Dept, Labour Section, *Annual Reports*. The following interpolations are made for periods where neither source offers any data:

* (1921 figures) from Huxley 1935 (D1), vol. II. p. 81.   ** (figures for early war years) from Powles diaries, RH: Mss. Afr.s. 1121.

†† (1920 figure) from PRO:CO 533/232, Bowring to Milner, 21 April 1920.

157

Table 4.9b. *Southern Rhodesia: recorded monthly wage rates for different categories of African unskilled labour*

Year	(1) Miners (underground, unskilled)		(2) Agricultural labourers (unskilled)		(3) Indices of money wages (1914 = 100)			(4) Indices of real wages (1914 = 100)[cd]		
	(a) Excluding allowance for value of food	(b) Including allowance for value of food supplied[a]	(a) Excluding allowance for value of food supplied	(b) Including allowance for food supplied	(a) Agriculture	(b) Mining	(c) Agriculture and mining composite[b]	(a) Agriculture	(b) Mining	(c) Composite
1899	20/- to 40/-	35/-	15/-	19/-	105	89	94			
1900			12/3	16/3	91		82			
1901			14/2	18/2	101		91			
1902	40/- to 80/-	70/-				179	161			
1903	40/- to 50/-	55/-	10/-	18/-	100	141	127			
1904										
1905		40/- to 60/-			114	128	146			
1906		40/- to 60/-	12/6	20/6	113	128	120			
1907			13/-	21/-			119			
1908										
1909		40/- to 45/-	10/-	18/-	100	109	106			
1910		30/- to 35/-	14/-	22/-	122	84	97			
1911										
1912										
1913										
1914	30/10	38/10	10/-	18/-	100	100	100	100	100	100
1915			13/9	21/9	121		121	81		81
1916			10/3	18/3	101		101	74		74
1917			10/-		111		111	70		70
			10/		111		111	64		64

Year										
1920		33/1	16/9	22/9	127	85	127	61	41	41
1921	30/-	37/6	15/-	21/-	116	96	106	45	37	41
1922	28/6	35/-	17/-	22/-	122	97	108	57	43	50
1923			18/3	23/3	129		114	65		58
1924			16/3	21/3	118		104	55		49
1925			14/3	19/3	107		95	51		52
1926			20/2	25/2	140	83	111	74		59
1927	30/-	36/6	21/3	26/3	146	89	117	89	44	68
1928	28/2	34/8					125		52	74
1929			20/-	25/-	138		110	94		
1930			17/6	22/6	125		100	91		73
1931			13/-	18/-	100		89	92		
1932	25/10	32/4	12/3	17/3	96	83	87	83	72	76
1933	22/11	29/5				76	80		68	74
1934	21/7	28/1				72	78		64	70
1935	21/1	27/11	10/3	15/3	85	71	78	78	65	72
1936	21/2	28/-				72	79		69	75
1937	22/-	28/6				73	80		69	75
1938	26/9	32/6	12/-	17/-	94	84	89	86	77	82
1939	26/6	34/6	14/-	19/-	105	84	94	99	77	95
1940	26/6	34/6				84	94		77	95
1941	25/5	35/5				91	101			
1942	26/-	36/-				92	102			
1943	27/5	39/5				101	12			
1944	28/1	40/1				103	114			(75)[e]
1945	31/6	45/5				116	128			

Table 4.9b. (cont.)

Year	(1) Miners (underground, unskilled)		(2) Agricultural labourers (unskilled)		Average earnings (in cash and kind) in specific sectors[d]					(3) Indices of money wages (1914 = 100)			(4) Indices of real wages (1914 = 100)		
	(a) Excluding allowance for value of food	(b) Including allowance for value of food supplied[a]	(a) Excluding allowance for value of food supplied	(b) Including allowance for food supplied	Mining	Domestic service	Manufacturing	European agriculture	Public services	(a) Agriculture	(b) Mining	(c) Agriculture and mining composite[b]	(a) Agriculture	(b) Mining	(c) Composite
1946					47/-		40/4	26/-		144	120	138	72	60	70
1947						44/6									
1948					58/4	42/-	58/6	36/-		200	150	187	96	72	90
1949						46/-									
1950					71/4	54/6	54/6	73/6		254	183	236	109	79	102
1951					81/8	61/7	90/-	50/8		282	210	264	98	73	91
1952					101/8	76/-	91/-	58/-		322	261	306	99	80	94
1953					105/-	94/-	99/2	62/2		349	269	326	106	83	100
1954					111/8	118/-	125/-	64/3		357	287	339	–	–	–
1955						125/-	140/1			–	–	–	–	–	–
1956					161/6	135/-	161/6	86/6		481	415	464	126	109	122
1957					171/6	140/-	180/-	82/6	143/-	458	441	453	120	116	119
1958					176/8	145/8	191/8	86/6	171/-	481	454	474	120	113	118
1959					185/-	142/6	208/4	88/2	193/4	482	475	480	120	118	120
1960					191/8	157/6	236/6	90/-	206/-	490	493	490	121	122	121
1961					203/6	164/-	272/3	92/6	260/-	500	523	505	140	125	121
										513	529	517	121	125	122

Notes :

[a] Value of miners' food is assumed to be 25 per cent in excess of farm rations throughout, as most mines supplied a meat ration, in addition to maize, to their African labour (others supplied considerably more, cf. note 3 above).

[b] Money wage indices for agriculture and mining are simply the figures in cols. 1b and 2b expressed as percentages of their 1914 level. The 'composite index' of agricultural and mining wages in col. 3c is a weighted average of the indices in cols. 3a and b, the weights being

    mining 2 : agriculture 1 until 1920
    mining 1 : agriculture 1 from 1920–1945
    mining 1 : agriculture 3 after 1945

these being approximations to the employment ratios in these industries (see Table 4.8a above). In years where a value of the wage index for *either* agriculture or mining only is reported, the value of the composite index is increased by the extent of the percentage change in the wage index for that activity.

[c] The real wage indices in col. 4 are computed by deflating the values given in cols. 3a to 3c by the price index of goods consumed by Africans given at the end of Appendix 3 above.

[d] Figures after 1946 are average African earnings all grades, and are not therefore strictly comparable with the average earnings for African unskilled workers ('marginal money wages') quoted by the pre-1950 sources. See p. 117.

[e] This interpolation is made on the assumption that nearly all the wartime price changes affecting Africans had fed through by 1944; see NAR : ZBJ 1/1/2, p. 977, evidence of I. Lasovsky to the 1944 Native Production and Trade Commission.

Sources :

Mining Industry, 1898–1920 – NAR : LO 4/1/4, 4/1/14, 4/1/19, 4/1/28, 4/1/30, A 8/1/10 : Reports of the Mining Commissioner, Bulawayo for year stated.

    1920–1936 – Southern Rhodesia, *Annual Reports of the Chief Native Commissioner.*
    1937–1945 – Southern Rhodesia, *Economic and Statistical Bulletin,* 21 June 1946.

Agricultural workers, to 1947 – Table 4.9a above.

All data (except price index, for which see note c), 1942–55 – Barber 1961 (D2), Table 4, p. 273.

1956–63 – Southern Rhodesia, *Monthly Statistical Digest 1971,* Table 14, 'Average and total earnings of African employees'.

161

Table 4.9c. *Kenya: recorded monthly wage rates for different categories of African unskilled labour*

Year	(1) Agricultural labourers (unskilled)^b		(2) Public works department construction^b		(3) Indices of money wages (1914 = 100)			(4) Indices of real wages (1914 = 100)^e		
	(a) Excluding allowance for value of food supplied	(b) Including allowance for value of food supplied	(a) Excluding allowance for value of food supplied^g	(b) Including allowance for value of food supplied	(a) Agri-culture	(b) Public Service	(c) Composite^d	(a) Agri-culture	(b) Public Service	(c) Agriculture and public service composite
1903	4.0	8.0								
1904										
1905										
1906	5.4	13.4			71		77			
1907	5.4	13.4	6.0	14.0	71		77			
1908	5.4	13.4			71	93	77			
1909	6.0	13.0			70		75			
1910	7.0	15.6			82		88			
1911	7.0	15.0			80		86			
1912	10.8	15.8	7.0	15.0	100		100			
1913	10.8	15.8			100		100			
1914	10.8	18.8	7.0	15.0	100	100	100	100	100	100
1915										
1916	8.0	16.0			85		85	62		62
1917	7.0	15.0			80		80	51		51
1918										
1919										
1920	8.0	15.0			80		80	40		40
1921	10.0	17.0			91		91	35		35

162

Year										
1923		18.0	12.0	17.0	96	113	100	50	59	50
1924		20.0	14.0	21.0	106	140	114	50	65	50
1925										
1926	16.0	23.0	23.0	30.0	122	200	141	65	104	75
1927	16.0	23.0	23.0	30.0	122	200	141	75	123	87
1928	16.0	23.0	23.0	30.0	122	200	141	74	121	85
1929	16.0	21.0	16.0	21.0	112	140	119	68	85	73
1930	16.0	21.0	15.30	20.30	112	135	118	76	91	80
1931	(13.0)ʃ	18.0	18.0	23.50	96	156	111	81	132	94
1932	(10.0)ʃ	15.0	18.50	23.50	80	156	99	68	133	84
1933	8.0	13.0	18.50	23.50	70	156	92	66	147	87
1934	9.0	14.0	17.50	22.50	75	150	93	64	127	79
1935	9.0	14.0	17.50	22.50	75	150	93	69	137	85
1936	9.0	14.0	17.50	22.50	75	150	93	77	153	95
1937	11.50	16.50			88		110	80		100
1938	11.50	16.25			86		108	78		103
1939										
1940										
1941										
1942										
1943	10.0	20.0			106		138			(93)ʃ
1944										
1945	12.0	24.0			128		162	67		(88)ʃ
1946	6.0	28.0		33.0	149	220	172	77	117	91
1947										
1948										
1949										

163

Table 4.9c. (cont.)

Year	(1) Agricultural labourers (unskilled)[b]		Statutory urban minimum (Nairobi)[c]		Average African monthly earnings (cash and kind)[a]			(2) Public works department construction[b]		(3) Indices of money wages (1914 = 100)			(4) Indices of real wages (1914 = 100)[e]		
	(a) Excluding allowance for value of food supplied	(b) Including allowance for value of food supplied	Wage	Housing allowance	European agriculture	Private industry and commerce	Public service employment	(a) Excluding allowance for value of food supplied[g]	(b) Including allowance for value of food supplied	(a) Agriculture	(b) Public Service	(c) Composite[d]	(a) Agriculture	(b) Public Service	(c) Agriculture and public service composite
1950															
1951					(33.0)			(63.0)	(78.0)	176	520	290	61	179	100
1952					(36.0)			(73.0)	(86.0)	192	573	319	59	176	98
1953			52.50	7.0	(40.0)			(81.0)	(101.0)	213	673	366	66	207	113
1954			62.50	11.0	(41.0)			(93.0)	(103.0)	219	686	374	70	205	96
1955			75.0	17.50	(51.0)			(103.0)	(120.0)	272	800	448	77	216	123
1956			82.50	17.50	(53.0)			(113.0)	(123.0)	394	820	469			
1957			85.0	20.0											
1958			85.0	22.50											
1959			95.0	24.50	(56.0)			(143.0)	(156.0)	299	1040	546	75	260	136
1960			102.0	26.0											
1961			102.0	26.0											
1962			107.0	26.0											
1963			115.0	35.0						104	417	800	104	417	208

164

Notes:

[a] Figures in brackets are average African earnings, all grades, and not therefore strictly comparable with the average earnings for African *unskilled* workers ('marginal money wages') quoted by the pre-1950 sources (see p. 117 above)

[b] Before 1920 wages were paid in rupees and have been converted to shillings at the rate of Sh. 1.33 = 1 rupee. Immediately after the First World War, the rupee appreciated sharply, and was stabilised in 1921 at the rate of 1 rupee = 2 shillings, the shilling then becoming the colony's currency. For 1920 only, the conversion has been made at this exchange rate.

[c] Minimum Nairobi wages and housing allowances after 1955 apply to adults over twenty-one only.

[d] Money wage indices for agriculture and African public service employment are simply the figures in col. 1b and 2b expressed as percentage of their 1914 level. The 'composite index' of agricultural and public sector wages in col. 3c is a weighted average of the indices in cols. 3a and b, the weights being

    agriculture 3 : public sector employment 1 before 1939
    agriculture 2 : public sector employment 1 after 1939

these being approximations to the employment ratios in those industries (see Table 4.8b). In years where a value of the wage index for *either* agriculture *or* public sector employment only is reported, the value of the composite index is increased by the extent of the percentage change in the wage index for that activity.

[e] The real wage indices in col. 4 are computed by deflating the values given in cols. 3a to 3c by the price index of goods consumed by Africans given at the end of Appendix 3 above.

[f] Wartime real wage data are interpolations, as the Mombasa African price index is silent in the years between 1939 and 1947. The agricultural wage figures for 1931 and 1932 are also interpolated.

[g] Where a range is given for wages, the mid-point is taken. This only applies between 1926–9 and 1931–6.

Sources:

Agriculture, to 1949 – Table 4.9a.

Public sector, to 1949 – Kenya. *Blue Books*, various, except 1946 figure which is from Labour Department *Annual Report*.

All data : After 1949 (except price index used in calculating real wage. for which see note[f]) – East Africa Statistical Dept 1961a (B3) except 1964 figures which are from Kenya, *Statistical Abstract*, 1965.

It will be apparent from our discussion so far that only a minority of Africans during the colonial period were able to break free, through wage employment or agricultural production, from the strait-jacket of a family cash income not exceeding 20 shillings per month at 1914 prices.[56] The one way in which they could hope to do this without leaving the country was self-employment within the complex of activities which it has now become fashionable to describe as the informal sector.[57]

It is important to note at the start that the African informal sector comprised *two* sub-sectors, the first involved in trade, transport and other services, the second involved in manufacturing. Both had flourished, as is now well documented, during the pre-colonial period; both laboured throughout the colonial period under the common handicap of an educational policy which gave very little training in the skills which they required and a land policy which compressed them into areas of operation well away from their main potential markets. But, as we relate in what follows, their fortunes during the colonial period were diverse. The colonial government's dismissal of the African informal sector as economically unproductive, however, reacted back on the quality of the data which it collected, so that the story has to be put together from a mixture of doubtful statistics and somewhat anecdotal archival material.

In the pre-First World War period, African manufacturing and (in Southern Rhodesia) mining crumbled away under the stress of low-cost European competition. The lament of the Native Commissioner, Mrewa, in 1911 describes what was happening in every African district:

> With the exception of basket making and the preparation of tobacco for sale, there are no native industries of any importance in this district. The native blacksmith and worker in iron has practically gone, there is no further use for him, the trader's store supplies all and more he could ever produce and at a quarter of his price, and in twenty years' time the smelting of iron carried on to quite a great extent twenty years ago will be a lost art. Why smelt iron ore when you can pick up the material ready to hand on any scrap heap on farm or mine ... The woman potter still carries on her trade, but this also is gradually going; grease tins, old paint pots and cheap enamel ware is [*sic*] taking its place. The manufacture of wooden platters and mugs was once quite a trade, today in almost every kraal you find enamel ware from a saucer to a soup tureen and bedroom ware, and in place of the beautifully moulded little clay pots an empty herring tin ...[58]

Likewise, the African gold-mining pioneers in Southern Rhodesia were no longer able to make a living after the beginning of the twentieth century.[59]

But in trade things were different. Many Africans were able to ride on the back of the peasant agricultural boom that immediately preceded the First World War by providing the link between the producer and the trader with head load, donkey cart or (in some of the more prosperous parts of Matebeleland) ox-cart. By this means they were able to avoid being sucked into the labour market by paying their tax out of the profits of trade.[60]

During the First World War and the depression following it the situation was reversed. The export economy, and thus the growth of petty commodity trade which depended on it, ceased to expand; at the same time, the old indigenous manufacturing sector came to be re-created at a lower level in the African reserves as African real incomes fell during the First World War: 'The high cost of all goods has, to a certain extent, induced the natives to attempt manufacturing several articles previously purchased by them. In Lower Gwelo reserve hats are being made from palm leaves, native-made pipes are also replacing the imported article, and skins are being more generally used in the place of blankets.'[61]

The whole cycle, so far as we can tell, repeated itself during the years 1923–34. In the late 1920s, certainly, African trade expanded once again on the back of export agriculture. The 1926 annual report for Fort Hall District, Kenya records that: 'The Kikuyu are born traders; their aptitude for trade seems to grow year by year. Ten years ago it was doubtful if there was one native owned shop in the Reserve; last year there were perhaps seventy; this year 126 have been counted.'[62]

In Southern Rhodesia too, there was a large expansion in African trade. Reports from the Marandellas District gave the following figures for the number of wagons owned by Africans:

1926	23
1927	36 (also 'one man has purchased a Ford car')
1928	49

(*Source*: NAR: S 235/504–6, Annual Report for Marandellas District for 1926–8).

Meanwhile, in the same decade the manufacturing part of the informal sector vanished from sight, at any rate in the sources consulted by this study. In the middle 1920s attempts were made by both the Southern Rhodesian Department of Native Development and the Kenya Education Departments to foster craft skills which might be usable in the reserves[63] – as distinct from the mechanical, carpentering and bricklaying skills which might make him useful to the European – but in both cases these met settler opposition which in the inter-war depression was successful in getting such training reduced to a nominal level.

In 1930 in Southern Rhodesia we get, for the first time, an attempt at a statistical catalogue of the informal sector, which is repeated each year until 1946. If we pick the story up in 1932 we may observe both the sector's variety in the depths of the depression, and the extent to which the manufacturing part of it, as in the 1914–20 period, had mushroomed during a lean period for both crop and wage incomes:

The following figures, which show details of the natives in the Colony engaged in earning their own livelihood in trades and businesses, have an indicative value:

Baker	1	Kaross (leather bed cover) makers	20
Barber	1	Laundrymen	43
Blacksmiths	9	Mechanics	2
Bootblacks	5	Midwives	4
Bricklayers	70	Musicians	2
Builders	394	Painters	83
Butcher	1	Photographers	2
Carpenters	201	Plasterers	3
Plumbers	24	Charcoal burners	3
Clerks	41	Rickshaw owners	32
Cobblers	281	Sieve makers	11
Cycle repairers	36	Tailors	83
Dairymen	4	Taxi owners	23
Thatchers	36	Eating house keepers	27
Upholsterers	29	Tennis court maker	1
Watch menders	7	Fence erector	1
Market gardeners	62	Transport riders	22
General dealers	7	Hat and basket makers	21
Hawkers	145	Well sinkers	61
Herbalists	20	Wire workers	34
		Wood sellers	22

The total is 1834, as compared with 1586 last year and 861 in 1930.[64]

If the number of 'natives earning their own livelihood in trades and businesses' is graphed against the modern sector real wage rate, as derived from Table 4.9b, it turns out that the periods of fastest growth in African self-employment (1930–5 and 1944–7) were also periods of falling real wages. This suggests that informal services and, to a very limited degree, manufacturing, became during these periods, as it had been during the First World War, a refuge for Africans unwilling to accept, or unable to make ends meet on, real wages which had fallen from an already meagre level; the growth of this sector tended during the 1930s, we have suggested, to blunt the observed supply response of the African participation rate to real wages when they finally rose. For Kenya, we have no statistics, but King records on the basis of oral evidence that 'it was during the 1930s that ... from the whole range of Indian small enterprise (garages, blacksmithing, tinsmithing, tailoring, furniture and building, to mention only a few) there began to emerge Africans who had acquired elements of Indian skill. In all likelihood, such Africans were the first generation in their families to engage in craft activity'.[65] In a Kenya Legislative Council debate on 11 January 1946 an anxious speaker referred to the fact that 'the clothing industry, men's shirts and women's and children's garments, has been almost entirely usurped by hefty young [African] lads with sewing machines sitting on verandas throughout the reserves';[66] he, like our own analysis (p. 124 above) drew a connection between the growth of this activity and the fact that even wage increases now sometimes did not elicit any increase in labour supplies.

The 1930s and 1940s were a period of rapid urbanisation, and during it what had previously been perceived as the problem of the 'detribalised native' came to be seen, definitively, as the urban native problem. Towards the end of it, in Southern Rhodesia, we have both the first sample social survey of the African population and the first systematic enquiry into African production and trade. The former, the Urban African Survey of 1942/3, found that 18 451 unmarried urban Africans out of a sample total of 26 494, or 69 per cent, were below a 'poverty line' of £2 per month; 973 out of 1076 married Africans, or 91 per cent, received less than the minimum requirements for a family of four of £4.15s.0d. per month.[67] These figures reinforce the impression of a drift into informal economic activity in the later war years as a desperate measure to make the family budget balance. The evidence to the latter, the Native Production and Trade Commission of 1944, gives an idea of the intensity of the competition within the urban informal sector:

> *Chairman:* What do you intend trading?
> *Charles Mzengele (Native Labour Party):* As a grocer.
> *Chairman:* Have you learned that trade somewhere?
> – I was doing it some time ago.
> – Trading on your own?
> – Yes.
> – Why did you stop?
> – I had some trouble and financial difficulty in 1941 and I lost the place I was renting. In Salisbury when we trade we have to hire our own buildings from the Indian people. I was paying £5 and somebody went behind my back and offered £6.10/-. Sometimes somebody will offer as much as £12.10/-.
> – You did not have enough capital?
> – I could not afford to pay rent. That was the trouble with the business, there was too much competition.
> – They did not give you a lease?
> – No, they knew what it would mean, and they preferred to make a gentleman's agreement.
> – Who took it from you?
> – Another African.
> – Is he still there?
> – No, they don't last there. They kick out one after another.[68]

At this point it is necessary to consider, briefly, the influence of land policy on the nature of the informal sector. In spite of warnings as early as the 1920s that 'in time the Natives will become industrialists',[69] neither Kenya nor Southern Rhodesia at this stage provided accommodation for the African except as labouring worker, and usually migrant worker at that. The possibility that he might require land in the town on which to cultivate or otherwise carry on his own business had been consciously foreseen and foreclosed by both Morris Carter Land Commissions.[70] In Southern Rhodesia, under the Land Apportionment Act, urban land was specifically demarcated on a racial basis; in Kenya, it was technically open to bids for the freehold by all races, but the barriers imposed by the cost of acquisition of land confined African small-scale production to waste ground and the surroundings of designated African market places. This is the historical context of King's statement (made in relation to Nairobi, but equally valid for Salisbury) that 'the very conspicuousness of the informal sector ... is the result of a town planning constraint from the colonial period which did not anticipate the rise of the African petty producer'.[71]

The post-Second World War period is distinctive as being the only period in the economic history of the settler economies in which the relation between informal manufacturing and the real wage was not inverse. As King notes: 'the period around the late 1950s and early 1960s saw a major move towards what could be called the creation of an [sc. informal] artisan layer in African society'.[72]

But this happened more quickly in Kenya than in Southern Rhodesia. In Kenya the emergency of 1952–7 brought about a labour shortage, a consequent increase in real wages and a scattering of African artisanal skills into the rural areas. In Southern Rhodesia, by constrast, in the absence of this internal shock to the economy and in the presence of the Land Apportionment Act, the vicious circle of largely migrant labour and standardised single-person accommodation unsuitable for workshop activity was harder to escape from. In neither country, it should be added, did the colonial government do anything to help the informal sector or treat it as an asset rather than a liability. Typical was the attitude of A.G. Dalgleish, Permanent Secretary in the Kenya Ministry of Commerce and Industry, as expressed only twenty years ago:

> Mention must be made of the *problem* presented by the large number of Africans who are seemingly unemployed, but who are frequently in self-employment, often of a kind which is perilously close to the borderline of legality. In Nyanza, in particular, there are many itinerant hucksters who *take advantage*, for example, of the large quantities of produce being brought in by gullible peasants to act as middlemen and to *bedevil* the marketing of produce.[73]

Such attitudes, almost universally held by the colonial authorities, have themselves bedevilled not only the growth of the African informal sector, but also all but the broad outlines of our knowledge concerning its growth.

5

European agriculture

5.1. INTRODUCTION

European agriculture in the settler economies is striking in that it does not conform to the principle, stated for example by Chenery (1960 (D3)), that agriculture declines in relative importance as economic development proceeds. In 1925 the share of European agriculture in Southern Rhodesian national income was estimated at 15.1 per cent; in 1955, after thirty years of rapid economic growth, it was still 14 per cent.[1] In Kenya European agriculture's share of total domestic *exports* in 1926 (we have no national income data) was 62.7 per cent; in 1961 the figure was 64.8 per cent.[2] However, within the sector there was a profound structural shift (Table 5.1) from a position in which maize occupied a predominant share of total acreage in the 1920s, to a position at the beginning of the 1960s in which European agriculture was dominated by plantation crops.

No systematic description of the European farming economy covering the colonial period has to our knowledge been attempted, although there do exist a general historical survey of agriculture in Kenya with a bias towards the European sector (Cone and Lipscomb 1972 (D1)) and an economic survey of post-Second World War European farming in Southern Rhodesia (Dunlop 1971 (D2)). However, as a by-product of studies of policy-making, African agriculture and other topics, a stereotype of the white farmer has emerged, which threatens to become almost as widespread as once the stereotype of the 'economically irrational African' was in the settler economies themselves. The principal elements of this stereotype are that the white settler-farmer was, first of all, inefficient, in relation both to other countries and what was necessary to keep him competitive on a free home market.[3] The elaborate structure of subsidies and restraints on competition set up to protect white farming in the 1930s, discussed in Chapter 2.2 above (pp. 43–58), is seen as both consequence[4] and continuing cause of this inefficiency. Secondly, the white settler-farmer was seen as under-capitalised, as a consequence of the colonial government's anxiety to promote settlement in any shape or form (discussed in Chapter 2.2 above);[5] and thirdly, he was labour-intensive (a condition accentuated by the perceived cheapness of African labour).[6]

170

Table 5.1a. *Southern Rhodesia and Kenya: share of particular farming activities in European agriculture by value of output*

	Southern Rhodesia					Kenya				
	Value of European agricultural production (£ million)	Percentage share of particular agricultural products in total value of output				Value of European agricultural exports (£ million)	Percentage share of particular agricultural products in total value of exports			
		Maize	Tobacco	Beef	Other		Maize	Coffee	Sisal	Other
1924	1.7	38.0	22.7	13.4	25.9	1.6	22.4	40.7	21.6	15.3
1961	55.6	13.8	55.7	12.4	18.1	22.8	4.5	19.7	17.9	57.9

Sources:
Southern Rhodesia – *Statistical Yearbook of the Colony of Southern Rhodesia for 1924*; *Agricultural Production in Rhodesia*, 1965 edition.
Kenya – *Agricultural Census*, 1924; Kenya and Uganda Customs Department, *Annual Report* 1924; East Africa Customs Department, *Annual Trade Report* 1961; Kenya, *European Agricultural Census* 1961.

Table 5.1b. *Southern Rhodesia and Kenya: share of particular farming activities in European agriculture (crop husbandry only)*

	Southern Rhodesia				Kenya				
	Total acreage under European cultivation (thousand acres)	Percentage share of particular crops in total acreage			Total acreage under European cultivation (thousand acres)	Percentage share of particular crops in total acreage			
		Maize	Tobacco	Other		Maize	Coffee	Sisal	Other
1922/3	167	79.9	3.3	16.8	274	36.4	19.0	14.2	30.4
1961/2	934	43.5	21.0	35.5	1204	13.1	6.1	22.6	58.2

Sources: as for Table 5.1a.

The principal purpose of this chapter is to examine, within the usual constraints of available data, the accuracy of this stereotype. Section 2 considers efficiency, the first element in the stereotype, and some of the political consequences of differences in efficiency; section 3 considers factor proportions, which embraces the second and third elements in the stereotype, their relationship to the policies of intervention in the market for factors of production discussed in Chapter 2, and some of the implications of the production function (i.e. set of factors of production) actually chosen for other sectors of the economy. The emphasis throughout will be on maize and beef production, these being the two sectors of the economy on which attention was focused in Chapters 2 and 3; but in order to try and counteract the inevitably biased picture of the sector which this procedure will give, we include where possible cross-references to the position in the principal 'plantation crops': coffee in Kenya, and tobacco in Southern Rhodesia.

5.2 ECONOMIC PERFORMANCE

Overall performance: the data

In Table 5.2a and b we compare mean yields per acre in maize and plantation crops (coffee and tobacco) as between the settler economies and other major producing countries. The data contradict the stereotype view that European agriculture in the settler economies was *uniformly* less efficient, on a basis of yield per acre, than elsewhere. In the inter-war period, maize yields are about the same in Kenya and Southern Rhodesia as those in the USA and Australia, superior to those of the Danube basin, and clearly inferior only to those achieved in Argentina. During the Second World War the settler economies begin to lag behind the USA and Australia, but Southern Rhodesia almost catches up due to increased use of hybrid seed in the later 1950s. Coffee yields on Kenyan coffee estates consistently equalled, and in the 1950s exceeded, those of Brazil. Southern Rhodesia tobacco yields were (except during the 1940s) about the same as in Australia, but consistently well below American levels.

Although mean levels of yield, therefore, were not except in the case of Southern Rhodesia tobacco lower than in the main producing countries of the world, the dispersion of yields around these mean levels does seem to have been wider than elsewhere – particularly in those activities such as maize farming and cattle rearing where there were relatively few minimum-capital-cost barriers to entry – and the concentration of production in the hands of a few big operators (i.e. the skewness of the distribution) greater than elsewhere.

For the period before 1950 these points have to be made impressionistically, as statistics on the distribution of European farmers by production and

172

Table 5.2a. *Maize, yields per acre: Southern Rhodesia and Kenya in relation to other producing countries, 1920–60 (five-year average)*

Period	Southern Rhodesia			Kenya			Other producing countries (yields in bags per acre)[b]				
	Acreage under maize (000 acres)	Production (000 bags of 200 lb)	Yield (bags per acre)[a]	Acreage under maize (000 acres)	Production (000 bags of 200 lb)	Yield (bags per acre)[a]	United States of America	Australia[a]	Argentina	S. Africa (European production)	Rumania
1920–4	211	1107	5.22	60	435	7.25	7.63	6.89			
1925–9	293	1584	5.42	169	1064	6.30	7.27	6.64	7.44	2.75	
1930–4	254	1494	5.81	174	1231	7.05	6.10	7.28			
1935–9	267	1658	6.21	108	856	7.92	6.89	6.17	8.26	3.38	4.78
1940–4	243	1723	5.91	101	495	4.90	8.81	6.93			
1945–9	290	1492	5.11	119	595	5.01	9.83	7.37	8.02	3.36	
1950–4	358	2283	6.34	152	828	5.22	10.62	7.63			
1955–9	353	3554	10.07	154	888	5.77	12.24	8.99			

Notes:
[a]The averages given in the case of Southern Rhodesia, Kenya and Australia are for the *crop years* which began in the year stated in the left-hand margin, i.e. the figures for '1920–4' are an average of the results from crop year 1920/1 to crop year 1924/5. For other countries they are calendar year figures.
[b]'Other producing countries' figures are converted from bushels at the rate 1 bushel = 56 lb.
Sources: Southern Rhodesia – Southern Rhodesia 1931 (B2), Appendix D; Federation of Rhodesia and Nyasaland 1963a(B2), Appendix II. Kenya, production figures – Kenya 1966(B3); acreage figures – *Kenya Agricultural Census*, various issues. Other countries – Southern Rhodesia 1950a(B2) pp. 51 and 125, supplemented by *Historical statistics of the US: colonial times to 1957* (US Department of Commerce, 1960), Tables K265–K273; *Official Year-book of the Commonwealth of Australia*, 1931, p. 491; 1941, p. 475; 1951, p. 438; 1961, p. 888; US Department of Agriculture, *Agricultural Statistics* 1953.

Table 5.2b. *Plantation crops, yields per acre: Southern Rhodesia and Kenya in relation to other producing countries, 1920–60 (five-year averages)*

| | Coffee | | | | | Tobacco (Virginia type only) | | | | |
| | Kenya | | | Other producing countries (yields in cwt per acre) | | Southern Rhodesia | | | Other producing countries (yields in lb per acre) | |
Period	Acreage under coffee (000 acres)	Exports (000 cwt)	Yield (cwt per acre)	Brazil	Colombia	Acreage under tobacco (000 acres)	Production (000 lb)	Yield (lb per acre)	USA	Australia
1920–4	43	115	2.67			8	3 030	378	790	
1925–9	76	168	2.21			21	11 027	525	772	
1930–4	99	254	2.56	3.56		35	16 613	474	785	419
1935–9[a]	97	319	3.28	3.14		49	25 390	518	882	508
1940–4	–	175	–			67	38 876	580	1020	685
1945–9[b]	57	176	3.05	3.17		125	73 493	587	1179	797
1950–4	69	274	3.98	3.06[c]		170	103 142	606	1291	805
1955–9	64	407	6.37	3.27	4.15[d]	196	156 123	796	1515	804

– no data

Notes:

[a] Three-year average, 1935, 1937 and 1939 (no census in even years).
[b] Three-year average, 1947–9 (no census in 1945 or 1946).
[c] Four-year average, omitting 1952.
[d] Three-year average, 1955–7.

Sources:

Kenya (before 1939, also 1955–9) – *Agricultural Censuses*, various; 1947–55 – Hill 1956 (D1). Appendix C, pp. 198–203 (where Coffee Marketing Board data is used).

Brazil – Instituto Brasileiro de Geografia e Estatística, *Anuario Estatístico de Brasil*, 1937, pp. 205, 209; 1950, p. 93; 1960, p. 56.

Colombia – FAO, *Coffee in Latin America*, vol. I (Colombia and El Salvador, 1958).

Southern Rhodesia – Agriculture Department, *Annual Report* (for data prior to 1945); *Annual Report and Accounts of the Rhodesia Tobacco*

yield are not available on a regular basis (see Appendix 6 below), but the collective weight of evidence is suggestive. On the matter of *dispersion*, the yield of Southern Rhodesia maize farmers varied so much as early as 1903 that 'figures on costs ranged from 2s. 7½d. [per 200 1b bag] to as high as 13s. 9d. per bag, according to a report in the *Rhodesia Herald* for 27 June 1903, and by 1907 5/- per bag was considered easily within the means of the bigger producers with 8/6d. as a fair average';[7] twenty-seven years later the range of yields on a sample of farms ran from 5.3 to 12.5 bags per acre, the mean level being estimated at 8 bags.[8] In Kenya in 1918 one farmer gave average costs of production at Sh. 10.50 per bag,[9] free on rail, but in the same year a telegram was to advise the Colonial Secretary that 'East Africa maize could not be sold at profit [by many farmers] at £3.50 per quarter',[10] i.e. Sh. 23.30 per bag. On the matter of *concentration*, in 1933 the four biggest stockowners in Southern Rhodesia (that is, 1.4 per cent of those on the role of the Stockowners' Association) owned 54 per cent of the European cattle herd.[11] The two biggest ranchers of the inter-war period in Kenya, Gilbert Colvile and Brian Curry, owned about one-third of the European herd.[12] In 1921 in Southern Rhodesia, the seventeen largest farmers (8 per cent of the members of the Maize Association) contributed 195 000 bags or almost half (45.4 per cent) of the total European crop.[13] In Kenya, one maize farmer alone, S.H. Powles, was producing in the 1930s 'an average of 50,000–80,000 bags'[14] out of a European crop which averaged, during the decade, under a million bags. We know, also, that the larger farmers

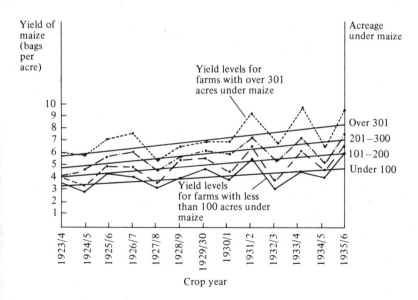

Fig. 5.1 Southern Rhodesia 1923–36: yield per acre by size of maize lands. *Source*: adapted from Southern Rhodesia 1939b (B2).

were the most efficient. Powles was, in 1943, 'rather disappointed' by a yield of 14 bags per acre, in a year when the average maize yield amongst European farmers was 5.6 bags per acre;[15] Colvile and Curry's steers killed out at an average of 900 lb whereas the average European animals killed out at between 400 and 600 lb;[16] most detailed of all, there exists a graph in the cyclostyled Report of the (Southern Rhodesia) Economic Development Committee of 1939, reproduced as Figure 5.1 here, which shows clearly that in the inter-war period the largest farmers were not only the most productive but also the most progressive in the sense that the trend rate of growth of their yields was highest. I have not, unfortunately, found it possible to trace the raw data on which this graph was based.

After 1948 the data improve. In Southern Rhodesia we have, for the first time, statistical returns which enable us to plot the distribution of maize farmers by yield. This is done in Figure 5.2 for *average* yields over the six crop years 1949/50 to 1954/5, in order to eliminate the effects of freak years (such as 1951, a drought year).

Figure 5.2 gives an indication of the skewness of the yield distribution: one-eighth of the growers reap 40 per cent of the crop (which is a slight levelling-up from the position in 1921); conversely, an estimated two-thirds of the growers[17] are below the mean yield level.

The dispersion of yields in grain crops was far greater than in crops which had to be traded on the world market; for example, Table 5.3 demonstrates that the dispersion (as measured by the coefficient of variation) of yields of

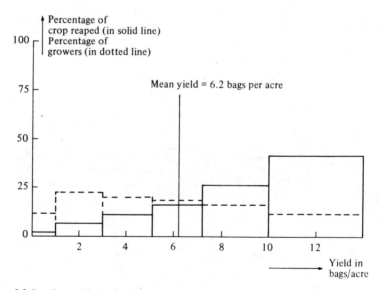

Fig. 5.2 Southern Rhodesia: European maize growers, six-year average 1949/50–1954/5, distribution by yield group and percentage of crop reaped. *Source*: as for Table 5.3.

Table 5.3. *Southern Rhodesia, European maize and tobacco growers: distribution by yield, average of crop years 1949/50 to 1954/5*

Maize growers				Tobacco growers			
Yield category	Number	Per cent of all maize growers	Per cent of total maize crop reaped	Yield category	Number	Per cent of all tobacco growers	Per cent of total flue-cured crop
10 bags per acre and over	512	12.6	41.1	1001 lb per acre and over	98	4.0	7.1
7 bags and under 10	622	15.3	25.4	701 to 1000 lb	662	27.2	38.8
5 bags and under 7	731	18.0	16.3	401 to 700 lb	1189	48.9	46.3
3 bags and under 5	813	20.0	10.9	Up to 400 lb	483	19.9	7.8
1 bag and under 3	909	22.4	5.7				
Under 1 bag	329	8.1	0.5				
No yield	139	3.4	–				
Totals	4055	100	100		2432	100	100

Mean yield = 6.20 bags per acre
Standard deviation of yield[a] = 3.88 bags per acre
Coefficient of variation = 62.61%

Mean yield = 627 lb per acre
Standard deviation of yield[a] = 251 lb per acre
Coefficient of variation = 40.08%

Notes: [a] To calculate standard deviation, data within closed class intervals are assumed to cluster at the mid-point. Data within uppermost (open) class interval are assumed to cluster at the mean yield for growers within that class interval, i.e. 12.72 bags per acre for maize, 1116 lb per acre for tobacco.

Source: Central African Statistical Office, *Report on the agricultural and pastoral production of Southern Rhodesia* 1955, Tables VII and XI.

Southern Rhodesian maize farmers was, during the period covered by Figure 5.2, half as large again as the dispersion of tobacco farmers' yields.

Our contention, therefore, is that what is truly distinctive of at any rate the maize growing part of the settler agricultural economy is not so much its low *average* efficiency (in the sense of output per acre)[18] as the very wide *range* of efficiency levels which it managed to contain and the skewness of the distribution within this range, with a minority of highly efficient, frequently foreign-owned[19] concerns counter-balancing (in the sense of total output) a majority of inefficient farmers who obtained below-average yields. It is this majority of inefficient, amateur, farmers in the tail of the yield distribution on whom previous scholarly, and popular,[20] writing on European agriculture has focused, and they supply the basis for the stereotype of the

177

settler-farmer described above. What the stereotype in fact described, it appears, is the modal farmer; not mean levels of achievement. There remains, however, the question of how the inefficient tail of the distribution was able not only to survive but to wag vigorously in face of the threats to its survival which it encountered in particular at times of depressed export prices. It turns out that a large part of the answer can be found in the political measures discussed in Chapter 2 above, and that the picture of political alignments on matters of economic policy presented there can be refined by considering the political relationship between the efficient and the inefficient producers.

Finance, marketing and their effects on European productivity

In the days before the network of branch railway lines was fully spread, and when the high cost of ox-cart transport caused the national maize market to be fragmented into a cluster of regional sub-markets each with a different ruling price for maize, the persistence of a wide spread between the most efficient and the least efficient producers, as noted in notes 7–10, is nothing surprising. With the extension of the railway network and the increased use of motor lorries during the 1920s, however, these markets became more integrated, and it became more easily possible for large and efficient producers to undercut small and inefficient ones – European and African – in supplying isolated local markets, e.g. mines and coffee plantations.[21] But the 1920s were a period of generally rising maize prices (see Table 4.3 above) and with the 1928/9 world price, for maize, at 11 shillings[22] it was comfortably possible for the farmer with a yield of six bags per acre to break even.[23] When the depression came, the fall in world prices to a 1930–40 average of 6.23 shillings per bag, free on rail, should in principle have weeded out those producers for the market who had yields of less than eleven bags per acre, assuming that all producers were able to hold costs at their 1930 levels. How far this was from happening is well demonstrated by Table 5.2: in Kenya European average maize yields rose, but only slightly, to 7.9 bags per acre in 1935–9; in Southern Rhodesia they stayed more or less constant, and averaged 6.2 bags per acre over that period. This owes much to policies in the field of agricultural credit and marketing, which we now examine.

Southern Rhodesia had had an agricultural bank, set up by the British South Africa Company, since 1912. Like the commercial banks operating there and in Kenya, it functioned on 'conventional commercial principles' – i.e. it advanced long-term credit only for development works, at commercial interest rates[24] against approved security, and thus was of little help to the farmer requiring short-term credit and without substantial capital assets to pledge. Joint-stock company development was similarly out of the question for such individuals, and there was thus a gap in the credit structure to be filled if the European areas of the colonies were to be developed on a basis of individually owned farms. In 1924 the Land and Agricultural Bank of

178

Southern Rhodesia was set up, lending at lower interest rates and against riskier securities, typically the farmer's crop of the following year. Seven years later, after a number of abortive petitions to the Colonial Office,[25] a Kenya Land Bank was set up on the basis of a loan raised in London with a capital of £240 000. It charged farmers $6\frac{1}{2}$ per cent interest as against the 8 per cent of the commercial banks, and three additional features of its policy are worth noting. Firstly, it lent, certainly during the depression years, largely for purposes of granting farmers relief from immediate financial distress, rather than for development; in its first full year of operations (1932), 18.7 per cent of loans were granted for permanent improvements, and 39 per cent specifically for the discharge of existing mortgages.[26] Secondly, Land Bank loans were confined to a ceiling of £3000, eventually raised to £5000 in 1936 after pressures from sisal and coffee planters; but, as Heyer notes, such small sums were of little use to the sisal planter whose machinery alone cost £8000.[27] Thirdly, *within* the group of maize, wheat and livestock farmers whom Land Bank loans were in a position to help it was the policy of the Agricultural Advances Board, administered by the Land Bank, 'to help as many farmers as possible with comparatively small amounts rather than a few with large sums'.[28]

The Southern Rhodesian Land Bank, also, operated according to the criteria of sheltering the neediest producers rather than encouraging the most efficient. In 1934, in fact, another bureaucratic tier of state agricultural credit had to be thrown beneath the existing one as the result of farmers' inability to repay their Land Bank advances. Following a recommendation of the Danziger Committee (Southern Rhodesia 1934 (B2)), a Farmers' Debt Adjustment Board, a majority of whose members consisted of the Board of the Land Bank, was set up to arrange where necessary the re-scheduling of repayments.

The Kenyan farmers tried, initially without success, to imitate this Rhodesian precedent. In 1936 they requested machinery for the discharge of existing obligations by means of government bonds, involving a virtual moratorium on repayment for five years.[29] This they were refused, but informally it was reported that 'the majority of secured creditors have extended a large measure of consideration to debtors during the period of depression. Rates of interest have in many cases been reduced or interest waived for a period, and few actions for foreclosure have been intensified'.[30] And in 1942, in addition, Kenya cereal farmers were granted the thickest insulation from market forces offered to any group of producers in the settler economies during the colonial period by means of the Guaranteed Minimum Return system, which offered not only a guaranteed pre-planting price but also 'advances of up to eighty per cent of the Guaranteed Minimum Return for the scheduled crops for which they have been given planting orders'[31] by the district production committees empowered under the Increased Production of Crops Ordinance to vet each European farmer's production plans.[32] The KFA also began, during the late 1930s, to offer its members credit

179

The settler economies

facilities. After 1945 the role of the Land Banks in propping up the inefficient parts of the European farming community waned, as high post-war
prices floated existing farmers away from the risk of bankruptcy and stringent
capital requirements were imposed on new settlers.[33] But their role in
preserving an otherwise non-viable segment of the settler community in the
period 1930–45 was clearly important, although it should be emphasised
that financial constraints precluded the possibility of Land Bank lending
being of a strictly counter-cyclical kind: it was in fact lower during the 1930s
depression than at other times.[34]

Supporting the Land Banks in the role of protecting the inefficient farmer
were government measures acting not on the input but on the output side, by
raising the price the European farmer received. As they relate to maize,
and cattle (to which they were largely confined, since only these and other
cereal crops were sold on the manipulable local market), these have been
described in Chapter 2 above.

The mere existence of protective measures, of course, tended to shelter
the inefficient; it is worth recalling, however, that some of them were explicitly conceived to give greater help to the smaller and therefore least efficient
farmers. The shares of Southern Rhodesia white maize farmers in the high-
priced local pool, under the Maize Control Amendment Act of 1934, were
inversely proportional to their size,[35] the Chairman of the Maize Board
making it clear at the time that the objective of the sliding scale was 'to
assist small producers and to reduce materially the surplus production of
large growers in excess of local requirements'.[36] The Southern Rhodesia
Cold Storage Commission's grazier scheme, and the destocking measures of
1938 which made it possible for European ranchers to obtain cattle at
artificially depressed prices, were explicitly conceived so as to help the small
ranchers who could not afford to buy from Africans on the open market. It
may therefore be said with some confidence that the distinctive credit and
marketing policies of the settler economies' governments, in particular in
the 1930s and 1940s, played an important part in preserving the distinctive
long 'tail' at the left-hand end of the yield distribution for locally marketed
foodstuffs, which market forces might otherwise have eliminated.

The politics of economic viability

By policies such as those just described the governments of the settler economies were able to give the objective of maximising the white population a
substantial boost in relation to the rival objective of economic efficiency, in
the sense of maximising output per unit input. The trade-off between size of
population and economic efficiency had particular emotional weight for
white Kenyan and Rhodesian agriculturists, because a policy of putting
economic efficiency first implied not only a risk to many of their own liveli-
hoods but also an enhancement of that settler's bogy, 'control from London'.
In 1938, when the local market was small, the latter policy, implying the

180

extinction of the individually run farm, seemed an inevitable outcome in Kenya to one influential observer, E.W. Bovill, the Secretary of Agriculture:

> The economic development apart from native production and secondary production by Europeans, will probably be along the following lines:
> (1) confining of each form of agriculture to the developments which have proved most suitable.
> (2) conversion of small holdings into large by expansion and amalgamation.
> (3) passing of primary production into the hands of those who control ample financial resources and insist on [applying] strict commercial principles to the whole production process.
> If development follows these lines it means that primary production will pass out of the hands of the owner-manager into those of plantation companies most of which would, we may presume, be under London control.
> To the majority of settlers this is a foul heresy which threatens all that they hold most dear. The average Kenyan farmer has sunk his all in the country to which he is in consequence closely attached. He is esentially an individualist (otherwise he would not be here) taking an intense pride in ownership and convinced that given a fair chance – at present denied him by superior authority and predatory combines – he can work out his own salvation.
> He rightly realises that the plantation system means that he, the farmer, must surrender his independence to become the servant of others, his cherished homestead become a mere manager's house – and an independent community pass under the tutelage of remote financial magnates of whose honesty of purpose he has the gravest suspicions.[37]

In Southern Rhodesia, where the local market was larger, the policy makers refused to contemplate the euthanasia of the 'homesteader', but they were sufficiently apprehensive of his survival, as we have seen, to propose the partitioning of the local market for food according to products between Europeans and Africans.[38]

The Second World War and post-war boom, of course, enlarged the local market, and lifted world prices to a point where the latent conflict between economic efficiency and a large white community, between 'homesteader' and international capital, no longer appeared as a zero-sum game. But it is worth exploring the various manifestations of that conflict a little further, not only because it reveals a political dimension to the ultra-wide distribution of farming abilities within the settler community, but also because it enables us to shed a little more light on the hitherto neglected and shadowy figure of the efficient agricultural settler. The two main elements of intra-settler conflict over economic policy were the extent of government intervention and wages policy. The latter has been discussed in Chapter 4 above, we now discuss the former, and it will help our exposition to identify the 'efficient' settlers and consider the stand which they took on these matters.

Stephen Powles was manager of a group of maize farms (among other interests: he also kept a sheep farm and rose to run the East African Standard groups of newspapers) on behalf of an English company, the Howard de Walden interests, in the Trans Nzoia region of Kenya from 1924 to 1963.

These farms were big enough for him to be able to consider, during the Second World War, that 'if we left the KFA we could dominate the European maize position'.[39] As an efficient farmer well to the right-hand end of the efficiency spectrum set out in Figure 5.2, he was 'astonished' by the low yields obtained by a number of European maize farmers[40] and was no more acquiescent to their demands for statutory protection than the coffee and sisal farmers had been when faced with a draft maize control bill in 1936.[41] Never sympathetic to the need for maize control in the first place,[42] he nonetheless accepted co-option to the Board of Maize Control in 1942 in the hope of exercising a moderating influence from within on upward pressures on the price. The story of his lack of success is best told in his own words:

> 15 January 1943. Attended a very hot meeting about the price of maize. I told them that I thought they were being absurd in asking for a 3/- increase [from the current posted price of 9 shillings] and that 11/- + increased costs would be a fair thing for the 1943 crop instead of the 12/- + which the meeting was demanding. As was to be expected I got a thoroughly rough time for my trouble. A resolution was passed asking me to resign from the Production and Maize Boards ...
>
> 21 January 1943. D[irector of] A[griculture] came to drinks. He told me that Government intended to give way to the clamour over maize prices – as I thought Government in the right and stood up for it this makes me feel rather sad and rather foolish.[43]

It was not only in the market for maize that Powles found himself professing *laissez-faire* in face of entrenched interests whose viability depended on an existing pattern of extra-market operations. In 1948 he 'Saw General Edwards of the Meat Marketing Board. He remained quite firm in his refusal to allow us to buy in Nandi, saying quite frankly, that if he is to feed the urban population, the Board must retain parts of its monopolistic position'.[44] But most radically of all, he deprecated the idea of a racially closed market in White Highland land. Twice he deplored the exercise of the Governor's veto on transfers of Highland land to Indians,[45] the second time explicitly on the grounds that it was *depressing* land values, but by 1952 he had come round to the view that it would be better 'to allow well-to-do Africans, not Indians, to buy land in the Highlands provided they came under the same control as Europeans against fragmentation of holdings and bad farming',[46] against the opposition of the white agrarian majority to whom the Highlands Order in Council was a Bill of Rights.

An appropriate Rhodesian analogue to Powles is Robert Gilchrist, a large-scale rancher from Hartley district and Member of the Legislative Assembly. Like Powles he was efficient enough to be able to espouse *laissez-faire* ideology (which, since in general Africans had everything to gain from an open market, enabled him to pose with more or less sincerity as sympathetic to their cause). In evidence to the 1925 Land Commission he protested, in face of the 'small men's' demands for tightened restrictions on African entry into the commercial beef market,[47] that 'if we are going to make a success of our export trade then we want every beast that a native can produce'.[48] Thirteen years later, in evidence to the Commission on Sales of Native Cattle, he was to deplore the discrimination between Africans and Europeans in the manner of marketing cattle, insisting that 'a fair price . . . is not . . . being paid to the natives'.[49]

Finally, like Powles, he was to advocate openness in markets other than the one in which he himself traded. In the debate over the first (1931) Southern Rhodesia Maize Control Bill he was to make himself highly unpopular by his suggestion that 'the prosperity of Rhodesian agriculture might well be based on maize grown at 4/- a bag – not by the European, but by the native'.[50] But Gilchrist's economic strength, like Powles', did not prevent his political failure. In defiance of his advocacy of a free maize market the Southern Rhodesian government was to show its implicit agreement with the counter-argument that state intervention was needed to preserve a 'viable' white agricultural community. Indeed, the *laissez-faire* pressure group of efficient white producers was politically potent only to the extent that the policy they desired corresponded with one of the *sectoral* interests described in Chapter 2 above, as in the case of the argument over statutory control of the Kenyan maize market in the 1930s. Only in areas which allowed of individual option, such as wage policy, was it possible for the 'large and efficient' group to adopt a line of economic policy which departed from the sectoral norm.

5.3 FACTOR PROPORTIONS AND THEIR RELATIONSHIP TO POLICY

The structure of this section is as follows. We present, in Table 5.4, a fragmentary picture of the 'production function' – the input structure – of European agriculture in the settler economies across the period 1923–55, using the agricultural economy of the USA and Britain as a basis for comparison. This enables us, in passing, to enquire to what extent the stereotypical picture of the settler economy as labour-intensive and undercapitalised is an accurate one. We then proceed to examine specific elements of the input structure, in particular the capital–labour ratio, and influences (above all policy-related ones) acting upon it.

The figures of Table 5.4, which list the stocks of certain important agricultural inputs (cultivated land, hired labour, tractors, combine harvesters) in relation to total output for each country and year, confirm the stereotype of labour-intensity and capital-scarcity, if US and British agriculture are taken as points of reference. The labour coefficients per £000 value of gross farm revenue for the USA, Britain, Southern Rhodesia and Kenya are in the ratio $1:1\frac{1}{4}:15:38$ in 1923; in 1955 these ratios are very similar, at $1:2:17:38$, since although the agricultural sectors of Britain and the USA have been progressively shedding labour and those of the settler economies

Table 5.4. *European agriculture in Southern Rhodesia and Kenya, with international comparisons: factor proportions*

	(1)	(2)	(3)	Labour intensity (a) (4)	Labour intensity (b) (5)
	Labour[a] (thousands)	Tractors (thousands)	Combine harvesters and threshing machines (thousands)	Labour per tractor	Labour per £000 of output[b]
Kenya					
1923	70.9	0.13	0.086	545.3	73.0
1930	120.2	1.39	0.302	86.4	–
1945	118.3	–	–	–	–
1955	246.1	5.06	–	48.6	15.0
Southern Rhodesia					
1923	59.0	–	–	–	35.0
1930	67.0	–	–	–	–
1945	130.6	–	–	–	–
1955	189.6	8.1	–	23.4	6.7
USA					
1923	3364	428	–	7.9	2.3
1930	3190	920	61	3.5	–
1945	2119	2354	375	0.9	–
1955	2017	4345	980	0.46	0.4
Great Britain					
1923	772	–	–	–	2.9
1930	–	–	–	–	–
1945	515	177	2.8	2.9	–
1955	505	334	21.1	1.51	0.62

– no data

Notes:

[a] Kenya and Southern Rhodesia: African labour only. USA: 'labourers and foremen'.
[b] For the purposes of calculating this column for USA figures, dollar values are converted to
£ sterling at the rate $4.86 = £1.00 (1923)
                    $4.00 = £1.00 (1930 and 1945)
                    $2.80 = £1.00 (1955)

Sources:

Kenya, labour – Table 4.8b; tractors and combine harvesters – *Agricultural Census.*
Southern Rhodesia, labour – Table 4.8a; tractors – Central African Statistical Office, *Report of the agricultural and pastoral production of Southern Rhodesia,* 1955.
USA, before 1955 – *Historical statistics of the US: colonial times to 1957* (US Department of Commerce, 1960), pp. 277, 280, 284, 285, 1955 – *Statistical Abstract of the US,* 1957.
Great Britain, 1923 – *Report of the agricultural production of England and Wales;* subsequent years – Ministry of Agriculture, Fisheries and Food, *Agricultural Statistics* 1963/4 and Central Statistical Office, *Annual Abstract of Statistics* 1952.

progressively taking on more, the rate of growth of gross farm revenue in the settler economies was higher. Kenyan European farmers use only half as many tractors per £000 of revenue in 1923 as American farmers, and in 1955 the ratio is less than half.

Much of the explanation of these differences can be attributed to relative factor prices. Considering as inputs to the farm production process, for the time being, only unskilled labour and agricultural machinery, we discover that in 1923, the year in which the estimates of Table 5.4 begin, the relative costs of these inputs in the United States and in the settler economies were as shown in Table 5.5. The ratio of *measured* capital cost to *measured* labour cost was, then, at this stage about ten times as high in the settler economies as it was in the USA, largely due to the lowness of the wages of African labour. However, this measured ratio almost certainly understates the true one.

In the early period (up to 1920) white farmers in the settler economies faced a climatic regime so unprecedented elsewhere in the world – a year divided into distinct periods of rainy and dry season[51] at a high altitude in the tropics – that there was no bank of available research experience available to tell pioneer farmers what crops would grow well in what locations with what treatments, and which implements would be appropriate

Table 5.5. *Southern Rhodesia, Kenya and USA : relative cost of agricultural machinery and labour, 1923*

		Southern Rhodesia	Kenya	United States
(1)	Agricultural machinery (landed cost farmer's station; price in £ per ton)	127.9	127.0	114.3
(2)	Farm labour (national average cost of unskilled labour, including allowance for food and housing; £ per man per month)	1.2	0.9	9.77
(1)/(2)	Ratio of capital to labour costs	106	141	11.6

Source : Price of agricultural machinery – the basis is the c.i.f. import cost into Kenya and Southern Rhodesia, as recorded in the import statistics of each country (for more detail see Appendix 6 below), i.e. £122 per ton in Kenya and £121 per ton in Southern Rhodesia. To this is *added*, to arrive at the Southern Rhodesian and Kenyan estimates, the 1923 per ton rail rate for agricultural machinery for 450 miles, which takes one into the centre of the European farming area for each country. From it is *subtracted*, to arrive at the US estimate, the 1923 ocean shipping rate for agricultural machinery from the US to Mombasa, i.e. £7.15s. per ton (Kenya 1929 (B3)). This indirect method of estimating US prices is used owing to the difficulty of working out an average US cost 'per ton of agricultural machinery'; it will differ from the true cost to the extent that the source of Kenya and Southern Rhodesia agricultural machinery was not the US.

Price (i.e. wage) of farm labour, Kenya and Southern Rhodesia – Table 4.9a. United States wage data – *Historical statistics of the US: colonial times to 1957* (US Department of Commerce, 1961), Table K 73–82.

to the conditions.[52] Until the reorganisation of the Department of Agriculture in 1908 the Southern Rhodesian European farmer had to make do with little or no help from government support services, and in Kenya this statement applies until after the First World War.[53] In such an environment experimentation with different crops and techniques assumed, more than usually, the role of a public good with a very low expected rate of return, and the only individuals willing to invest in it were the two with outstanding quantities of capital at their disposal: Rhodes in Southern Rhodesia and Delamere in Kenya.[54] The rate of agricultural failure particularly among farmers was high[55] and therefore there was a very high risk premium to be attached to measured capital cost.[56] No less than the African farmers discussed in Chapter 3, therefore, did they need to have recourse to a 'survival algorithm';[57] a set of rules of thumb which afforded the best hope of keeping the farm going, sustaining one's existing way of life, and keeping risk to a minimum. On the output side, one element in such a survival algorithm (as the figures of Table 5.1 reflect) was reliance on maize, a crop which required a relatively small commitment of capital and was relatively resistant to disease; another was the combination of farming as a means of making a living with other means of earning an income. Thus many early agricultural settlers in Rhodesia were prospectors, or alternated periods on the land with periods in retailing or government employment;[58] and of the early Kenyan white farmers, who had settled in Kikuyuland by 1902, 'most ... did other things: Boedeker and Atkinson were physicians; McQueen was a blacksmith: Watcham and others cut wood for the railway; and so it went'.[59]

On the input side, survival algorithms for most farmers dictated the avoidance, where possible, of heavy commitments of capital, more particularly since the system of agricultural finance was undeveloped and the cost of transport from railhead to farm before the 1920s very high indeed.[60]

Thus there were not only quantitative factors but also qualitative ones (in particular the underdevelopment of agricultural finance and the riskiness of increasing one's capitalisation and one's fixed cost burden) which help to explain the fact that European agriculture in the settler economies before 1920 started off with highly labour-intensive production techniques. Some farmers well off the line of rail, indeed, started off with a capital coefficient insignificantly different from zero. A bemused Governor of Kenya described the way of life of the South African immigrants on the Uasin Gishu plateau in 1913 in the following manner:

> Having rigged up a shanty infinitely less attractive than a Connemara shebeen, and having scratched over a sufficiency of soil to supply mealies for the family consumption, his domestic exertions are ended. Thereafter the antelopes provide him with more meat than he can consume, their hides supply him with rugs, shoes and harness material, and having laid out what funds he possesses in a wagon and a team of oxen, he is equipped for a career of profit making [sc. transport riding] entailing little or no further outlay ...[61]

Other farmers suffering from no constraints of capital availability, such as Delamere, nonetheless switched from a capital- to a labour-intensive process of production as a result of their early experimentation, finding it simply the more efficient. As he described the process,

> When I went to Njoro [his first wheat farm, in 1903] there was no method of traction for ploughs. A traction engine was bought and used for the first plough on the property, but was found to be unsatisfactory because it packed the soil underneath, creating a pan. A thousand young bullocks were bought in Kavirondo, and after getting a lesson from a South African Dutchman in the breaking of the first three or four, I spent many months breaking the rest . . . [62]

Considerations of risk and 'non-visible' capital outlays such as transport delays also help to explain the form of capitalisation which took place. Characteristically capital equipment was not imported in mint condition but either improvised *in situ*:

> It would have amused the present day farmers to have seen the primitive methods we were forced to adopt to work the land at all. The writer managed to get a plough from Mr Edwards (the store-keeper), but harrows had to be made out of thorn trees cut to some shape, and triangles made of hard wood and with wooden teeth . . . [63]

or alternatively imported second-hand, a process often recommended today for less developed countries with abundant labour and scarce capital if new machines fitting the 'optimal' ratio of labour to capital are not available.[64] For example, the processes of shelling and milling maize were carried out on Rhodesian farms in the 1920s with a maximum of African labour in the processes of transport, loading, stacking, etc. and second-hand equipment already obsolete in the countries from which it had been imported.[65] There has been a tendency in much writing about settler societies to emphasise the extent to which their members looked back towards the values and life-style of an earlier age,[66] and to cite the use of outdated equipment as the technical analogue to this traditionalism, but in fact some of these machines, inefficient though they may be in an engineering sense, were a highly appropriate technology to use in the situation of cheap labour, dear capital, and high risk which characterised the early settler period. Significantly, it was the large and efficient farmers who showed keenest awareness of the potentialities of what we would now call 'intermediate' technology. Delamere's experiments in the use of stationary steam engines and other implements for ploughing are described above, and Stephen Powles, unlike some of his less percipient neighbours, quickly reverted from tractor to ox-ploughing at the start of the 1930s depression to keep the burden of his capital costs down when they were rising relatively to his income.[67]

The real ratio of capital cost to labour cost was, therefore, at the start of the colonial period well above even what is indicated by Table 5.5, being

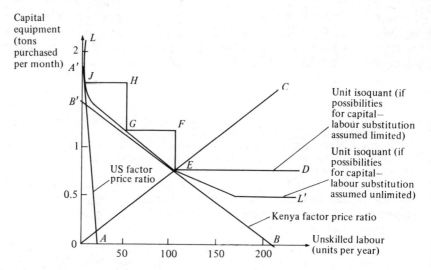

Fig. 5.3 Kenya and USA 1923: factor prices and technical options in European agriculture. The 'budget lines' show what could be purchased by farmers with an annual 'budget' of £2400. *Source*: Table 5.5.

inflated by transport costs, loan capital constraints and a risk premium; the position may be summarised by Figure 5.3, which is drawn to scale with estimated 1923 price ratios.

We now consider change over time in factor proportions in white agriculture. Table 5.6 sets out the basic data, which are poor and broken in the inter-war period, particularly in the area of agricultural capital stocks. The following rather confusing pattern emerges from the data.

(1) During the inter-war period there is no discernible relationship in Kenya, and very little visible relationship in Southern Rhodesia, between factor prices and factor intensity. In both countries the relative price of imported capital inputs rises to a peak in 1930, then falls back. But in Kenya the capital–labour ratio responds *perversely* to this trend, also rising to a peak in the early 1930s and then falling back. In Southern Rhodesia there is very little that can be said, as there are only occasionally reliable statistics on agricultural labour, but in the years that such statistics do exist the capital–labour ratio fluctuates wildly and independently of the factor-price ratio which is fairly stable for most of the period 1932–48.

(2) After the Second World War the capital–labour ratio seems to be much more responsive to factor prices. During the period 1948–56 in Southern Rhodesia, and 1951–6 in Kenya, there is a gradual decline in the relative price of capital to labour (prices of imported inputs were indeed rising, but not nearly as fast as money wages) and a gradual increase in capital intensity; during 1956–60 the relative price of capital to labour is

188

on an upward tendency, and capital intensity falls in Kenya, and increases much less fast in Southern Rhodesia.

It is, however, possible to make some sense of the data by taking note of factors already discussed. First, constraints and imperfections in the credit market: until after the Second World War many farmers were unable to afford capital improvements out of current income,[68] and lending by the Land Banks tended largely to be devoted to the meeting of existing obligations rather than capital development.[69] Second, lack of incentive: labour remained so cheap throughout the inter-war period, any shortages as we have seen being easily resolved by increased recruitment or by small wage increases, that there was little incentive to resolve them by the alternative route of changing technology.[70] 'In the tobacco world', wrote a correspondent to the journal *Rhodesia Mines and Industries* in 1941, 'there has not been necessity enough to mother invention'.[71] The same argument might be applied to the entire agricultural sector of both countries,[72] and indeed not until 1946 did the capital cost/labour cost ratio rise above its 1925 level. Third, the interlinkage of factor proportions and input cost through the squatter system: we have seen that the squatter system provided not only a flexible and cheap method of hiring and firing labour *pari passu* with output, but also 'free or at nominal cost such ... products as manure, milk and actual stock'.[73] These external benefits of a labour-intensive production function no doubt helped to discourage many farmers between the wars from moving off it in a capital-intensifying direction, even if tempted to do so by small increases in labour's relative cost. After the Second World War, however, the position changed, and by the 1950s it was only relatively impoverished white farming districts that still relied a great deal on resident labour.[74] Thus until 1939 European agriculture in the settler economies, having rationally adopted a production function which was labour-intensive even by the standard of other less developed countries,[75] found itself largely locked into that production pattern[76] with only a small group of efficiently and highly capitalised farmers managing to escape from it. The post-Second World War boom in agricultural prices provided release for many more.

Consideration of these factors brings us to the following composite hypothesis:

(1) In European agriculture, the factor proportions adopted depended not only on factor prices but also on (a) the level of credit provided by the Land Bank and (b) the farmer's level of income.

(2) The responsiveness of factor proportions to factor prices was greater after the Second World War, both because this was the first instance of a large discontinuous 'jump' in the ratio of labour to capital cost and because by then the risk factor had diminished.

This hypothesis is put to a highly tentative test in the regression equation whose results are reported in Table 5.7. The results are consistent with both parts of the hypothesis: Land Bank credit and European agricultural exports are significant positive influences on capital intensity, and the ratio of the

189

Table 5.6. *Southern Rhodesia and Kenya: factor proportions and factor prices in European agriculture, 1925–63*

	Southern Rhodesia								Kenya							
	Factor prices (1925 = 100)			Factor inputs			Measures of capital/labour ratio		Factor prices (1925 = 100)			Factor inputs			Measures of capital/labour ratio	
Year	P_K	P_L	P_K/P_L	K_1	K_2	L	K_1/L	K_2/L	P_K	P_L	P_K/P_L	K_1	K_3	L	K_1/L	K_3/L
1925	100	100	100						100	100	100	170	86	78	2.18	1.10
1926	153	130	117		142				153	113	135			84		
1927	138	136	101		216				138	113	122			102		
1928	146	128	114		137				146	113	129	1 162	170	114	10.19	1.49
1929	147	117	125		117				147	113	130			100		
1930	168	117	143		84	72		1.16	168	103	163			125		
1931	116	93	124		102				116	103	112	1 381	302	120	11.50	2.51
1932	90	89	101		126				90	89	101	1 360	275	104	13.07	2.64
1933	73				160				73	73	100	1 277	268	105	12.16	2.55
1934	74				171				74	65	113	1 133	267	107	10.58	2.49
1935	79	79	100		183				79	70	112					
1936	73				214	83		2.57	73	70	104			101		
1937	99				190	87		2.18	99	70	141					
1938	89	88	101		244	92		2.65	89	81	109			111		
1939	89				269	93		2.89	89	80	111					
1940	145				245											
1941	165				206									101		
1942	209				153									122		
1943	203				105	114		0.92								
1944	152				305	123		2.47						118		
1945	141				398	130		3.06						118		
1946	125	130	96		423	135		3.13						108		
1947	154			1 155	386	147		2.62						122		

	P_K	P_L (SR)	P_L (K)				K_1 (SR)				L (SR)	L (K)			
1948	185	186	99				2 116				147	14.4			138
1949	210	237	88				3 448				165	20.9			161
1950	231	263	88	162	142		4 484				160	28.0			149
1951	224	300	75	177	126		5 184				171	30.3			141
1952	236	326	73	197	119		5 905				173	34.1			140
1953	231	333	69	202	114		6 610				177	37.3			139
1954	294	449	65	251			7 318				183	39.9			158
1955	394	428	92	272		108	8 151	4 799	884		189	43.1			133
1956	413	449	92				9 053	5 794	1 227		191	42.3			148
1957	343	450	76				9 745	5 863	1 131		192	50.7			153
1958	349	457	76		276	124	10 327	6 126	1 095		197	52.4	30.37	5.59	157
1959							11 438	6 232	1 094		200	57.1	43.56	9.22	170
1960							12 115	6 403	1 052		208	58.2	39.61	7.64	
1961							12 567	6 422	1 021		208	60.4	40.03	7.15	
1962							12 848	6 418	1 026		208	61.8	39.69	6.96	
1963							13 442	6 111	936				37.66	6.18	

Notes:

P_K = price index of capital inputs into European agriculture; 1925 = 100. Goods considered are: motor spirit and fuel oil; fertilisers and manures; agricultural machinery. Weights used are: 1923 weights for 1923–30; 1931 weights for 1931–40; 1941 weights for 1941–50; 1951 weights for 1951–60. The same index is used for both Kenya and Southern Rhodesia, as until 1930 Southern Rhodesia import data do not give sufficient detail, and after 1930 there are insignificant differences between the two countries' import prices and weights; the source used is Kenya (after 1948 East Africa) Customs Department, *Annual Trade Reports*.

P_L = index of nominal cash wages, including food, paid to African unskilled agricultural labourers; 1925 = 100. Source, for Southern Rhodesia, Table 4.9b; for Kenya, Table 4.9c.

K_1 = number of tractors owned by European farmers; source, for Southern Rhodesia, Central Statistical Office, *Agricultural Production in Rhodesia* (annual); for Kenya, *Agricultural Censuses* for years stated.

K_2 = imports of fertiliser (Southern Rhodesia only). These are given in value terms by the original sources, which are *Yearbook of the Colony of Southern Rhodesia*, 1924, 1930, 1932, and *Statistical Year Book of Southern Rhodesia*, 1938, 1947, and here deflated by the P_K index to give an estimate of physical usage (in the form of an index, 1925 = 100). No data are quoted after 1947, as in that year local production of fertilisers by the African Explosives Co. began, and import figures thus become misleading as a measure of input.

K_3 = number of threshing machines and combine harvesters owned by European farmers (Kenya only); source, Kenya, *Agricultural Censuses* for years stated.

L = adult male African labour, in thousands, employed in European agriculture; source, for Southern Rhodesia, Table 4.8a; for Kenya, Table 4.8b.

191

Table 5.7. *Determinants of capital intensity in white agriculture: results of regression analysis*

Period covered by analysis	Constant	P_K/P_L	Real value of European agricultural exports (index 1925 = 100)	Value of Land Bank loans (in £000)	r^2	D.W.
Southern Rhodesia						
1948–60, excluding 1955 (12 observations)	100.1 (3.22)	− 0.75* (2.01)			0.2886	0.3731
1948–60, excluding 1955 (12 observations)	7.92 (0.46)	− 0.16 (0.99)	0.13** (7.59)		0.9039	1.2480
Kenya						
1925, 1928, 1931–4, 1955–60 (12 observations)	− 42.7 (− 0.80)	0.59 (1.26)			0.1379	0.4923
1925, 1928, 1931–4 *only* (6 observations)	− 25.9** (12.13)	0.15 (0.99)	0.12** (17.3)	0.031** (14.6)	0.9064	2.7932
1955–60 *only* (6 observations)	28.9 (1.61)	− 0.69** (4.08)	0.13** (4.98)	0.096** (4.07)	0.9550	3.0651

Note: Dependent variable: ratio of tractors/African agricultural (adult male) labour (index 1925 = 100). Regression coefficients on independent variables (Student's t statistics in parentheses).

* denotes significance at the 5 per cent level
** denotes significance at the 1 per cent level

price of capital to the price of labour is a negative influence only after the Second World War (significant in the Kenyan and insignificant in the Southern Rhodesian case). Too much should not be read into this, as the results are based on only twelve observations in each case and the Durbin–Watson statistics indicate the presence of serial correlation in the residuals. It can be said, however, that until after the Second World War there is little evidence that the low initial level of capital intensity in European agriculture was responsive to factor prices.

CONCLUSION

We have now come some way from the idea, which the settlers themselves did much to perpetuate,[77] of white farming communities in Africa as being an amateurish, profligate, cohesive group, forced by the threat of bankruptcy into reliance on primitive techniques and state assistance. The profligate amateurs certainly existed, but they were outnumbered, at least in terms of their contribution to output, by professionals, often the employees of multi-national companies with agrarian interests. This schism between the competent and the incompetent farmers frequently broke down even the appearance of cohesiveness within the white farming group, a unity which as we have seen[78] was already threatened by conflicts of interest between farmers growing different crops. Settler farming, finally, was indeed labour-intensive, but it had good economic reason to be, given the cheapness of labour and the high money cost and risks associated with the use of capital equipment. This labour-intensiveness had an important implication for the incipient manufacturing base of the settler economies: it restricted the market for 'backward linkage industries', i.e. local industries manufacturing agricultural inputs, and accentuated the consumer goods orientation of manufacturing industry.[79] And settler agriculturists were by no means enthusiastic for local businessmen to supply even such market as there was, fearing the effects on their cost structure. We develop the implications of this point for manufacturing industry in our next chapter.

APPENDIX 6 A NOTE ON THE DATA FOR CHAPTER 5

For nearly all of the statistical material in this chapter the source is a census of the activities of European farmers carried out under the authority of a Statistics Act and to which replies were mandatory. As a consequence the response rate was high, and even when a farm did not send in a return for a given year it was usually possible to use the previous year's estimate, reducing the proportion of questionnaires where pure guesswork was necessary to a small figure. The response rates recorded by the collecting authorities were published in certain years as shown in the table.

	Kenya			Southern Rhodesia		
	Proportion of farms			Proportion of farms		
		Not sending in a return			*Not sending in a return*	
		estimate of	estimate of		estimate of	estimate of
	Sending in	output	output not	Sending in	output	output not
	a return	possible	possible	a return	possible	possible
1923	90	10				
1938				96	2	2
1947				94	2	4
1960	94	3	3			

The problem with these census data is thus not so much that they are not reliable as that, firstly, they do not exist for all years (Kenya published results for 1919–34, 1936, 1938, 1940 and 1954–60 only; Southern Rhodesia published results for 1923 to date), and, secondly, they ask questions of limited scope, e.g. we have no worthwhile information on the ownership of fixed capital assets in Southern Rhodesia before 1946 or on the inter-farm distribution of crop yields in Kenya for any year.

The only data in this chapter not drawn from Agricultural Census material are as follows.

(i) The estimates of agricultural wages used in Tables 5.5, 5.6 and 5.7. These are worked out mainly from administrative officers' reports; for a full account of the methods used and of the limitations on the reliability of the data, see respectively Appendices 4 and 3 above.

(ii) The data on prices of imported capital equipment used in Tables 5.5 and 5.6. These are all derived from trade data, which are accurate estimates of the c.i.f. landed cost of the inputs listed. In Table 5.6 no attempt is made to go from this to an estimate of prices actually paid by farmers, as what is needed for that table is an index of changes over time in input prices rather than their absolute levels; any inaccuracy which may exist here, therefore, derives from incompleteness in the list of inputs considered, which is derived from farm cost surveys. In Table 5.5 absolute magnitudes *are* important and what is worked out is the average cost per ton of agricultural machinery after a 450 mile haul from the coast, which is probably the best guess one can make at the variable we are trying to measure. i.e. average landed cost at the European farmer's station.

6

Secondary industry

Of the West Indian colonies perhaps Jamaica affords the most interesting comparison. The population of Jamaica, which is 98% coloured and black, is almost the same in numbers as our native population. But the landed cost of imports into Jamaica was something like £4 million, whereas the corresponding figure for this colony was about £1 210 000 which with the addition of local purchases represents a purchasing power of about 30s. per head. Now supposing that only 25 per cent of our native population increased their purchasing power from 30s. to 70s. per head, the Jamaican level, this would mean an increase in the value of the native trade of at least £500 000 per annum ... Surely then, on commercial grounds alone, apart from any moral obligation, it should be the policy to encourage the native in the attainment of higher standards.

(NAR: S 1216/SC 1/100/110, Governor (of Southern Rhodesia)
to Associated Chambers of Commerce, 10 March 1933)

6.1 INTRODUCTION: THE PROBLEM TO BE RESOLVED

Secondary industry in Africa, unlike mining and most forms of agriculture, has always depended for its market largely on the local economy and on that of neighbouring territories, rather than on exports outside Africa. And at this point, many writers have alleged, a major contradiction arises in the development process of settler economies. For if the incomes of the mass of the population are kept down by near-subsistence wages and by prohibitions on the growing of lucrative cash crops, then this will surely impose an insuperable constraint on the home market and hence on the growth of a locally based industrial sector.

This line of argument is not confined to the 'underdevelopment school'. True, Arrighi has maintained that:

A necessary condition for industrialisation was an expanding internal demand whereas the deterioration of peasant productive capacity inevitably was to lead to the opposite viz. an internal demand, if not stagnant, growing at a negligible rate ... Thus, notwithstanding increased government intervention to foster economic growth, the system lacked an *internal* force sufficient to start industrial development.[1]

195

Also, many Latin-American writers of the 'dependency' school have attributed deficient industrial growth to the low purchasing power of the mass of the population.[2] But over and above these contributions, Chenery, in his 1960 study of patterns of industrial growth, noted that there were downward deviations from the regression line relating the share of manufacturing in GDP to income per capita 'in countries such as South Africa, Kenya and Peru, in which predominantly European communities have much higher per capita incomes than the larger native communities'.[3] Pearson's survey of industrial development in East Africa asserts that 'the size of the market for manufactures increases with the slope of the Pareto curve, other things being equal',[4] and we can safely assume that the Governor of Southern Rhodesia, quoted at the head of this chapter, was free from the influence of Marxist thinking when he formulated his remarks.

But at this point a paradox arises. For industrial growth was, in fact, anything but backward in the settler economies. As Table 6.1 shows, secondary industry increased steadily through time as a proportion of national income, in other words, it grew faster than national income: the average real rate of industrial growth in Southern Rhodesia was 8.7 per cent between 1948 and 1963 as against 6.4 per cent for the economy as a whole, and in Kenya it was 5 per cent between 1954 and 1963 as against 3 per cent for the economy as a whole.[5] In other words, the industrial sector, so far from acting as a brake on the economy as a whole, actually appears to have served as an engine of growth. Moreover, industrial growth in Kenya and Southern Rhodesia was not, as one might expect, biased away from the consumer goods sector if one compares it with the process of growth in

Table 6.1. *Kenya and Southern Rhodesia: share of secondary industry (manufacturing, construction, electricity and water) in national income, 1924–64*

	Southern Rhodesia		Kenya	
	Value (£000)	% share in national income	Value (£000)	% share in national income
1924	999	9.4		
1931	1 160	13.2		
1943	5 108	16.5		
1947			4 500	8.5
1949	17 500	23.7		
1955	39 600	24.7		
1956			21 000	13.1
1964	89 000	27.2	45 400	18.7

Sources: Southern Rhodesia, 1924–43 – Southern Rhodesia 1946 (B2). 1949 and 1955 – Southern Rhodesia 1958b (B2). 1964 – *National Accounts and Balance of Payments of Rhodesia*, 1965.
Kenya, 1947, 1965 – Hope-Jones 1958 (D1), p. 317. 1964 – Kenya, *Statistical Abstract*, 1965.

less developed economies which have a more equal internal income distribution.[6]

In this chapter, we attempt to resolve the paradox. In the next section we set out a simple explanatory model and with its help take up the implicit invitation of the Governor of Southern Rhodesia to embark on a comparison between industrial structure in 'settler' and 'peasant export' economies. The implications of our analysis are considered in the concluding section.

6.2 INDUSTRIES PRODUCING FOR FINAL DEMAND: INCOME INEQUALITY AND INDUSTRIAL DEVELOPMENT

A simple model

Consider the following three-equation model which attempts to reduce the problem to its simplest terms. The demand for a manufactured consumer good,[7] D_i, depends on disposable national income (Y_h), export demand (Y_f) and inequality in national income, as measured by its variance (σY_h):

$$D_i = a + b Y_h + c(\sigma Y_h) + d Y_f \tag{6.1}$$

and this demand can be satisfied either from imports (M_i) or from domestic production (P_i):

$$D_i \equiv P_i + M_i \tag{6.2}$$

and finally, the level of domestic production for any industry depends on size of market in relation to minimum optimum scale (P_i^*):

$$P_i = \begin{bmatrix} 0 \text{ if } D_i < P_i^* \\ f(D_i) \text{ if } D_i > P_i^* \end{bmatrix} \quad \text{all } i \quad (f' > 0) \tag{6.3}$$

If assumptions (6.1)–(6.3) are true, which we believe to be the case, four factors at least may cause a country in which income is unequally distributed (high σY_h) to have a higher level of industrial production (ΣP_i) than a country with identical GNP and a more equal distribution of income:

(a) The coefficient c in (6.1) may in fact be *positive*.
(b) The country with unequal distribution of income may have a demand pattern with a lower average import threshold (average P^*) than the country with more equal distribution of income.
(c) The function f in (6.3) may be such that the country with more unequal distribution of income takes advantage of a higher proportion of import substitution opportunities $\left(\text{has a higher } \dfrac{\Sigma P_i}{\Sigma D_i} \right)$ than the country with more equal distribution of income.
(d) Export demand for manufactures ($d Y_f$) may be higher in the country with more unequal distribution of income.

In the remainder of this chapter we investigate these four sources of slippage empirically, with emphasis on the first and the last. But before we proceed, a word about intermediate goods. Since the demand for intermediate goods, like all other factors of production, is a derived demand it is intuitively likely that the growth of this sector of manufacturing would depend on the growth of the economic activities which it supplies – most of them primary production activities dependent on export demand – and not in any sense on the internal distribution of income. That is, the appropriate demand equation for intermediate goods is likely to be, not a form such as (6.1), but rather

$$D_i = a + bP_j \qquad\qquad (6.1a)$$

where D_i = demand for intermediate good, (e.g. explosives), P_j = production level in the industry which it supplies (e.g. mining). In the few cases where we have adequate statistics, hypothesis (6.1a) stands up well.[8] But we do not have sufficient data on industrial production to warrant a full-scale study of the growth of intermediate goods industries.[9] Hence in what follows we assume that the consumer goods sector is the only one sensitive to income distribution effects and confine ourselves to this area.

The shape of the demand function for manufactures: Evidence from cross-section data

Only in the decade of the 1950s do we have the kind of information on household budgets which would enable us to compute, even approximately, the shape of the consumption function from this source. Even then, all we have are sample surveys of the urban African, and in Southern Rhodesia also the European, population. The consumption behaviour of rural Africans, numerically the largest part of the population, went without statistical investigation in the settler economies during the colonial period but fortunately there was a very thorough survey of rural African consumption habits by Chalmers Wright (Great Britain 1955a (B1)) next door in Nyasaland and Tanganyika, and this can be used as a check on our *pis aller* assumption that the consumption habits of rural and urban Africans with similar incomes did not differ.

The data which are available on household budgets in the 1950s are set out in Table 6.2a and b for Africans and Table 6.2c for Europeans. They do suggest that in Southern Rhodesia and Kenya in the 1950s, there existed, within the African community, a continually decreasing average propensity to consume manufactured goods; but this tendency is clearer in Southern Rhodesia than in Kenya, where in fact the propensity of urban Africans to consume manufactures *rises* between the third and fourth quartiles. The tendency is also apparent amongst the rural Africans surveyed by Chalmers Wright.[10] Hence there is some presumption that a progressive *intra*-African community redistribution of income might have broadened the market for manufactures, since such a redistribution would have transferred income

Table 6.2a. *Southern Rhodesia 1957/8: average monthly income and expenditure (shillings and pence) of unrationed African families in rent-free accommodation in Salisbury*

Expenditure categories	Income groups (arranged by quintiles)					Change in percentage of income spent on expenditure item as income increases[a]
	(1) Up to 167/- per month	(2) 167/6 to 199/6 per month	(3) 200/- to 247/- per month	(4) 247/6 to 315/- per month	(5) 315/- and over per month	
1. Foodstuffs						
Mealie meal	13/2	18/10	20/6	22/9	23/4	−
Meat	29/4	34/6	41/2	45/8	58/0	−
Bread	19/0	22/9	26/9	27/4	38/3	−
Sugar	11/0	13/4	15/1	16/3	21/2	−
Fish	3/0	2/11	3/7	4/9	3/3	−
Milk	7/1	7/1	10/0	10/11	16/4	−
Other	18/8	20/1	26/9	25/5	44/4	−
2. Fuel and light	7/9	9/2	9/0	10/2	10/2	−
3. Drink and tobacco	9/9	9/2	10/0	12/5	20/0	−
4. Cycle	0/11	1/11	2/3	2/7	4/7	−
5. Clothing and footwear	15/7	18/3	21/3	34/6	43/9	−
6. Household stores[b]	9/8	8/3	10/9	11/7	20/2	−
7. Miscellaneous[c]	13/1	11/6	14/6	28/6	55/0	+
8. Total expenditure	158/-[d]	177/9	211/7	252/10	358/4	−
9. Average income	140/2	179/11	219/4	271/7	450/6	
10. Expenditure on manufactured goods (2 + 3 + 4 + 5 + 6)	43/8	46/9	53/3	71/3	98/8	
11. Expenditure on manufactured goods as a proportion of income (10/9)	0.307	0.259	0.242	0.261	0.219	−

Notes: Total number of respondents = 640 (roughly a $5\frac{1}{2}$ per cent sample).

[a] Entry in this column is − if share of item of consumption in total income has declined by more than one percentage point between col. 1 and col. 5, + if it has increased by more than one percentage point, blank otherwise.

[b] 'Household stores' includes soaps, blankets, linen, furniture, crockery, etc.

[c] 'Miscellaneous' is mostly services: it includes stationery, entertainment, fares, chemists' sundries, doctors' and herbalists' fees, taxes, licences, etc.

[d] 'Families with incomes up to £8.7.0. per month reported an overspending of income on the average and stated that they obtained the money by gifts and borrowing from friends and relatives and by drawing on savings. It is however believed that some of the repeated borrowings and drawings from savings were, in fact, incomes from sources the recipients were unwilling to disclose.' Southern Rhodesia 1959a (B2), p. 9.

Source: Southern Rhodesia 1959a (B2), Tables VII and VIII.

Table 6.2b. *Kenya 1957/8: average monthly income and expenditure (shillings and cents) of Africans in Nairobi*

Expenditure categories	Income groups (arranged by quartiles)				
	(1)	(2)	(3)	(4)	Change in percentage of income spent on expenditure item as income increases[b]
	Up to Sh. 130 per month	Sh. 131 to Sh. 170 per month	Sh. 171 to Sh. 220 per month	Sh. 221 to Sh. 320 per month[a]	
1. Food	91.63	106.68	108.72	124.89	–
2. Non-alcoholic liquor	0.53	0.74	0.88	1.53	
3. Alcoholic liquor	3.93	6.32	6.14	12.31	+
4. Tobacco and snuff	3.94	4.58	4.81	5.67	–
5. Clothing	8.45	8.28	12.04	19.58	
6. Footwear	0.79	0.77	1.93	2.36	–
7. Rent and water charges	17.60	24.62	27.57	27.83	–
8. Fuel and light	6.98	8.31	8.07	10.19	–
9. Furniture and furnishings	3.84	4.14	7.51	7.84	
10. Household operation	2.48	2.67	2.15	4.28	
11. Personal care and health	1.25	2.48	3.33	5.46	+
12. Transport and communication	3.18	3.39	3.62	8.07	
13. Recreation and entertainment	0.57	1.48	1.90	4.33	+
14. Miscellaneous services	1.65	1.77	0.88	2.00	–
15. Total expenditure	146.82	176.24	189.53	236.35	–
16. Average income	116.16	146.94	191.52	268.60	
17. Expenditure on manufactured goods (2 + 3 + 4 + 5 + 6 + 8 + 9 + 10)	30.94	35.81	43.53	63.98	
18. Expenditure on manufactured goods as a proportion of income (17/16)	0.266	0.243	0.227	0.238	–

Notes: Total number of respondents = 393.
[a] The survey excludes Africans earning more than Sh. 320 per month, also domestic servants and police, prison and hospital employees.
[b] Entry in final column is – if share of item of consumption in total income has declined by more than one percentage point between col. 1 and col. 4, + if it has increased by more than one percentage point, blank otherwise.
Source: East African Statistical Department 1959 (B3), Tables 3, 7 and 8.

Table 6.2c. *Southern Rhodesia 1950/1: distribution of European families by income and expenditure groups*

Average income per month	Number of families with an average expenditure per month of									Row totals
	Less than £40	£40 to £50	£50 to £60	£60 to £70	£70 to £80	£80 to £90	£90 to £100	£100 to £110	More than £110	
Less than £40	2		2							4
£40 to £50	1	4	2							7
£50 to £60		4	5	3	1					13
£60 to £70			10	29	4	2	1			46
£70 to £80			2	11	20	10	4			47
£80 to £90				6	22	12	8	5	1	54
£90 to £100				1	4	11	6	4	1	27
£100 to £110				1	1	3	1	4		10
Column totals	3	8	21	51	52	38	20	13	2	208

Note: Total number of respondents = 208
Source: Southern Rhodesia 1952b (B2), Table 15, p. 9.

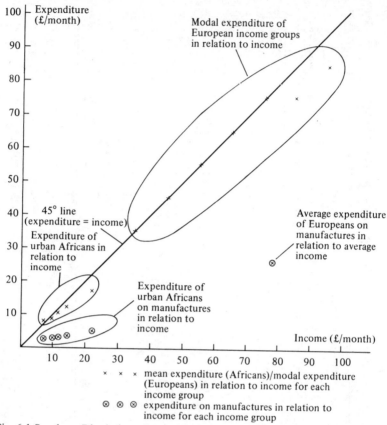

Fig. 6.1 Southern Rhodesia: urban Africans 1957/8 and Europeans 1950/1, patterns of expenditure in relation to income. Within each income class, income and expenditure are assumed to cluster at the mid-point. *Sources*: Tables 6.2a and 6.2c.

from one set of Africans to another, poorer, set with higher propensities to consume.[11] But the scanty available evidence on European consumption patterns (Table 6.2c) suggests that among the bottom two-thirds of the Southern Rhodesian European income distribution (those earning more than £80 per month, in 1951)[12] far more overspent than underspent their income. The average propensity to consume out of current income for these 'poorer' Europeans is thus in excess of one, that is, far greater than the APC for the most prosperous Africans.[13] In other words, as Figure 6.1 above illustrates for Southern Rhodesia, it appears to be the case that although *within* each racial group the consumption function had a slope of less than one, the *overall* consumption function, up to and including the seventh decile of the European population, had a slope insignificantly different from one.[14] It is thus unlikely that an *inter*-racial redistribution of income would have broadened the market for goods as a whole or for manufactures in particular;[15] indeed, it appears on the available evidence that a redistribution from poorer Europeans to richer Africans would almost certainly have narrowed it. In other words, the coefficient c in equation (6.1) above, which measures the relationship between inter-racial variance of personal income and the demand for industrial products, is probably a positive figure in the 1950s.

The shape of the demand function for manufactures: time-series evidence

We can gain additional information about the nature of the relationship between consumption of manufactures and income by looking at the time series of imports of certain manufactures in relation to the time series of African crop and labour income. In many ways this is a less satisfactory exercise than that carried out in Table 6.3, since imports are an imperfect proxy for consumption and since the data series on crop and labour income are less than ideal, a problem fully discussed in Appendices 2 and 3. But it does give us an insight into the stability of demand patterns denied us, of course, by the cross-section approach.

Table 6.3 illustrates the relationship between African cash income and imports of two major manufactures consumed almost exclusively by Africans – cotton piece goods and bicycles – into Kenya between 1926 and 1953. Between them, they almost certainly accounted for more than half the African import trade before the Second World War in both settler economies;[16] unfortunately, no satisfactory series for African crop income in Southern Rhodesia before 1945 exists, hence comparison between the two economies is not possible.

The data described give in all cases a close and significant fit to a direct linear relationship with a *negative intercept*. Since negative values of consumption are meaningless, this should almost certainly be interpreted as a linear approximation to a 'threshold' type consumption function in which consumption is zero up to a certain critical level of income, and proportionate to income in excess of this critical level. A consumption function of this type is presented as (1′) in Appendix 8 below. As is there demonstrated, this type of function is characterised by an increasing average propensity to consume the commodity in question as income increases.[17] Were the estimated functions set out in Table 6.3 also to hold good at a moment in time, then there would be inconsistency with the results of Table 6.2 and we would conclude that even a progressive income redistribution *within the African community* would actually reduce the size of the market for the goods in question.[18] But the making of cross-sectional predictions from results based on time-series data has been shown to be notoriously risky in Britain and America,[19] and what is much more likely is that as for those countries the cross-sectional relationships set out, for example, in Tables 6.2a and b, which are characterised by a falling APC, were subject to an upward float as the range of wants and market outlets widened. But certainly the time-series data do not cast doubt on our earlier conclusion that the

Table 6.3. *Kenya 1926–52: results of regression analysis linking imports of cotton piece goods and bicycles to African cash income*

Equation number	Constant	Regression coefficients on independent variables			r^2	D.W.
		Crop income (in £)	Labour income (in £)	Sum of crop and labour income (in £)		
(a) *Dependent variable: imports of cotton piece goods (value in £)*						
1a	− 549098*	2.25**			0.8725	1.8385
	− (2.18)	(12.54)				
1b	− 583549**		10.21**		0.9107	1.5707
	− (2.79)		(15.31)			
1c	− 555166*			1.82**	0.8639	1.8301
	− (2.32)			(13.23)		
(b) *Dependent variable: imports of bicycles (value in £)*						
1d	− 33085*	0.089**			0.7403	1.9199
	− (2.11)	(8.09)				
1e	− 37996**		0.425**		0.8300	1.9786
	(− 3.01)		(10.59)			
1f	− 33954*			0.073**	0.7598	1.9410
	− (2.26)			(8.52)		

Notes: Figures in brackets beneath coefficients are Student's t-statistics;
** denotes significance at 1% level, * significance at 5% level.
Number of observations: 25 (no crop income estimates are available for 1939 and 1940).
Sources: African crop income – Kenya Agricultural Department *Annual Reports*, 1931, p. 36; 1932, p. 45; 1936, p. 101; 1938, p. 123; 1945, p. 16; and thereafter annually. (Figures for 1941–3 have had to be estimated from export figures by treating as African all agricultural exports except coffee, sisal, pyrethrum, tea, butter, wheat, flax, sugar and the European maize export cited in Table 3.6.)
African labour income – Tables 4.8 and 4.9.
Imports of bicycles and cotton piece goods to 1948 – Kenya and Uganda Customs Department, *Annual Reports* (total domestic imports of item stated, less Uganda imports), various. 1946–52 – East African Customs Department, *Annual Reports*. (N.B. after 1952 the classification of cotton piece goods becomes too elaborate for the total to be reliably threaded onto the pre-1952 series, hence the termination of the analysis in this year.)

effects of income inequality on demand for manufactures are unlikely to be positive.

This conclusion is further strengthened by a comparison of the import data just analysed with the corresponding data for a cluster of 'peasant export economies'. It is a widely publicised assertion that in the inter-war period demand for certain manufactures bought by Africans (notably bicycles) in Uganda and on the west coast of Africa was far higher than that

Table 6.4. *Kenya, Southern Rhodesia and three 'non-settler economies':*
size of market for manufactures in relation to national income, early 1960s

	(1) Market size for consumer goods (current £ million)	(2) Money national income in year stated (current £ million)	(3) = (1)/(2) Size of market for manufactures as percentage of national income
Settler economies			
Southern Rhodesia (1964)	84.3	320.4	26.3
Kenya (1961)	45.6	224.8	20.3
Non-settler economies			
Uganda (1963)	24.0	176.0	13.6
Jamaica (1960)	55.8	240.0	23.3
Ghana (1959)	42.2	507.5	8.3

Sources: *Market size* – Appendix 7 below: 'Sub-total I: total consumer goods'
from each individual country table.
Money national income (includes in all cases an estimate for the non-monetary
sector) *Statistical Abstracts* for countries and years listed.

in Kenya, with an African population of broadly similar size. An Asian
member of the Kenya Legislative Council, Isher Dass, advised European
merchants and traders during the debate on the Kenya Land Commission:

> not to forget the fact that they cannot possibly thrive so long as the great bulk
> of the native peasantry remain wage slaves, merely capable of purchasing a
> little salt and snuff now and then, and a cheap blanket and a small supply of
> beads once a year. In countries possessing a prosperous native peasantry, such
> as Uganda and the West Coast of Africa, you can sell, not only salt and cheap
> blankets, but motor cycles and motor cars in their thousands, besides dinner
> suits and dress suits, building materials, footwear, headwear and all the other
> paraphernalia of modern civilisation.[20]

Let us attempt a formal test of this proposition by considering the 'size
of the market' (domestic production plus imports less exports) for consumer
goods in relation to national income in the late 1950s, both in the settler
economies and also in a cluster of economies where income was more
equally distributed – the 'peasant export economies' of Uganda and Ghana,
as suggested by Isher Dass, and Jamaica, as suggested by the Chairman of
the Rhodesia Federated Chambers of Commerce.[21] This is shown in Table
6.4. The market for manufactured consumer goods (as a proportion of
national income) in the two settler economies appears to be much larger
than the market for such goods in either of the two peasant export economies,
and it is not significantly different from the market for consumer goods in

Jamaica. On the assumption, which seems to be empirically correct,[22] that income is less equally distributed in the settler than in at any rate the peasant export economies (we have no data for Jamaica), this is yet further evidence against the proposition that inequality of income exerts as such a substantial downward pressure on the market for manufactures, or in terms of the notation of equation 6.1 above, that the coefficient c in that equation is negative.

So far we have only considered equation. (6.1) – the demand side – of the simple model set out above. It remains now to consider, briefly, the supply side: equations 6.2 and 6.3.

Country	Domestic production (including export) as a proportion of total market size
Settler economies	
(1964) Southern Rhodesia	97.0
(1961) Kenya	87.2
Non-settler economies	
(1963) Uganda	86.7
(1960) Jamaica	79.1
(1959) Ghana	21.0

Source: Appendix 7 below. Col. 3 (domestic production) is divided by col. 4 (total market size) in respect of total consumer goods in each individual country (Table 6.10).

The data of Appendix 7 suggest that the proportion of the total market supplied by local manufacturing[23] was higher in the settler economies than in the other three. We have already suggested that three separate factors may be responsible for these inter-country differences:

(1) Differences in import structure: thus it may be that the imports of the peasant export economies are less easily substitutable than the imports of the settler economies.
(2) Differences in entrepreneurship proper: i.e. differences in willingness of businessmen to take advantage of a given market opportunity.
(3) Differences in businessmen's willingness to take advantage of *export* opportunities, which could buttress the home market and in some cases enable them to jump over the constraint imposed by minimum optimum scale of plant.

Of these factors, the third is considered in the final section of this chapter, on manufactured exports; thus we confine ourselves here to the first and second.

Factor (1) does not appear to be relevant. This conclusion is derived from an examination of each country's imports which are 'shiftable' in the

	(1) Total imports of consumer goods (£000)	(2) 'Shiftable' imports of consumer goods (£000)	(3) Percentage of imports 'shiftable'
Settler economies			
(1964) S. Rhodesia	19 619	17 563	89.5
(1961) Kenya	17 501	12 539	71.6
Non-settler economies			
(1963) Uganda	8 051	6 274	77.9
(1960) Jamaica	15 954	15 274	95.7
(1959) Ghana	33 485	32 719	97.7

Source: Appendix 7 below. Imports are given as col. 1 in each country Table (6.10)
'Thresholds for domestic production' are given at the beginning of Appendix 7, and the
imports of a given country are defined as 'shiftable' if their imports of a given product for
the years stated exceed these thresholds. For a note on the limitations of the concept, see
note 24 below.

sense that they exceeded the average output per plant – which we take as an
indication of minimum optimum scale[24] – in South Africa, the one country
in Africa which produced, at this time, the full range of consumer goods.

From these data there is nothing to suggest that the settler economies
have an advantage over the others in terms of the 'shiftability' of their
existing imports – if anything the reverse. But these are a poor surrogate
for the shiftability of past imports – the thing we really want to know;
also, the coarse statistical mesh of the import statistics makes the concept
itself risky of application. Hence we advance our conclusion with great
tentativeness.

This brings us to the 'entrepreneurial' factor (2). Analytical discussion
of this factor is difficult, and of its 'animal spirits' component impossible,
with the statistics which we have; we attempt no serious discussion here.
But the level of protection and state assistance to secondary industry, in
the case of Kenya and Southern Rhodesia, does greatly exceed the level
of such support granted in the case of 'peasant export economies'. The
members of the East African and Central African customs arrangements
(Uganda, Tanganyika, Nyasaland, Northern Rhodesia) which did not
have as vocal a settler-producer lobby as Kenya and Southern Rhodesia,
spent much time complaining about the high level of protective duties on
consumer goods,[25] and in practice frequently charged lower rates; the
Chairman of the Uganda Chamber of Commerce actually went so far, in
1931, as to assert that 'Kenya is protectionist, whereas we are not protectionist'.[26] From the inception of the common federal external tariff in 1955
it was no longer possible for Northern Rhodesia and Nyasaland to opt
out from such protectionism, but within the arrangements of the East
African Common Market it remained possible for some protective duties

to be effective in Kenya only.[27] There was some state entrepreneurship in the Second World War in Kenya (acids, pottery and oil and fats) and Southern Rhodesia (steel and cotton spinning); in Uganda and Ghana, however, within our sample group of 'peasant export economies' there was none. In general it seems true to say that the supply side of the market for manufactured consumer goods received more help from the state in settler than in peasant export economies. The influence of this on entrepreneurship, and thence on function f in (6.3) above, is impossible to calculate, but it is probably positive.

To summarise so far, it appears that of the three possible factors mentioned above that may have caused the settler economies to take advantage of a higher proportion of import substitution opportunities than non-settler economies, the first – differences in import structure – is probably insignificant, and the second – differences in government policy – is probably of some importance. In the next section we consider the influence of the third factor, namely differences in the pattern of manufactured exports.

6.3 INDUSTRIAL DEVELOPMENT AND THE MARKET OF NEIGHBOURING COUNTRIES

The structure of economic policy built up after the First World War was conceived with the primary producer, not the industrialist, in mind. This applied as much to measures of economic integration with neighbouring countries as to tariffs and railway rates. When in 1917 the Economic Commission recommended the removal of customs barriers between Kenya and Uganda, the extension of country produce rates and the institution of certain protective tariffs, the ostensible purpose was the encouragement of the European farmer.[28] When Captain Bertin argued for the construction of a direct railway link between Salisbury and the Copperbelt in 1929, urging, 'the transport charges to get [local produce] to a market render it almost valueless, unless a local market can absorb it. So if this development which is taking place in the North [sc. the copper discoveries] turns out as we expect it to do, what a splendid opportunity there is for us there!' it was the European potato farmers and ranchers of Mashonaland whose cause he was pleading.[29] But railway rates and customs agreements which made the local market easier to reach helped the secondary industrialist as much as the primary producer, indeed were even more important to him, inasmuch as it was more difficult, indeed impossible, for him even in the 1920s to unload surplus production at a profit on markets outside Africa. By 1930, however, the relationship of neighbouring economies to secondary industry in the settler economies involved very much more than the dumping of a surplus. In Southern Rhodesia exports of manufactures to neighbouring countries accounted for 23.7 per cent of net output in manufacturing in 1930,[30] and from both settler economies a wide range of consumer goods

Table 6.5a. *Kenya and Southern Rhodesia: exports of manufactures, 1930*

	Exports of manufactures (£000)[a]	Exports to neighbouring countries		Exports to neighbouring countries as a percentage of total exports
		N. Rhodesia and Nyasaland	South Africa	
Southern Rhodesia				
Intermediate goods				
Cement	60.6	51.8	—	85.4
Timber	7.6	7.6	—	100.0
Iron and steel manufactures	12.9	11.0	0.4	85.2
Bricks	4.4	2.5	—	56.8
Printed matter	15.0	13.4	—	89.3
Other	3.8	2.3	0.5	73.6
(I) Total intermediate goods	104.3	88.6	0.9	85.9
Consumer goods				
Maize meal	90.6	67.7	1.8	76.7
Butter	72.2	26.0	7.7	45.7
Cigarettes and manufactured tobacco	73.7	73.0	—	99.0
Beer and stout	52.6	51.8	—	98.4
Wheat flour	38.8	32.4	1.2	86.5
Clothing – outer garments	35.2	31.6	3.4	99.4
Soap and candles	18.7	17.0	0.4	93.0
Other consumer goods	8.7	4.2	0.7	56.3
(II) Total consumer goods	390.5	303.7	15.2	81.4
(I) + (II) Total manufactured exports	494.8	392.3	16.1	82.1
		Tanganyika	Uganda	
Kenya				
Intermediate goods				
Wood and timber	67.3	10.0	12.3	33.1
(I) Total intermediate goods	67.3	10.0	12.3	33.1
Consumer goods				
Maize meal	35.6	14.1	20.9	98.3
Butter	45.8	6.5	0.7	15.7
Ale, beer and stout	1.9	—	1.3	68.4
Wheat flour	55.1	32.0	21.9	97.8
Aluminium hollow ware	0.4	0.4	—	—
Soap and candles	47.9	9.8	36.8	97.2
Bacon and ham	10.5	1.1	3.2	40.9
(II) Total consumer goods	197.2	63.9	84.8	75.4
(I) + (II) Total manufactured goods	264.5	73.9	97.1	64.6

– not available

[a] Kenya and Uganda operated a joint customs administration. Hence Kenya exports must be calculated as domestic exports of Kenya and Uganda *less* export of Uganda plus inter-territorial sales by Kenya.

Table 6.5b. *Kenya and Southern Rhodesia: exports of manufactures, 1951*

	Exports of manufactures (£000)	Exports to neighbouring countries		Exports to neighbouring countries	
				As a percentage of total exports	As a percentage of gross output
		N. Rhodesia and Nyasaland	South Africa		
Southern Rhodesia					
Intermediate goods					
Intermediate goods	136	125	0	91.9	5.5
Wood products	480	117	254	77.2	21.7
Iron and steel					
manufactures	350	225	87	87.0	3.9
Steel windows	139	112	0	80.5	–
Printed matter	77	71	2	94.8	4.1
Fertilisers	173	170	0	98.2	–
Other	514	368	56	82.4	–
(I) Total intermediate goods	1869	1188	399	84.9	–
Consumer goods					
Clothing	2826	323	2217	89.8	58.7
Cigarettes and					
manufactured tobacco	793	605	0	76.2	18.4
Preserved meat	555	101	281	68.8	8.6
Footwear	340	172	112	83.5	–
Cotton piece goods	333	89	209	89.4	18.3
Furniture	258	185	4	73.2	21.2
Aluminium hollow ware	108	13	87	92.5	–
Other	2821	1434	1017	86.8	–
(II) Total consumer goods	8034	2922	3927	85.2	
(I) (II) Total manufactured					
exports	9903	4110	4326	85.1	16.5
Kenya		Tanganyika	Uganda		
Intermediate goods					
Builders' woodwork	322	4	4	2.4	–
Sisal sacks and twine	269	90	179	100.0	–
Insecticides	268	23	13	13.4	–
Iron and steel					
manufactures	110	43	65	9.8	–
Other	292	92	104	67.1	–
(I) Total intermediate goods	1261	252	365	49.0	–
Consumer goods					
Wheatmeal and flour	1252	348	388	58.7	10.3
Beverages and tobacco	236	102	82	86.8	4.2
Footwear and other					
leather products	321	174	126	93.4	41.6
Aluminium hollow ware	195	75	77	77.9	–
Other	575	208	301	88.5	–
(II) Total consumer goods	2579	907	974	72.9	
(I) and (II) Total					
manufactured exports	3840	1159	1339	65.0	7.1

Table 6.6. *Kenya and Southern Rhodesia: sales of manufactures to neighbouring countries as a percentage of total industrial production, 1930–64*

	Southern Rhodesia Exports of manufactures to Northern Rhodesia, Nyasaland and South Africa as a percentage of		Kenya Exports of manufactures to Uganda and Tanganyika, expressed as a percentage of gross output in manufacturing	Source
	(a) Net output in manufacturing	(b) Gross output in manufacturing		
1930	23.7			Note 30 above
1951	38.7	16.5	7.1[a]	Table 6.5 above
1961			20.3	Appendix 7 below
1964		18.1		

Note: [a] 1951 exports divided by 1954 gross output.

was being exported to neighbouring countries in that year, as illustrated by Table 6.5.

In the 1930s, exports by secondary industry to neighbouring countries expanded rapidly, in Southern Rhodesia faster than national income;[31] in that country this growth took place under the particular stimulus of the abrogation of the customs agreement with South Africa in 1935, following which tariffs were imposed in Southern Rhodesia on South African goods and a number of South African manufacturing firms set up in production in Southern Rhodesia behind the tariff barrier.[32] Many of the industrialists who set up in production during this decade testified to the importance of the local export market in their decision to do so, in particular the General Manager of the Rhodesian Iron and Steel Commission, who claimed that the demand of the Northern Rhodesian copper mines was critical to sustain

Notes:

0 zero or insignificant (i.e. less than £1000)

– not available

[a] For many categories of manufactures it has not been possible to match up industrial production data with export data (in general the export data have a much finer statistical mesh). In this event, the symbol – is entered in the final column.

Sources:

Southern Rhodesia – trade data from *Annual Statistics of the Trade of Southern Rhodesia 1952* (Salisbury, 1953), Tables XVII and XIX;

Industrial production data from Southern Rhodesia, *Census of Industrial Production 1953*.

Kenya – trade data from East African Statistical Dept. *Annual Trade Report* 1951, Tables 1 and 5; industrial production from East African Statistical Dept, *Survey of Industrial Production Kenya 1954*, Table 1.

211

his Bulawayo works at an economic level of production.[33] It was not surprising, therefore, that in both countries in the wartime period the main tool by which governments sought to win the allegiance of industrial interests was the promise of an extension of the customs union after the war. In Southern Rhodesia, as may be expected from our argument so far, the Rhodesian Federated Chamber of Commerce was under the control of enthusiastic advocates of close political relations with the British colonies to the north,[34] and in Kenya this argument was extended as far as a proposal for a ministry which would plan commerce and industry on an East African basis.[35] Although this was not achieved, commercial interests in Kenya were successful in getting industrial licensing organised on an East African basis; in the same year, 1948, the United Party government in Southern Rhodesia committed itself to seeking federation with the northern territories of Northern Rhodesia and Nyasaland.[36] Table 6.5b, read in conjunction with Table 6.5a, takes stock of the changes which had occurred in the settler economies' trade in manufactures with neighbouring countries since 1930. In both countries the export of intermediate goods, of negligible importance in 1930, has grown at least as fast as the export of consumer goods over the period to 1951, in spite of the relative competitive advantage which consumer goods were given by tariff policy and in spite of import substitution by the peripheral countries (Northern Rhodesia, Uganda, Tanganyika) in those intermediate goods with high transport costs: cement, bricks, timber. A second notable trend in Southern Rhodesia is a diversification of the local export market after the Second World War: South Africa, unimportant as a consumer of Southern Rhodesia manufactures in 1930, takes more than Northern Rhodesia and Nyasaland combined in 1951. Her importance as a market for Southern Rhodesian industry lies particularly in the textiles and clothing sector where it was possible for the Gatooma manufacturers to take advantage of the trade agreement with South Africa signed in 1949 to capture a large part of the native clothing trade. This trade on its own, in fact, accounted for 77.6 per cent of Southern Rhodesia's exports of clothing, cotton piece goods, and cotton yarn in 1951, and indeed for 35.4 per cent of her gross production.

In the 1950s manufacturing, still growing rapidly up to the end of the decade in both settler economies, becomes still more dependent on the market of neighbouring countries, in Kenya dramatically so. Table 6.6 documents the secular shifts in this dependence from 1930 to the early 1960s. Certain sectors (cotton fabrics, rubber products and paper products in Kenya; 'jam and canned juice', also 'cooking oil and margarine' in Southern Rhodesia) appear to depend for their existence on this market, in the sense that 1961 industrial production, net of sales to neighbouring territories, falls short of the 'threshold' plant size as defined in Appendix 7 below. Because of the shallowness of the 'threshold' concept this conclusion must be put forward tentatively; what is certain, however, is that in a number of industrial sectors over and above these (tobacco manufacturing,

Table 6.7. *'Settler' and 'non-settler' economies: manufactured exports in relation to gross output in manufacturing, early 1960s*

	Manufactured exports (£ million)		Gross value of manufacturing production	Manufactured exports as a percentage of gross value of manufacturing production	
	(1) Total	(2) To neighbouring countries	(£ million)	(1) Total	(2) To neighbouring countries
Settler economies					
Southern Rhodesia (1964)	35.6	27.1	149.5	23.8	18.1
Kenya (1961)	16.5	11.6	57.2	28.8	20.3
Peasant export economies					
Uganda (1963)	5.5	5.1	30.8	17.8	16.5
Ghana (1959)	4.9	0.2	21.5	22.7[a]	0.9
Jamaica (1960)	5.0	0.8	56.9	8.8	1.4

Note: [a] Nearly all (98 per cent) of Ghana's manufactured exports consisted of raw or simply worked timber, which is treated as part of 'secondary industry' by the criteria of Appendix 7, but arguably should not be.
Source: Appendix 7 below, which see for definition of 'neighbouring countries' used here.

furniture, insecticides, cigarettes in Kenya; rubber products, household utensils, electrical machinery in Southern Rhodesia; clothing in both countries) the local export market contributed more than 25 per cent of sales and was thus a significant determinant of demand.[37] The local export market was important not only in the sense of enlarging the market, and thus enabling firms to jump the barrier of minimum optimum size but also in the sense of *stabilising* it: for if faced with a downturn in local sales, as occurred at the end of the 1950s in both Kenya and Southern Rhodesia, it was frequently possible for a firm which already had a foothold in a local export market to expand its sales there.[38]

The local export market, and exports generally, are a more important factor in the demand for manufactures in the settler economies than in the 'peasant export economies' discussed earlier: Table 6.7 gives summary details. The export demand factor (Y_f, in the notation of equation 6.1 above) may therefore be significant in explaining the relatively more advanced role of manufacturing industry in the settler economies than in the peasant export economies in the early 1960s.

The influence of the 'neighbouring country market', however – we may note in conclusion – was not confined to manufacturing but influenced the orientation of the entire economy. In 1914 both Kenya and Southern Rhodesia approximated to the classical model of the colonial economy in that over half their imports came from, and more than half of their exports went to, their 'imperial overlord' the United Kingdom; at this stage inter-LDC trade of any sort was trivial. But by 1951, as is evident from Table 6.8,

Table 6.8. *Kenya and Southern Rhodesia: direction of export trade, 1914–64*

	Southern Rhodesia — Percentage of total export trade by value					Kenya — Percentage of total export trade by value			
	(1)	(2)	(3) To other British Dominions		(4)	(1)	(2)	(3)	(4)
	To UK	To South Africa	Total	Northern Rhodesia and Nyasaland	To other countries	To UK	To other British Dominions and colonies	To Uganda and Tanganyika	To other countries
1914	84.0	4.9	3.6		7.3	46.3[a]	8.0[a]	N/A	45.7[a]
1930	44.5	22.9	13.3		19.0	23.3	29.8	11.9	35.0
1941	61.5	4.4	23.2		10.8	25.7	23.1	13.5	37.7
1951	38.7	15.3	29.7	12.2	16.1	16.8	13.4	21.0	48.8
1964	25.5	7.4	38.4	30.4	28.5				

Note: [a] 1914 data are for Kenya and Uganda combined.

Source: Southern Rhodesia – *Annual Statement of the Trade of Southern Rhodesia for 1952*, Table II; Rhodesia, *Annual Statement of External Trade 1964* (Salisbury, 1965)

Kenya – East Africa Protectorate, *Annual Report of the Chief of Customs for the year 1917/18*; East Africa Customs and Excise, *Annual Trade Report of Kenya, Uganda Tanganyika (Tanzania)* for 1951 and 1964.

other countries in the British empire had become more important than the UK as destinations for exports, and of these 'other countries' the most significant single group was the neighbouring countries (Uganda, Tanganyika; Northern Rhodesia, Nyasaland) which by 1953 was incorporated into customs unions with Kenya and Southern Rhodesia. With these countries, as we have seen, the major part of the trade consisted of manufactures[39] for which the market was highly monopolistic,[40] rather than primary products for which the producer simply had to take whatever price world markets dictated. Thus the shift from primary producing to diversified economy involved, in both cases, a movement away from an economically dependent status in the direction of establishing the settler economies as 'regional metropolises'. It is futile to establish any date as a watershed in this process, although it is interesting to note that the period of sharpest

Table 6.9. *Kenya and Southern Rhodesia: balance of trade, 1914–64*

Year	Southern Rhodesia Balance of trade[a] (£000)		Kenya Balance of trade[a] (£000)	
	With all countries	With Northern Rhodesia and Nyasaland	With all countries	With Uganda and Tanganyika
1914	368			
1922	773			
1926	223		− 2 920	
1930	− 42		− 1 500	178
1934	3 105	1 016	500	182
1938	3 203	1 608	− 400	308
1942	6 998			− 329
1946	733	1 329	− 7 340	− 54
1948	− 13 426	2 287	− 17 742	− 407
1950	− 10 621	2 436	− 12 055	1 286
1952	− 33 790	3 650	− 28 467	1 128
1954[b]			− 36 026	1 534
1958[b]			− 21 777	7 531
1962[b]			− 14 366	
1964	9 770	28 555	− 8 520	

Notes:
[a] Balance of trade is defined as exports of merchandise less re-exports less imports (which includes in the Kenya case before 1948 'government imports'. For Kenya before 1948 it has been necessary to deduct Ugandan imports and exports from a composite total.
[b] Federal period. No separate data for Southern Rhodesia available.
Sources: Reports on the Trade of Southern Rhodesia, various (n.b. the 1952 edition was used for years before 1950); Kenya and Uganda Customs Department (after 1948, East African Customs Dept), *Annual Trade Report*, various.

shift away from British markets and sources of supply was, in Kenya at any rate, the inter-war and not the wartime and post-war period.[41]

In the post-Second World War period the economic counterpoise which the neighbouring countries offered to the settler economies gained an added importance. For during this time the settler economies were, for the first time since the inter-war depression (Table 6.9), in persistent balance-of-payments deficit with the rest of the world, and one of the most important factors in keeping these deficits within reasonable bounds and preventing them from constraining the growth of the economy was the persistent and increasing surpluses (up to 1953 in Southern Rhodesia, after which inter-territorial transfers within the Federation are not recorded) which the settler economies ran with surrounding territories.

CONCLUSION

The evidence presented in this chapter suggests that the extreme inequality in domestic income distribution in the settler economies did not act as an effective brake on industrialisation for the home market. Partly this was because the propensity to consume manufactures seems to have been as high amongst the rich as amongst the poor; partly also, however, it was because businessmen in the settler economies were able to swamp the markets of still poorer developing economies with exports of manufactures. Warren was correct when he wrote in his famous essay 'that the ties of dependence binding the Third World to the imperialist countries have been, and are being markedly loosened',[42] but he overstated the case when he wrote that 'the leading sector for the majority of less-developed economies in post-war development has been manufacturing based precisely and dominantly on the home market'.[43] For the settler economies the building up of relations of commercial dominance with other less favoured Third World countries was as important as the home market as a means of loosening the ties of dependence binding them to Britain and to Europe.

APPENDIX 7: A COMPARISON OF EARNINGS AND INDUSTRIAL STRUCTURE IN THE SETTLER ECONOMIES AND THREE NON-SETTLER ECONOMIES IN THE EARLY 1960s

This appendix provides data on earnings, and also on industrial production, exports and imports in particular industrial categories which are used in the argument of Chapter 6 above.

Trade and industrial structure

An important analytical distinction used in the argument of Chapter 6 which cuts across the conventional (ISIC and Brussels Convention) taxonomies of industrial activity is that between goods produced for final consumption and 'intermediate' goods which are inputs to other industries. The following definition of consumer goods and intermediate goods is adopted here.

216

Consumer goods (ISIC category)		Threshold for domestic production (£000)	Intermediate goods (ISIC category)	
011–13	Meat and meat products fresh, frozen and chilled	116		
022	Milk, cream, baby foods	430	243	Timber
023, 024	Butter and cheese	219	27	Crude fertilisers
046, 047	Milled cereals and cereal preparations	225	511–12	Basic industrial chemicals
048	Bakery products	71	531–3	Paints and varnishes
053, 055	Canned fruit and vegetables	341	599.01	Explosives and manufactured fertilisers
062	Confectionery	238		Structural clay products
111	Non-alcoholic drinks		66	Glass
		202		Cement and other non-metallic minerals
112	Alcoholic drinks		681	Iron and steel basic industries
122	Cigarettes and manufactured tobacco	566	682	Non-ferrous metals
411, 412, 413	Cooking oil and margarine	1121	699	Metal products (not machinery)
541, 551	Perfumes, cosmetics and drugs	135	71	Non-electrical machinery (except 716.11)
552	Soap and candles	396	72	Electrical machinery
651.01, 652.01	Cotton fabrics		732, 734, 735	Other transport equipment (except 733.01)
652.02, 653.02	Woollen fabrics	583	812	Plumbing, heating, lighting fittings
651.01, 651.06, 653.05	Silk and artificial fibres		Part of 89	Printing and publishing Scientific instruments
656.03	Blankets	612		
699.13, 699.14	Household utensils	94		
716.11	Sewing machines	37		
733.01	Bicycles	37		
821	Furniture	48		
84	Clothing	128		
851	Footwear	245		

Table 6.10a. *Secondary industry, Southern Rhodesia, 1964: imports, exports, and domestic production*

		(1) Imports 1964 (£000)	(2) Exports 1964 (a) Total (£000)	(2) Exports 1964 (b) Total to neighbouring countries[c] (£000)	(3) Domestic production 1964 (gross output in £000)	(4) = (1) + (3) − (2a) Total 'market size' (£000)	(5) = (2b)/(3) Exports to neighbouring countries as a proportion of total industrial production (%)
Consumer goods							
011–013	Meat products	348	2 050	399	12 869	11 167	3.1
022	Dairy products	452	(100)[a]	447	5 286	5 489	7.4
023, 024	Butter and cheese	51	(200)[a]	30		9 913	0.3
046, 047	Cereals (milled)	582	(200)[a]	155	9 531		2.8
048	Bakery products	218	(200)[a]		5 361	5 379	
053, 055	Jam, canned fruit and vegetables	486	(200)[a]	174	300	586	29.6
062	Confectionery	298	200	171	(included in 048)		
111	Non-alcoholic drinks	11	230		1 654	1 533	
112	Alcoholic drinks	779	460	133	5 090	5 409	2.6
122	Cigarettes and manufactured tobacco	169	1 764	1 435	9 030	7 435	15.8
411–13	Cooking oil and margarine	556	623	616	1 200	1 133	51.3
541, 551	Perfumes, cosmetics and drugs	1 655	442	372	1 378	2 591	51.3
552	Soap and candles	305	952	934	5 071	4 424	21.1
651.01 651.02 652.02	Cotton fabrics	3 238					

Code	Item						
652.02 / 653.02	Woollen fabrics	890	1 348	1 300	9 199	15 611	14.1
651.01 / 651.06 / 653.05	Fabrics of silk and artificial fibres	3 632					
656.03	Blankets	82	100	(included in 651–3)	(included in 651–3)	(−18)[b]	
699.13 / 699.14	Household utensils	223	372	389	400	251	89.7
716.11	Sewing machines	300	–	–	(included in 733)	300	
733.01	Bicycles	388	100	38		288	
821	Furniture	147	587	558	2 856	2 416	19.5
84	Clothing	3 739	5 306	5 165	12 579	10 414	64.7
851	Footwear	1 070	1 668	1 582			
	(I) Total consumer goods	19 619	17 102	13 898	81 804	84 321	17.0
Intermediate goods							
243 + 631	Timber and wood products	1 001	898	593	(included in 642)	103	
27	Crude fertilisers				(included in 599.01)		
511–12	Basic industrial chemicals	2 333	439	436	7 185	9 079	6.1
531–3	Paints and varnishes		583	555	1 462	(879)	37.9
599	Explosives, fertilisers, dips	3 149	860	818	(included in 511)	(2 289)	
629	Rubber products	543	972	929	3 204	2 775	28.9
641–2	Pulp and paper	2 572	838	733	3 677	5 411	19.9
	Structural clay products						
66	Glass	850	636	555	4 263	4 477	13.0
	Cement and other non-metallic minerals						

Table 6.10a. (cont.)

		(1) Imports 1964	(2) Exports 1964		(3) Domestic production 1964	(4) = (1) + (3) − (2a) Total 'market size'	(5) = (2b)/(3) Exports to neighbouring countries as a proportion of total industrial production
			(a) Total	(b) Total to neighbouring countries[c]	(gross output in £000)		
		(£000)	(£000)	(£000)	(£000)	(£000)	(%)
681	Iron and steel basic industries	5 244	4 505	1 166	9 609	10 348	12.1
682	Non-ferrous metals	1 568	1 079	301	1 879	2 368	16.0
699	Metal products (not machinery)	908	2 231	1 911	10 922	9 599	17.4
71	Non-electrical machinery	12 531	652	577	1 799	13 678	32.0
72	Electrical machinery	4 016	2 042	1 943	4 764	6 738	40.7
733	Motor vehicle assembly and repair	8 731	1 937	1 923	8 475	15 269	22.6
732, 734, 735	Other transport equipment	2 778	268	259	5 104	7 614	5.0
	Printing and publishing ⎫ Stationery ⎬ Scientific instruments ⎭						
89		1 021	593	549	5 423	5 851	8.2
	(II) Total intermediate goods	47 245	18 533	13 248	67 766	96 478	19.5
	(I) + (II) Total manufactured goods	66 864	35 635	27 146	149 570	180 799	18.1

− negligible (less than £10 000).

Notes:

[a] Arbitrary breakdown of a total of 1100 for 'miscellaneous foods'.

[b] A notional figure, due to the fact that the production figure for blankets is included in industrial classification 651–3.

[c] Neighbouring countries are South Africa, Nyasaland (Malawi) and Northern Rhodesia (Zambia).

220

Table 6.10b. *Secondary industry, Kenya, 1961: imports, exports, and domestic production*

	(1) Imports 1961 (£000)	(2) Exports 1961 (a) Total (£000)	(2) Exports 1961 (b) Total to neighbouring countries[a] (£000)	(3) Domestic production 1961 (gross output in £000)	(4) = (1) + (3) − (2a) Total 'market size' (£000)	(5) = (2b)/(3) Exports to neighbouring countries as a proportion of total industrial production (%)
Consumer goods						
011–013 Meat products	64	2 163	437	5 544	3 445	7.8
022 Dairy products	382	88	468	4 430	3 688	12.6
023, 024 Butter and cheese	62	1 098				
046, 047 Cereals (milled)	62	850	785	8 612	7 824	10.0
048 Bakery products	49	181	161	1 870	1 738	9.2
053, 055 Jam, canned fruit and vegetables	343	552	80	747	538	14.8
062 Confectionery	233	27	27	123	329	9.3
111 Non-alcoholic drink	6	52	40	1 095	1 049	3.8
112 Alcoholic drink	741	710	696	3 677	3 708	18.7
122 Tobacco manufactures	218	1 909	1 904	3 001	1 310	63.4
411–13 Cooking oil and margarine	⎱ 684		⎱ 425			
511 Basic industrial chemicals	⎰		⎰ 93			
541 Medical and pharmaceutical products	1 569	756	⎱ 62 ⎰ 76	5 027[b]	6 524	13.0
551 Perfumes and cosmetics						
552 Soap and candles	312	926	914	2 409	1 795	37.9

Table 6.10b. (cont.)

| | | (1) Imports 1961 | (2) Exports 1961 | | (3) Domestic production 1961 | (4) = (1) + (3) − (2a) Total 'market size' | (5) = (2b)/(3) Exports to neighbouring countries as a proportion of total industrial production |
| | | | (a) Total | (b) Total to neighbouring countries[a] | (gross output in £000) | | |
SITC		(£000)	(£000)	(£000)		(£000)	(%)
651.04, 652.01, 652.02	Cotton fabrics	5 130					
651.02, 653.02	Woollen fabrics	(included in 656.03)	250	249	737	8 828	33.7
651.01, 651.06, 653.05	Fabrics of silk and artificial fibres	3 211					
656.03	Blankets	973	46	46	(included in 651)		
699.13	Household utensils	(included in 699)	205	205	(included in 699)	722	35.7
716.11	Sewing machines	306	–	–	–	306	
733.01	Bicycles	213	13	11	(included in 732–5)	200	
821	Furniture	231	213	193	435	453	44.3
84	Clothing	2 416	881	874	2 141	3 164	78.2
851	Footwear	296	808	802			
	(I) Total consumer goods	17 501	11 728	8 548	39 848	45 621	21.4

Intermediate goods

SITC	Industry						
243 + 631	Timber and wood products	339	247	103	1 184	1 276	8.7
27	Crude fertilisers				(included in 599.01)		
532. 533	Dyeing, tanning, colouring materials	950	1 009	234			
599.02	Fertilisers, insecticides, dips		228	179	1 213	926	34.8
629	Rubber products	(400)	194	192	454	660	42.2
642	Pulp and paper, paper products	(1 500)	517	494	1 261 / 481	2 244	39.1
66	Structural clay products / Glass / Cement and other non-metallic minerals	872	1 379	912	3 358	3 332	23.7
681	Iron and steel basic industries	4 412	182	182	(included in 699)	(4 230)	–
682	Non-ferrous metals	3 721	120	120	3 741	6 672	14.7
699	Metal products (not machinery)	7 681	670	433	657		
71	Non-electrical machinery	2 596	69	59	212	8 269	8.9
72	Electrical machinery		11	11		2 797	5.1
733	Motor vehicle assembly and repair	4 613	–	–	279	4 892	–
732–5	Transport equipment	6 886	12	9	3 252	10 126	–
89	Printing, publishing	(included in 642)	163	145	1 261	1 098	11.5
	(II) Total intermediate goods	33 970	4 801	3 073	17 353	46 522	17.7
	(I) + (II) Total manufactured goods	51 471	16 529	11 621	57 201	92 143	20.3

– negligible

Note: [a]Uganda and Tanganyika.

Sources: Imports, exports – East Africa Customs Dept. *Annual Trade Report*, 1961.

Industrial production – Kenya, *Census of Manufacturing*, 1961.

Table 6.10c. *Secondary industry, Uganda, 1963: imports, exports, and domestic production*

	(1) Imports 1963 (£000)	(2) Exports 1963 (a) Total (£000)	(b) Total to neighbouring countries[a] (£000)	(3) Domestic production 1963 (gross output in £000)	(4) = (1)+(3) − (2a) Total 'market size' (£000)	(5) = (2b)/(3) Exports to neighbouring countries as a proportion of total industrial production (%)
Consumer goods						
011–013 Meat products	7	107	75	492	392	1.3
022 Dairy products	243	–	–	250	429	–
023, 024 Butter and cheese	6	70	–			–
046, 047 Cereals (milled)	12	54	54	1 116	1 074	5.0
048 Bakery products	8	–	–	1 342	1 350	–
053, 055 Jam, canned fruit and vegetables	78	–	–	–	78	–
062 Confectionery	52	65	65			
111 Non-alcoholic drink	1	31	25	7 981	6 718	18.9
112 Alcoholic drink	166	70	70			
122 Tobacco manufactures	29	1 345	1 342			
411–13 Cooking oil and margarine	297	856	768	3 944	(3 961)	19.8
541 Medical and pharmaceutical products	590	14	15			
551 Perfumes and cosmetics						
552 Soap and candles	362	242	242	1 130	1 250	
651.04 652.01 652.02 Cotton fabrics	1 991					
651.02 653.02 Woollen fabrics	(included in 656.03)	1 907	1 899	4 160	6 357	21.4
651.01 651.06 Fabrics of silk and artificial fibres	2 113					

			[illegible]	[illegible]	[illegible]	251	42.0
733.01	Bicycles	161	–	–	28	189	–
821	Furniture	72	19	8	257	310	3.1
84	Clothing	1 236	27	27	(included in 651)	(1 209)	–
851	Footwear	175	22	19		(153)	–
(I) Total consumer goods		8 051	4 934	4 714	20 950	24 067	22.5
Intermediate goods							
243, 631	Timber and wood products	68	193	55	998	873	5.5
511/2	Basic industrial chemicals	252	15	10	243	480	4.0
532	Dyeing, tanning, colouring materials	138	4	4	–	134	–
599	Fertilisers, insecticides, dips	152	–	–	–	152	–
629	Rubber products	600	3	3	346	943	
641	Pulp and paper, paper products	479	6	6	–	473	–
66	{Structural clay products, Glass, Cement and other non-metallic materials}	512	173	152	1 323	1 662	11.4
681	Iron and steel basic industries	1 007	41	41	–	966	–
699	Metal products (not machinery)	514	136	126 }			
71	Non-electrical machinery	2 044	35	35 }	4 701	7 915	3.4
72	Electrical machinery	827		}			
733	Motor vehicle assembly and repair	4 712	–	–	1 351	6 063	–
731–5 (excl. 733)	Transport equipment				(included in 71 & 72)		
892	Printing, publishing	216	–	–	898	1 114	–
(II) Total intermediate goods		11 521	606	432	9 860	20 775	4.4
(I) + (II) Total manufactured goods		19 572	5 540	5 146	30 810	44 842	16.7

– negligible

Note: [a] Kenya and Tanganyika.

Source: Import and export data – East African Customs Dept, *Annual Trade Report*, 1963.
Industrial production – Uganda, *Survey of Industrial Production*, 1963, Table III.

Table 6.10d. *Secondary industry, Jamaica, 1960: imports, exports, and domestic production*

| | | (1) Imports 1960 | (2) Exports 1960 | | (3) Domestic production 1960 | (4) = (1) + (3) − (2a) Total 'market size' | (5) = (2b)/(3) Exports to neighbouring countries as a proportion of total industrial production |
| | | | (a) Total | (b) Total to neighbouring countries[a] | | | |
		(£000)	(£000)	(£000)	(gross output in £000)	(£000)	(%)
Consumer goods							
011–013	Meat products	1 790	7	4			
022	Dairy products	499	33	6			
023, 024	Butter and cheese	1 079	–	–			
046, 042	Cereals (milled)	} 3 046					
048	Bakery products		549	–			
053, 055	Jams, canned fruit and vegetables		5	–	18 599	24 419	–
062	Confectionery		–	20			
111	Non-alcoholic drink	521	15	15	7 728	6 651	–
112	Alcoholic drink		1 583	39	4 308	4 745	–
122	Tobacco manufactures	916	479	15	–	234	
411–13	Cooking oil and margarine	235	1	1			
541	Medical and pharmaceutical products	}					
551	Perfumes and cosmetics	1 494	309	78	2 212	3 397	2.3
552	Soap and candles						
651.04 / 652.01 / 652.02	Cotton fabrics	} 2 059					
651.02 / 653.02	Woollen fabrics	385	129	3	5 243	8 759	–
651.01 / 651.06 / 653.05	Fabrics and silk and artificial fibres	} 1 201					

Code	Product						
821	Furniture	679	52	48	2 217	2 844	1.7
84	Clothing[b]	1 002	991	26	1 329[b]	1 340	1.9
851	Footwear	676	166	99	2 581	3 091	3.8
	(I) Total consumer goods	15 954	4 319	354	44 217	55 852	0.8
Intermediate goods							
243, 631	Timber and wood products	500	10	2	541	1 031	0.4
511/2	Basic industrial chemicals	(1 000)	48	8	2 212	3 164	–
53	Dyeing, tanning, colouring materials	341	258	78	389	472	20.0
599	Fertilisers, insecticides, dips	853	3	3	(included in 511)	850	–
629	Rubber products	500	–	–	104	604	–
642	Pulp and paper, paper products	2 241	61	60	805	2 985	7.4
66	Structural clay products / Glass / Cement and other non-metallic minerals	1 004	116	113	1 615	2 503	6.9
681 / 699	Iron and steel basic industries / Metal products (not machinery)	2 940	250	247	–	2 690	–
71 / 72	Non-electrical machinery / Electrical machinery	2 333	–	–			
733 / 732–5	Motor vehicle assembly and repairs / Transport equipment	8 049	–	–	5 351	15 733	4.6
89	Printing, publishing	–	–	–	1 708	1 708	–
	(II) Total intermediate goods	19 761	746	511	12 725	31 740	1.6
	(I) + (II) Total manufactured goods	35 715	5 065	865	56 942	87 592	1.5

– negligible

Notes: [a] All Caribbean countries. [b] Sum of 'dressmaking' and 'tailoring'

Sources:

Imports and exports – Jamaica, *Annual Abstract of Statistics*, 1960. Table 41.

Production – Jamaica, *Industrial activity: mining, manufactures, construction: report on a survey of establishments* (Kingston: Department of Statistics, 1963).

Table 6.10e. *Secondary industry, Ghana, 1959: imports, exports, and domestic production*

		(1) Imports 1959	(2) Exports 1959 (a) Total	(2) Exports 1959 (b) Total to neighbouring countries	(3) Domestic Production 1959	(4) = (1)+(3) −(2a) Total 'market size'	(5) = (2b)/(3) Exports to neighbouring countries as a proportion of total industrial production (%)
		(£000)	(£000)	(£000)	(gross output in £000)	(£000)	
Consumer goods							
011–013	Meat products	1 654	–	– ⎱	272	3 173	–
022	Dairy products	1 067	–	– ⎰			–
023, 024	Butter and cheese	180	–	–			–
046, 047	Cereals (milled)	71	1	1	1 359	1 429	–
048	Bakery products	188	–	–		188	–
053, 055	Jam, canned fruit and vegetables	567	–	–	(included in 011)	567	–
062	Confectionery	273	–	–		273	–
111	Non-alcoholic drinks	12	–	– ⎱			–
112	Alcoholic drinks	2 616	–	–	6 600	9 588	–
122	Tobacco manufactures	360	–	– ⎰			–
411–13	Medical and pharmaceutical products	2 210	4	–	–	2 206	–
551	Perfumes and cosmetics		–	–	–		–
552	Soap and candles	2 949	–	–	–	2 949	–
651.4	Cotton fabrics	11 011	–	–	⎱		–
652.01 652.02							
651.02	Woollen fabrics	451	–	–	–	14 487	–
653.02							
651.06	Fabrics of silk and				⎰		

Code	Item						
699.13	Household utensils	1 275	–	–	142	1 275	–
716.11	Sewing machines	182	–	–	–	182	–
733.01	Bicycles	240	2	–	–	240	–
821	Furniture	434	2	2	365	797	–
84	Clothing	3 006	44	–	253	3 215	13.8
851	Footwear	1 572	–	35	–	1 572	0.1
	(I) Total consumer goods	33 485	51	38	8 849	42 283	
Intermediate goods							
243, 631	Timber and wood products	228	4 878	–	7 926	3 276	1.8
511	Basic industrial chemicals	415	–	146	–	4 892	–
53	Dyeing, tanning, colouring materials	816	–	–	1 007	–	–
599	Fertilisers, insecticides, dips	2 662	–	2 }	–	2 441	–
629	Rubber products	2 172	8	–	269	–	–
641/2	Pulp and paper, paper products	1 195	–	–	–	1 195	–
	Structural clay products }						
66	Glass	4 791	–	–	310	5 101	–
	Cement and other non-metallic minerals }						
681	Iron and steel basic industries	4 288	–	–	–	4 288	–
699	Metal products	4 526	–	–	–	4 526	–
71	Non-electrical machinery	9 088	–	–	382	9 470	–
72	Electrical machinery	3 870	–	–	–	3 870	–
733	Motor vehicle assembly and repair }	12 646	5	5	1 910 }	14 551	–
732–5 (exc. 733)	Transport equipment				890	1 737	–
892	Printing and publishing	847	–	–			–
	(II) Total intermediate goods	47 544	4 891	153	12 694	55 347	1.2
	(I) + (II) Total manufactured goods	81 029	4 942	191	21 543	97 630	0.9

Note: [a]All West African countries (Sierra Leone, Ivory Coast, Dahomey, Nigeria, Togo, Mali, Liberia, Upper Volta, Senegal).

Sources: Exports and imports – Ghana, *Trade Report for 1959 and 1960* (Accra: Central Bureau of Statistics, 1960). Production – Ghana, *Industrial Statistics 1959 and 1959* (Accra: Central Bureau of Statistics, 1959).

The 'threshold for domestic production' is average sales per plant in the industry stated, South Africa, 1961, and is intended to give a rough indication of the 'shiftability' of import categories. Its significance and limitations are discussed in the text above, p. 207 and in particular note 24. The source is South Africa, *Industrial census 1950–1961* (Pretoria: Bureau of Statistics, 1961). In the case of most products in this table the classification to be adopted is intuitively obvious but three arbitrary cut-offs in it should be noted at once.

(1) Food processing *mainly or wholly for export* (e.g. tea, coffee processing, and in some countries sugar processing too) is counted as part of the industrial sector by the national accounts systems of some countries (e.g. Uganda) and excluded by others (e.g. Kenya) on the grounds that it is part of the agricultural sector. We exclude it.
(2) All drugs (ISIC sub-sector 551) are counted as consumer goods. This obviously oversimplifies the position.
(3) With the exception of sewing machines and bicycles, all machinery (ISIC sub-sector 7) is classified as intermediate goods. Again, this obviously exaggerates the position. On the above classification, the data are as shown in Table 6.10.

The earnings distribution

The essential difference between the labour markets of the settler economies of Africa and those of the peasant export economies was that the former contained a significant amount of European skilled and, in Southern Rhodesia, also unskilled labour. This labour commanded so high a premium above the rates which it could command in Europe,[44] particularly in Southern Rhodesia where it was protected by legislation which effectively excluded Africans from skilled jobs,[45] that average real white earnings in the settler economies were scarcely, if at all, lower than in the peasant export economies where the white presence was largely confined to administrative and managerial roles.[46] Average black real earnings *from employment*,[47] and thus the black/white earnings *differential*, were similar as between settler and peasant export economies. But this similarity in African non-African differentials is sharply offset by a higher share of whites in the total wage bill (more than half in Kenya and Southern Rhodesia, against 42 per cent in Uganda and 16 per cent in Ghana). Table 6.11 sets out the data.

Table 6.11. *'Settler economies' and peasant export economies: racial distribution of incomes from employment, 1960*

	Africans		Non-Africans		
	(1)	(2)	(3)	(4)	(4)/(2)
	Number of employees	Average annual earnings from employment (£; cash and kind)	Number of employees	Average annual earnings from employment (£; cash and kind)	Ratio of average African to average non-African earnings from employment
Settler economies					
Southern Rhodesia	640 000	94	89 400	1 134	12.1
Kenya	553 204	68	58 880	781	11.5
Peasant export economies					
Uganda	219 695	68	15 163	738	10.9
Ghana	326 664	166	6 234	1 694	10.2

Source: As for Figure 6.2.

230

Cumulative
distribution
of income
(%)

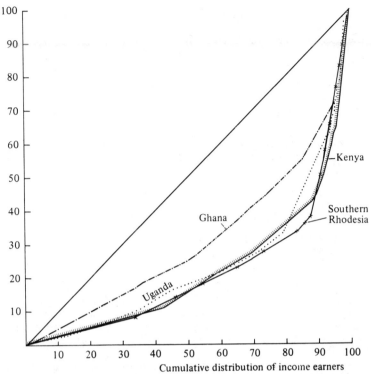

Cumulative distribution of income earners

Fig. 6.2 Kenya, Southern Rhodesia and two 'peasant export economies': Lorenz curve estimate of distribution of incomes from employment, 1960. *Sources*: Rhodesia, *Monthly Statistical Digest*, May 1972, Tables 11, 12, 14, 15; East African Statistical Dept 1961a (B3), text Table 4 and appendix Table 1; Uganda, *Statistical Abstract* 1961, Section UP; Ghana, *Labour Statistics* 1960, Analysis of recorded number of employees, 31 December 1960.

As a result, the earnings distribution is more unequal in the 'settler' than in the 'peasant export' economies. Figure 6.2 presents Lorenz curve estimates of the earnings distribution for the same four countries; they are rather crude estimates since for the African population in Southern Rhodesia and Kenya and for the non-African population in all four countries, it is necessary to base them on the assumption that earnings within occupational groups clustered around the group mean. The Ghanaian Lorenz curve is consistently outside that of the settler economies, and although the Uganda curve does entwine itself with the Kenyan one at one point towards the upper end of the African part of the earnings structure, it also lies for the most part above both settler economy curves, and its Gini coefficient of inequality is a good deal lower.[48] We conclude that income *from employment* was substantially more unequally distributed in the settler economies than in the peasant export economies. We do not have the data with which even to make a guess at the distribution of overall incomes, but it seems almost certain that if we did, this difference in inequality would show up even more sharply, since African average income from sale of agricultural produce was so much higher in the peasant export economies, and non-African average income from such sources so much lower.[49]

231

The settler economies

APPENDIX 8 INCOME INEQUALITY AND THE DEMAND FOR
MANUFACTURES (AFTER PEARSON AND OTHERS)

Pearson (1969 (D1) p. 77) asserts that 'the size of the market for manufactures increases with
the slope of the Pareto curve, other things being equal'.

This is demonstrated by an arithmetical example in which a demand function for 'manufactured goods' estimated against Southern Rhodesia data for Europeans and urban Africans
in 1960 and 1963/4:

(1) log Y $\qquad$ = 0.13758 + 0.82154 log X
(expenditure on $\qquad\qquad$ (total personal
manufactured goods) $\qquad\qquad$ income)

is applied to two hypothetical communities, with equal total and per capita income:
country A, consisting of
100 000 'high' incomes of £500 p.a. each,
totalling $\qquad\qquad$ £50 million

900 000 'low' incomes of £67 p.a. each,
totalling $\qquad\qquad$ £60 million

country B, consisting of
500 000 'high' incomes of £200 p.a. each,
totalling $\qquad\qquad$ £100 million
500 000 'low incomes of £20 p.a. each,
totalling $\qquad\qquad$ £10 million

'Substituting in equation (1) and summing', he writes, 'we find that the demand for manufactures
in country A will be, in round figures, £36 million, and in country B £62 million. Thus even
though total and average incomes and population sizes are the same in both countries, the
market for domestic industry is getting on for twice the size in country B than in country A'
(Pearson, *ibid.*).

Accepting for the time being that incomes are 'more equally distributed' in B rather than in
A – as Pearson obviously intends – it is by no means necessarily true that this relationship will
hold. For instance, if the estimated demand function for manufactures were, not (1) but

(1') Y = 0.8 (X − 200) $\quad$ (if X > 200)
$\quad$ Y = 0 $\qquad\qquad$ (if X < 200)

where Y is consumption of manufactures and X is individual income, then consumption of
manufactures would of course be zero in B and £24 million in A. This kind of relationship, in
which consumption of manufactured goods only starts at a certain 'threshold' level of income,
seems to be the one in the mind of many Latin American underconsumptionists.[50]

In short, the effects of income distribution on demand are highly sensitive to the shape of the
consumption pattern. In particular, if the cross-sectional consumption function is linear, cuts
the vertical axis and has a slope of less than 45°,[51] it is true that a minor[52] internal redistribution
from one group to a poorer group will increase aggregate demand, since a consumption function of this sort is characterised by a continually falling average propensity to consume as
income rises. (This was a result well known by the 'stagnation theorists' of the 1940s, who
predicted that the post-war Western economy would suffer from chronic deficiency of demand on
account of a chronically falling APC as living standards rose.)[53] But if this condition is not
satisfied, and in particular if the consumption function has a slope of 45° or more over any part
of its length (as appears to be the case in Southern Rhodesia in the 1950s, see pp. 198–204 and
Figure 6.1 above), then this result will not necessarily hold, and a redistribution from a richer to a
poorer group may lower the aggregate propensity to consume.

232

The case becomes more complex when we turn from the effect on demand of redistributing income within a country, to the effect of moving from one country to another with a different income distribution. For different countries will not necessarily have identical consumption functions, and if one moves from country A into a country B that has the same per capita and total income, but a more equal income distribution, then the demand for manufactures (or any other goods) may change *either* because the *different income distribution* causes a change in the average propensity to consume manufactures (this, as we have seen, need not necessarily be a fall), or because a *differently shaped consumption function* causes a change in the average propensity to consume manufactures. A sufficient condition for the move from A to B to increase demand is that the consumption function in B does not have a smaller average propensity to consume than that in A in the neighbourhood of the current average income level, and that the consumption function in B is linear, non-proportional and has a slope of not more than 45°.

These two slips, therefore, intervene between the cup of a more equal income distribution and the lip of a higher demand for manufactures. They mean that the arithmetic sign which has to be attached to the income distribution term in a demand for manufactures equation such as (6.1) is highly uncertain, in spite of the claims of Pearson and Chenery (see above) and the spokesmen of commercial interests in the settler economies in the 1930s (e.g. Isher Dass and Rhodesia Chamber of Commerce: pp. 195 and 205 above). Those spokesmen, of course, were comparing respectively Kenya and Uganda, and Southern Rhodesia and Jamaica: countries which differed in both total and per capita income (cf. Table 6.4 above), giving rise to sources of variation additional to those analysed above.

7

Conclusions

The principal purpose of this study has been to set the facts of Kenyan and Southern Rhodesian economic history against a stereotypical view of the evolution of the economy and economic policy in 'settler economies'.[1] According to this stereotype, European agriculture is unable to compete, and European enterprise of all kinds unable to secure a labour force, without the help of a thicket of protective and coercive measures. But although economically weak, the rural bourgeoisie, according to this stereotype, is so politically dominant that it can implement these measures without effective opposition from colonial bureaucracy, metropolitan ministry for the Colonies or indigenous population. The measures bring about a continuous reduction in the productivity of the African population, and this so effectively flattens out the curve of labour supply that shortages of African labour, when they arise, can be eliminated purely by political and not by economic means. But the subsistence level wages which this process implies hamstring any industrialisation which is based on the home market, and hence the economy remains ossified in its dependence on primary exports far longer than is normal for a country enjoying its level of average income, until eventually rescued by state intervention.

The research reported in Chapters 2 to 6 above suggests that if the data on which we have to depend give an accurate impression, this picture of the long-term development of a settler economy must be modified at many points in its application to Kenya and Southern Rhodesia. Indeed, in some areas, it is simply inaccurate. The maize growing, coffee growing and tobacco growing sectors of the European rural bourgeoisie were not on average, at most periods for which data exist, less efficient than the principal growing regions in other parts of the world. However, the governments of Kenya and Southern Rhodesia were at all times exposed to pressure to protect the weak farmers as well as the strong, in the interests of maximising the size of the European rural population. In many cases this pressure was successful, and this kept many inefficient farmers in being. In some cases, however, the pressure was unsuccessful, on account of conflicts within the European community. These conflicts reflected, at the start, principally the split between large concessionaires and small individual producers, but increasingly their basis shifted to reflect *sectoral* conflicts of interest

234

between producer and producer, or producer and consumer, and schemes to circumvent them by 'buying off the losers' were themselves more and more constrained, as time wore on, by the dwindling tolerance of the African majority on whom the cost of such schemes was often visited. Nor, to the extent that policies repressive of African agriculture were implemented, did they bring about a 'progressive deterioration' of the productivity of the African peasantry in most districts. That productivity, so far as we can tell from the rather poor data, fluctuated about no clear trend[2] during the colonial period; but during the periods when it increased, such as the 1920s, and late 1930s, it pushed up the supply price of labour and required some economic mechanisms, i.e. increases in the wage level, to be used to ease labour shortages in supplementation of the existing political measures. Nor does the low productivity and pay of unskilled African labour seem to have exerted an effective constraint on industrialisation for the home market, in large part because the limitations of low demand could be circumvented by unloading an ever-increasing proportion of consumer goods production on the markets of neighbouring, and less industrially developed, countries.

None of these conclusions does anything to rehabilitate the old economic historiography, in which underdevelopment in the African economy was ascribed to the absence of a spirit of economic rationality in the African, and colonial governments exercised 'trusteeship' over him by assisting the growth of this spirit: they simply suggest that to a considerable extent the colonial economy was able to elude the deterministic traps, the 'contradictions', that some versions of Marxist analysis set for it. The analysis of all the chapters of this study has in fact been underpinned by models based on the assumption that all parties pursued their own rational economic interests, which in the case of European food producers meant the suppression of African competition, as far as this was necessary and possible. But the very existence of empirical support for these models suggests that the versions of underdevelopment theory which have been applied to settler-colonial societies in Africa are shot through with irrationalities of their own. The European farming community has been accused of economic incompetence and irrationality,[3] leading to the need for political intervention, whereas we have argued that the adoption of a labour-intensive production function was a highly rational response to a situation in which capital was dear and labour, thanks partly to economic policy itself, was cheap. The African peasantry stands implicitly accused of irrationality, in the sense of inability to adapt, in face of declining per capita acreage and of competition in product markets, whereas we have argued that in many districts it was successful, at any rate until absenteeism became a severe problem in the 1940s, in adopting the perfectly rational response of intensifying agricultural production as land became scarcer.

However, one of the contentions of this study, which would bear a great deal more testing than we have been able to give it here, is that rationality itself takes on a specialised meaning in a policy environment which is perceived as hostile. To the writings of the last ten years which emphasise the importance of risk aversion and survival strategies in traditional agriculture it is necessary to add the gloss that in Kenya and Southern Rhodesia rational behaviour seems to have been seen by African economic actors not only as a game against nature but also against the government.[4] This appears to explain much of the observed reluctance by Africans to adopt technical change in agriculture – particularly maize cultivation and livestock improvement, in which they were competitive with the European farmer. In principle, one may expect to see agriculturists involved in such games against the government in all less developed countries today; but in settler economies additional antagonism was added to the 'game' by the rivalry between African and European farmers in food production.

To what extent – generalising the last point – should the 'settler economy' be seen as a distinctive economic system? The answer seems to be that it is easier to identify a distinctive pattern of 'extra-market operations', or interventions in the market, than a distinctive economic structure. If we go back to the twelve countries in Table 1.1, we find that they, unlike other countries, were characterised in the twentieth century by the making of vast concessions to white colonists, by racial division of land, by labour tenancy on white farms, and in some cases by racial discrimination in the markets for skilled labour and agricultural produce. But if we compare wage levels (Table 6.11) and industrial development (Chapter 6, in particular Table 6.4) between settler and non-settler economies it turns out that generalisations about differences between patterns of evolution of the *economy* are very difficult to make. The indigenous wage level may be higher in 'peasant export economies' than the near-subsistence level of settler economies (Ghana); or it may not (Uganda). The level of demand for consumer manufactures may be almost as high, in relation to national income, in non-settler as in settler economies (Jamaica) or it may be well below (Ghana). Invariably, however, the settler economy is marked by a highly unequal income distribution.

The settler economy has proved a transient species, and certainly, of the twelve specimens listed in Table 1.1, only one, South Africa, could be said to survive more or less intact. Patterns of evolution since independence and the end of the formal settler era for the others have been bifurcated between attempts to take over the existing structure of production and landholding unaltered into African hands, as in Kenya and Zaire, and attempts to transform it in a socialist direction, as in Angola, Mozambique and Algeria, with extensive nationalisation and equalitarian programmes of land reform. A year after the achievement of formal independence in 1980, the government of Zimbabwe appears to be about to follow the second course; but as a comparison between the declarations of 'African Socialist' rhetoric made in Kenya shortly after independence and the present stance of her economic policy will readily remind us, this present indication offers little guide to the long-term future.

Notes

1. Introduction

1 Colonisation of underdeveloped areas by European producers who became economically dependent on the indigenous population. This definition distinguishes 'settler colonies' from 'peasant export' colonies where the white immigrant population was purely administrative (e.g. Uganda, Gold Coast, Nigeria) and from colonies such as Australia and Canada where the indigenous population was so sparse as to be unimportant either as a market or as a factor of production in the colonial economy. For elaboration, see Chapter 1.2.

2 This has been noted particularly by Arghiri Emmanuel 1972 (D3), p. 36, who argues that traditional Marxist theories of imperialism have failed 'to recognise a factor that intervenes between imperialist capitalism and the peoples of the exploited countries, i.e. the colonists themselves'.

3 For example, on settler economies generally: Good 1976 (D3); on East Africa: Brett 1973 (D1); on Kenya: Wolff 1974 (D1); on Southern Rhodesia: Arrighi 1973 (D2) and Clarke 1975 (C); on land policy: Palmer 1977 (D2) on Southern Rhodesia, Sorrenson 1968 (D1) on Kenya.

4 See Chapter 4, p. 117.

5 As Jones puts it (1960 (D3), p. 108), 'just as some nineteenth-century Americans denied the Negro a soul in an attempt to justify slavery, so have some twentieth-century Europeans denied the African an economic spirit in an attempt to justify colonial rule'. For more findings appearing to refute this myth in the present study, see p. 91.

6 See discussion in Chapter 3.1.

7 Arrighi 1967 (D2), p. 20.

8 E.g. Redley 1977 (C) and Murray 1970 (D2).

9 See Chapter 3, pp. 91–6 and 101–9 for cases in which policy seems to have been governed by a false (ideologically distorted) perception of the actual state of the economy in the field of agricultural supply response.

10 See Chapter 3, pp. 101–9, for an example of this. A model which shows the selling behaviour of Kenyan African cattle owners as a simple instantaneous response to price appears to support the hypothesis of perverse supply response. But a model which includes the influence of policy factors on the supply side of the market negates this simple hypothesis.

11 All except the first ten years in the case of Southern Rhodesia and the first five in the case of Kenya. The 1890s are omitted from this study as there are few serviceable statistical data for the period.

12 For an influential example of this distinction, see Myint 1967 (D3).

13 Arrighi 1973 (D2), p. 222.

14 Uganda and Tanganyika (Tanzania) have been intentionally excluded from this list, al-though there were a few white-owned farms and estates in both countries, on the grounds that they were not economically significant, and the representation of white unofficials in their legislature was always minimal. Latin America is also excluded from discussion here; but the patterns of policy adopted in the early colonial period (vast concessions to the first settl-ers, labour tenancy, and coercive methods to secure a labour force) are almost indentical as between the settler economies of Africa and the Andean areas of Peru, Bolivia and Colombia.

15 Clearly, figures of land acreage per head of population are misleading, inasmuch as the fertility of land varied enormously within and across the sample in Table 1.1. Kenya is a good case in point; whites in 1960 owned only 7 per cent of the land, as the table shows, but are estimated to have owned 18 per cent of the high-potential land, i.e. that land with rainfall exceeding thirty inches. Van Zwanenberg and King 1975 (D1), p. 30.

16 See tsetse fly map in Hailey 1957 (D3), p. 877.

17 For the Belgian Congo: Jewsewiecki 1978 (D3) *passim*. For Malaya: Silcock and Fisk 1963 (D3). For Ceylon: Oliver 1957 (D3).

18 But sometimes the capital requirements barriers had to be artificially augmented by policy; see Chapter 2, pp. 39–41.

19 For a brief comparison of labour market policies in settler and non-settler economies, see Chapter 6, pp. 230–1.

20 The changes in the composition of the Kenyan and Southern Rhodesian legislatures during our period were as follows:
Southern Rhodesia: 1898: five officials nominated by British South Africa Company, four elected unofficials
1908: six nominated officials, eight elected unofficials
1914: six nominated officials, twelve elected unofficials
1923: thirty elected unofficials
Kenya: 1906: six officials, two (later four) nominated unofficials
1916: twelve officials, eleven unofficials elected by 'British subjects of European descent'
1920: two elected Asians added
1927: five elected Asians added
1944: one elected African added
1946: one elected African added

21 Hailey 1957 (D3), p. 275.

22 Until 1951 the qualification for the franchise was income of £120 or property of £500. In 1951 the income qualification was doubled. 'By 1953 only 431 Africans had been register-ed as voters, though a very much larger number were said to be eligible for the vote' (Hailey 1957 (D3), p. 185).

23 This point is forcibly put by RH: Mss. Afr.s.510, *Official economic management in Kenya* by V. Liversage, p. 6.

24 Elspeth Huxley helped to explain this when making her own, admittedly value-laden, distinction between 'true settler' and 'plantation' economies according to the criteria of Lord Delamere, the pioneer Kenya settler:

> The planter comes to earn a living, to make a fortune if he can, and to retire as soon as he can to some remembered corner of the British Isles. He comes to a country to exploit it for his own benefit. But the settler who means to live and die there is thinking of the future. He has his children to consider. When he makes the colony his home he ceases to be a mere exploiter; he becomes, for good or ill, a builder. He transfers to the country of his adoption many of those loyalties and emotions which bound him before to the country of his birth. The colony becomes *his*; he is making it, and his descendants will inherit it.   (Huxley 1935 (D1), vol. I, pp. 97–8)

Hence the settler's possession, and the planter's absence, of interest in the politics of the colony.

2. The political constraints on economic behaviour

1 K.W. Rothschild, preface to Rothschild 1971 (D3), p. 7.
2 Murray 1970 (D2), p. 95.
3 More formally, extra-market operations are 'those extra-market activities which are directed towards ends which may be sought also through operations in the market'. This definition is taken from Walker (1943 (D3)), excerpts from Chapter 6 of which appear in Rothschild 1971 (D3), pp. 36–55.
4 Arrighi 1967 (D2), pp. 22–5; Good 1976 (D3), p. 605.
5 For more detail of the economics of colonisation see Mosley 1974 (D3).
6 Sorrenson 1968 (D1), p. 19.
7 The 1893 prediction for the line's earnings when operational was an import revenue of £16 550, and an export revenue of £19 075; Great Britain, *Parliamentary Papers*, vol. 62 (1893) C. 7025, pp. 60–1. The 1903 out-turn was an import traffic of £53 562 and an export traffic of £6612; Great Britain, *Parliamentary Papers*, vol. 73 (1904).
8 Wolff 1974 (D1), p. 50.
9 For details of these schemes, see Huxley 1935 (D1), vol. I, Chapter 6.
10 Source for Kenya data: *Blue Book* 1914; for Southern Rhodesia data: Wilson Fox 1913 (D2), p. 2.
11 In the words of an early settler in the Mazoe Valley, 'individual farming enterprise was not encouraged, and the Administration appeared to be Company-minded to the exclusion of all else'. RH: Mss.Afr.s.875, *Memories of an early settler in Rhodesia* by C.W.R. Southey, JP.
12 In Southern Rhodesia in 1913 'companies' held 9 out of 21 million acres alienated (Wilson Fox 1913 (D2), p. 2); in Kenya in 1909 'rather more than half' of the alienated area was occupied by large concessionaires (Montgomery (Commissioner of Lands) to Colonial Secretary, 8 May 1909, in PRO: CO 533/59).
13 Of the concessionaires in Table 2.2, Willoughby's Consolidated Company set up an enterprise for the supply of electric light to Bulawayo; the South African-owned Mashonaland Agency owned several large gold mines; Delamere invested in grain milling, butchering and plant breeding; and Grogan built a tramway to carry timber, which also benefited other producers.
14 NAR: L 2/1/134/4, 'The Liebig Extract of Meat Company's properties', 17 November 1913.
15 Southern Rhodesian data from Rooney 1968 (C), p. 106, South African data from Hodder-Williams 1971 (D2), note 85.
16 In the first Crown Lands Ordinance of 1902, ninety-nine year leases were made available for the first time, and in the second such Ordinance of 1915 provision was made for 999 year leases.
17 Huxley 1935 (D1), vol. I, p. 88.
18 Church of Scotland Mission Society papers, Edinburgh: Watson to Alexander, 30 November 1897, cited in Sorrenson 1968 (D1), p. 177. In 1901 and 1902 'Government allowed and ratified purchase by Europeans from native owners of lands': evidence of J.W. Arthur to 1934 Kenya Land Commission, in Great Britain 1934b (B1), vol. I, p. 470.
19 Church of Scotland Mission Society papers, Edinburgh: Watson's diary, 16 May 1898.
20 Great Britain 1934a (B1), p. 96. Compare the case of the United States land market in the mid-nineteenth-century 'frontier days'. Gates 1973 (D3), p. 10, relates that 'one cession in Arkansas [in 1833] was appraised at $0.05 an acre by the government witness and $2 by the witness for the Indians'.
21 Palmer 1977 (D2), p. 67.
22 In Kenya in 1905 a Land Committee actually debated the question of whether existing land policy should be revised in favour of the 'smaller man', for example by tighter development conditions. It decided against, not surprisingly in view of the fact that concessionaires

dominated the commission (Delamere was Chairman). Some of the correspondence surrounding the 1905 Commission is preserved in PRO: CO 533/441 (1934), 'Papers relating to British East Africa, 1907'.

23 Wilson Fox 1913 (D2), p. 1.
24 BSAC, *Annual Report* for 1913/14, p. 10.
25 Sorrenson 1968 (D1), p. 135.
26 E.g. speech by Lord Delamere to Convention of Associations, August 1913, reproduced in Huxley 1935 (D1), vol. I, p. 278.
27 The Exploring Lands and Minerals Company sold ranchland to soldier-settlers in 1917 at an average price of 3s. to 5s. per acre; the Crescent Mines and Land Company sold dairying land near Gwelo at 8s. per acre; and the Fife Scott Ranching Syndicate Ltd sold dairying land near Gwelo at an average price of 10s. to 16s. per acre. These figures are to be set against an auction realisation for 1915 (the 1917 price was almost certainly lower) of 11s. 9d. PRO: CO 417/617, Booklet 'War settlement in Southern Rhodesia', December 1917. For a complaint that excessively high land prices were hindering post-war settlement see PRO: CO 417/621, Memorandum by R.H.B. Dickson, Umtali, to Director of Land Settlement.
28 PRO: CO 417/657, Memorandum by Dickson, enclosed in H.C. Cape Town to Colonial Secretary, 19 January 1921.
29 Huxley 1935 (D1), vol. II, p. 55.
30 In 1913, 161 000 acres out of 21 million alienated to whites in Southern Rhodesia were under cultivation (Wilson Fox 1913 (D2); the total was only 237 000 by 1920. In Kenya in 1920, 176 000 acres out of a total of 7.3 million alienated to whites were under cultivation (PRO: CO 533/232, Bowring to Milner, 21 April 1920).
31 Brown, *SRLAD*, 25 June 1908, p. 98.
32 Letter from Rhodesia Chamber of Mines, cited in *SRLAD*, 25 June 1908, p. 65.
33 Machingaidze 1978 (D2), p. 7.
34 Palmer 1977 (D2), p. 135.
35 Redley 1977 (C), Chapter 3.
36 McGregor Ross 1927 (D1), p. 161.
37 A previous attempt to impose a tax on undeveloped land failed in 1914. For the debate on the 1928 proposals, see *SRLAD*, 25 June 1928.
38 E.g. the annexation of native reserve land intervening between the Tokwe and Nuanetsi ranches (see Great Britain 1922 (B1), p. 10).
39 Southern Rhodesia 1925 (B2), p. 8.
40 E.g. when Chaplin, Administrator of Southern Rhodesia, wrote to London on behalf of the BSAC in response to the situation in Gwanda where Europeans were applying for land adjoining the already overcrowded reserve, suggesting that Africans be given the first option of buying land. PRO: CO 417/671, Chaplin to Malcolm, 22 December 1920. The use of policy towards Africans generally as a consensus-building instrument was common. In introducing the Land Apportionment Bill the Minister for Native Affairs expressed the hope 'that there should be no question of party politics when we touch on the native question [Hear, hear]', *SRLAD*, 25 April 1929, col. 91.
41 Southern Rhodesia 1925 (B2), p. 13.
42 E.g. Cripps 1927 (D2), p. 180.
43 Arrighi 1973 (D2), p. 185.
44 Sorrenson 1968 (D1), p. 168.
45 Great Britain 1934a (B1), p. 113.
46 However, a generous transition period was stipulated over which rent agreements could be phased out, and as Table 2.4 shows they persisted vestigially until the middle 1950s.
47 In Kenya 'about forty or fifty thousand acres': Commissioner of Lands, *KLC Debs.*, 17 September 1942, col. 575.

48 RH: Mss.Afr.s.1121, Diaries of S.H. Powles, entry for 24 November 1943.

49 See Table 2.3.

50 This is a figure given by Clayton and Savage 1974 (D1), p. 348. It is, however, incompatible with the estimates of Table 2.4; either the former is too high, or the latter are too low.

51 Great Britain 1934a (B1), p. 12.

52 Great Britain 1934b (B1), vol. I, p. 1057, 'Record of an informal meeting of Provincial Commissioners held at Nyeri, 26 January 1933'.

53 For Southern Rhodesia see the statement of C.A. Carbutt, Chief Native Commissioner, to a Native Demonstrators' conference at Domboshawa, reported in the *Rhodesia Herald* for 14 July 1933 (Steele 1972 (C), Chapter 8, note 26). For Kenya see Sorrenson 1967 (D1), p. 60, who quotes P. Wyn Harris, a Land Settlement Officer, as saying, 'it would be wholly contrary to the interests of Africans if individual titles to land were ever granted to them'.

54 Sorrenson 1967 (D1), p. 225.

55 See Tables 4.8a and 4.8b above.

56 See e.g. *KLC Debs.*, 24 November 1959, col. 504.

57 Aitken-Cade, *SRLAD*, 24 July 1958, col. 522.

58 Cf. the following excerpt from the diary of S.H. Powles: 'There seems to be little doubt that we could get £200 an acre for the remaining 170 acres of LR37 if it were not for the racial restrictions covenant on the rest of the property.' RH: Mss.Afr.s.1121, entry for 24 May 1947.

59 Ox-wagon transport cost about 1s. per 100 lb. for ten miles in 1902, and average working expenses of gold production were calculated at 27s. 6d. per ton of ore. The gold price in that year was equivalent to 31s. 6d. per ton of ore at the prevailing grade of five pennyweights gold per ton of ore. NAR: MB 6/1/1, Report of Mining Commissioner, Bulawayo, for year ended 31 March 1902.

60 The Kenya–Uganda Railway (whose finances were, until 1921, merged with those of the colony's administration) had a monopoly of railway operation in Kenya. In Southern Rhodesia until 1923 five separate railway companies operated under the umbrella of the Rhodesian Railways Trust in which the BSAC held a controlling interest; they merged in that year.

61 For samples of settler opinion on railway policy in Kenya, see PRO: CO 533/63, Girouard (Governor of Kenya) to Colonial Secretary, 12 November 1909. In Southern Rhodesia a particularly good source is the attack by the Rhodesian Agricultural Union on the Acworth Report, at PRO: CO 417/617, 3 April 1919.

62 The opinion 'that the aim of the railway tariff was to secure the maximum tonnage for conveyance over its lines' was actually stated by J.H. Allen, the General Manager of Rhodesia Railways: Hawkins 1963 (C), p. 98.

63 For examples of this line of argument see Mitchell (MLA for Bulawayo N.), *SRLAD*, 2 May 1919, col. 156: 'I can hardly conceive . . . that in a country like America they would ever allow a railway to be run for twenty years carrying so many empty trucks from a country that was capable of supplying produce.'

64 Freights on the Uganda railway, for example, were as shown here.

| | (000 tons) | |
	Up	Down
1903–4	10.6	5.7
1907–8	39.2	15.5
1913–14	112.7	76.7

Source: Uganda Railway, *Administration Report*, 1914–15

65 For details of these cuts see Table 2.14. Note, in passing, that within the Southern Rhodesian rail users' lobby there was already a quarrel between concessionaires and small farmers over the distribution of these cuts, paralleling the quarrel over land policy already described. J.G. Macdonald (PRO: CO 417/605, 27 May 1919) described railway rate policy as being 'primarily in the interests of the concessionaires and largely at the expense of the people who were induced to come into the territory'. For further attacks on the concessionary rates for coal and chrome, see Rhodesian Agricultural Union Congress 1921, reported in enclosure to PRO: CO 417/659, High Commissioner Cape Town to Churchill, Colonial Secretary, 8 April 1921.

66 Cf. letter from Alladina Visram to H.M. Sub-Commissioner, 22 April 1907, cited in KNA: PC/NP/1/3, Nyanza Province Annual Report for 1906/7; also RH: Mss.Afr.s.1467, Minutes of Nairobi Chamber of Commerce MGM for 27 March 1919.

67 Frankel 1938 (D3), p. 380: 'Hardly a railway exists in Africa which has been managed purely on the principles which govern the policy of a private railway undertaking. In one way and another all the railways have been used as the economic instruments of Governments.'

68 See note 65 above. There was also wrangling, in Southern Rhodesia, between tobacco and maize farmers; for an example of this, see PRO: CO 417/659, speech of P.H. Gresson to 1921 Rhodesian Agricultural Union Annual Conference, enclosed in Connaught (High Commissioner Cape Town) to Churchill (Colonial Secretary), 8 April 1921.

69 Hill 1949 (D1), p. 292. For more discussion of the Uasin Gishu settlers, see Chapter 5, p. 186.

70 McGregor Ross 1927 (D1), p. 241.

71 Hill 1949 (D1), p. 411. The survey is available at PRO: CO 533/259, enclosure in Northey (Governor of Kenya) to Churchill (Colonial Secretary), 21 May 1921.

72 J.E. Coney, *KLC Debs.*, 17 December 1924, p. 113.

73 Bertin, *SRLAD*, 20 June 1928, cols. 1333–4.

74 Leys 1931 (D1), p. 48. The losses on the various Kenyan branch lines were as shown here.

	Thomson's Falls line	Kisumu-Butere line	(£000) Kitale line	Solai line	Nanyuki line	Total
1920			26.1	9.4	26.7	62.2
1928			21.2	15.7	31.2	68.0
1930	27.8	4.4	96.4	45.9	45.5	207.3

The outward traffic on all these lines, except the Nanyuki line, was mainly maize. Compare the statement of Mr Stewart, the MLA for Salisbury Town, that 'the export traffic that leaves (the Shamva and Sinoia branch lines] is, of course, largely maize, and we have a statement from the General Manager [of the railways] that maize is not a payable traffic'. *SRLAD*, 26 May 1921, col. 1201.

75 RH: Mss.Afr.s.1467, Minutes of Nairobi Chamber of Commerce meeting of 18 October 1935, D.D. Puri. NAR: RH 12/2/4/2/9, Minutes of Annual General Meeting for 1954.

The railways were aware of this point too. The East African Railways *Annual Report* for 1956 notes that

Only under favourable conditions can road transport costs be reduced below 40 cents per ton-mile. It can be argued theoretically that if the railway is left to fight its way on a solely competitive basis it could eliminate any road transport competition by applying a flat rate equivalent to the overall cost of rail transport – somewhere around 20 cents per ton-mile. But this is no more than theory because in practice the railways' tariff is necessary to the agricultural and industrial development of East Africa. (p. 9)

76 In 1936, a year of particularly depressed export prices, the Kenya–Uganda railway administration did, however, waive a part of the export rail rate for maize farmers.
77 The precise list of adjustments during the 1950s is as follows:
Rhodesia Railways
1952 General increase, with the 'increases in rates at lower tariffs more substantial than those at higher tariffs' (Hawkins 1963 (C), p. 91).
1954 New tariff book: tariffs 1–10 raised 15 per cent, tariffs 11–14 raised 30 per cent.
1960 Following the Harragin Report: *cuts* in tariffs 1–10 (e.g. tariff 1 from 3940 to 3720 pence per ton, tariff 10 from 1220 to 1060 pence per ton); increases in tariffs 11–14 (e.g. tariff 14 from 316 to 330 pence per ton).
East African Railways
1951 Increases for 'coffee, cotton, fertiliser, wattle, timber, bacon, dairy produce, corrugated iron' (all low-rated products).
1953 General increase 20 per cent.
1959 'To meet competition with road transport the highest class rates were reduced to a maximum of 40 cents per ton-mile. To compensate, the rates on commodities in the lower half of the tariff were raised five per cent' (*Annual Report*, 1959).
78 Brett 1973 (D1), p. 92.
79 Leys 1931 (D1), Chapter 3; Leys 1975 (D1), p. 34.
80 The above analysis covers only producers' *outputs*; it is thus biased to the extent that European producer inputs paid cheaper rail rates than African inputs.
81 In 1952 a tobacco barn cost £200 to build, or more than twenty times the average annual African farm income in Southern Rhodesia; one barn was needed for every six to eight acres of tobacco.
82 On the difficulties of Kikuyu small-holders realising their expressed desire to grow tea, see KNA: DC/KBU/18, Kiambu District Annual Report 1925, p. 19.
83 Southern Rhodesia 1947 (B2), p. 45. As from 1918 every coffee grower in Kenya had to acquire an annual licence costing fifteen rupees (£1): Kenya *Official Gazette* 1918, pp. 1 and 178, cited McGregor Ross 1927 (D1), p. 101. In 1932 the licence fee was raised to £10 and coffee growing by Africans explicitly banned except for experimental plantings of one hundred acres apiece in three areas (Embu, Meru and Kisii) 'declared by the Director of Agriculture as suitable for the purpose' (*KLC Debs.*, 20 December 1932, col. 504) on account of their remoteness from European coffee growing areas.
84 'Some years back the Prime Minister issued a circular in which he used the words that the native was to be discouraged from growing wheat', NAR: ZBJ 1/1/3, Evidence to the Native Production and Trade Commission 1944, p. 1439, evidence of A.J. Cripwell, NC Gutu (see also testimony of E.D. Alvord at p. 144 of the same evidence). In evidence to the same commission the Chief Native Commissioner said that he 'did not consider cotton to be a Native crop', NAR: ZBJ 1/1/1, p. 33.
85 See PRO: CO 533/309, Coryndon (Governor of Kenya) to Thomas (Colonial Secretary) 27 March 1924.
86 Great Britain 1934b (B1), vol. III, p. 3054, evidence of Alex Holm, Director of Agriculture.
87 Blunt (Director of Agriculture), *KLC Debs.*, 11 September 1942, col. 412.
88 E.g. Major Joyce, *KLC Debs.*, 18 June 1938, col. 180; NAR: S 235/510, Report of the NC Victoria for the year 1932.
89 This point is eloquently made by Lonsdale and Berman 1979 (D1).
90 On this trade see, for Kenya, van Zwanenberg and King 1975 (D1), Chapter 8; for Southern Rhodesia, the chapter by Beach in Palmer and Parsons 1977 (D3), also 'The nineteenth century in Southern Rhodesia' by T.O. Ranger in Ranger 1968 (D2).
91 See e.g. Kenya 1920 (B3).
92 Great Britain 1934b (B1), vol. III, pp. 3169ff, evidence of F.J. McCall, Chief Veterinary Officer, Tanganyika.

93 In 1925 there were 188 dip tanks in Kenya and over 2000 in Southern Rhodesia: C. Eickhoff, *SRLAD*, 8 May 1929, col. 500.

94 PRO: CO 533/310 and 311, Notes by Calder and Bottomley on Coryndon to Thomas, 10 April 1924, and reply, Thomas to Coryndon, 3 June 1924.

95 For complaints on the absence of markets, see NAR: S 138/38, NC Zaka to SN Victoria, 4 May 1925, and Cripps to Downie, 17 October 1925.

96 These organisations were: for maize, the Kenya Farmers' Association and the Rhodesia Farmers' Cooperative; for beef, the Rhodesia and Kenya Stockowners' Associations. The Kenya Stockowners' Association never found an export market in chilled meat, but there were so few white Kenyan ranchers that this did not lead to problems of a glutted home market.

97 A Rhodesian rancher wrote that in the 1920s, 'by trading locally I could buy for about five or six shillings a sack; the railhead price would have been more than double for inferior stuff, plus the time and wages cost of long wagon transport through the bush'. Robertson 1935 (D2), p. 41.

98 E.g. J.H. Smit, *SRLAD*, 30 April 1931, col. 1368.

99 NAR: S 1216/SC 1/100/110, H.E.F. Aylmer, Secretary to the Maize Association, to E.R. Jacklin, Secretary of the Maize Control Board, 15 March 1933.

100 *SRLAD*, debate of 28 April 1931, cols. 1388, 1253 and 1213 respectively. The original draft of the Maize Control Bill, with no exempted areas, was opposed by twenty-seven out of thirty constituencies in the country; Gilchrist, *SRLAD*, 7 June 1933, col. 2449.

101 R.D. Gilchrist, *SRLAD*, 28 April 1931, col. 1221. European maize production costs were estimated by the Maize Commission of Enquiry (Southern Rhodesia 1931 (B2), paragraph 33) at 65s. per acre, i.e. an average of just over 8s. a bag on the assumption of a mean yield of eight bags per acre. The export price at the time was 4s. 3d.

102 NAR: S 1561/38, Telegram Scouts, Mazoe, to CNC, Salisbury, July 1931.

103 NAR: ZBJ 1/1/1, Evidence to the Native Production and Trade Commission 1944, p. 888, evidence of E.R. Jacklin.

104 M. Danziger, *SRLAD*, 7 June 1933, col. 2439.

105 African maize farmers frequently received a great deal more than the export parity; see, for example in 1912 in Southern Rhodesia, when the f.o.r. export parity was 8s. 5d. African producers were reported by District Annual Reports as receiving anything between 7s. 6d. and 40s. per bag of maize.

106 Trader-producers selling to the export pool were instructed not to pay more than 5s. (the export realisation was 6s.) to Africans in 1934. NAR: S 1216/SC 1/100/29, Minutes of Maize Control Board meeting, 13 July 1934.

107 Southern Rhodesia, Maize Control Board, *Annual Report* 1937/8.

108 Two entries in the Maize Control Board minutes may stand for hundreds: (1) *Lonely Mine* 'request for reduced rake-off on traded maize. Proposed by Mr Goodenough and seconded by Mr Sanderson: That the rake-off be 3/- per bag [normally it was 4s. 6d. to 5s.]. Matter to be kept confidential. Agreed.' NAR: S 1216/SC 1/100/29, Minutes for 9 August 1934. (2) *Devuli Ranch* 'allowed maize for rations on clean cross-entry terms [i.e. to purchase from Africans without paying any 'rake-off' at all]. Agreed.' NAR: S 1216/SC 1/100/242, Minutes for 20 September 1935.

109 This sliding scale was a sop to the small maize growers of the Midlands, who although not exporting much themselves had been roped into sharing the export loss burden with the exporters of Mashonaland under the arrangements of 1931.

110 Southern Rhodesia, Maize Control Board *Annual Report* 1937/8. Subsequent scholars who have stated that Africans enjoyed a genuine 25 per cent stake in the local pool include Yudelman 1964 (D3), p. 279.

111 The 'rake-off' might be less than 5s. if the maize, coming from a remote district and hence already heavily loaded with transport costs, posed no competitive threat. The Board was frank in its admission that the prevention of this threat was the main function of the rake-

off on trader-producers' 'local pool' maize: 'The Board imposes a levy of up to 5/- a bag, its criterion of the amount being not now a contribution by the natives towards export subsidy, but the prevention of native maize entering in competition with that actually surrendered to the Board.' NAR: S 1215/1090/246, Minutes of Maize Growers' Conference, 8 September 1936.

112 NAR: S 1215/1090/103, Comment by Bullock, Chief Native Commissioner, on Jacklin to Secretary of Agriculture, undated, almost certainly 1938.

113 One of these (Director of Marketing to Secretary of Agriculture, 1938) suggested that Africans should have a monopoly of the marketing of sorghum, millets and rice, and that in return Europeans should be given a monopoly of the sale of tobacco (Turkish and Virginia); citrus, apples and pears; wheat, barley and oats; onions and Irish potatoes. The other (Secretary of Agriculture to Minister of Agriculture, 31 May 1938) added groundnuts to, and subtracted rice from, the first list. Both proposals are in NAR: S 1215/1090/103.

114 RH: Mss.Afr.s.510, *Official economic management in Kenya* by V. Liversage, p. 92. Such compulsory pooling had been achieved under the Sale of Wheat Act 1930.

115 RH: Mss.Afr.s.510, *Official economic management in Kenya* by V. Liversage, p. 84.

116 On 24 November 1932 A.C. Tannahill, a Nairobi businessman, claimed that 'a certain industry [sc. maize] asks every other industry to subsidise it in order that it can make extra profit. I don't know why they should.' RH: Mss.Afr.s.1467, Minutes of Nairobi Chamber of Commerce, 2 November 1932. For the opposition of the coffee and sisal producers, see minutes of the same Chamber for 20 May and 27 May 1933.

117 G.M. Riddell (a coffee producer, speaking for the Coffee Board), *KLC Debs.*, 30 December 1935, col. 1043. See also Coffee Board of Kenya, *Annual Proceedings of Coffee Conference 1936*, p. 69.

118 Kenya 1935 (B3), D.D. Puri, Note of Dissent to Kenya Government; J.H. Smit, *SRLAD*, 6 June 1933, col. 2429.

119 RH: Mss.Afr.s.510, *Official economic management in Kenya* by V. Liversage, p. 104.

120 RH: Mss.Afr.s.1121, Powles diaries, entry for 3 February 1940. The KFA's advertised local selling price at the time was Sh. 12. Pig farmers were also offered concessionary maize. This bonus, unlike that offered to coffee planters, persisted into the 1960s (Kenya 1966 (B3), p. 20).

121 Minutes of the Maize Conference on 4 June 1941, cited by Kenya 1943 (B3), p. 13. The passage in brackets is a paraphrase.

122 *KLC Debs.*, December 1941, cited Kenya 1943 (B3), p. 12.

123 It was estimated that 180 000 bags were traded in this way in 1942, against a total of 690 000 sent to the Board; D.L. Blunt (Director of Agriculture), *KLC Debs.*, 21 August 1942, col. 323.

124 C.J. Wilson, *KLC Debs.*, 21 August 1942, col. 312.

125 This was mediated either through a 'rake-off' on squatter-to-farmer transactions or through a fixed buying price for maize offered directly to the Maize Control.

126 C.J. Wilson, *KLC Debs.*, 21 August 1942, col. 313. Compare the operation of the 1934 Rhodesian Maize Control Amendment Act, as described by the Native Commissioner, Darwin:

> The natives are frankly not enthusiastic [about control]. The trouble is that prior to the passing of this year's Amendment Act consumers were only too keen to put up any maize offered by natives at anything up to 7/6 a bag as it was so much cheaper than the Board [selling] price. Trader producers ... buying grain for resale have more or less been told that they are not to pay more than 4/- a bag [see p. 46 above]. It amounts to a command as they have to pay 6/- per bag if they exceed the figure of 4/- given to the Board. One trader has informed me that the most he can pay to make anything is 3/6. Natives having in mind last year's price are not too keen on this. (NAR: S 1542/M2, NC Darwin to CNC, 7 July 1934)

127 Vincent, *KLC Debs.*, 22 March 1943, col. 119. Once again, compare the operation of the 1934 (Southern Rhodesia) Maize Control Amendment Act: 'Prior to the introduction of Control Mr Rutherford [of the Marandellas Farmers' Association] and a few other farmers had always purchased their maize from natives at a cost of about 4/- a bag. The maize was now being carted past their doors and sold to traders in Marandellas.' NAR : S 1216/SC 1/100/242, Minutes of Maize Control Board meeting, 6 February 1936.

128 Notably the East African Royal Commission (Great Britain 1955b (B1)) and the Urban African Affairs Commission (Southern Rhodesia 1958b (B2)).

129 Estimated cattle numbers were as shown.

	Kenya		Southern Rhodesia	
	European	African	European	African
1925	216 000	3 200 000	1 006 086	1 095 841
1930	226 861	4 965 000	910 343	1 558 075

130 '*Mr Macarthur* I would rather see rejected cattle scrapped or burned rather than being brought back on to the local markets of Rhodesia.' NAR : S 1215/1324/3, Minutes of the Rhodesia Stockowners' Association AGM, 2 May 1933.

131 Figures from Minister of Agriculture, *SRLAD*, 27 March 1921, col. 152.

132 Somerville, *SRLAD*, 26 March 1935, col. 460.

133 Colonial Secretary 1922, cited Grogan, *KLC Debs.*, 20 April 1939, col. 220. My italics.

134 It must be noted that Liebig's keenness to manufacture in Africa almost certainly rose during the 1920s, as a consequence of the growth of the South African compound market.

135 Phimister 1976 (D2), p. 29.

136 NAR : Hist.Mss. DO 1/1/1, Downie to Moffat, 6 February 1933.

137 NAR : S 1215/1324/3, Annual General Meeting of the Rhodesia Stockowners' Association on 2 May 1932 ; Downes, *SRLAD*, 8 May 1934, col. 1264.

138 NAR : ZAX 1/1/1, Evidence to Commission on Sales of Native Cattle 1938, p. 91, evidence of L.A. Levy, cattle buyer, on 31 October 1938.

139 A monopoly so far as Africans were concerned, that is. It was true that by the end of 1938, as one white rancher testified, 'you [could] evacuate cattle from the prohibited area by riding them in motor lorries . . . to the railhead at Victoria, [but] I don't think I need emphasize how entirely impossible it is for the native to take advantage of those arrangements under which I, at any rate, am evacuating cattle'. NAR : ZAX 1/1/1, R.D. Gilchrist MLA, Evidence to Commission on Sales of Native Cattle, evidence of 1 November 1938, p. 64.

140 For example:

> *Chairman*: Do you think that those private buyers are in any way working in league with Liebig's own buyers?
>
> *B.V. Brewer* (trader): Well, I have no proof of that, but I will say that when Liebig's buyers come you will always find the same buyers with them. On the day of [one sale in Matibi No. 2 reserve] five other buyers rolled up. They were not invited, Liebig's didn't buy any cattle at all till those five buyers had finished. Immediately the native cattle had finished, Liebig's rebought from them. Those buyers circulated £300 between them in one day. (NAR : ZAX 1/1/1, Evidence of 8 November 1938, p. 69)

141 Evidence of R.D. Gilchrist MLA to Commission on Sales of Native Cattle:

> *Chairman*: We have been assured that Liebig's always, as a matter of policy, instruct their buyers to pay a certain price, and the price given to us was 6/- per 100 liveweight?
> – I suppose this is in camera?
> – I am pretty sure that [the advertised] prices are 50% above Liebig's actual prices.
> (NAR : ZAX 1/1/1, evidence of 1 November 1938, p. 68)

246

Notes to pp. 55–62

142 Cf. evidence of A.C. Jackson, NAR: ZAX 1/1/1, evidence of 31 October 1938, Mr Gains, *ibid.*, evidence of 1 November 1938, p. 54; Mrs Comberbach, *ibid.*, evidence of 7 November 1938, p. 4; and finally Mudene, NAR: ZAX 1/1/2, evidence of 15 November 1938, p. 13: '[Mr du Plessis, the dip supervisor,] told me that I had to dispose of these other three head of cattle, otherwise I would be fined 2/6 a head and would have to go to gaol for 3 months.'
143 Evidence of General Manager of Liebig Rhodesia Ltd to Native Production and Trade Commission, NAR: ZBJ 1/1/3, p. 1993.
144 Evidence of A.R. Jackson, NAR: ZAX 1/1/1, evidence of 7 November 1938, p. 101; A. Gelman *ibid.*, evidence of 1 November 1938, p. 6.
145 Kenya 1937 (B3), p. 10.
146 KNA: C/VET 2/10/7/7, Colonial Secretary to Managing Director, Liebig Rhodesia Ltd, 8 August 1936.
147 W. Harragin, *KLC Debs.*, 21 April 1939, col. 242.
148 Ordinance No. 3 of 1926, Crop Protection and Live Stock Rules: 'The Governor in Council may from time to time make rules which shall be applicable to such area or areas as may be named therein for the following purposes ... (h) for defining or limiting the number, kind, ages and sexes of the livestock to be carried on any area. ... (j) for the disposal of surplus and undesirable livestock.'
149 Acting Director of Veterinary Services, *KLC Debs.*, 17 August 1938, col. 297. Compare the similar statement on maize policy on pp. 43–4 above.
150 E.g. Kenyatta, *Manchester Guardian*, 11 August 1938, and *New Statesman*, 25 June 1938.
151 Kenya Chief Secretary to Nairobi Chamber of Commerce, 8 July 1938, cited in *KLC Debs.*, 20 April 1939, col. 227.
152 In 1944 fifty out of the ninety-eight Southern Rhodesian African reserves were said to be over-stocked (Southern Rhodesia 1945 (B2), p. 28). This also applied to three out of the five main Kenyan pastoral reserves: the Kamba, Suk and Kamasia.
153 Southern Rhodesia 1952a (B2), p. 10.
154 An envious Kenyan Director of Veterinary Services commented thus on the Southern Rhodesian grazier scheme in 1947: 'These [Grazier] agreements have proved immensely successful, many farmers taking fifty or one hundred head on which they usually realise some three pounds a head' (Kenya 1947c (B3), p. 7). The Cold Storage's average buying price from Africans in 1947 was some Sh. 45 for a 400 lb animal.
155 Under the Southern Rhodesian Agreement the price for the following five years was based on a price of 20s. a bag for the 1945/6 crop, and was to be moved up or down in accordance with changes in the cost of production. This agreement was, with amendments, renewed or extended until finally abrogated in May 1962. The Kenyan agreement of 1951 was based on an award made by an external arbitrator, L.G. Troup: Troup was only shown the accounts for less efficient maize farmers and based his award on their high cost of production (interview S.H. Powles (E), 17 November 1979). The Troup formula was used for fixing maize prices until the 1957/8 crop year.
156 Kenya 1943 (B3), p. 47.
157 Federation of Rhodesia and Nyasaland 1956 (B2), p. 30, Kenya 1966 (B3), p. 20.
158 Southern Rhodesia, *Grain Marketing Board Annual Report* 1958/9, p. 9.
159 Evidence of J.D. Otiende, MP, to Kenya 1966 (B3).
160 Federation of Rhodesia and Nyasaland 1963a (B2), p. 21; Kenya 1963b (B3), p. 38. The argument for retaining the system of guaranteed producer prices was generally the 'instability' of African deliveries of maize (cf. p. 96 where this hypothesis is examined).
161 Africans were not allowed to act as graders at the sales or even read the weight on the grounds that 'this would not be satisfactory to both buyer and seller' (Southern Rhodesia 1952a (B2), pp. 8–9).
162 Kenya Meat Commission, *Annual Report* 1956; anonymous memo attached to Kenya 1947c (B3), p. 9; Cavendish-Bentinck, *KLC Debs.*, 27 January 1950.

247

163 E.g. KNA:PC/SP 1/2/4, Annual Report, Masai Province for the year 1951: '5341 cattle were bought [by Kikuyu traders] at an average price of 130/-' (the Kenya Meat Commission bought 148 at an average price of Sh. 80).

164 Interview R.O. Hennings (E), 31 January 1980 and KNA:PC/SP 1/2/3, Annual Report, Masai Province for the year 1947.

165 Samburu and the entire Northern Frontier Province, apart from Garissa District.

166 Kenya 1956a (B3), paragraph 108.

167 Cold Storage Commission of Southern Rhodesia, *Annual Report* 1956.

168 Federation of Rhodesia and Nyasaland 1963b (B2), Appendix 2, p. 129. The export realisation in 1961/2 was 125s. per 100 lb, against offered prices as shown in the table (Prices varied according to month of delivery.)

	Rhodesia's Best	Imperial	Standard A	GAQ
Minimum	147/-	133/-	122/-	106/-
Maximum	184/-	172/-	160/-	144/-

169 This hypothesis is formalised in Appendix 1.

170 See p. 39 above.

171 Arrighi 1967 (D2), pp. 22–5; Good 1976 (D3), p. 605 (my italics).

172 Murray 1970 (D2), Chapter 2; Peacock and Wiseman 1961 (D3).

173 This is also true of the state's role in secondary industry: see Chapter 6 above.

174 Typical left-wing views are presented in Leys 1975 (D1) and van Zwanenberg 1975 (D1); typical right-wing views in Smith 1972 (D1).

175 Cf. the plea of E.W.L. Noaks, MLA for Lomagundi, Southern Rhodesia, in 1931: 'can the country afford a big crash in the maize belt? I do not believe the country can.' *SRLAD*, 28 April 1931, col. 1257.

3. African agricultural development

1 Arrighi 1967 (D2), p. 32.

2 Good 1976 (D3), p. 606.

3 Palmer 1977 (D2), p. 241 (emphasis added). The statement is repeated by Palmer, more or less word for word, in Palmer and Parsons 1977 (D3), p. 243. In general the evidence used by the underdevelopment school to support this contention of decline fits into one of three main categories. There is evidence of *declining relative shares* (e.g. it has been shown that the proportion of African to total agricultural sales declined from over 90 per cent at the beginning of the century to just over half in the early 1920s; e.g. Arrighi 1973 (D2), Table 4, p. 205); there is evidence of *declining rural self-sufficiency* (in the sense that many previously autonomous farm families were reduced to dependence on non-farm sources of income; e.g. Arrighi 1973 (D2), p. 207); finally, there is *impressionistic verbal evidence* of 'growing chaos' as population pressure and land erosion built up (e.g. Palmer 1977 (D2), especially quotations keyed by notes 103, 105, 119, 121, 124 to Chapter 8). The accuracy of these pieces of evidence in themselves is not questioned; what is questioned is the verbal sleight of hand by which they are used to prove a contention – i.e. that there was a decline in absolute agricultural productivity over the period 1900–39 – which in fact they do not prove. For more on this point see Mosley 1982 (D3).

4 The indices of output per capita in columns 6 and 12 of Table 3.1 are figures of output per head of *total* African population. That is, they understate output per head of African *farm* population, for which we have no figures in Kenya and an incomplete series in Southern Rhodesia. What is more, it is almost certain (though it cannot be proved) that the

degree of understatement increases continuously over time as the non-farm/farm population ratio grows. To this extent, the basic argument of this section, i.e. that there was no drastic decline in African farm productivity, is strengthened.

5 Proportion of high-value cash crops to total African exports, 1936:

Kenya	8.7
Southern Rhodesia	5.0 (1950)
Nyasaland	57.5
Uganda	95.5
Gold Coast	100

Source: Southern Rhodesia 1947 (B2).
High-value cash crops are defined as: cotton, cotton seed, coffee, tobacco, tea, palm oil, cocoa.

6 As a fairly recent example of this genre from the region presently under discussion: '[In the Bantu societies of Eastern and Southern Africa] intra-tribal trade is non-existent. Men do not dig; chief and witch doctor determine time of planting and sowing; manure is dried and used as fuel ... Thus the manipulation of supernatural forces in the interest of the cultivator takes the place of methods which harness the forces of nature to increase productivity.' Sadie 1960 (D3), p. 295.

7 E.g. Lipton 1968 (D3).

8 E.g. all the writers listed in notes 1 to 3 above.

9 Boserup 1965 (D3), p. 118.

10 In particular, the stipulation of reserves for African use followed by restrictions of gradually increasing severity on African tenure in non-African areas; see Chapter 2, pp. 25–7.

11 'The natives [of the district] have sown largely of every kind of Kaffir grain, except Kaffir corn. The crops sown are rupoko [*Eleusine* millet], munga [*pennisetum* millet], mealies [maize] and rice. Other crops they have planted are sweet potatoes.' NAR: N 9/1/7, Report of the Native Commissioner Marandellas District for the year ended 31 March 1901.

12 Johnson 1968 (C), p. 57.

13 In Southern Rhodesia the available reserve land area in 1911 was 33.4 thousand square miles, the estimated population 705 000, and the average population density thus at most 20.9 persons per square mile; the most densely populated district was Bulawayo, with twenty-four persons per square mile of reserve land. In Kenya the estimated African population density in North Nyanza in 1909 was eighty-one persons per square mile, and in Kisumu district 187 persons per square mile (KNA: PC/NP/1/5, Annual Report, Nyanza Province for 1909).

14 Thomson 1887 (D1), p. 284.

15 Barber 1961 (D2), Chapter 4.

16 Spencer 1974 (C), p. 15.

17 Masefield 1950 (D3), p. 76.

18 KNA: PC/NP/1/4, Annual Report, Nyanza Province for the year 1907/8.

19 In Southern Rhodesia in 1926 African population density and plough ownership in the four reserves for which data are given in Table 3.3 are as shown here.

	Estimated population density	Plough ownership
Victoria	22	1108
Marandellas	15	1080
Mazoe	15	880
Mrewa	7	56

In Kenya in 1927 it was reported that 'The increased use of labour-saving devices is becoming more general in native reserves. Nyanza still leads the way in this respect but in South Kikuyu more interest is being evinced in wheeled transport and a number of ploughs, mills and cultivators have been purchased by the natives.' Kenya Agriculture Department, *Annual Report* 1927, p. 17.

20 Some extremist groups of settlers attempted to use the plough's character as an indivisible input (cf. the Kenyan coffee licence fee and the Southern Rhodesian 'rakc-off' on trader-producer maize for the local pool, see pp. 40 and 46) to tax or ban its use by Africans in order to force them into the labour market. See NAR: S 235/515, Annual Report of the NC Marandellas for 1936, and Kasim, *KLC Debs.*, 15 September 1942, col. 404.

21 In his 'Economic survey of Kikuyu proper' (Great Britain 1934b (B1), pp. 993 and 1024), S.H. Fazan estimated the 1933 cost of a plough at Sh. 60.75, whereas *average* annual cash income in Kikuyu Province per capita was Sh. 21.86 (£180 067 from sale of crops, £413 872, not all of which came back to the reserve, from wage employment, plus £67 083 from sale of non-agricultural produce, divided by a population of 604 516).

22 Number of observations: thirty in each case (all districts whose boundaries changed between 1913 and 1938 have been omitted from the regression); source for all data Southern Rhodesia, *Annual Report of the Chief Native Commissioner*, 1913 and 1938, except for data on arable land holdings by district which are drawn from Southern Rhodesia 1930a (B2), Table C 'Agricultural status of reserve natives'. Figures in brackets beneath coefficients are Student's *t*-statistics; *denotes significance at 5 per cent level, **denotes significance at 1 per cent level. No statistics of this sort are available for Kenya.

23 Duesenberry 1949 (D3) for the original theory; Livingstone 1972 (D3) for an application to the supply of effort and economic development.

24 NAR: S 235/507, Report of the Native Commissioner Mrewa for the year 1929.

25 NAR: ZAY 2/2/28, Evidence to the Economic Commission 1939, evidence of T.L. Ball, Native Commissioner, Gutu.

26 Characteristic is the report of the Native Commissioner, Victoria: 'The plough [as used by native families] is merely a device for saving manual labour, and not a device for improved tillage.' NAR: S 235/504, Report of the Native Commissioner, Victoria District for the year 1926.

27 In the years 1901 to 1950, during which Southern Rhodesian *de facto* farm population is estimated to have risen by about 140 per cent, cultivated acreage was extended by 260 to 270 per cent; Yudelman 1964 (D3), p. 237.

28 NAR: S 235/503, Report of the Native Commissioner Mrewa for 1925.

29 That it was the increase in labour cost which deterred African agriculturalists from using manure on their lands, and the plough for that matter in some cases, is not in doubt from the accounts of agricultural administrators: 'One major reason for not manuring is ... that fragmentation makes an adequately compact holding the rare exception. The average family has several shambas, and to manure them would require the carrying of loads from one place to another. The Kikuyu woman does enough load carrying without adding yet another task to her present duties.' Kenya 1945a (B3), p. 53.

30 KNA: PC/NZA/1/33, Annual Report for Nyanza Province for the year 1938. Emphasis added.

31 NAR: S 235/515, Annual Report of the NC Marandellas for the year 1936.

32 As late as 1949 there were fewer than 200 farm carts owned by Southern Rhodesian Africans (Johnson 1964 (D2), p. 186).

33 Levi (1976 (D3)) has recently argued that population density is a poor proxy for population pressure in districts where shifting cultivation and free migration are possible. But in Kenya and Southern Rhodesia, as we have argued, not only had African population densities risen by the late 1920s to a point where in most reserves shifting cultivation was impracticable save in isolated, remote areas, but land legislation meant that the African *as cultivator* could not migrate freely from his reserve; his only option apart from migration

into employment was squatter tenancy on a European farm, which was subject to restriction in Southern Rhodesia from 1930 and in Kenya from the mid-twenties onward.

34 Number of observations: thirty in each case. Figures in brackets beneath coefficients are Student's *t*-statistics; *denotes significance at 5 per cent level, **at 1 per cent level. Sources: as for Table 3.1a and 3.1b.

35 To test this hypothesis, I have re-run equation (3.2b) with the acreage under Native Purchase Areas (*NPA*) as an additional independent variable. This increased the predictive power of the equation, but gave insignificant results for this particular variable, viz.

$$Y = 1.89** + 6.634* \ X + 0.0058 \ (NPA)$$
$$r^2 = 0.4202$$

where *NPA* = area of land (in thousand acres) classed as Native Purchase Areas in each district. (Source for these data, Palmer 1977 (D2), Appendix I.) On absenteeism there are no Rhodesian figures for the inter-war period, but the 1929 figures for Kenya, as argued in Table 3.5, suggest a *positive* relationship at this time between absenteeism and agricultural output by districts.

36 See the account by Alvord 1958 (D2), p. 5.

37 The development of demonstration work in the African reserves is well documented: for Southern Rhodesia by Johnson 1968 (C) and Steele 1972 (C), and for Kenya in the period before 1929 by Spencer 1974 (C).

38 In the article by Alvord (Southern Rhodesia 1930a (B2)) a photograph depicting contemporary methods of agricultural extension shows a copious maize crop grown by 'progressive' methods, and in front of this crop a very spruce African farmer wearing a European-style hat, jacket and tie; this farmer is arm-in-arm with a young European child in an obvious gesture of 'adoption'. Next to this tableau is a stunted, diseased maize crop, and standing in front of this crop is an African wearing rags, obviously intended to stand for a 'primitive native'.

39 NAR: S 235/515, Annual Report of the NC Victoria for the year 1936.

40 Southern Rhodesia 1945 (B2), p. 25. A similar resistance was met by demonstrators attempting to persuade Africans to upgrade their cattle (in the comparatively rare cases where this was attempted before 1945). The Superintendent of Natives, Fort Victoria, reported in 1925 that: 'Some time ago I was discussing with one of the Nuanetsi chiefs the question of supplying him with a grade bull to improve his cattle. He replied that he did not want a grade bull, because he thought if he improved his cattle they would become desirable in the white man's eyes and would be taken from him.' NAR: S 138/38, Superintendent of Natives, Fort Victoria, to Chief Native Commissioner, 12 January 1925.

41 Great Britain 1934b (B1), p. 1052, evidence of C.O. Oates, Agricultural Officer, Fort Hall. Much of this fear of land confiscation in Kikuyuland appears to have been 'due to the newspaper "Mwigwithania", the editor of which is one Johnston Kenyatta [as he was then known], warning natives that unless they utilised land in the Reserve it would be taken from them by Government.' KNA: DC/KBU/21, Annual Report, Kiambu District for the year 1928.

42 Selukwe. The others (Inyanga, Mrewa, Bubi, Gutu) were areas of relatively sparse European settlement.

43 In the Kikuyu districts, 100 000 acres of land originally occupied by Africans had been sold or given away to Europeans; but in Nyanza Province only 900 acres had been alienated. Great Britain 1934a (B1), section 337.

44 See pp. 16–22 and 43–58 above.

45 The effect which these policies, and their anticipated continuation, exerted on survival algorithms may be deduced from the following testimony concerning maize control:
Before the [Maize Control] Act came into force in the Fort Victoria and Matabeleland

areas, the demonstration work was really going ahead in leaps and bounds, and in certain areas, the demonstrators were able to cope with the large numbers of natives interested in better methods of farming. There were 141 plot holders [agriculturalists who had agreed to follow certain improved farming practices] on Zimutu Reserve last year, and I regret to report that this year there are only sixty-seven. I have spoken to the natives to try and encourage them to continue with the better methods of farming that they have been taught, but they simply refuse and say "Why should we grow crops and sell them at less than we used to" and another favourite remark is "Yes, we told you when you first brought demonstrators on to other reserves that they had come to try out our land, and later the government would either take it or our crops." (NAR: S 1542/M2, Assistant Agriculturalist, Salisbury, to Chief Native Commissioner, 19 January 1935.)

46 We are here crediting the African producer with 'rational expectations' regarding the future course of government policy, which lead him in part to frustrate that policy. There is an analogy with businessmen or employers faced with what seems to them a prohibitively high marginal tax rate, and from workers who believe that any productivity gains they achieve will be confiscated by the employer rather than being added to their wage.

47 See Chapter 6, p. 196.

48 KNA: DC/NN.1/36, Notes for 1955 Annual Report, North Nyanza District, by P.G.P.D. Fullerton, District Officer, Southern Division.

49 Barber 1961 (D2), pp. 186–7.

50 Absenteeism and population data: Southern Rhodesia 1950b (B2). Total sales, cash-crop sales and cultivated acreage: Southern Rhodesia, *Annual Report of the Chief Native Commissioner*, 1951, Report of the Under-Secretary, Native Economics and Markets Division, Annexure 'C', 'Agricultural production and marketing, 1951'. Figures in brackets beneath coefficients are Student's t-statistics; **denotes significance at 1 per cent level.

51 See Chapter 2, pp. 27–8.

52 The Rhodesian Native Land Husbandry Act of 1951 imposed a floor of eight acres on individual family holdings (Floyd 1960 (C), Chapter 7). 'In Kenya, the Agricultural Department insisted (though without similar legislative sanction) on a minimum holding of seven acres' (KNA: DC/NN.1/36, Notes for North Nyanza District Report 1955 by P.G.P.D. Fullerton, p. 11).

53 Massell and Johnson (1968 (D2)) compared the farming patterns of Africans in the early 1960s in Darwin, a Native Purchase Area, and Chiweshe, a reserve area twenty-five miles from Salisbury. They found (in their Table 4.7) that Darwin farmers averaged 3251 hours of labour per annum on land improvement fairly evenly spread through the year, whereas the Chiweshe figure was zero; also that Darwin farmers averaged 285 hours per year on manure application, again evenly spread through the year, whereas Chiweshe farmers averaged only fifty-three hours, concentrated in the pre-planting months of September to November.

54 Coffee and pyrethrum grew best at altitudes above 5000 feet which were relatively common in the African areas of Central Province, relatively rare in the African areas of Nyanza Province. Also, Central Province was the fountainhead of the 'Mau Mau' rebellion of the early 1959s, and what is now a large literature interprets the concentration on Central Province in the Swynnerton Plan (of intensified rural development in the African areas) as an attempt to pre-empt this rebellion by economic means. For an example of this literature, see Leys 1975 (D1), pp. 69–71.

55 Of course, these data can be misinterpreted, as they neglect the large quantities of grain traded, legally or illegally, other than through the marketing board. Something is said about this problem on pp. 97–100.

56 For a general survey of this point, see Elkan 1973 (D3), p. 38; and for specific examples of it in the Kenya context, see van Zwanenberg 1974 (D1).

57 A formal demonstration of this point is given by Livingstone 1977a (D3).
58 Cf. the Kenya government's argument in favour of retaining price guarantees for European
farmers in its Sessional Paper no. 6 of 1957/8:

> in order to feed the Colony's African labour force with their families it would be most
> imprudent to rely on deliveries by peasant growers whether in Kenya or neighbouring
> territories. While Africans in certain areas, especially Nyanza, have come to rely on
> maize to a considerable extent as their cash crop, it still remains true that the majority
> of the 600 000 African farmers in Kenya plant maize primarily for family subsistence
> and only secondarily for cash. Thus the surplus available for delivery to markets is
> only a small fraction of the whole and is liable to fluctuate widely from season to
> season according to weather conditions ... Since these deliveries cannot be relied
> upon, the only other sources of maize are from overseas or from farmers in the Schedul-
> ed Areas ... (Kenya 1958 (B3), pp. 32–3)

For a similar argument in Southern Rhodesia, see Southern Rhodesia 1934 (B2), p. 1, and
for an academic argument along similar lines, see Allan 1965 (D3), pp. 39 and 353.
59 Sources: European price – average payout, local and export pools, for 1938/9 pool year,
from Maize Control Board *Annual Report* for 1938/9. African price – mid-point of range
cited by G.M. Higgins to Minister of Agriculture, NAR: S 1215/1090/103, 22 June 1938.
60 This result is obtained by substituting a price of 9s. 4d. for a price of 5s. 3d. in the equation
$D = -338 + 46.1\,P$, where D = African deliveries to Maize Control Board, in thousands
of bags, and P = price received by farmer (in shillings per bag), as estimated against data
for 1948/9 to 1961/2 in Table 3.7a (equation 2).
61 See p. 51 above.
62 C.J. Wilson, *KLC Debs.*, 15 April 1942, p. 18.
63 Kenya 1949 (B3), p. 6. The low producer price of meat in Kenya after the Second World
War (p. 62) also contributed to this result.
64 See note 45 above.
65 Cold Storage Commission of Southern Rhodesia, *Annual Report* 1941.
66 KNA: DC/MKS/1/1/25, Annual Report, Machakos District 1933 (D. Storrs-Fox),
p. 23.
67 For instance, in 1937 it was not easy to persuade a Masai 'who can get 50/- to 70/- for a
beast at the local markets on the east or west boundaries that for the sake of the permanent
[sc. Nairobi Abattoir] market he ought to take that same beast some hundreds of miles
and get half the price' (KNA: PC/SP 1/2/2, Annual Report, Masai Province 1937). Fourteen
years later the Kenya Meat Commission, set up in response to insistent pleas that a certain,
fixed price would improve supplies, was to complain that 'purchases on a liveweight basis
of African owned cattle were seriously curtailed by the ability of traders to offer considerably higher prices than those the Commission were authorised to pay. The Commission
has suffered greatly in this respect since its inception and has found it quite impossible to
compete with traders supplying cattle to the African consuming areas.' Kenya Meat
Commission *Annual Report* 1951.
68 Occasionally, of course, he was refused permission, under the Kenyan Crop Production
and Livestock Rules 1926, to sell maize outside the district, and during the depression he
often found difficulty in selling his maize for cash; see p. 44 above.
69 'Das höchste Gluck der Masai ist ein möglichst grosser Viehbesitz, sein ganzes Denken
und Tun gilt der Erhaltung und Vergrösserung der Herden' (The greatest happiness of the
Masai lies in the possession of as many cattle as possible; all his thoughts and actions are
bound up with retention and enlargement of his herds). Merker 1904 (D1), p. 157, cited
in Herskovits 1926 (C) (my translation).
70 Steele (1977 (D2)) notes that in Southern Rhodesia in 1930 the Post Office interest rate
stood at 3.5 per cent; whereas the net rate of increase in the African cattle population
between 1913 and 1932 was 7.38 per cent per annum.

71 KNA: DC/MKS/1/1/13, Annual Report, Machakos District for 1920/1 (R.G. Stone), p. 25; NAR: ZBJ 1/1/1, Evidence to the Native Production and Trade Commission 1944, p. 19, evidence of Mr Munro, rancher.

72 During the period 1934–41 cattle deliveries do follow cattle prices quite closely, but prices were themselves partly determined, of course, by the number and kind of market outlets that the government chose to open.

73 KNA: PC/SP 1/2/2, Annual Report, Masai Province for 1927/8. For similar complaints see the Annual Reports also for 1922/3, 1923/4, 1928/9, 1930/1, 1931/2.

74 KNA: DC/MKS/1/1/33, Annual Reports, Machakos District, 1955 and 1956.

75 See notes 58, 65, 66 above.

76 For more information on the practices of traders, see for Southern Rhodesia, Kosmin 1974 (C), and for Kenya to 1929, Spencer 1974 (C).

77 NAR: N 3/3/8, Acting Superintendent of Natives, Victoria, to Native Commissioner, Gutu, 2 July 1921. I am indebted to Dr Murray Steele for this reference.

78 Chief Native Commissioners' Circulars, no. 7 of 1913 (NAR: N 4/1/1); cited in Johnson 1969 (D2), p. 6.

79 Martin 1949 (D1).

80 Great Britain 1934b (B1), vol. I, p. 961, evidence of Fazan. NAR: S 235/501, Edwards, Native Commissioner Mrewa, Annual Report for Mrewa District for 1923.

81 In 1926–31 and 1941–6 there were large spurts in the Southern Rhodesian tax registers, which it is hard to imagine corresponding to changes in the adult male population.

82 J.E. Goldthorpe, in Great Britain 1955a (B1), Appendix VIII, p. 464.

83 From United Nations 1962 (D3).

84 These figures differ slightly from those given in Lury's tables, presumably due to a computing error.

4. The labour market

1 The phrase used by Lewis (1954 (D3)) to denote a supply curve of labour to the 'modern sector' which is flat at or around the real purchasing power of rural incomes.

2 Arrighi's series is criticised at p. 118.

3 The reliability of the data collected is considered at Appendix 3, and the series themselves are given in full at Appendix 4.

4 The basic ration for the resident African labour force was 2 lb of maize meal per day, and many employers before the Second World War, perhaps a majority, gave no more than this; however, some employers gave considerably more. Thus in 1907 the Wankie Colliery Company gave its African employees:

$2\frac{1}{2}$ lb maize meal or $1\frac{1}{4}$ lb rice per diem
$3\frac{1}{2}$ ounces of salt per week
1 lb meat per week
2 lb vegetables per week
plus any *one* of the following: 20 oz of lard
                             20 oz of monkey nuts
                             Kaffir beer

NAR: A 3/18/30/45, 'Conditions of service applying to natives engaged ... at the Wankie Coal Mine', 16 December 1907. During and after the Second World War the issue of a meat ration became general.

5 For the value of this, see Appendix 3, Tables 4.9a, b and c.

6 No series on African agricultural wages before 1945 has, to my knowledge, been put forward either for Kenya or Southern Rhodesia. Van Zwanenberg (1971 (C), p. 117) offers a series based on the Kenya Blue Books, which are also my source, but does not state what economic

sector it is based on, or whether rations are included; Arrighi (1973 (D2), p. 190) offers a table of money wages in Southern Rhodesia, but this contains only two figures for agricultural wages, applying to 1922 and 1926.

7 Unaccountably, cotton piece goods and blankets were omitted from the only previous exercise in this genre, that by Arrighi (1973 (D2), p. 190). Yet they formed 70 to 75 per cent of the 'native trade' in Rhodesia in 1944 (obviously they were a lesser proportion of total African consumption): NAR: ZBJ 1/1/2, Evidence to the Native Production and Trade Commission 1944, pp. 856–8, evidence of C.D. Dryden and J.W. Luffman. They were in general, to judge from the annual trade reports, about one-third of the total import trade of Kenya in the inter-war period.

8 'From the point of view of the effect of economic development on wages, the supply of labour is practically unlimited. *This applies only to unskilled labour.*' Lewis 1954 (D3), p. 145 (my emphasis).

9 Arrighi 1973 (D2), p. 183.

10 For more detail on this see Table 4.9b, cols. 2a and 2b.

11 This episode has been surprisingly little commented on by the underdevelopment school (who mostly confine their attention to events before 1914); it was however, noted by the Southern Rhodesian Chief Native Commissioner in his report for 1920. He noted that:
the average increase in wages since 1914 has been as follows:

Mines	Farms	Domestic service
13%	21%	21%

Meanwhile, the average increase in cost of the articles purchased by natives was 165 per cent. Farm labourers, whose average wage is less than that of other classes, appear to have been particularly handicapped; many are wearing grain bags for want of better apparel.

12 Arrighi 1973 (D2), pp. 192, 212–13.

13 Lewis 1954 (D3), pp. 409, 431–2. The estimated regression equations for the data in our sample are:

for Southern Rhodesia (29 observations, i.e. 1914–38, 1944, 1946–7, 1952–3, 1956–9, the years for which we have information on both variables):

$$w_u = -15.3 + 41.6 \quad w_R; \quad r^2 = 0.2137, \quad D.W. = 0.4239$$
$$(0.64) \quad (1.75)$$

for Kenya (25 observations, i.e. 1921, 1923–4, 1926–38, 1944, 1946–7, 1952–6, 1958, the years for which we have information on both variables):

$$w_u = 48.8^{**} + 0.29^{**} \quad w_R; \quad r^2 = 0.4120, \quad D.W. = 0.9395$$
$$(4.71) \quad (4.01)$$

where w_u = value of modern sector real wage index, 1914 = 100 (from Appendix 4, Table 4.9)

w_R = (Southern Rhodesia) estimate of grain produced per head of rural population (from Table 4.3, col. 3)

= (Kenya) *sales* of products of African origin per head of total African population, deflated by the export price of a bag of maize, 1925 = 100 (from Table 4.3, col. 8)

**denotes significance at the 1 per cent level

Numbers in parentheses below coefficients are Student's *t*-statistics

The correlation is significant only in Kenya; and in Kenya less than half, and in Southern Rhodesia less than a quarter, of variations in the wage index are explained by variations in the volume of per capita rural production.

14 Arrighi 1967 (D2), p. 32.

15 Note that for Southern Rhodesia the participation rate being measured is the proportion of indigenous Africans employed to the total male labour force, as for non-indigenous Africans the supply price would be average product in their rural area of origin, and not average product in Southern Rhodesia agriculture (w_R) as set out in Table 4.3.

16 E.g. Kenya 1913 (B3), evidence of witnesses 42, 51, 129 and 214; and Major Hastings, *SRLAD*, 7 June 1939, col. 1106: 'It must never be forgotten that the native does not respond to economic stimuli in the same way as the European.'

17 E.g. Wolff 1974 (D1), p. 96: 'In essence, European settlers confronted a backward-bending supply curve of labour'; also van Zwanenberg 1971 (C), p. 85.

18 Arrighi 1973 (D2), p. 191 (italics in original). For what it is worth (bearing in mind the exceptionally low correlation coefficients in equations 4.3a and 4.3b) the exercise of splitting the data sets used in those regressions into two halves yields in each case *lower* regression coefficients in the second half of the data, i.e. the latter time period.

19 Southern Rhodesia, *Annual Reports of the Chief Native Commissioner*, 1932–7.

20 For an examination of rigidity in factor proportions in European agriculture, see Chapter 5, pp. 188–92 above.

21 The operations of the resident labour system in Rhodesia were modified by the Land Apportionment Act of 1930; for details see Chapter 2, p. 24.

22 For complaints of this sort, see NAR: N 9/1/23, report of the NC Gwanda 1920; NAR: ZBJ 1/1/3, p. 1759, evidence of P. Ibbotson to the Native Production and Trade Commission 1944; KNA:PC/RVP6A/25/1, *A note on the squatter problem* by V.M. Fisher, Principal Inspector of Labour.

23 Tow 1960 (D2), p. 105.

24 Source for Southern Rhodesian data: *Statistical Yearbooks* – various issues. 'Mineral production' covers gold, chrome ore and coal; weights are those of the beginning of the relevant decade. Source of Kenyan data: Kenya Agriculture Department, *Annual Reports* ('non-African exports' the 'total exports' less 'exports of African origin'). Numbers in parentheses below coefficients are Student's *t*-statistics; **denotes significance at the 1 per cent level.

25 Note however that of all the years in which wages rise in apparent response to excess demand, all except 1928 and 1938 (in Southern Rhodesia) were years of increasing real African agricultural productivity, the alternative explanatory variable in equation (4.3′). But this, of course, itself acted on supply and hence on labour shortage. It must be accepted that agricultural productivity and labour shortage are multi-collinear and that it is extremely difficult to separate their effects on wages.

26 We consider only those years which count as 'excess demand' years both on the evidence of Table 4.4 and on the definition of the Chief Native Commissioner.

27 Wilson 1972 (D3), p. 68.

28 Arrighi 1973 (D2), p. 184, suggests that in Southern Rhodesia after 1903 'market mechanisms were largely discarded in the determination of wages'. Clayton and Savage 1974 (D1), p. 49, likewise insist that 'the requirement that labour remain cheap prevented any operation of the laws of supply and demand'.

29 Cf. this testimony from Marandellas, which comes from as late as 1946: 'In regard to the new comers [sc. post Second World War settlers], some of them have been so *desperate* that it has been alleged that they have enticed away labourers from some of the more affluent farmers ... by offering them higher wages. The Police have investigated some of the complaints of the latter farmers but have not been able to get sufficient evidence to justify prosecution of the alleged enticers.' NAR: S 235/518, Annual Report of the NC Marandellas for the year ended 31 December 1946.

For earlier complaints about farmers who increased wages, and attempts to get wages legally standardised throughout the country, see for Kenya, RH: Mss.Afr.s.1618, Minutes of Rongai Farmers' Association, 26 March 1934, and for Southern Rhodesia, NAR: Hist.Mss. BI 1/1/1, Minutes of Bindura Farmers' Association meeting for 9 October 1926. In the Southern Rhodesia legislative assembly on 7 June 1939, col. 1110, Major Hastings described competition between employers for the services of African employees as being 'demoralising' for the employee.

30 For Kenya: PRO: CO 533/90, (Governor) Girouard to (Colonial Secretary) Harcourt, 25 September 1911. For Southern Rhodesia: Agriculture Department, *Annual Report* 1909; PRO: CO 417/467, Rhodesia Chamber of Mines to Milton, 12 March 1909, enclosed in (High Commissioner) Hely Hutchinson to (Colonial Secretary) Crewe, 8 September 1909.

31 In Southern Rhodesia there are peaks in the tax registers of 1921, 1931 and 1946, of which the first and last were years of labour shortage by both our criteria (CNC's testimony and the calculation of Table 4.4), whereas the second is a shortage year also on the calculations of Table 4.4. In Kenya, for direct evidence that the tax collection effort was stepped up in the years of labour shortage, see van Zwanenberg 1971 (C), Chapter 6.

32 E.g. Arrighi 1973 (D2), p. 194; Good 1976 (D3), p. 603.

33 In Uganda the Native Authority Ordinance of 1919 authorised the use of compulsory paid labour (*kasanvu*) for sixty days in the year, which was widely used in the construction of the road system; and under the Gold Coast Colony Labour Ordinance of 1935 Provincial Commissioners could require able-bodied men to render twenty-four days' paid labour a year on public works projects. Hailey 1957 (D3), pp. 615 and 620.

34 Duignan 1961 (C), p. 171.

35 That is 18.4 thousand out of a total labour force of 130 thousand; 1921–3 averages. 1921–3 was not a period of labour shortage in agriculture, which was experiencing a period of depressed production and prices, but it was a period of rapid expansion of the railway network.

36 For fuller discussion, see Chapter 2, p. 20.

37 NAR: N 9/1/16, Report of the NC Chilimanzi for the year 1913. For testimony that the 1918 Resident Labour Ordinance in Kenya had a similar effect, see PRO: CO 533/238, Northey (Governor of Kenya) to Milner (Colonial Secretary), 11 December 1920.

38 See Table 2.4, col. 4.

39 As Prime Minister Coghlan of Southern Rhodesia maintained (and the point would have had even more force in Kenya, whose links with the Colonial Office were so much tighter): 'We cannot make the [Rhodesian Native Labour] Bureau a Government concern. To do so would be to discredit ourselves in the eyes of the United Kingdom Government and to lay ourselves open to the charge of using forced labour.' NAR: S 235/40, Prime Minister to Minister of Mines and Works, 20 August 1925.

40 Van Zwanenberg 1971 (C), p. 373. The Assistant District Commissioner for Kisii, C. Rimmington, wrote that 'when a man, whatever his nationality, has failed in the exercise of other professions, he turns naturally to labour recruiting'. KNA: PC/NZA/3/20/2/1, cited van Zwanenberg 1971 (C), p. 374.

41 The capitation fee charged by one of the more respectable recruiters, John L. Riddoch, in 1926 was a mere 20s. to 34s. a head, or about two months' wages, by comparison with the twelve months' wages charged by the RNLB. The RNLB rates were described as 'prohibitive and quite beyond the means of the average employer in this country' in Kenya 1925 (B3); a conclusion to which the same colony's Labour Bureau Commission had previously come in 1921 when deciding whether to encourage the setting up of a labour bureau with a monopoly of recruiting in some areas along the lines of the RNLB (Kenya 1921 (B3)).

42 In general the rate of pay earned by Rhodesia Native Labour Bureau contract labour was some 25 per cent below that earned by 'free flow' labour. As an indication, at Wankie

Colliery in 1918 the average wages of voluntary and recruited labour were as shown in the table.

	Underground strength	Average length of service	Average rate of pay per month
Voluntary labour	365	3 yrs 1½ mths	40/-
RNLB	570	5 mths	29/3

Source: NAR: A 3/17/12/3, A.R. Thomson to Secretary to Administrator, letter dated 6 August 1918.

43 See note 42 above.

44 Van Zwanenberg 1971 (C), p. 378; see also Kenya Labour Department, *Annual Reports*, 1938, 1946.

45 E.g. on Southern Rhodesia mica mines, cf. Phimister 1975 (C), p. 151; and as surface workers in the Kenya gold mines in the 1930s. In 1937 the Medical Officer of Health for North Nyanza related that in the gold mines he had seen 'a gang of children ... carrying dirt on their heads some hundred yards to the sluice box. In the "paddock" they were struggling up to their knees in thick grey slush. Ninety trips are made daily on a ticket of thirty days to earn a monthly wage of three shillings ....' KNA: DC/NN.1/19, North Nyanza District, Annual Report 1937, p. 49.

46 Cf. the evidence of the going wage rate for mining in Kenya in 1937 as quoted in the previous note. More systematic data are given by the Kenya Labour Department and Southern Rhodesian Native Commissioner as shown in the table.

	Southern Rhodesia		Kenya		
	Juvenile rate	Adult males (national average)	Juvenile rate	Women	Adult males
1927	6/- to 10/-	21/3	6.0 to 8.0	10.0 to 12.0	16.0
1934			3.0 to 6.0		9.0
1938			6.0		11.10

Sources: NAR: S 235/505, Annual Report of NC Lomagundi for 1927; Appendix 4; Kenya Labour Department *Annual Report*.

47 See, for example, *Rhodesia Mines and Industries*, August 1940, p. 9; also Riddoch, *KLC Debs.*, 16 December 1954, col. 1239.

48 Arrighi 1973 (D2), p. 184.

49 Arrighi 1973 (D2), p. 214. 'Real wages remained at a level which promoted capitalist accumulation not because of the forces of supply and demand, but because of political-economic mechanisms that ensured the "desired" supply at the "desired" wage rate.'

50 The increase in compulsory labour was mainly associated with railway building projects; however, these like the labour shortage of 1923 were the result of the same phenomenon, namely post-war agricultural settlement and the growth of agricultural production.

51 Kenya Agriculture Department, *Annual Report*, 1946.

52 For 1905–9 we only have money wage data, suggesting about a 20 per cent fall during the period (see Appendix 4, Table 4.9b).

53 For good examples of public debate about methods of relieving labour shortage, see *KLC Debs.*, 11 January 1946 and 16 December 1954; also *SRLAD*, 7 June 1939 and 10 October 1946.

54 United States of America, Bureau of the Census, *Historical Statistics of the US: colonial times to 1957*, (US Department of Commerce, 1961) Notes on Series K73–82, p. 280.

55 On change in the Southern Rhodesia African labourer's diet, see Howman 1942 (D2).

56 Cf. King 1977 (D1), p. 99: 'The decision to protect at all costs settler agriculture against African cash crop competition so reduced the rewards of local production that African aspirations were usually directed elsewhere.'

57 Coined by Hart 1973 (D3) and given great emphasis in the policy recommendations of the International Labour Organisation's mission to Kenya. The term 'sector' is a little misleading, however, as many 'informal' activities represent part-time employment undertaken by agriculturists or wage-workers.

58 NAR: N 9/1/14, Report of Native Commissioner, Mrewa District, for year ended 31 March 1911. For a similar comment in Nyanza, Kenya that the manufacture of hoes for African use had passed almost entirely from African into Indian hands, see KNA: PC/NZA/1/7, Annual Report, Nyanza Province for 1912.

59 *Rhodesia Mines and Industries*, May 1940, p. 17.

60 For Kenya: KNA: DC/MKS/1/1/5, Annual Report, Machakos District for 1912/13; for Southern Rhodesia, NAR: N 9/1/7, Annual Report, Mrewa District for year ended 31 March 1901.

61 Southern Rhodesia, *Annual Report of the Chief Native Commissioner*, 1920, p. 4.

62 KNA: DC/FH, Annual Report, Fort Hall District, 1926.

63 These attempts are described in the case of Kenya by King 1977 (D1), pp. 142–53; in the case of Southern Rhodesia by Steele 1972 (C), pp. 304–52.

64 Southern Rhodesia, *Annual Report of the Chief Native Commissioner* 1932, p. 7.

65 King 1977 (D1), p. 26.

66 *KLC Debs.*, 11 January 1946, col. 771.

67 Ibbotson 1945 (D2), p. 41. Cf. Kenya Labour Department, *Annual Report* 1945: 'Average wages in the towns are not sufficient to support a family in this town ...'

68 NAR: ZBJ 1/1/2, pp. 999–1000, evidence of Charles Mzengele to Native Production and Trade Commission 1944.

69 NAR: ZAH 1/1/1, paragraph 1137, evidence of John White to Land Commission 1925.

70 Cf. testimony of G.M. Huggins, later Prime Minister, to 1925 Land Commission:

> *Chairman*: You do not approve of native industries in the white towns?
> *Huggins*: That is so: [I only approve of] employment by white men in the white men's townships, with villages under control for the natives to live in.

NAR: ZAH 1/1/1, evidence to the Land Commission 1925, paragraph 449.

71 King 1977 (D1), p. 198.

72 King 1977 (D1), p. 210.

73 Kenya 1960 (B3), p. 9. Emphasis added.

5. European agriculture

1 Source for 1925, Southern Rhodesia 1946 (B2), Table IV, p. 15; for 1955, Southern Rhodesia 1958a (B2).

2 Source for 1926, Kenya and Uganda Customs Department, *Annual Report*; for 1961, Kenya, *Statistical Abstract* 1961.

3 Van Zwanenberg 1971 (C), pp. 44–7; van Zwanenberg 1972 (D1), *passim* but in particular pp. 8–9; R. Palmer, 'The agricultural history of Rhodesia', in Palmer and Parsons 1977 (D3), p. 240.

4 Typical is Wasserman's judgment on the Kenya settlers: '[Their] intense drive for political influence and their conflicts with the metropole largely derived from the need to correct the unviability of their economic condition through political supports' (1976 (D1), p. 23).

5 Van Zwanenberg 1971 (C), pp. 42ff; Remole 1959 (C), Chapter 3; Murray 1970 (D2), p. 60.

6 Leys 1975 (D1), pp. 29ff; Furedi 1972 (D1).

7 Rooney 1968 (C), p. 116.

8 Southern Rhodesia 1931 (B2), Appendix B.

9 PRO: CO 533/208, evidence of F.W. Baillie to Economic Development Commission, 1919.

10 PRO: CO 533/229, telegram Acting Governor of Kenya to Colonial Secretary, 24 February 1918.

11 The 'big four' were:
> Rhodesia Land and Cattle Ranching Company, Nuanetsi (BSAC majority share-holding) (90 000 cattle)
> Willoughby's Consolidated (40 434 cattle)
> Liebig's Extract of Meat Company (17 214 cattle)
> Devuli Ranch (21 000 cattle)

The 244 other ranches on the Stockowners' Association roll ran, between them, a total of 195 603 cattle. NAR: S 1215/1324/3, Rhodesia Stockowners' Association to Secretary of Agriculture, 29 December 1933.

12 Interview R.O. Hennings, 31 January 1980 (E).

13 PRO: CO 417/659, Memo by Mr Duthie, The Maize Association, to Resident Commissioner of Southern Rhodesia, enclosed in Frederick (High Commissioner, Capetown) to Churchill (Colonial Secretary), 8 April 1921.

14 Interview S.H. Powles, 17 November 1979 (E).

15 RH: Mss.Afr.s.1121, Diary of S.H. Powles for 14 January 1943.

16 Matheson and Bovill 1950 (D1), p. 131.

17 All that can be said with precision is that between 54 and 72 per cent of growers were below the mean level as the relevant class interval covers yields between five and seven bags per acre. The estimate of 66 per cent is a *pro rata* interpolation.

18 Output per acre is the only measure of efficiency considered here. In the sense of output per *man employed* the settler economies come far worse out of international comparisons (cf. note 75 below), but we argue that this reflects mainly a high level of labour intensity that stems in turn from low relative labour costs and high risk levels.

19 All the 'big four' Rhodesian ranchers mentioned in note 11 above represented companies incorporated outside Rhodesia, as did Stephen Powles (note 14). However, we push this line of analysis no further, not only because data on nationality of ownership (particularly in the agricultural sector) are so poor but also because of doubt about what they mean: should Lord Delamere, whose capital was derived exclusively from landownership in England but who lived in Kenya from 1903 onwards, be treated as a 'local' or 'foreign' capitalist?

20 For the latest example in the latter genre, see Best (1979 (D1)). One may hazard an analogy between white farming in the settler economies and the English cricket profession until the early 1960s: the professionals or 'players' kept the activity viable, but the amateurs or 'gentlemen' received the lion's share of attention in the media and of official favour.

21 Cf. Chapter 2, p. 41.

22 12s. 1d. per bag average export price less 1s. 1d. per bag (12s. per ton) railage and export charges; Southern Rhodesia 1931 (B2), p. 14 and Appendix D.

23 Average production cost (labour and other inputs) per acre in Southern Rhodesia in 1930 was estimated at 65s., i.e. 10s. 10d. per bag, or just below the export parity pay-out on a six-bag yield; Southern Rhodesia 1931 (B2), p. 9.

24 In 1919 its terms were 7 or 8 per cent interest, payable half-yearly in advance. These onerous terms were blamed for the high rate at which soldier-settlement scheme farms were being abandoned in 1919. PRO: CO 417/621, enclosure in Chaplin (Administration of Southern Rhodesia) to Buxton (High Commissioner, Cape Town), 25 June 1919.
25 For these, see Huxley 1935 (D1), vol. II, p. 243.
26 Kenya, *Annual Report of the Land and Agricultural Bank*, 1932, p. 10.
27 Heyer 1960 (C), p. 176.
28 Kenya 1935 (B3), p. 8.
29 Heyer 1960 (C), p. 209.
30 Kenya 1936 (B3), p. 13.
31 Kenya 1953 (B3), p. 10.
32 RH: Mss. Afr.r. 114, *No signposts* by J.F. Lipscomb, p. 80.
33 Recall Chapter 2, p. 14. The minimum capital requirement for post-Second World War settlers in Kenya was £15 000. RH: Mss.Afr.r.114, *No signposts* by J.F. Lipscomb, Chapter 8.
34 The table gives summary details of Land Bank lending. It will be noted, in particular, that as the depression of the 1930s deepened the Southern Rhodesia Land Bank did not much reduce the *number* of its loans from the average 1920s level, but it sharply reduced their average value.

	Southern Rhodesia		Kenya	
Year	Number of Land Bank advances	Value of Land Bank advances (£000)	Number of Land Bank advances	Value of Land Bank advances (£000)
1924	286	327		
1928	443	321		
1932	292	166	158	195
1936	215	141	88	117
1940	150	130	(297)[a]	(295)[a]
1944	134	129		
1950	929	1182	140	248
1955	1157	1828	161	447

Note: [a] 1940–5 total.
Source: Land and Agricultural Banks of Kenya and of Southern Rhodesia, *Annual Reports*.

35 Local pool quotas were:

Size category (number of bags)	Proportion of deliveries taken by local pool (%)	
1–100	80	
101–200	75	
201–300	70	
301–500	70	of triennial average of sales
...		
4001–6000	30	
more than 6000	20	

NAR: S 1216/SC 1/100/130, Chairman of Maize Board to Secretary of Agriculture, 5 April 1934.
36 NAR: S 1216/SC 1/100/130, Chairman of Maize Board to Secretary of Agriculture, 5 April 1934. It is of interest that in the 1930s the Southern Rhodesia fiscal system was

adapted so as to give small producers in the mining industry, also, preferential treatment. The Gold Premium Tax of 1932 was imposed on monthly outputs of more than 300 ounces only, from mines realising a grade of more than two and a half pennyweights per ton of ore (Phimister 1975 (C), p. 158), and the Que Que Roasting Plant, which consistently ran at a loss until 1948 (Southern Rhodesia 1953 (B2)), was set up in 1937 largely for the benefit of the low-grade gold mines.

37 KNA: SC.AGR. 56/4, E.W. Bovill, memorandum, 'Economic development in East Africa' to Secretary of Agriculture, November 1938. I am grateful to Dr John Lonsdale for this reference.

38 Cf. p. 47 above.

39 RH: Mss.Afr.s.1121, Diaries of S.H. Powles, entry for 18 March 1943.

40 Powles' diaries (*ibid.*), entry for 12 February 1943. Powles' yields were more than double the European average (recall p. 176 above).

41 See p. 47 above.

42 In July 1942 he noted in his diary that maize control was 'quite unnecessary' and in December 1950 argued unavailingly with the Governor that 'it was time maize was de-controlled for the reason that the benefits we are receiving under control, are not worth $\frac{1}{2}$ million a year'. RH: Mss.Afr.s.1121, Diaries of S.H. Powles, entries for 13 July 1942 and 11 December 1950.

43 Powles' diaries (*ibid.*), entries for 15 and 21 January 1943.

44 Powles' diaries (*ibid.*), entry for 2 March 1948.

45 Powles' diaries (*ibid.*), entries for 4 March 1934 and 28 May 1947.

46 Powles' diaries (*ibid.*), entry for 28 November 1952.

47 For which, see p. 54.

48 NAR: ZAH 1/1/3, evidence of R.D. Gilchrist to the Land Commission 1925, paragraph 5508.

49 NAR: ZAX 1/1/1, evidence of R.D. Gilchrist to the Commission on Sales of Native Cattle 1938, p. 68. For the detail of market discrimination in beef, see pp. 52–8.

50 Gilchrist, *SRLAD*, 28 April 1931, col. 1221.

51 In Southern Rhodesia the rainy season is from November to April; in Central Kenya there are two rainy seasons, from end March to May and from November to December, which merge into one as one moves westward.

52 As Delamere noted,

> With implements ... the difficulty of getting the right articles in a country where you have no-one to copy is not understood. Even in the case of ploughs it took a consider-able period to get implements suited to the country, and many were tried. Mowers, reapers and binders, Australian strippers and Australian harvesters were tried for harvesting wheat before a satisfactory solution was arrived at.
>
> (PRO: CO 533/345, enclosure in Grigg (Governor) to Strachey (Assistant Under-Secretary of State, Colonial Office), 14 January 1926)

53 In 1904 Odlum, the Agricultural Assistant, was to explain the position in the following terms:

> At the present time we have a so-called experimental farm near Salisbury, but I fail to see how it is in any particular of value to us or to the country. We have some make-shift buildings (the tobacco barn is a disgrace to the Department), we have no orchard, we have no herd or flocks, we have but few implements, our experiments are conducted in a hit or miss manner. The farmer is quick to observe this and concludes that we either do not know our business or that we do not care ...
>
> (NAR: G 1/4/3, Odlum to Secretary, Department of Agriculture, 21 December 1904)

For the Kenya case, see Spencer 1974 (C).

54 In Southern Rhodesia, Rooney (1968 (C), p. 158) argues that 'the main efforts to carry out early experimental work were carried out on the farms belonging to Cecil Rhodes'; for Delamere's experimental work, see Huxley 1935 (D1), vol. I, especially pp. 170–6.

55 The position in Kiambu District, Kenya, in 1917 was that the district 'started on the small man principle. Where are the original settlers? A few who had capital remain and flourish; many who had capital have "made good" in the army or professionally; the rest, the majority, have gone.' KNA: DC/KBU/10, Annual Report, Kiambu District for 1916/17.

56 The risk factor is emphasised by Palmer 1978 (D2), p. 2.

57 Cf. Chapter 3, p. 85.

58 'Except in certain areas largely settled by Afrikaners from the south the majority of farmers were migratory and speculative. A man might own a farm one year and abandon it the next while he tried his luck at mining, storekeeping, or took a safe but unrewarding post with the railways or with the company's administration.' Clements and Harben 1962 (D2), p. 66.

59 Remole 1959 (C), p. 180.

60 There were three elements in the reduction in costs after the First World War: the improvements of some roads to all-weather standard; the advent of the motor lorry in place of the ox-cart; and the extension of branch railway lines.

61 PRO: CO 533/116, Report on a visit to the Uasin Gishu Plateau by Sir H.C. Belfield, Governor of Kenya, 10 April 1913. Huxley (1959 (D1), vol. 1, p. 67), notes that on the Uasin Gishu, the Afrikaner (settler community) cut by hand with sickles, and bound by hand not with twine, but with the straw; and at the same time in Southern Rhodesia,

> A survey of farmers in the Marandellas district carried out [in 1914] by two officials of the Chartered Company revealed that many of them were penniless, waiting to receive money for their tobacco, which was stacked in the warehouse or being hawked around London. while their other assets were pathetically few – a wagon, a few oxen, one or two ploughs, the total value of which would be well below that of one light modern tractor.   (Clements and Harben 1962 (D2), p. 80)

62 PRO: CO 533/116, Report on a visit to the Uasin Gishu Plateau by Sir H.C. Belfield, Governor of Kenya, 10 April 1913.

63 RH: MSS.Afr.s.875, *Reminiscences of an early settler in Rhodesia* by C.W.R. Southey, JP, p. 9. Similar technical adaptations occurred among small-workers in the Rhodesian mining industry at this time: 'Our working gear was made of eland hide, several strands cut wet and twisted into a rope, and the buckets were made of the same material. The windlass was a Msasa trunk and the handles of Msasa branches with a good angle in them.' Phimister 1975 (C), p. 52, quoting N. Jones, *Rhodesian genesis* (Bulawayo, 1953), p. 47.

64 Sen 1962 (D3); Pack 1978 (D3); Cooper and Kaplinsky 1974 (D2).

65 Information from Mr George Watkins, Centre for the Study of the History of Technology, University of Bath.

66   Aristocrats like Delamere took with them 'something of the grand manner of an age already dying, and tried, perhaps unconsciously, to create ... a replica of the feudal system of their fathers'. Two other aristocrats, who settled in the Protectorate before 1914, were described by Karen Blixen as 'outcasts' from England: 'It was not a society that had thrown them out, ... but time had done it, they did not belong to their century. No other nation than the English could have produced them, but theirs was an earlier England, a world which no longer existed.'
Sorrenson 1968 (D1), p. 231, quoting Huxley, *Settlers of Kenya* (London: Chatto and Windus, 1948), p. 20 and Blixen 1964 (D1), p. 228.

67 Interview S.H. Powles, 17 November 1979 (E). Vincent Liversage, the Kenya government

agricultural economist, also emphasised (interview 25 November 1979 (E)) that 'a lot of the most successful people stuck to the bullock for cultivation', and after the Second World War official reports (e.g. Kenya 1953 and 1961b (B3)) continued to emphasise that over-mechanisation was the cause of low yields on a number of farms.

68 The implementation of the Kenya Cattle Cleansing Ordinance of 1924, requiring compulsory dipping of African cattle, had to be delayed until 1937 because so few farmers could afford a dip tank, which at £150 in 1925 (Carnegie 1931 (D1), p. 213) was one of the cheapest of agricultural capital items.

69 See p. 179 above.

70 The argument here is that if the production function was discontinuous (e.g. a step-function such as *DEFGHJL* in Figure 5.3 rather than the smooth isoquant *LL'*) then *small* increases in the ratio of labour cost to capital cost would not justify the adoption of a more capital-intensive technique.

71 *Rhodesia Mines and Industries*, February 1941.

72 The position in mining was similar: in evidence to the Wankie Coal Commission of 1949 R. Lechmere-Oertel, Managing Director of Powell Duffryn Technical Services, insisted that there was no rational alternative to the current methods of hand-got pillar and stall mining. The alternative, mechanisation, 'is scarcely one that would have been considered, at any rate up to the war period, in view of the abundant supply of relatively cheap labour that has hitherto been available'. Anglo-American archives, Salisbury: Box 67, Evidence to Wankie Coal Commission, p. 4.

73 KNA: PC/RVP 6A/25/1, *A note on the squatter problem* by V.M. Fisher, Principal Inspector of Labour, Kenya, 1932.

74 The figures for the main European farming districts of Kenya in 1954, although crudely aggregative, are suggestive of an inverse correlation between the prosperity of European agriculture and the importance of squatter tenancy.

District	% of squatters to total agricultural labour force	Average gross farm revenue by district (shillings/acre) 1956–60
Machakos	21.5	37
Uasin Gishu	20.2	76
Laikipia	14.3	18
Trans Nzoia	14.0	89
Naivasha	13.9	69
Nakuru	10.9	110
Nairobi	8.4	760
Kericho/Sotik	8.1	600
Thika	6.1	240

Sources: Squatters: East African Statistical Department, *Kenya Agricultural Census* 1954–5, Table X; revenue: East African Statistical Department, *Kenya Agricultural Census* 1960, text Table 99

75 'It is a significant fact', noted the Kenya Native Affairs Department, Labour Section, *Annual Report* for 1925, 'vide the Report of the Senior Coffee Officer re his visit to South America, that whilst in Kenya an average of six units per ten acres of coffee is required, in Guatemala the average is four units, and in Costa Rica one unit.' In the 1940s two articles published in the Agricultural Journals of the respective settler economies (Maher 1942 (D1) and Wadsworth 1950 (D2)) deplored, and the latter estimated, the extent of 'wasted labour' in European agriculture; but this exercise was largely irrelevant, as the 'waste' of labour followed directly from its cheapness.

76 I.e. in terms of Figure 5.3, moving out along the ray *OC* if output were increased, and not deviating from this ray even in the event of an increase in relative labour cost. (The tight link between output and employment in European agriculture has been noted and estimated in Chapter 4, p. 126.) It might be suggested that in times of labour scarcity the African labour coefficient could be reduced by Europeans doing more manual work. But sociological factors precluded this: 'Would the honourable member like me to recommend', asked W. Cdr Eastwood in the Southern Rhodesia Legislative Assembly on 9 June 1943, 'that the European farmer of Southern Rhodesia should accept the same standard of living as the farmers of Rumania, Bulgaria, Yugoslavia and Poland?' *SRLAD*, 9 June 1943, col. 1613.

77 Including the Governor of Kenya, Sir Robert Brooke-Popham, when he asserted in 1939 that 'Where most ... people make a mistake is to imagine that Kenya Colony is primarily a money-making organisation. It isn't. There is no reason why a settler with good farming knowledge shouldn't make a decent living, but the main object of most people in coming out here is to live in fine scenery, a good climate, and amongst friends.' KNA: SC.AGR. 56/4, 'Development of agriculture in settler areas'. I am indebted to Dr John Lonsdale for this reference.

78 See for example pp. 180–3 above.

79 This complements the point made by Baldwin (1963 (D3)) that plantation economies are poor generators of external economies through the route of demands for skilled labour.

6. Secondary industry

1 Arrighi 1967 (D2), p. 36.

2 Furtado 1970 (D3), p. 147; Baer and Maneschi 1971 (D3), *passim*. For a critical survey of 'under-consumptionist' arguments as applied, in particular, to Brazil see Wells 1977 (D3).

3 Chenery 1960 (D3), p. 646.

4 Pearson 1969 (D1), p. 77. The assumptions underlying Pearson's statement are discussed in Appendix 8.

5 Pearson 1969 (D1), p. 166.

6 The relevant data for the five countries considered in Appendix 7 are shown in the table.

	Proportion of consumer goods manufacture to total manufacturing	Gini coefficient of inequality (%)
Settler economies		
Southern Rhodesia	55.1	62.1
Kenya	69.6	58.6
Peasant export economies		
Uganda	67.9	53.1
Ghana	41.0	40.6
Jamaica	77.6	—

—no data
Source: For derivation of data, see Appendix 7.

7 For data on income distribution see Appendix 7. The demand function (equation 6.1) can only be expected to apply to consumer goods. For a brief discussion of intermediate goods, see p. 198.

8 E.g. for Southern Rhodesia 1938–52 and 1955–62, where P_j = construction, estimated

regression equations are:

P_i = cement

$$P_i = 254.04 + 0.087** P_j$$
$$(1.50) \quad (17.46)$$
$$r^2 = 0.9356$$

P_i = structural
clay products

$$P_i = 153.53* + 0.023** P_j$$
$$(2.36) \quad (12.26)$$
$$r^2 = 0.8774$$

* = significance at the 5 per cent level
** = significance at the 1 per cent level

where all variables are gross output in current £000. There are negligible imports of cement and structural clay products in the years mentioned, so that $P_i \simeq D_i$ in both cases.

9 Data on Southern Rhodesian industrial production run from 1938 to 1962, but are highly aggregated (e.g. 'chemicals' and 'metal manufacture' are the limit to which disaggregation is taken). For Kenya we have industrial census data only in 1954, 1955 and 1961.

10 Chalmers Wright (Great Britain 1955a (B1), p. 14) considers that:

Typical sources of cash expenditure among rural householders in the Kahama district of Western Province, Tanganyika, may have varied with the income group approximately as follows in 1952:

less than 50 shillings – tax, plain cloth*, salt, hoe-heads*, a few beads, native beer
50 to 100 shillings – same as above, plus coloured cloth* (*khangas*), blankets*, aluminium cooking pots*, lamp oil*, cigarettes
100 to 250 shillings – same as above, plus other metal pots and pans*, more expensive beads*, ready-made shorts* and shirts*, bottled beer
250 to 500 shillings – same as above, plus a bicycle*, simple furniture (locally made)*, hair oil, more expensive clothing*, door and window frames (locally made)*, or, in livestock areas, a cow
over 500 shillings – same as above, plus bride price for another wife, or in livestock areas, more cattle.

If it is assumed that no savings were in cash form, then the marginal propensity to consume manufactures (marked * in the list above) is one, between a cash income of 50 and 250 shillings. Thereafter it sinks below one as items of non-manufactured, durable investment goods enter the budget.

11 This argument depends on the assumption that the income redistribution does not itself alter the level of the average propensity to consume of the gainers and the losers from the redistribution; for more detail, see Appendix 8.

12 135, or 64.9 per cent of the Europeans in the sample analysed in Table 6.2c had family incomes of less than £80 per month in 1951.

13 A precise statement of the APC for particular income groups is not possible since precise average and total expenditures by income group are not given in the 1951 survey. But the overall APC is, in fact, just over one since average monthly expenditure for all families sampled was £77.3s.2d. whereas average monthly income was £77.3s.4d. (Southern Rhodesia 1952b (B2), Table 12, p. 7). Since most families earning more than £80 per month underspent their income (see Table 6.3c) it is therefore more than likely that the APC for *poorer* European families was in excess of one.

14 This is, of course, support for the stereotype of the white colonist family as 'conspicuous consumers': Baran 1973 (D3), pp. 211–15.

15 The Southern Rhodesia survey of European household budgets in 1951 gives no information on the allocation of expenditure by income groups (Southern Rhodesia 1952b (B2)). But for all income groups together the average propensity to consume manufactures (fuel

and light, household stores, linen, consumer durables, clothing and footwear, drink and tobacco, motor cycles, cycles) is (£25.10s. out of an average income of £77.2s.4d.) = 0.326, compared with an APC for manufactures for the richest African income group (cf. Table 6.2a) of 0.219.

16 See Chapter 4, note 7.
17 This is obviously the kind of 'discontinuous' demand function which Furtado has in mind to describe the Brazilian market for manufactures in the 1950s (1970 (D3), p. 147).
18 Cf. Appendix 8, pp. 232–3.
19 Cf. Ackley 1961 (D3), pp. 246–9.
20 Isher Dass, *KLC Debs.*, 19 October 1934, col. 589. For similar testimony, see Archdeacon Owen (in Great Britain 1931 (B1) vol. II, p. 97) who referred to 'a hum of prosperity on the Uganda side of the border where there is stagnation on the Kenya side'. In fact both Dass and Owen over-stated their case. Imports of cotton piece goods and bicycles into Kenya were in some years less than into Uganda, in some years more. The table, showing a random sample of import figures, illustrates this (figures in £000).

	Cotton piece goods		Bicycles	
	Kenya	Uganda	Kenya	Uganda
1929	537	524	14	47
1934	325	365	7	38
1939	259	346	14	62
1944	1588	951	12	7
1949	7429	2528	286	209

Source: Kenya and Uganda Customs Department, *Annual Reports*, various.

21 See quotation at the head of this chapter.
22 For Gini coefficients see note 6 above, and for their derivation see Appendix 7.
23 $\Sigma P_i/\Sigma D_i$, in the notation of p. 197 above.
24 There are two problems with this definition. First, cost structures may differ drastically between the country whose industrial structure is being taken as a reference point – here South Africa – and that where import substitution is being considered. Thus, it is important to emphasise that in this context 'shiftability' means simply that size of market alone presents no barrier to import substitution: cost factors, such as absence or high cost of the necessary skilled labour, may present such a barrier, although to some extent this can be overcome by protection of the domestic market.
   Second, there is the problem posed by the aggregative nature of the categories used to classify imports and industrial production. Often there is a wide dispersion of plant sizes within these categories; on the one hand, this may lead us to infer that an entire category is 'shiftable' when only part of it is, but on the other, it may lead us to discard other industrial categories as being entirely unshiftable on this criterion, whereas in fact some small plants within these categories would be entirely viable in the economies under discussion. We may hope, in the absence of evidence to the contrary, that these opposite biases will cancel one another out.
25 Great Britain 1931 (B1), vol. II, paragraphs 285ff and 322ff, evidence of Uganda and Tanganyika Chambers of Commerce to Joint Committee on Closer Union; and also NAR: ZAY 2/2/12, evidence of J. H. Brown to Economic Development Commission 1939.
26 Great Britain 1931 (B1), vol. II, p. 290, evidence to the Joint Committee on Closer Union.
27 This applied in 1956 to the duties on frozen meat (suspended); glass bottles; other glass

containers; motor spirit (this was purely a revenue duty); and rice. East Africa High Commission 1956b (B3) pp. 46ff, Appendix II.

28 PRO: CO 533/210, Report of the Economic Commission 1917, p. 26.

29 Bertin, *SRLAD*, 8 May 1929, col. 484.

30 Sales to Northern Rhodesia, Nyasaland and South Africa in 1930 £410 123 (source: Table 6.6); national income in manufacturing £1 724 000 (source: Southern Rhodesia 1946 (B2), Table IV, p. 14).

31 Between 1930 and 1938 Southern Rhodesian money national income increased by 53 per cent, from £13 million to £20 million; its exports to Northern Rhodesia and Nyasaland, however, all but doubled, from £392 000 (Table 6.5a) to £762 000.

32 In particular this happened in the field of producers' goods, e.g. explosives, mining machinery, steel: see NAR: ZAY 2/2/12 and 2/2/41, evidence to the Economic Development Commission 1939.

33 NAR: ZAY 2/2/23, evidence to the Economic Development Commission 1939, evidence of C. W. Ridge, General Manager RISCOM. See also evidence to the same commission by T. Y. Craster, maker of steel castings, and B. Jolson, maker of steel windows.

34 Murray 1970 (D2), p. 185; see also NAR: Hist. Mss. RH 12/2/4/2/2, Minutes of Rhodesia Federated Chamber of Commerce meetings for 27 February 1945, 11 March 1947 (urging 'that a Goodwill Mission be sent under Government sponsorship to the Eastern and Central African colonies at the earliest possible date', and 'that all restrictions on Exports to Northern Rhodesia be removed in respect of general merchandise imported or manufactured locally'), and Annual General Meeting 1950.

35 Rankine (Chief Secretary), *KLC Debs.*, 13 January 1948, col. 825.

36 Murray 1970 (D2), p. 186.

37 Cf. Tables 6.10a and 6.10b.

38 Cf. the accompanying figures for Kenyan exports of cement (in thousand tons).

| Year | Local (Kenya) consumption | Exports to | | | Total production |
		Uganda	Tanganyika	Elsewhere	
1958	164.3	8.3	59.5	4.0	236.1
1960	182.1	7.7	104.7	42.4	335.8
1961	118.3	6.5	106.5	93.6	324.3
1962	123.2	11.1	100.8	103.9	338.1
1963	116.4	16.8	97.0	108.9	338.3
1964	82.7	13.2	148.6	171.4	415.4
1965	96.6	7.1	176.2	196.3	476.2

Source: Zajadacz 1970 (D1).

39 The 1951 data are illustrative.

Kenya	(1) Total exports of manufactures to Tanganyika and Uganda (£000)	(2) Total exports to Tanganyika and Uganda (£000)	(1)/(2)%
	2589	3722	69.5

Southern Rhodesia	(1) Total exports of manufactures to Northern Rhodesia and Nyasaland (£000)	(2) Total exports to Northern Rhodesia and Nyasaland (£000)	(1)/(2)%
	4110	5144	79.8

Source: As for Table 6.5b.

40 Eglin 1975 (D1); Tow 1960 (D2).
41 Contrary to the contention of van Zwanenberg who insists that the inter-war period was a period of 'intensification of the process of deeper integration of metropole and periphery economies' (1975 (D1), p. 3).
42 Warren 1973 (D3), p. 4.
43 Warren 1973 (D3), p. 17.
44 In 1930 Professor Henry Clay's report on industrial relations in Southern Rhodesia (Southern Rhodesia 1930b (B2), p. 33) reported the following hourly rates:

	London	Bulawayo
Bricklayers	1s. 9d.	4s.
Carpenters	1s. 9d.	4s. 4½d.
Linotype operators	2s. 0d.	4s. 5d.
Railway platelayers	10s. 10d.	20s. 6d. (per day)

45 The Industrial Conciliation Act of 1934 (eventually repealed in 1958) prevented Africans from bargaining collectively with white employers, by excluding them from the definition of 'employee' under the Act, made it impossible for Africans to take up apprenticeships with European masters, and stipulated equal pay for equal work as between Africans and Europeans, which prevented Africans from using the cheapness of their labour as a means of making progress in the labour market.
46 The emphasis of this statement is on real *white* earnings: money earnings from employment of both Africans and Europeans were higher, after the Second World War, in Ghana than in British East and Central Africa (cf. Table 6.11) but prices were higher there also. In Kenya and Uganda average non-African earnings are pulled down by the relatively low earnings of Asians.
47 Black earnings per capita from cash-crops were of course higher in peasant export economies.
48 The Gini coefficient is a summary measure of inequality. It measures the ratio of the area between the plotted Lorenz curve and the 45° diagonal line, to the total area under the diagonal line; it is measured

$$G = 1 - \sum_{i=1}^{n} (X_i - Y_i)(X_{i-1} - X_{i+1})$$

where X_i are cumulative population shares, Y_i are cumulative earnings shares, and there are n income classes. It is constrained within the limits $0 < G < 1$. The estimated values of G for the countries in Figure 6.2 are as follows:

Southern Rhodesia	62.1%
Kenya	58.6%
Uganda	53.1%
Ghana	40.6%

49 The approximate value of sales of agricultural produce per househ
may be estimated as follows.

Southern Rhodesia: African agricultural sales £4.5 million; number of African households 707 000; sales per household = £6.36.

Kenya: African agricultural sales (exports only) £8.26 million; number of African households 2 390 000; sales per household (export) = £3.45.

Ghana: African agricultural sales (cocoa export only) £66.4 million; number of African households 1 609 000; sales per household (cocoa exports only) = £41.26.

Uganda: African agricultural sales (cotton and coffee exports only) £31.9 million; estimated number of African households 1 914 000; sales per household = £16.66.

50 E.g. 'The bottom 50% of the population has only marginal access to manufactured goods, the next 40% of the population, the mass of the urban working-class, only has access to non-durable consumers' goods. Between these groups large differences in average income are responsible for substantial discontinuities in patterns of consumption.' C. Furtado, *The Analysis of the Brazilian model* (in Portuguese) summarised by Wells 1977 (D3), p. 262.

51 I.e. if the consumption function is written $c = a + bY$, it must satisfy the condition $0 < b < 1$.

52 I.e. small enough to prevent individual propensities to consume being unaltered by the redistribution *itself*.

53 Ackley 1961 (D3), pp. 509–12.

7. Conclusions

1 This stereotype has not been articulated in full by any one person – though Good 1976 (D3), and Arrighi 1967 (D2) come close to it – but is a consistent amalgam of the views of a number of authors, for instance those cited in note 3 of Chapter 1 above. It may be argued that the stereotype in question is an emaciated and unsophisticated version of under-development theory which does no justice to its sociological dimensions, as do the versions of Andre Gunder Frank and many Latin Americanists. This is true; however, each of the propositions in it has been advanced for the case of Kenya and Southern Rhodesia, and they also have the merit of being testable. Frequently, the researcher wishing to apply a test of 'underdevelopment theory' to a particular country is faced with the choice between a version which is crude but operational and a version which is more sophisticated but tautologically true, so that by definition no test is possible. Inevitably he is forced, as we have been, up the first road.

2 This statement holds good for a comparison between 1914 (the first year when usable economic data become available in the settler economies) and 1955, both of which marked peaks in economic activity in the local and world economies. Of course it is possible to arrive at other conclusions by judicious choice of time period – the 'underdevelopment' theorist desirous of proving decline in the African agricultural economy can compare 1912 and 1922, the 'liberal' determined to show that there was improvement can compare 1922 and 1955 – but the description of 'no trend' seems the fairest.

3 This assumption is common ground between those inside the 'underdevelopment' camp and those outside it. For examples of the former group, see note 3 to Chapter 5 above; for examples of the latter, see Wrigley's statement (1965 (D1), p. 247) that in the European Highlands of Kenya 'marginal revenue did not need to equal marginal cost'.

4 This concept is also in fact implicit in much writing on worker consciousness in Southern Africa (e.g. van Onselen 1976 (D2), Phimister 1975 (C), Perrings 1979 (D3), which effectively sees many worker responses as 'games' with a hostile employer.

Bibliography

This bibliography is laid out according to the following pattern:
A. Manuscript sources
  1. Public Record Office, London (PRO)
  2. National Archives of Rhodesia (now Zimbabwe), Salisbury (NAR)
  3. Kenya National Archives, Nairobi (KNA)
  4. Rhodes House, Oxford (RH)
B. Printed primary sources
  1. Publications of Her Majesty's Stationery Office, London
  2. Official reports and publications of the Southern Rhodesia government, Salisbury
  3. Official reports and publications of the Colony and Protectorate of Kenya, Nairobi
  4. Southern Rhodesia Legislative Assembly Debates (*SRLAD*)
  5. Kenya Legislative Council Debates (*KLC Debs.*)
C. Unpublished theses
D. Secondary material
  1. Books and articles on Kenya
  2. Books and articles on Southern Rhodesia
  3. Background
E. Interviews

A Manuscript sources

A1 Public Record Office, London (PRO)
The archives consulted here fall exclusively under two headings: the CO 417 series (Africa, South, 1884–1925: despatches from the High Commissioner, Cape Town, to the Colonial Secretary in London, many of them enclosing letters from the Administrator of Southern Rhodesia and Southern Rhodesia government internal correspondence) and the CO 533 series (East Africa Protectorate, later Kenya: despatches from the Governor or his deputy to the Colonial office).

A2 National Archives of Rhodesia (now Zimbabwe), Salisbury (NAR)

Archives
A 3/17/12/3: Administrator's correspondence, 1918
A 3/18/30/1–46: Administrator's correspondence: Labour, 1900–23
A 8/1/3–9: Civil Commissioners' reports, 1907–22
G 1/4/3: Department of Agriculture: correspondence, 1904

Bibliography

L 2/1/134/4: 'The Liebig Extract of Meat Company's properties', 17 November 1913
MB 6/1/1: Report of Mining Commissioner, Bulawayo, for year ended 31 March 1902
N 9/1/4–25: Annual Reports of the Native Commissioners, 1898–1922 (Mashonaland only until 1912)
NB 6/1/1–12: Annual Reports of Matabeleland Native Commissioners, 1901–12
S 138/38: Native cattle, 1923–6
S 138/189b: Cotton growing in Native reserves, 1923–4
S 235/40: Prime Minister's Office: Correspondence, 1925
S 235/501–18: Annual Reports of Native Commissioners, 1923–38 and 1946
S 1051: Native Commissioners' reports, 1946–8
S 1089: Estates Department register of land sales
S 1215/1090/85: Maize Control Board, minutes, 1940–2
S 1215/1090/103: Marketing of native agricultural produce
S 1215/1090/125: Maize Control Board, minutes, 1939
S 1215/1090/172: Maize Control Board, minutes, 1937–9
S 1215/1090/246: Maize Growers' Conference, September 1936
S 1215/1324/3: Rhodesia Stockowners' Association, claims under Cattle Levy Act
S 1215/1324/14: Export of meat policy, 1940–2
S 1215/1326/15: Conferences of Rhodesia Stockowners' Association (all 1930s)
S 1216/SC 1/100/29: Maize Control Board, meetings, minutes, 1933–4
S 1216/SC 1/100/110: Maize Control Board, correspondence, 1933
S 1216/SC 1/100/130: Maize Control Board, correspondence, 1934
S 1216/SC 1/100/214: Conference of Maize Producers held in Salisbury on 4 October 1932
S 1216/SC 1/100/242: Maize Control Board, minutes, 1935–6
S 1216/SC 7: Rhodesia Stockowners' Association, minutes of executive committee meetings, 1941–3
S 1542/M2: Correspondence re Maize Control Act 1934
S 1542/N2: Local Native Councils, minutes, 1931–9
S 1561/38: Telegram Scouts, Mazoe, to CNC, Salisbury, July 1931
SA 5/1/4: Minutes of Salisbury Chamber of Commerce meeting, 2 July 1910

Historical manuscripts
BI 1/1/1: Bindura Farmers' Association papers
DO 1/1/1–7: Correspondence and other papers of John Wallace Downie, Minister of Agriculture 1925–7 and Minister of Mines and Public Works 1927–30
ME 1/1/1: Reminiscences of John Meikle, pioneer trader, prospector and farmer
RH 12/2/4/2/1–9: Rhodesia Federated Chambers of Commerce: minute books, 1919–57
SM 4/1/1: Correspondence of J.H. Smit, Mayor of Salisbury 1927–8 and Minister of Finance 1933–42
UM 1/3/1: Umvukwe Farmers' Association minute books

Evidence to commissions
ZAH 1/1/1–4: Land Commission 1925, oral and written evidence
ZAX 1/1/1–2: Commission on Sales of Native Cattle 1938, oral evidence
ZAY 2/2/1–46: Economic Development Commission 1939, oral and written evidence
ZBJ 1/1/1–4: Native Production and Trade Commission 1944, oral evidence
ZBJ 1/2/1–2: Native Production and Trade Commission 1944, written memoranda

A3 Kenya National Archives, Nairobi (KNA)
Files marked with an asterisk are also available on microfilm at Rhodes House, Oxford.
AA/13/4/8/2: Annual Reports, Nyanza Province, 1957–62*
ARC(MAA) 2/3/10 I: Annual Report, Nyanza Province, 1939*

ARC(MAA) 2/3/10 II: Annual Reports, Nyanza Province, 1940 and 1941*
ARC(MAA) 2/3/10 III: Annual Reports, Nyanza Province, 1942–5*
ARC(MAA) 2/3/10 IV: Annual Reports, Nyanza Province, 1946 and 1947*
ARC(MAA) 2/3/10 V: Annual Reports, Nyanza Province, 1948 and 1949*
ARC(MAA) 2/3/10 VI: Annual Report, Nyanza Province, 1950*
ARC(MAA) 2/3/10 VII: Annual Report, Nyanza Province, 1951*
ARC(MAA) 2/3/10 VIII: Annual Reports, Nyanza Province, 1952–4*
ARC(MAA) 2/3/41 II: Annual Reports, Masai Province, 1940–2*
DC/FH: Annual Reports, Fort Hall District*
DC/KBU/9–49: Annual Reports, Kiambu District, 1915/16 to 1962*
DC/KER: Annual Reports, Kericho District
DC/MKS/1/1/1–34: Annual Reports, Machakos District, 1908/9 to 1942/3*
DC/NN.1/1–40: Annual Reports, North Kavirondo District (subsequently North Nyanza District), 1917/18 to 1961*
DC/NYI: Annual Reports, Nyeri District
PC/NP/1/1–6: Annual Reports, Nyanza Province, 1905/6 to 1910/11*
PC/NZA/1/7–33: Annual Reports, Nyanza Province, 1912–38*
PC/RVP 6A/5/22: Correspondence re Lord Moyne's report on Kenya's taxation system, 1932
PC/RVP 6A/7/1: Correspondence re squatters in Rift Valley, 1932–6
PC/RVP 6A/15/29: Masai grazing facilities circa 1933
PC/RVP 6A/25/1: Squatters in Rift Valley, 1931–8
PC/SP 1/2/2: Annual Reports, Masai Province, 1914/15 to 1939*
PC/SP 1/2/3–4: Annual Reports, Masai Province, 1943–51*

A4 Rhodes House, Oxford (RH)

753.14 r.5: C. Speller, *European agriculture in Kenya Colony*, 30 June 1931
Mss. Afr.r.114: J.F. Lipscomb, *No signposts: the story of European agricultural settlement in Kenya*, no date (1965?)
Mss.Afr.s.510: V. Liversage, *Official economic management in Kenya, c. 1930–1945*, no date
Mss.Afr.s.875: C.W.R. Southey, JP, *Memories of an early settler in Rhodesia*
Mss.Afr.s.1121: S.H. Powles, Estate manager's diaries, 1928–54
Mss.Afr.s.1410: Mervyn W.H. Beech, *Kikuyu system of land tenure*, reprinted from the Journal of the Royal African Society, 1917
Mss.Afr.s.1467: Nairobi Chamber of Commerce minute books, 14 vols., covering 1909–61
Mss.Afr.s.1618: Rongai Farmers' Association, minutes, 1933–6

B Printed primary sources

B1 Publications of Her Majesty's Stationery Office, London

Serials
Board of Trade, Department of Overseas Trade, *Reports on the trade and commerce of East Africa* (subsequently *Review of Commercial Conditions in East Africa*), 1922–
Colonial Office, *Annual Report* on Kenya, 1905–

Blue Books and other non-serial publications
Great Britain, 1917, *Papers relating to the Southern Rhodesia Native Reserves Commission 1915*. Cd. 8674
1921, Report on the Railway System of Kenya, Uganda and Tanganyika by Lt-Col. F.D. Hammond
1922, *Correspondence with the Anti-Slavery and Aborigines' Protection Society relating to the native reserves in Southern Rhodesia*. Cmnd. 547

Bibliography

1929, *Report of the Commission on Closer Union of the Dependencies in East and Central Africa* (chairman: Sir Hilton Young). Cmnd. 3234

1931, *Report of the joint committee on closer union in East Africa*, vol. I: report, House of Lords 184 of 1931; vol. II: oral evidence, House of Lords 29 of 1930; vol. III: written memoranda, House of Lords 29 of 1930

1932, *Report by Mr Roger Gibb on railway rates and finance in Kenya, Uganda and Tanganyika Territory*. Cmnd. 4235

1934a, *Report of the Kenya Land Commission* (September 1933), Cmnd. 4580

1934b, *Kenya Land Commission: evidence and memoranda*, 3 vols., Colonial no. 91

1955a, *African consumers in Nyasaland and Tanganyika: an enquiry into the distribution and consumption of commodities among Africans carried out in 1952–53*, by F. Chalmers Wright, Colonial Research Studies 17

1955b, *Report of the East Africa Royal Commission 1953–1955*, Cmnd. 9475 (reprinted 1966)

1961, *East Africa: report of the economic and fiscal commission* (chairman: Sir J. Raisman)

B2 Southern Rhodesia government (and federal government) publications, Salisbury

Serials

Annual Reports of the Agriculture Department 1909–

Annual Reports of the Chief Native Commissioner 1913–

Annual Reports of the Cold Storage Commission of Southern Rhodesia

Annual Reports of the Grain Marketing Board

Annual Reports of the Land Bank

Annual Reports of the Maize Control Board

Annual Yearbooks of the Colony of Southern Rhodesia

Central African Statistical Office, *Report on the agricultural and pastoral production of Southern Rhodesia*

Development Co-ordinating Commission, First interim report, 8 March 1948; Second interim report, 1 February 1949; Third interim report, 23 March 1949

Industrial Development Advisory Committee, Second report, 1 September 1942–31 March 1944

Industrial Development Commission, First report, 1 February–31 December 1945; Second report, 1 January–31 December 1946; Third report, 1 January–31 December 1947; Fourth report, 1 January 1948–31 March 1949

National Accounts and Balance of Payments of Rhodesia Statistical Yearbooks

Reports and other non-serial publications

Southern Rhodesia, 1918, *Report of Mr. William Mitchell Acworth, Commissioner appointed to enquire into railway questions in Southern Rhodesia*

1925, *Report of the Land Commission* (chairman: Sir Morris Carter)

1926, *Report by Brigadier-General F.D. Hammond on the railway system of Southern Rhodesia* (CSR-2 of 1926), 3 vols.

1928, *Proceedings of a conference of Superintendents of Natives and Native Commissioners* (Salisbury, 13 December 1927 and succeeding days)

1930a, *Agricultural development work on native reserves* by E.D. Alvord, Department of Native Development, occasional paper 3

1930b, *Report on industrial relations in Southern Rhodesia* by Professor Henry Clay

1931, *Report of the Maize Enquiry Committee 1930* (CSR-2 of 1931)

1934, *Report of the committee of enquiry into the economic position of the agricultural industry of Southern Rhodesia* (chairman: M. Danziger) (CSR-16 of 1934)

1938a, *Report of the commission on sales of native cattle* (chairman: R.J. Hudson)

1938b, *Nyasaland native labour in Southern Rhodesia* by G.N. Burden, Government Labour Officer, Salisbury

1939a, *Report of the committee to enquire into the preservation, etc. of the natural resources of the Colony* (CSR-40 of 1939)

1939b, *Report of the economic development committee*

1945, *Report of the native production and trade committee 1944* (chairman: W.A. Godlonton) (CSR-2 of 1945)

1946, *Report of the committee of enquiry into the protection of secondary industries* (chairman: W. Margolis)

1947, *Report on a visit to certain African colonies to study problems of native production, marketing and co-operation* by A. Pendered

1950a, *Report on the agricultural development of Southern Rhodesia* by Professor Sir Frank Engledow (CSR-23 of 1950)

1950b, *Sample census of African agriculture*

1952a, *Report of a commission of enquiry into the Cold Storage Commission of Southern Rhodesia* (CSR-29 of 1952)

1952b, *Report on family expenditure survey 1950/51*

1953, *Report of the commission of enquiry into certain aspects of the operation of the Roasting Plant, Que Que* (CSR-39 of 1953)

1954, *Report of the Commissioners appointed to inquire into the iron and steel industry of Southern Rhodesia*

Federation of Rhodesia and Nyasaland, 1956, *Report of a commission on the marketing of cattle for slaughter and sale of beef in Southern Rhodesia* (C. Fed. 31–1956)

Southern Rhodesia, 1958a, *Economic appraisal of the broad prospects for African agriculture in Southern Rhodesia* by S. Makings

1958b, *Report of the Urban African Affairs Commission* (chairman: R.P. Plewman)

1959a, *Report on African household budget survey 1957/58*

Federation of Rhodesia and Nyasaland, 1959b, *Report of the Commission of Enquiry into the rating structure of Rhodesian railways* (Harragin Report)

Southern Rhodesia, 1960a, *Problems of the cattle country* by A. Hunt, Native Affairs Department

1960b, *Second report of the select committee on settlement of natives* (chairman: H.J. Quinton)

1962, *Report of the Advisory Committee on the development of the economic resources of Southern Rhodesia with particular reference to the role of African agriculture* by J. Phillips, J. Hammond, L.H. Samuels, R.J.M. Swynnerton (CSR-15 of 1962)

Federation of Rhodesia and Nyasaland, 1963a, *Report of the Commission of Enquiry into the maize and small grains industry of Northern and Southern Rhodesia*

Federation of Rhodesia and Nyasaland, 1936b, *Report of the Commission of Enquiry into the beef cattle industry of Northern and Southern Rhodesia*

B3 Kenya government publications, Nairobi

Serials

Agriculture Department, *Annual Reports*, 1912/13 onward

Blue Books of the Colony, 1903 onward

East African Statistical Department, *Kenya Agricultural Census*, 1919–34, then 1936, 1938, 1954–

Kenya Meat Commission, *Annual Reports*

Kenya and Uganda Customs Department (after 1948, East Africa Customs Department), *Annual Reports*

Labour Department, *Annual Reports*, 1945–

Land and Agricultural Bank of Kenya, *Annual Reports*

Maize Control, *Balance Sheets*, 1942–58

Bibliography

Native Affairs Department, Labour Section, *Annual Reports*, 1923–6, 1934–8, 1940–5
Proceedings of the Stockowners' Conference, 1927, 1930, 1936
Statistical Abstracts
Uganda Railway (Kenya–Uganda Railway after 1921, East African Railways after 1948), *Annual Reports*

Non-serial publications
Kenya, 1905, *Report of the Land Committee*
    1913, *Native Labour Commission 1912–13: report and evidence*
    1920, *Report of a conference of the veterinary departments of Kenya Colony, Uganda Protectorate and Tanganyika Territory*
    1921, *Report of the Labour Bureau Commission*
    1925, *Report of the economic and finance committee on native labour*
    1929, *Report of the agricultural commission, 1929* (chairman: Sir Daniel Hall)
    1930, *Soil deterioration in Kenya* by V.A. Beckley, Government Chemist
    1935, *Report of the economic development committee*
    1936, *Report of the agricultural indebtedness committee*
    1937, *Report of the meat and livestock enquiry committee* (Chairman: W. Harragin)
    1939, *Report on a visit to Kenya* by Dr I.B. Pole-Evans (grasslands expert, South Africa)
    1943, *Report of the Food Shortage Commission of Enquiry*, Nairobi
    1945a, *The Kikuyu lands: the relation of population to the land in South Nyeri* by N. Humphrey
    1945b, *Conscription of African labourers*
    1946, *Report on agricultural marketing in Kenya* by R.H. Bassett
    1947a, *Economic survey of resident labour in Kenya* by J.H. Martin
    1947b, *The Liguru and the land: sociological aspects of some agricultural problems of North Kavirondo*
    1947c, *A report on marketing of livestock in Southern Rhodesia and Tanganyika and the Cold Storage Commission of Southern Rhodesia with proposals for the reorganisation of the livestock industry in Kenya* by D.E. Faulkner
    1949, *The improvement of livestock in Kenya* by H.R. Bisschop
    1952, *Report of the committee on the marketing of maize in Kenya* (chairman: W. Ibbotson)
    1953, *Enquiry into the general economy of farming in the Highlands having regard to capital invested and long- and short-term financial commitments whether secured or unsecured; excluding farming enterprises solely concerned with the production of sisal, wattle, tea and coffee*, Commissioner, L.G. Troup, OBE
    1954, *Report of the commission on African wages, 1954* (chairman: F.W. Carpenter)
    1956a, *Report of the enquiry into the Kenya meat industry 1956* (chairman: C. Nevile)
East Africa High Commission, 1956b, *Some notes on industrial development in East Africa*
Kenya, 1958, *The maize industry*, Sessional paper no. 6 of 1957/8
East African Statistical Department, 1959, *Patterns of income, expenditure and consumption of Africans in Nairobi 1957/58*
Kenya, 1960, *Survey of unemployment* by A.G. Dalgleish
East African Statistical Department (Kenya Unit), 1961a, *Reported employment and wages in Kenya 1948–1960*
Farm Economic Survey Unit, 1961b, *Report on an economic survey of farming in the Trans Nzoia area 1959–60* by J.D. MacArthur and W.J. England
Kenya, 1963a, *Census of manufacturing 1961,* Ministry of Finance and Economic Planning
    1963b, *Report on the Kenya maize industry* by V.G. Mathews
    1966, *Report of the maize commission of enquiry*

B4 Southern Rhodesia Legislative Assembly debates
We list here debates to which reference is made in the text. Only the opening day of the debate is cited; frequently debates were subsequently adjourned until much later in the session.

22 June 1908	Private Locations Ordinance
4 May 1916	Railway policy
16 April 1917	Railway policy
23 April 1917	Land policy
17 May 1918	Land policy and soldier settlement scheme
2 May 1919	Land policy and soldier settlement scheme
3 May 1921	Railway policy
18 May 1921	Land policy
18 November 1926	Railway rate policy
21 May 1928	Umboe Railway Bill
23 May 1928	Agreement with Imperial Cold Storage Co. Ltd
27 May 1929	Land Apportionment Bill
28 May 1929	Umvukwes Railway Bill
27 March 1931	Cattle Levy Bill
10 April 1931	Unemployment
28 April 1931	Maize Control Bill
7 June 1933	Maize Control Amendment Bill
8 May 1934	Beef Export Bounty Bill
7 June 1939	Native labour
14 June 1939	Protection for secondary industries
1 May 1940	Industrial development
6 November 1940	Meat industry
5 June 1942	Iron and Steel Bill
2 June 1943	Minimum wages for adult Africans
17 November 1944	Industrial Development Bill
28 November 1944	Native policy
22 April 1947	Rhodesia Railways Bill
29 November 1948	Union Trade Agreement Bill
11 April 1951	Native Land Husbandry Bill
23 June 1952	Federation
6 July 1955	African labour
4 April 1956	Turner Cattle Commission
17 July 1958	Report of Urban African Affairs Commission
3 March 1959	Industrial Conciliation Amendment Bill

B5 Kenya Legislative Council debates
Only the opening day of each debate is given.

25 November 1912	Plague and African housing in Nairobi
19 January 1915	Crown Lands Ordinance
12 February 1917	Resident Native Labourers Bill
14 May 1924	Land policy
26 May 1924	Branch railway policy
14 June 1928	Native Lands Trust Bill
20 June 1928	Land Bank Bill
4 April 1930	Railway rating policy
28 August 1930	Sale of Wheat Bill
20 November 1930	Maize industry
8 June 1931	Butter Levy Bill
18 June 1931	Railway rating policy
20 December 1932	Coffee Industry Bill
7 December 1933	African Artisans
19 October 1934	Kenya Land Commission Report

Bibliography

11 July 1935	Railway rate policy
6 December 1935	Railway policy
30 December 1935	Guaranteed maize export price proposal
16 August 1938	Agricultural policy
17 November 1938	Railway policy
20 April 1939	Liebig's
21 April 1939	Highlands Order in Council
15 April 1942	Increased Production of Crops Bill
21 August 1942	Maize Control
15 September 1942	Native production and welfare policy
17 September 1942	Post-war reconstruction
22 March 1943	Colony's food position and maize controls
5 February 1944	Food Shortage Committee of Enquiry Report
11 January 1946	Native policy
4 February 1947	Customs Tariff Bill
15 March 1948	Industrial Licensing Bill
25 November 1948	Customs agreement with Uganda and Tanganyika
27 January 1950	Kenya Meat Commission Bill
8 July 1952	Workings of the Kenya Meat Commission
4 June 1954	Customs tariff
16 December 1954	Carpenter Report on African wages
14 Novemver 1957	Government agricultural policy in African areas
13 June 1958	Customs tariff amendment
24 November 1959	Nairobi African housing

C Unpublished theses

Barber, W.J. 1957, 'The economy of Rhodesia and Nyasaland 1930–1955', PhD, Oxford

Breen, R.M. 1976, 'The politics of land: the Kenya Land Commission 1932–3 and its effects on land policy in Kenya', PhD, Michigan State University

Clarke, D.G. 1975, 'The political economy of discrimination and underdevelopment in Rhodesia, with special reference to African workers 1940–1973', PhD, St Andrews

Duignan, P. 1961, 'Native policy in Southern Rhodesia 1890–1923', PhD, Stanford

Engholm, G.F. 1968, 'Immigrant influences on the development of policy in Uganda', PhD. London

Floyd, B.N. 1960, 'Changing patterns of African land use in Southern Rhodesia', PhD, Syracuse University, New York

Fry, J. 1974, 'An analysis of employment and income distribution in Zambia', PhD, Oxford

Gupta, D.B. 1974, 'Labour supply and economic development in Kenya', PhD, London

Hawkins, A.M. 1963, 'Railway policy in Southern Rhodesia', Blitt., Oxford University

Herskovits, M. 1926, 'The cattle complex in East Africa', PhD, Columbia University

Heyer, J. 1966, 'Agricultural development and peasant farming in Kenya', PhD, London

Heyer, S.S. 1960, 'The development of agriculture and the land system in Kenya 1918–1939', MSc. London

Johnson, R.W.M. 1968, 'The economics of African agriculture in Southern Rhodesia: a study in resource use', PhD. London

Kosmin, B. 1974, 'Ethnic and commercial relations in Southern Rhodesia', PhD, University of Rhodesia

Lee, M.E. 1974, 'Politics and pressure groups in Southern Rhodesia 1898–1923', PhD, London

Munro, W.H. 1973, 'An economic study of maize marketing in Kenya 1952–1966', PhD, University of Michigan

Phimister, I. 1975, 'History of mining in Rhodesia to 1950'. PhD. University of Rhodesia

Redley, M.G. 1977, 'The politics of a predicament: the white community in Kenya 1918–1932', PhD, Cambridge

Remole, R.A. 1959, 'White settlers, or the foundation of European agricultural settlement in Kenya', PhD, Harvard

Rooney, M. 1968, 'European agriculture in the history of Rhodesia 1890–1907', MA, University of South Africa, Pretoria

Sabot, R.H. 1973, 'Economic development, structural change and labour migration: a study of Tanzania', PhD, Oxford

Schutz, B.M. 1972, 'The theory of fragment and the political development of white settler society in Rhodesia', PhD, University of California, Los Angeles

Simon, H.J. 1936, 'The criminal law and its administration in South Africa, Southern Rhodesia and Kenya', PhD, London

Spencer, I.R.G. 1974, 'The development of production and trade in the reserve areas of Kenya 1895–1929', PhD, Simon Fraser University, Vancouver

Steele, M.C. 1972, 'The foundations of a "native" policy: Southern Rhodesia 1923–1933', PhD, Simon Fraser University, Vancouver

Swainson, N. 1978, 'Foreign corporations and economic growth in Kenya', PhD, London

van Zwanenberg, R. 1971, 'Primitive colonial accumulation in Kenya 1919–1939', PhD, Sussex

D Secondary material

D1 Books and articles on Kenya and East Africa

Best, N. 1979, *Happy Valley: the story of the English in Kenya*, London: Secker and Warburg

Blixen, K. 1964, *Out of Africa*, London: Jonathan Cape

Brett, E.A. 1973, *Colonialism and underdevelopment in East Africa*, London: Heinemann

Carnegie, V.M. 1931, *A Kenya farm diary*, Edinburgh: Blackwood

Clayton, A. and D. Savage, 1974, *Government and labour in Kenya 1895–1963*, London: Frank Cass

Cone, L.W. and J.F. Lipscomb, 1972, *The history of Kenya agriculture*, Nairobi: University Press of Africa

Eglin, R. 1975, 'Economic aspects of early industrialisation in Kenya', paper presented to conference on the Political Economy of Kenya 1929–1952, Cambridge, June

Forbes Munro, J. 1975, *Colonial rule and the Kamba: social change in the Kenya Highlands 1889–1939*, London: Oxford University Press

Furedi, F. 1972. *The Kikuyu squatter in the Rift Valley, 1918–29*, Institute of Commonwealth Studies, mimeo

Hill, M.F. 1949, *Permanent way: the story of the Kenya and Uganda Railway*, Nairobi: East African Railways and Harbours

1956, *Planters' progress: the story of coffee in Kenya*, Nairobi: Coffee Board of Kenya

1961, *Magadi: the history of the Magadi Soda Co.*, Birmingham: Kynoch Press

Hope-Jones, A. 1958, 'Secondary industry in Kenya', *East Africa and Rhodesia*, pp. 317–28

Huxley, E. 1935, *White man's country: Lord Delamere and the making of Kenya*, 2 vols., London: Chatto and Windus

1957, *No easy way: the story of the Kenya Farmers' Association*, Nairobi: East African Standard Publications

1959, *The flame trees of Thika*, Harmondsworth: Penguin

King, K. 1977, *The African artisan*, London: Heinemann

Leys, C. 1975, *Underdevelopment in Kenya: the political economy of neo-colonialism*, London: Heinemann

Leys, N. 1931, *A last chance in Kenya*, London, Hogarth Press

Bibliography

Lonsdale, J. and B. Berman, 1979, 'Coping with the contradictions: the development of the colonial state in Kenya 1895–1914', *Journal of African History*, vol. 20, pp. 487–506

Lury, D.A. 1965, 'African population estimates: back projections of recent census results', *East African Statistical Department Economic and Statistical Review*, September

McGregor Ross, W. 1927, *Kenya from within: a short political history*, London: Allen and Unwin

Maher, C. 1937, 'Soil erosion and land utilisation in the Ukamba reserve (Machakos)', unpublished paper, Rhodes House, Oxford (Mss.Afr.s.755)

1942, 'African labour on the farm in Kenya Colony', *East African Agricultural Journal*, 7 (April), pp. 228–38

Martin, C.J. 1949, 'East African Population Census 1948, planning and enumeration', *Population Studies* 3 (December), pp. 303–24

Matheson, J.K. and E.W. Bovill, 1950, *East African agriculture*, Oxford: University Press

Merker, G. 1904, *Die Masai: Ethnographische Monographe eines Ostafrikanischen Semitenvolkes*, Berlin

Pearson, D.S. 1969, *Industrial development in East Africa*, Nairobi: Oxford University Press, East Africa

Redley, M. 1975, 'The White Highland land market 1919–1939', unpublished paper

Smith, A.B. 1972, 'Economic centralisation in Kenya 1929–1937', unpublished paper, Institute of Commonwealth Studies, University of London

Sorrenson, M.P.K. 1967, *Land reform in the Kikuyu country*, Nairobi: Oxford University Press, East Africa

1968, *The origins of European settlement in Kenya*, Nairobi: Oxford University Press, East Africa

Thomson, J. 1887, *Through Masailand*, London: Sampson Low

van Zwanenberg, R. 1972, *The agricultural history of Kenya*, East Africa Publishing House (Historical Association of Kenya: Paper No. 1)

1974, 'The development of peasant commodity production in Kenya 1920–1940', *Economic History Review* 27 (August), pp. 442–54

1975, 'Industrialisation and the growth of the Kenya state 1929–1952', paper presented at conference on the Political Economy of Kenya 1929–1952, Trinity College, Cambridge, June

and King, A. 1975, *An economic history of Kenya and Uganda 1800–1970*, London: Macmillan

Wasserman, G. 1976, *Politics of decolonisation: Kenya Europeans and the land issue 1960–1965*, Cambridge: University Press.

Wolff, R. 1974, *The economics of colonialism: Britain and Kenya, 1870–1930*, New Haven: Yale University Press.

Wrigley, C.C. 1965, 'Kenya: the patterns of economic life 1903–1945', in V. Harlow and E.M. Chilver, eds., *History of East Africa*, vol. 2, London: Oxford University Press.

Yoshida, M. 1966, 'The historical background to maize marketing in Kenya and its implications for future marketing reorganisation', unpublished paper, Makerere University

Zajadacz, P. 1970, *Studies in production and trade in East Africa*, Munich: Weltforum Verlag.

D2 Books and articles on Southern Rhodesia

Alvord, E.D. 1958, *Development of native agriculture in Southern Rhodesia*, unpublished manuscript, copies in Rhodes House Library, Oxford

Arrighi, G. 1967, *The political economy of Rhodesia*, The Hague: Mouton

1973, 'Labour supplies in historical perspective: a study of the proletarianisation of the African peasantry in Rhodesia', in G. Arrighi and J. Saul, eds., *Essays on the Political Economy of Africa*, New York: Monthly Review Press (originally published in *Journal of Development Studies*, vol. 6 (1970), pp. 198–233)

Barber, W.J. 1961, *The economy of British Central Africa*. London: Oxford University Press

Clarke, D.G. 1974a, *Contract workers and underdevelopment in Rhodesia*, Gwelo: Mambo Press

1974b, *Domestic workers in Rhodesia: the economics of masters and servants*, Gwelo: Mambo Press

Clements, F. and E. Harben, 1962, *Leaf of gold: the story of Rhodesian tobacco*, London: Methuen

Cooper, C. and R. Kaplinsky, 1974, *Second-hand equipment in a less-developed country*, Geneva: ILO

Cripps, A.S. 1927, *An Africa for Africans*. London: Longmans

Dunlop, H. 1971, *The development of European agriculture in Rhodesia 1945–1965*, University of Rhodesia, Department of Economics: Occasional Paper 5

Hodder-Williams, R. 1971, 'The British South Africa Company in Marandellas: some extra-institutional constraints on government', *Rhodesian History*, vol. 2

Howman, R. 1942, 'The native labourer and his food', *NADA* (Native Affairs Department Annual), pp. 3–24

Ibbotson, P. 1945, 'The urban native problem', *NADA* (Native Affairs Department Annual)

Johnson, R.W.M. 1964, 'African agricultural development in Southern Rhodesia 1945–1960', *Food Research Institute Studies*, vol. 4, pp. 165–223

1969, 'African population estimates: myth or reality?', *Rhodesian Journal of Economics*, 3 (March), pp. 5–16

Machingaidze, V. 1978, 'Company rule and agricultural development: the case of the BSA Company in Southern Rhodesia 1908–1923', paper presented at conference of African Studies Association of UK, Oxford, September

Massell, B.F. and R.W.M. Johnson, 1968, 'The economics of smallholder farming in Rhodesia', *Food Research Institute Studies*, special supplement to vol. 8

Murray, D.J. 1970, *The governmental system in Southern Rhodesia*, London: Oxford University Press

Palmer, R. 1977, *Land and racial domination in Rhodesia*, London: Heinemann

1978, 'White farmers in Central Africa: a study in brevity', paper presented at conference of African Studies Association of UK, Oxford, September

Pearson, D.S. 1968, 'Industrial development in Rhodesia', *Rhodesian Journal of Economics*, vol. 5, pp. 5–27

Phimister, I. 1974, 'Peasant production and underdevelopment in Southern Rhodesia, 1890–1914', *African Affairs*, vol. 73, pp. 217–28.

1976, 'Meat and monopolies: beef cattle in Southern Rhodesia 1890–1938', Paper presented at South Africa Labour and Development Research Unit Conference, Cape Town, 1976

Ranger, T. 1968 (ed.), *Aspects of Central African history*, London: Heinemann

Robertson, W. 1935, *Rhodesian rancher*, London: Blackie

Steele, M. 1977, 'The economic function of African-owned cattle in Southern Rhodesia 1914–43', University of Rhodesia, unpublished paper

Tow, L. 1960, *The manufacturing economy of Southern Rhodesia*, Washington: National Academy of Sciences

van Onselen, C. 1976, *Chibaro: African mine labour in Southern Rhodesia*, London: Pluto Press

Wadsworth, V.M. 1950, 'Native labour in agriculture', *Rhodesia Agricultural Journal*, part 1: vol. 47 (June), pp. 234–53; part 2: vol. 47 (November), pp. 486–93; part 3: vol. 48 (May 1951), pp. 267–75

Wilson Fox, H. 1913, *Memorandum upon Land Settlement in Rhodesia*, London: privately printed for board of British South Africa Co. (Royal Commonwealth Society Library)

D3 Background

Ackley, G. 1961, *Macro-economic theory*, New York: Collier-Macmillan

Adams, J. 1975, 'The economic development of African pastoral societies: a model', *Kyklos*, vol. 28, pp. 852–65

Allan, W. 1965, *The African husbandman*, Edinburgh: Oliver and Boyd

Andrews, W.G. 1962, *French politics and Algeria*, New York: Appleton-Century-Crofts

Arrighi, G. 1970, 'International corporations, labour aristocracies, and economic development in tropical Africa', in G. Arrighi and J. Saul, eds., *Essays on the political economy of Africa*, New York: Monthly Review Press

Baer, W. and A. Maneschi, 1971, 'Import-substitution and structural change: an interpretation of the Brazilian case', *Journal of Developing Areas*, January

Baldwin, R. 1963, 'Export technology and development from a subsistence level', *Economic Journal*, vol. 73, pp. 80–92

　1964, *Economic development and export growth: a study of Northern Rhodesia 1920–1960*, Los Angeles: University of California Press

Baran, P. 1973, *The political economy of growth*, Harmondsworth: Penguin

Bennett, M.K. 1962, 'An agroclimatic mapping of Africa', *Food Research Institute Studies*, May

Biebuyck, D. 1960, *African agrarian systems*, studies presented and discussed at the second International African Seminar, Leopoldville, January

Boserup, E. 1965, *The conditions of agricultural growth: the economics of agrarian change under population pressure*, London: Allen and Unwin

Breton, A. 1974, *The economic theory of representative government*, London: Macmillan

Chenery, H.B. 1960, 'Patterns of industrial growth', *American Economic Review*, vol. 50, pp. 624–54

Cyert, R.M. and J.G. March, 1963, *A behavioural theory of the firm*. Englewood Cliffs, NJ: Prentice-Hall

Demsetz, H. 1967, 'Towards a theory of property rights', *American Economic Review*, vol. 57, pp. 347–59

Duesenberry, J. 1949, *Income, saving and the theory of consumer behavior*, Cambridge, Mass.: Harvard University Press

Eckaus, R. 1955, 'The factor-proportions problem in underdeveloped areas', *American Economic Review*, vol. 45

Ehrlich, C. 1973, 'Building and caretaking: economic policy in British tropical Africa 1890–1960', *Economic History Review*, vol. 26, pp. 649–67

Elkan, W. 1973, *An introduction to development economics*, Harmondsworth: Penguin

Emmanuel, A. 1972, 'White-settler colonialism and the myth of investment imperialism', *New Left Review*, vol. 73, pp. 35–57

Frankel, S.H. 1938, *Capital investment in Africa*, Oxford: University Press

Fry, J. 1979, 'A labour turnover model of wage determination in developing economies', *Economic Journal*, vol. 89, pp. 353–69

Furtado, C. 1970, *Economic development of Latin America: a survey from colonial times to the Cuban revolution*, Cambridge: University Press

Gann, L.H. and P. Duignan, 1962, *White settlers in tropical Africa*, Harmondsworth: Penguin

Gates, P.W. 1973, *Landlord and tenant on the prairie frontier*, Ithaca: Cornell University Press

Gerschenkron, A. 1962, *Economic backwardness in historical perspective*, Cambridge, Mass.: Harvard University Press

Good, K. 1976, 'Settler colonialism: economic development and class formation', *Journal of Modern African Studies*, vol. 14, pp. 597–620

Hailey, Lord, 1957, *An African survey: revised 1956*, London: Oxford University Press

Hart, K. 1973, 'Informal income opportunities and urban employment in Ghana', *Journal of Modern African Studies*, vol. 11 (March)

282

Heyer, J., J.K. Maitha and W.M. Senga, 1976, *Agricultural development in Kenya: an economic assessment*, Nairobi: Oxford University Press, East Africa

Hirschman, A.O. 1958, *The strategy of economic development*, New Haven: Yale University Press

1968, 'The political economy of import-substituting industrialisation in Latin America', *Quarterly Journal of Economics*, vol. 82, pp. 1–32

Hooker, W.H. 1924, *The handicap of British trade with special reference to East Africa*, London: John Murray

Hornby, H.E. 1936, 'Overstocking in Tanganyika territory', *East African Agricultural Journal*, vol. 5 (March)

Ilchman, W.F. and N. Uphoff, 1969, *The political economy of change*, Berkeley: University of California Press

Jarvis, L.S. 1974, 'Cattle as capital goods and ranchers as portfolio managers: an application to the Argentine cattle sector', *Journal of Political Economy*, vol. 87

Jewsewiecki, B. 1978, 'Le colonat agricole europeen au Congo belge, 1910–1960: problèmes politiques et économiques', paper presented at conference of African Studies Association of UK, Oxford, September

Jones, W.O. 1960, 'Economic man in Africa', *Food Research Institute Studies*, vol. 1, pp. 107–34

1972, *Marketing staple food crops in tropical Africa*, Ithaca: Cornell University Press

Kjekshus, H. 1977, *Ecology control and economic development in East African history*, London: Heinemann

Knight, J.B. and G. Lenta, 1980, 'Has capitalism underdeveloped the labour reserves of South Africa?', *Oxford Bulletin of Economics and Statistics*, vol. 42, pp. 157–202

Lessing, D. 1958, *Going Home*, London: Michael Joseph

Levi, J.F.S. 1976, 'Population pressure and agricultural change in the land-intensive economy', *Journal of Development Studies*, vol. 13, pp. 61–78

Lewis, W.A. 1954, 'Economic development with unlimited supplies of labour', *Manchester School of Economic and Social Studies*, vol. 22, pp. 139–91

Lipton, M. 1968, 'The theory of the optimising peasant', *Journal of Development Studies*, vol. 4, p. 327–51

Little, I., T. Scitovsky and M. Scott, 1970, *Industry and trade in some developing countries: a comparative study*, Oxford: University Press for OECD Development Centre

Livingstone, I. 1977a, 'Supply responses of peasant producers: the effect of own-account consumption on the supply of marketed output', *Journal of Agricultural Economics*, vol. 28, pp. 153–8

1977b, 'Economic irrationality among pastoral peoples: myth or reality?' *Development and Change*, vol. 8, pp. 209–30

Maitha, J. 1974, 'A note on distributed lag models of maize and wheat production response: the Kenya case', *Journal of Agricultural Economics*, vol. 25, pp. 183–8

Mannoni, O. 1964, *Prospero and Caliban: the pyschology of colonisation*, 2nd edn, New York: Praeger

Masefield, G.B. 1950, *A short history of agriculture in the British colonies*, London: Oxford University Press

Miracle, M. 1965, *Maize in tropical Africa*, Madison: University of Wisconsin Press

Miracle, M. and B. Fetter, 1977, 'Backward-sloping labour supply functions and African economic behaviour', *Economic Development and Cultural Change*, vol. 18, pp. 399–407

Monod, T. 1975, *Pastoralism in tropical Africa*, Oxford: University Press for International African Institute

Mosley, P. 1974, 'The economics of colonialism: 1870–1939', *Journal of Economic Studies*, n.s. 1:2 (November), pp. 150–61

283

1976, 'Towards a "satisficing" theory of economic policy', *Economic Journal*, vol. 86, pp. 59–73

1980, 'The political economy of industrial development in settler economies', unpublished paper

1982, 'Agricultural development and government policy in settler economies: the case of Kenya and Southern Rhodesia, 1900–60', *Economic Theory Review*, vol. 35, pp. 390–408

Myint, H. 1967, *The economics of the developing countries*, London: Hutchinson

Naipaul, V.S. 1967, *The mimic men*, Harmondsworth: Penguin

Nerlove, M. 1956, 'Estimates of the elasticities of supply of selected agricultural commodities', *Journal of Farm Economics*, vol. 38, pp. 496–509

Oliver, H.M. Jr. 1957, *Economic opinion and policy in Ceylon*, Durham, NC: Duke University Press

Orde Browne, G. St J. 1933, *The African labourer*, 1st edn. Oxford University Press for International African Institute; 2nd edn. New York: Barnes and Noble, 1967

Pack, H. 1978, 'The optimality of used equipment', *Economic Development and Cultural Change*, 26 (January)

Palmer, R. and N. Parsons, 1977, *The roots of rural poverty in Central and Southern Africa*, London: Heinemann

Peacock, A. and J. Wiseman, 1961, *The growth of public expenditure in the United Kingdom*, London: Allen and Unwin

Perham, M. 1959, 'White minorities in Africa', *Foreign Affairs*, vol. 37, pp. 637–48

Perrings, C. 1979, *Black mine workers in Central Africa*, London: Heinemann

Robinson, K.E. 1965, *The dilemmas of trusteeship*, London: Oxford University Press
  and A.F. Madden, 1963, *Essays in imperial government*, Oxford: Basil Blackwell

Rotberg, R.I. 1964, 'The federation movement in East and Central Africa 1889–1953', *Journal of Commonwealth Political Studies*, vol. 3, pp. 141–60

Rothschild, K.W. 1971, *Power in economics: selected readings*, Harmondsworth: Penguin

Sadie, J.L. 1960, 'The social anthropology of economic underdevelopment', *Economic Journal*, vol. 70, pp. 294–303

Saint–Germès, J. 1950, *Economie algérienne*, Algiers: La Maison des Livres

Sandbrook, R. and R. Cohen, 1975, *The development of an African working class: studies in class formation and action*, London: Longmans

Schultz, T.W. 1963, *Transforming traditional agriculture*, New Haven: Yale University Press

Seers, D. 1963, 'The limitations of the special case', *Oxford Bulletin of Economics and Statistics*, vol. 25, pp. 77–98

Sen, A.K. 1962, 'On the usefulness of used machines', *Review of Economics and Statistics*, 44 (August), pp. 346–8

Silcock, T.H. and E.K. Fisk, eds., 1963, *The political economy of independent Malaya*, London: Angus and Robertson

Simkins, C. 1981, 'Agricultural production in the African reserves of South Africa 1918–1969', *Journal of Southern African Studies*, vol. 7, pp. 256–83

Todaro, M. 1969, 'A theory of rural-urban migration in Africa', *American Economic Review*, vol. 59

United Nations, 1962, *Methods for population projections by sex and age*, New York: United Nations

Walker, E.R. 1943, *From economic theory to policy*, Chicago: University of Chicago Press

Warren, W. 1973, 'Imperialism and capitalist industrialisation', *New Left Review*, vol. 81, pp. 3–45

Weeks, J. 1975a, 'Uncertainty, risk and wealth and income distribution in peasant agriculture', *Journal of Development Studies*, vol. 7, pp. 28–35

  1975b, 'Policies for expanding employment in the informal urban sector of developing economies', *International Labour Review*, vol. 111, pp. 1–13

Wells, J. 1977, 'The diffusion of durables in Brazil and its implications for recent controversies concerning Brazilian development', *Cambridge Journal of Economics*, vol. 1, pp. 259–80

Wilson, F. 1972, *Labour in the South African gold mines 1911–1969*, Cambridge: University Press

World Bank, 1961, *The economic development of Ceylon*, Washington DC: World Bank

Yudelman, M. 1964, *Africans on the land: economic problems of African agricultural development in Southern, Central and East Africa, with special reference to Southern Rhodesia*, Cambridge, Mass: Harvard University Press

E Interviews

Craster, T.Y. Managing Director, W.S. Craster Ltd, engineers at Salisbury since 1937. Interviewed at Salisbury, Zimbabwe, on 14 April 1978

Girdlestone, J.A.C. Economist, Association of Rhodesia and Nyasaland Industries. Interviewed at Salisbury, Zimbabwe, on 12 April 1978

Hennings, R.O. 1935–47, District Officer in pastoral areas of Kenya; 1947–62, Livestock Development Officer and then Permanent Secretary, Ministry of Agriculture, Kenya. Interviewed at Great Chesterford, Essex, on 31 January 1980.

Liversage, V. Economist with Ministry of Agriculture, Kenya, from 1930 to 1945. Interviewed at Bally Carry, Northern Ireland, on 25 November 1979

Powles, S.H. Estate Manager for the Howard de Walden interests in Kenya, and eventually Chairman, from 1928 to 1963. Interviewed at Andover, Hants., on 17 November 1979

Index

References to material in the end-notes (pp. 237–70) are italicised, thus: *245*